2009

Astrological
Pocket Planner

ISBN-13: 978-0-7387-0772-3

Cover design by Ellen Dahl
Designed by Susan Van Sant
Edited by Ed Day

A special thanks to Aina Allen for astrological proofreading.

Astrological calculations are performed by the Kepler 7.0 astrology
software program, specially created for Llewellyn Publications, and with
the kind permission of Cosmic Patterns Software, Inc.
Re-use is prohibited.

Published by
LLEWELLYN WORLDWIDE
2143 Wooddale Drive, Dept. 978-0-7387-0772-3
Woodbury, MN 55125-2989, U.S.A.

Printed in the United States of America
Typography property of Llewellyn Worldwide, Ltd.
Llewellyn is a registered trademark of Llewellyn Worldwide, Ltd.

Table of Contents

Mercury Retrograde 2009

	DATE	ET	PT			DATE	ET	PT
Mercury Retrograde	1/11	**11:43 am**	8:43 am	—	Mercury Direct	2/1	**2:10 am**	11:10 pm (1/31)
Mercury Retrograde	5/7	**1:00 am**	10:00 pm (5/6)	—	Mercury Direct	5/30	**9:21 pm**	6:21 pm
Mercury Retrograde	9/7	**12:45 am**	9:45 pm (9/6)	—	Mercury Direct	9/29	**9:13 am**	6:13 am
Mercury Retrograde	12/26	**9:38 am**	6:38 am	—	Mercury Direct	1/15/10	**11:52 am**	8:52 am

Moon Void-of-Course 2009

Times are listed in Eastern time in this table only. All other information in the *Pocket Planner* is listed in both Eastern time and Pacific time. Refer to "Time Zone Conversions" on page 7 for changing to other time zones. Note: All times are corrected for Daylight Saving Time.

Last Aspect		Moon Enters New Sign			Last Aspect		Moon Enters New Sign			Last Aspect		Moon Enters New Sign		
Date	Time	Date	Sign	Time	Date	Time	Date	Sign	Time	Date	Time	Date	Sign	Time
JANUARY					**FEBRUARY**					**MARCH**				
3	3:50 am	3	♈	4:50 am	1	1:08 pm	1	♉	5:08 pm	2	5:42 pm	3	♊	2:59 am
4	9:44 pm	5	♉	10:46 am	3	8:27 pm	3	♊	9:14 pm	4	9:10 pm	5	♋	6:07 am
7	1:05 am	7	♊	1:11 pm	5	12:44 pm	5	♋	11:05 pm	6	7:29 pm	7	♌	8:24 am
9	1:39 am	9	♋	1:14 pm	7	2:07 pm	7	♌	11:43 pm	9	3:56 am	9	♍	11:34 am
10	11:26 pm	11	♌	12:41 pm	9	2:28 pm	10	♍	12:38 am	11	1:48 am	11	♎	2:46 pm
13	1:38 am	13	♍	1:33 pm	11	11:17 pm	12	♎	3:33 am	13	6:39 pm	13	♏	8:22 pm
15	9:37 am	15	♎	5:30 pm	14	9:46 am	14	♏	9:50 am	15	8:43 pm	16	♐	5:21 am
17	9:46 pm	18	♏	1:20 am	16	4:37 pm	16	♐	7:53 pm	18	1:47 pm	18	♑	5:18 pm
19	10:36 pm	20	♐	12:30 pm	18	8:36 pm	19	♑	8:25 am	20	4:06 pm	21	♒	6:06 am
22	11:23 pm	23	♑	1:18 am	21	4:01 am	21	♒	9:06 pm	23	8:09 am	23	♓	5:08 pm
25	4:08 am	25	♒	1:56 pm	23	9:08 pm	24	♓	7:59 am	25	12:53 pm	26	♈	1:03 am
27	12:12 pm	28	♓	1:12 am	26	1:09 am	26	♈	4:24 pm	27	10:17 pm	28	♉	6:09 am
30	4:23 am	30	♈	10:25 am	28	12:51 pm	28	♉	10:33 pm	30	2:00 am	30	♊	9:36 am

Moon Void-of-Course 2009 (cont.)

APRIL

Last Aspect Date	Time	Moon Enters New Sign Date	Sign	Time
1	5:03 am	1	♋	12:30 pm
3	4:59 am	3	♌	3:32 pm
5	11:38 am	5	♍	7:01 pm
7	12:52 pm	7	♎	11:22 pm
9	9:45 pm	10	♏	5:23 am
12	1:28 pm	12	♐	2:00 pm
15	12:07 am	15	♑	1:27 am
17	12:42 pm	17	♒	2:19 pm
19	6:15 pm	20	♓	1:55 am
22	9:29 am	22	♈	10:09 am
24	8:11 am	24	♉	2:46 pm
26	11:42 am	26	♊	5:02 pm
28	12:22 pm	28	♋	6:38 pm
30	12:45 pm	30	♌	8:56 pm

MAY

Last Aspect Date	Time	Moon Enters New Sign Date	Sign	Time
2	6:08 pm	3	♍	12:37 am
4	9:31 pm	5	♎	5:51 am
6	7:00 am	7	♏	12:48 pm
9	2:48 pm	9	♐	9:49 pm
12	1:55 am	12	♑	9:09 am
14	8:58 pm	14	♒	10:01 pm
17	6:40 am	17	♓	10:17 am
19	5:43 pm	19	♈	7:30 pm
22	6:36 pm	22	♉	12:40 am
24	8:48 pm	24	♊	2:34 am
26	9:17 pm	26	♋	2:58 am
27	11:06 pm	28	♌	3:44 am
30	4:18 am	30	♍	6:17 am

JUNE

Last Aspect Date	Time	Moon Enters New Sign Date	Sign	Time
1	4:32 am	1	♎	11:17 am
3	2:00 pm	3	♏	6:43 pm
5	10:18 pm	6	♐	4:23 am
8	9:51 am	8	♑	3:59 pm
10	11:31 pm	11	♒	4:52 am
13	5:04 pm	13	♓	5:32 pm
15	9:17 pm	16	♈	3:51 am
18	5:35 am	18	♉	10:20 am
20	8:02 am	20	♊	1:00 pm
22	8:20 am	22	♋	1:12 pm
24	7:24 am	24	♌	12:50 pm
26	8:28 am	26	♍	1:46 pm
28	11:26 am	28	♎	5:24 pm
30	5:59 pm	7/1	♏	12:18 am

JULY

Last Aspect Date	Time	Moon Enters New Sign Date	Sign	Time
6/30	5:59 pm	1	♏	12:18 am
3	6:03 am	3	♐	10:10 am
5	3:17 pm	5	♑	10:07 pm
8	5:43 am	8	♒	11:03 am
10	10:17 pm	10	♓	11:44 pm
13	4:03 am	13	♈	10:40 am
15	11:07 am	15	♉	6:30 pm
17	4:48 pm	17	♊	10:41 pm
19	6:12 pm	19	♋	11:51 pm
21	10:34 pm	21	♌	11:27 pm
23	4:28 pm	23	♍	11:22 pm
25	7:14 pm	26	♎	1:25 am
27	10:53 pm	28	♏	6:56 am
30	8:54 am	30	♐	4:10 pm

AUGUST

Last Aspect Date	Time	Moon Enters New Sign Date	Sign	Time
2	1:42 am	2	♑	4:08 am
4	9:21 am	4	♒	5:08 pm
6	8:19 pm	7	♓	5:34 am
8	8:44 am	9	♈	4:23 pm
11	4:03 pm	12	♉	12:49 am
13	11:17 am	14	♊	6:25 am
16	2:19 am	16	♋	9:13 am
18	3:09 am	18	♌	9:56 am
20	6:01 am	20	♍	10:00 am
22	7:44 am	22	♎	11:12 am
24	2:10 pm	24	♏	3:16 pm
26	2:34 pm	26	♐	11:16 pm
28	1:26 am	29	♑	10:44 am
31	2:09 pm	31	♒	11:43 pm

SEPTEMBER

Last Aspect Date	Time	Moon Enters New Sign Date	Sign	Time
3	1:19 am	3	♓	11:58 am
5	12:53 pm	5	♈	10:14 pm
7	8:12 pm	8	♉	6:17 am
10	3:17 am	10	♊	12:17 pm
12	7:30 am	12	♋	4:19 pm
14	9:57 am	14	♌	6:39 pm
16	12:10 pm	16	♍	7:56 pm
18	7:56 pm	18	♎	9:26 pm
20	2:43 pm	21	♏	12:52 am
22	11:32 pm	23	♐	7:43 am
25	10:15 am	25	♑	6:19 pm
27	11:33 pm	28	♒	7:06 am
30	7:34 am	30	♓	7:26 pm

OCTOBER

Last Aspect Date	Time	Moon Enters New Sign Date	Sign	Time
2	11:29 pm	3	♈	5:20 am
5	1:46 am	5	♉	12:33 pm
7	1:19 pm	7	♊	5:46 pm
9	9:35 pm	9	♋	9:48 pm
11	9:37 pm	12	♌	1:02 am
13	5:20 pm	14	♍	3:45 am
16	6:18 am	16	♎	6:29 am
18	1:33 am	18	♏	10:22 am
20	2:57 pm	20	♐	4:49 pm
23	1:13 am	23	♑	2:39 am
25	2:14 pm	25	♒	3:08 pm
28	3:22 am	28	♓	3:45 am
30	12:56 am	30	♈	1:56 pm

NOVEMBER

Last Aspect Date	Time	Moon Enters New Sign Date	Sign	Time
1	8:29 am	1	♉	7:44 pm
3	1:04 pm	3	♊	11:53 pm
5	10:47 pm	6	♋	2:42 am
7	5:26 pm	8	♌	5:23 am
9	9:43 pm	10	♍	8:30 am
12	2:13 am	12	♎	12:22 pm
14	6:10 am	14	♏	5:24 pm
16	2:14 pm	17	♐	12:22 am
18	9:46 pm	19	♑	10:00 am
21	10:04 pm	21	♒	10:11 pm
23	10:35 pm	24	♓	11:07 am
26	9:17 am	26	♈	10:10 pm
28	6:32 pm	29	♉	5:34 am

DECEMBER

Last Aspect Date	Time	Moon Enters New Sign Date	Sign	Time
1	8:39 am	1	♊	9:23 am
3	5:27 am	3	♋	11:00 am
5	12:08 am	5	♌	12:07 pm
7	3:57 am	7	♍	2:05 pm
9	5:04 am	9	♎	5:47 pm
11	12:44 pm	11	♏	11:31 pm
13	8:17 pm	14	♐	7:25 am
16	7:02 am	16	♑	5:32 pm
18	3:07 pm	19	♒	5:38 am
21	7:53 am	21	♓	6:42 pm
24	3:09 am	24	♈	6:39 am
26	6:44 am	26	♉	3:26 pm
28	12:54 pm	28	♊	8:13 pm
30	3:29 pm	30	♋	9:45 pm

How to Use the *Pocket Planner*

by Leslie Nielsen

This handy guide contains information that can be most valuable to you as you plan your daily activities. As you read through the first few pages, you can start to get a feel for how well organized this guide is.

Read the Symbol Key on the next page, which is rather like astrological shorthand. The characteristics of the planets can give you direction in planning your strategies. Much like traffic signs that signal "go," "stop," or even "caution," you can determine for yourself the most propitious time to get things done.

You'll find tables that show the dates when Mercury is retrograde (℞) or direct (D). Because Mercury deals with the exchange of information, a retrograde Mercury makes miscommunication more noticeable.

There's also a section dedicated to the times when the Moon is void-of-course (v/c). These are generally poor times to conduct business because activities begun during these times usually end badly or fail to get started. If you make an appointment during a void-of-course, you might save yourself a lot of aggravation by confirming the time and date later. The Moon is only void-of-course for 7 percent of the time when business is usually conducted during a normal workday (that is, 8:00 am to 5:00 pm). Sometimes, by waiting a matter of minutes or a few hours until the Moon has left the void-of-course phase, you have a much better chance to make action move more smoothly. Moon voids can also be used successfully to do routine activities or inner work, such as dream therapy or personal contemplation.

You'll find Moon phases, as well as each of the Moon's entries into a new sign. Times are expressed in Eastern time (in bold type) and Pacific time (in medium type). The New Moon time is generally best for beginning new activities, as the Moon is increasing in light and can offer the element of growth to our endeavors. When the Moon is Full, its illumination is greatest and we can see the results of our efforts. When it moves from the Full stage back to the New stage, it can best be used to reflect on our projects. If necessary, we can make corrections at the New Moon.

The section of "Planetary Stations" will give you the times when the planets are changing signs or direction, thereby affording us opportunities for new starts.

The ephemeris in the back of your *Pocket Planner* can be very helpful to you. As you start to work with the ephemeris, you may notice that not all planets seem to be comfortable in every sign. Think of the planets as actors, and the signs as the costumes they wear. Sometimes, costumes just itch. If you find this to be so for a certain time period, you may choose to delay your plans for a time or be more creative with the energies at hand.

As you turn to the daily pages, you'll find information about the Moon's sign, phase, and the time it changes phase. You'll find icons indicating the best days to plant and fish. Also, you will find times and dates when the planets and asteroids change sign and go either retrograde or direct, major holidays, a three-month calendar, and room to record your appointments.

This guide is a powerful tool. Make the most of it!

Symbol Key

Planets:	☉ Sun	⚳ Ceres	♄ Saturn
	☽ Moon	⚴ Pallas	⚷ Chiron
	☿ Mercury	⚵ Juno	♅ Uranus
	♀ Venus	⚶ Vesta	♆ Neptune
	♂ Mars	♃ Jupiter	♇ Pluto
Signs:	♈ Aries	♌ Leo	♐ Sagittarius
	♉ Taurus	♍ Virgo	♑ Capricorn
	♊ Gemini	♎ Libra	♒ Aquarius
	♋ Cancer	♏ Scorpio	♓ Pisces
Aspects:	☌ Conjunction (0°)	⊻ Semisextile (30°)	⚹ Sextile (60°)
	□ Square (90°)	△ Trine (120°)	☍ Opposition (180°)
	⚻ Quincunx (150°)		
Motion:	℞ Retrograde	D Direct	
Best Days for Planting: 🌱		Best Days for Fishing: 🐟	

World Map of Time Zones

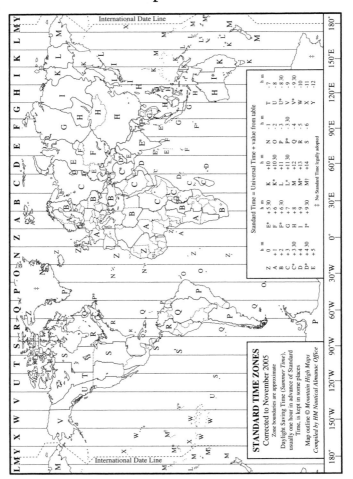

Time Zone Conversions

World Time Zones
Compared to Eastern Standard Time

( ) From Map	(Y) Subtract 7 hours	(C*) Add 8.5 hours
(S) CST/Subtract 1 hour	(A) Add 6 hours	(D*) Add 9.5 hours
(R) EST	(B) Add 7 hours	(E*) Add 10.5 hours
(Q) Add 1 hour	(C) Add 8 hours	(F*) Add 11.5 hours
(P) Add 2 hours	(D) Add 9 hours	(I*) Add 14.5 hours
(O) Add 3 hours	(E) Add 10 hours	(K*) Add 15.5 hours
(N) Add 4 hours	(F) Add 11 hours	(L*) Add 16.5 hours
(Z) Add 5 hours	(G) Add 12 hours	(M*) Add 18 hours
(T) MST/Subtract 2 hours	(H) Add 13 hours	(P*) Add 2.5 hours
(U) PST/Subtract 3 hours	(I) Add 14 hours	(U*) Subtract 3.5 hours
(V) Subtract 4 hours	(K) Add 15 hours	(V*) Subtract 4.5 hours
(W) Subtract 5 hours	(L) Add 16 hours	
(X) Subtract 6 hours	(M) Add 17 hours	

World Map of Time Zones is supplied by HM Nautical Almanac Office, © Center for the Central Laboratory of the Research Councils. Note: This is not an official map. Countries change their time zones as they wish.

Planetary Stations for 2009

	JAN	FEB	MAR	APR	MAY	JUN	JUL	AUG	SEP	OCT	NOV	DEC
☿	1/11–2/1				5/7–5/30				9/7–9/29			12/26–1/15
♀			3/6–4/17									
♂												12/20–3/10
♃						6/15–10/13						
♄		12/31–5/16										
♅							7/1–12/1					
♆					5/29–11/4							
♇				4/4–9/11								
⚷					5/30–10/31							
♊	1/11–4/12											
◇	10/26–1/14											
✳								8/9–11/3				
⟫												

8

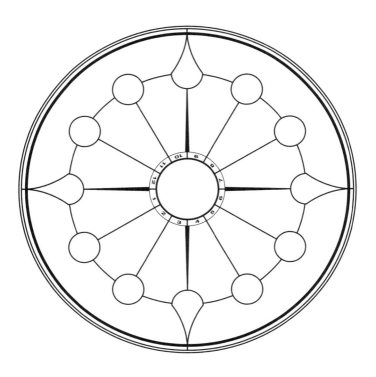

29 Monday

1st ♑
| ☽ V/C | **4:20 am** | 1:20 am |
| ☽ enters ♒ | **7:42 am** | 4:42 am |

Hanukkah ends
Islamic New Year

30 Tuesday

1st ♒

31 Wednesday

1st ♒
♄ ℞	**1:08 pm**	10:08 am
☽ V/C	**1:34 pm**	10:34 am
☽ enters ♓	**7:27 pm**	4:27 pm

New Year's Eve

1 Thursday

1st ♓
| ☿ enters ♒ | **4:51 am** | 1:51 am |

New Year's Day • Kwanzaa ends

Eastern time in bold type
Pacific time in medium type

2 Friday
1st ♓

3 Saturday
1st ♓

☽ V/C	**3:50 am**	12:50 am
☽ enters ♈	**4:50 am**	1:50 am
♀ enters ♓	**7:35 am**	4:35 am

4 Sunday
1st ♈

2nd quarter	**6:56 am**	3:56 am
☽ V/C	**9:44 pm**	6:44 pm

December 2008								January 2009								February 2009					
S	M	T	W	T	F	S		S	M	T	W	T	F	S		S	M	T	W	T	F	S
	1	2	3	4	5	6						1	2	3		1	2	3	4	5	6	7
7	8	9	10	11	12	13		4	5	6	7	8	9	10		8	9	10	11	12	13	14
14	15	16	17	18	19	20		11	12	13	14	15	16	17		15	16	17	18	19	20	21
21	22	23	24	25	26	27		18	19	20	21	22	23	24		22	23	24	25	26	27	28
28	29	30	31					25	26	27	28	29	30	31								

5 Monday

2nd ♈
♃ enters ♒ **10:41 am** 7:41 am
☽ enters ♉ **10:46 am** 7:46 am

6 Tuesday

2nd ♉
☽ V/C   10:05 pm

7 Wednesday

2nd ♉
☽ V/C   **1:05 am**
☽ enters ♊   **1:11 pm** 10:11 am

8 Thursday

2nd ♊
☽ V/C   10:39 pm

Eastern time in bold type
Pacific time in medium type

9 Friday

2nd ♊
》 V/C   **1:39 am**
》 enters ♋   **1:14 pm** 10:14 am

10 Saturday

2nd ♋
Full Moon   **10:27 pm** 7:27 pm
》 V/C   **11:26 pm** 8:26 pm

11 Sunday

3rd ♋
♃ ℞   **8:06 am** 5:06 am
☿ ℞   **11:43 am** 8:43 am
》 enters ♌ **12:41 pm** 9:41 am

December 2008								January 2009								February 2009					
S	M	T	W	T	F	S		S	M	T	W	T	F	S		S	M	T	W	T	F	S
	1	2	3	4	5	6						1	2	3		1	2	3	4	5	6	7
7	8	9	10	11	12	13		4	5	6	7	8	9	10		8	9	10	11	12	13	14
14	15	16	17	18	19	20		11	12	13	14	15	16	17		15	16	17	18	19	20	21
21	22	23	24	25	26	27		18	19	20	21	22	23	24		22	23	24	25	26	27	28
28	29	30	31					25	26	27	28	29	30	31								

12 Monday
3rd ♌
☽ V/C   10:38 pm

13 Tuesday
3rd ♌
☽ V/C   **1:38 am**
☽ enters ♍   **1:33 pm** 10:33 am

14 Wednesday
3rd ♍
☿ D   **2:51 pm** 11:51 am

15 Thursday
3rd ♍
☽ V/C   **9:37 am** 6:37 am
☽ enters ♎ **5:30 pm** 2:30 pm

Eastern time in bold type
Pacific time in medium type

16 Friday
3rd ♎

17 Saturday
3rd ♎
4th quarter **9:46 pm** 6:46 pm
☽ V/C **9:46 pm** 6:46 pm
☽ enters ♏ 10:20 pm

18 Sunday
4th ♎
☽ enters ♏ **1:20 am**

December 2008						
S	M	T	W	T	F	S
	1	2	3	4	5	6
7	8	9	10	11	12	13
14	15	16	17	18	19	20
21	22	23	24	25	26	27
28	29	30	31			

January 2009						
S	M	T	W	T	F	S
				1	2	3
4	5	6	7	8	9	10
11	12	13	14	15	16	17
18	19	20	21	22	23	24
25	26	27	28	29	30	31

February 2009						
S	M	T	W	T	F	S
1	2	3	4	5	6	7
8	9	10	11	12	13	14
15	16	17	18	19	20	21
22	23	24	25	26	27	28

19 Monday

4th ♏

☉ enters ≈ **5:40 pm** 2:40 pm
☽ V/C **10:36 pm** 7:36 pm

Sun enters Aquarius
Birthday of Martin Luther King, Jr. (observed)

20 Tuesday

4th ♏

☽ enters ♐ **12:30 pm** 9:30 am
☿ enters ♑ 9:36 pm

Inauguration Day

21 Wednesday

4th ♐

☿ enters ♑ **12:36 am**
⚷ enters ≈ **6:58 am** 3:58 am

22 Thursday

4th ♐

☽ V/C **11:23 am** 8:23 am
☽ enters ♑ 10:18 pm

Eastern time in bold type
Pacific time in medium type

23 Friday
4th ♐
☽ enters ♑ **1:18 am**

24 Saturday
4th ♑

25 Sunday
4th ♑
☽ V/C   **4:08 am** 1:08 am
☽ enters ♒ **1:56 pm** 10:56 am
New Moon   11:55 pm

Solar eclipse 6° ♒ 30' • 11:59 pm PST

December 2008							January 2009							February 2009					
S	M	T	W	T	F	S	S	M	T	W	T	F	S	S	M	T	W	T	F	S
	1	2	3	4	5	6					1	2	3	1	2	3	4	5	6	7
7	8	9	10	11	12	13	4	5	6	7	8	9	10	8	9	10	11	12	13	14
14	15	16	17	18	19	20	11	12	13	14	15	16	17	15	16	17	18	19	20	21
21	22	23	24	25	26	27	18	19	20	21	22	23	24	22	23	24	25	26	27	28
28	29	30	31				25	26	27	28	29	30	31							

Eastern time in bold type
Pacific time in medium type

26 Monday

4th ≈
New Moon   **2:55 am**

Chinese New Year (ox)
Solar eclipse 6° ≈ 30' • 2:59 am EST

27 Tuesday

1st ≈
☽ V/C   **12:12 pm**   9:12 am
☽ enters ♓   10:12 pm

28 Wednesday

1st ≈
☽ enters ♓   **1:12 am**

29 Thursday

1st ♓

30 Friday

1st ♓
☽ V/C   **4:23 am**   1:23 am
☽ enters ♈ **10:25 am**   7:25 am

31 Saturday

1st ♈
☿ D   11:10 pm

1 Sunday

1st ♈
☿ D   **2:10 am**
☽ V/C   **1:08 pm** 10:08 am
☽ enters ♉ **5:08 pm**   2:08 pm

January 2009						
S	M	T	W	T	F	S
				1	2	3
4	5	6	7	8	9	10
11	12	13	14	15	16	17
18	19	20	21	22	23	24
25	26	27	28	29	30	31

February 2009						
S	M	T	W	T	F	S
1	2	3	4	5	6	7
8	9	10	11	12	13	14
15	16	17	18	19	20	21
22	23	24	25	26	27	28

March 2009						
S	M	T	W	T	F	S
1	2	3	4	5	6	7
8	9	10	11	12	13	14
15	16	17	18	19	20	21
22	23	24	25	26	27	28
29	30	31				

Eastern time in bold type
Pacific time in medium type

2 Monday

1st ♉
2nd quarter **6:13 pm** 3:13 pm
♀ enters ♈ **10:41 pm** 7:41 pm

Groundhog Day • Imbolc

3 Tuesday

2nd ♉
☽ V/C **8:27 pm** 5:27 pm
☽ enters ♊ **9:14 pm** 6:14 pm

4 Wednesday

2nd ♊
♂ enters ≈ **10:55 am** 7:55 am

5 Thursday

2nd ♊
☽ V/C **12:44 pm** 9:44 am
☽ enters ♋ **11:05 pm** 8:05 pm

Eastern time in bold type
Pacific time in medium type

6 Friday
2nd ⊗

7 Saturday
2nd ⊗
☽ V/C   **2:07 pm** 11:07 am
☽ enters ♌ **11:43 pm** 8:43 pm

8 Sunday
2nd ♌

January 2009						
S	M	T	W	T	F	S
				1	2	3
4	5	6	7	8	9	10
11	12	13	14	15	16	17
18	19	20	21	22	23	24
25	26	27	28	29	30	31

February 2009						
S	M	T	W	T	F	S
1	2	3	4	5	6	7
8	9	10	11	12	13	14
15	16	17	18	19	20	21
22	23	24	25	26	27	28

March 2009						
S	M	T	W	T	F	S
1	2	3	4	5	6	7
8	9	10	11	12	13	14
15	16	17	18	19	20	21
22	23	24	25	26	27	28
29	30	31				

9 Monday

2nd ♌
Full Moon	**9:49 am**	6:49 am
D V/C	**2:28 pm**	11:28 am
D enters ♍		9:38 pm

Lunar eclipse 20° ♌ 52' • 9:38 am EST/6:38 am PST

10 Tuesday

3rd ♌
D enters ♍ **12:38 am**

11 Wednesday

3rd ♍
D V/C **11:17 pm** 8:17 pm

12 Thursday

3rd ♍
D enters ♎ **3:33 am** 12:33 am

Eastern time in bold type
Pacific time in medium type

13 Friday
3rd ♎

14 Saturday
3rd ♎

D V/C   **9:46 am**   6:46 am

D enters ♏ **9:50 am**   6:50 am
☿ enters ≈ **10:39 am**   7:39 am

Valentine's Day

15 Sunday
3rd ♏

January 2009						
S	M	T	W	T	F	S
					1	2	3
4	5	6	7	8	9	10
11	12	13	14	15	16	17
18	19	20	21	22	23	24
25	26	27	28	29	30	31

February 2009						
S	M	T	W	T	F	S
1	2	3	4	5	6	7
8	9	10	11	12	13	14
15	16	17	18	19	20	21
22	23	24	25	26	27	28

March 2009						
S	M	T	W	T	F	S
1	2	3	4	5	6	7
8	9	10	11	12	13	14
15	16	17	18	19	20	21
22	23	24	25	26	27	28
29	30	31				

16 Monday

3rd ♏

4th quarter	**4:37 pm**	1:37 pm
☽ V/C	**4:37 pm**	1:37 pm
☽ enters ♐	**7:53 pm**	4:53 pm

Presidents' Day (observed)

17 Tuesday
4th ♐

18 Wednesday
4th ♐

| ☉ enters ♓ | **7:46 am** | 4:46 am |
| ☽ V/C | **8:36 pm** | 5:36 pm |

Sun enters Pisces

19 Thursday

4th ♐

| ☽ enters ♑ | **8:25 am** | 5:25 am |

Eastern time in bold type
Pacific time in medium type

20 Friday

4th ♑

21 Saturday

4th ♑
☽ V/C **4:01 am** 1:01 am
☽ enters ♒ **9:06 pm** 6:06 pm

22 Sunday

4th ♒

January 2009						
S	M	T	W	T	F	S
				1	2	3
4	5	6	7	8	9	10
11	12	13	14	15	16	17
18	19	20	21	22	23	24
25	26	27	28	29	30	31

February 2009						
S	M	T	W	T	F	S
1	2	3	4	5	6	7
8	9	10	11	12	13	14
15	16	17	18	19	20	21
22	23	24	25	26	27	28

March 2009						
S	M	T	W	T	F	S
1	2	3	4	5	6	7
8	9	10	11	12	13	14
15	16	17	18	19	20	21
22	23	24	25	26	27	28
29	30	31				

Eastern time in bold type
Pacific Time in medium type

23 Monday

4th ≈
☽ V/C   **9:08 pm** 6:08 pm

24 Tuesday

4th ≈
☽ enters ♓   **7:59 am** 4:59 am
New Moon   **8:35 pm** 5:35 pm

Mardi Gras (Fat Tuesday)

25 Wednesday

1st ♓
☽ V/C   10:09 pm

Ash Wednesday

26 Thursday

1st ♓
☽ V/C   **1:09 am**
☽ enters ♈   **4:24 pm** 1:24 pm

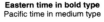

Eastern time in bold type
Pacific time in medium type

27 Friday
1st ♈

28 Saturday
1st ♈
☽ V/C   **12:51 pm**   9:51 am
☽ enters ♉   **10:33 pm**   7:33 pm

1 Sunday
1st ♉

February 2009						
S	M	T	W	T	F	S
1	2	3	4	5	6	7
8	9	10	11	12	13	14
15	16	17	18	19	20	21
22	23	24	25	26	27	28

March 2009						
S	M	T	W	T	F	S
1	2	3	4	5	6	7
8	9	10	11	12	13	14
15	16	17	18	19	20	21
22	23	24	25	26	27	28
29	30	31				

April 2009						
S	M	T	W	T	F	S
			1	2	3	4
5	6	7	8	9	10	11
12	13	14	15	16	17	18
19	20	21	22	23	24	25
26	27	28	29	30		

Eastern time in bold type
Pacific time in medium type

2 Monday
1st ♉
☽ V/C   **5:42 pm** 2:42 pm
☽ enters ♊   11:59 pm

3 Tuesday
1st ♉
2nd quarter   11:46 pm
☽ enters ♊ **2:59 am**

4 Wednesday
1st ♊
2nd quarter **2:46 am**
☽ V/C   **9:10 pm** 6:10 pm

5 Thursday
2nd ♊
☽ enters ♋ **6:07 am** 3:07 am

Eastern time in bold type
Pacific time in medium type

6 Friday

2nd ♋
♀ ℞   **12:17 pm**   9:17 am
☽ V/C   **7:29 pm**   4:29 pm

---

7 Saturday

2nd ♋
☽ enters ♌   **8:24 am**   5:24 am

---

8 Sunday

2nd ♌
☿ enters ♓   **2:56 pm** 11:56 am

Daylight Saving Time begins at 2 am

February 2009						
S	M	T	W	T	F	S
1	2	3	4	5	6	7
8	9	10	11	12	13	14
15	16	17	18	19	20	21
22	23	24	25	26	27	28

March 2009						
S	M	T	W	T	F	S
1	2	3	4	5	6	7
8	9	10	11	12	13	14
15	16	17	18	19	20	21
22	23	24	25	26	27	28
29	30	31				

April 2009						
S	M	T	W	T	F	S
			1	2	3	4
5	6	7	8	9	10	11
12	13	14	15	16	17	18
19	20	21	22	23	24	25
26	27	28	29	30		

9 Monday

2nd ♌
☽ V/C   **3:56 am** 12:56 am
☽ enters ♍ **11:34 am** 8:34 am

10 Tuesday

2nd ♍
Full Moon   **10:38 pm** 7:38 pm
☽ V/C   10:48 pm

Purim

11 Wednesday

3rd ♍
☽ V/C   **1:48 am**
☽ enters ♎ **2:46 pm** 11:46 am

12 Thursday

3rd ♎

Eastern time in bold type
Pacific time in medium type

13 Friday

3rd ♎︎
☽ V/C   **6:39 pm**   3:39 pm
☽ enters ♏︎ **8:22 pm**   5:22 pm

14 Saturday

3rd ♏︎
♂ enters ♓︎ **11:20 pm**   8:20 pm

15 Sunday

3rd ♏︎
☽ V/C   **8:43 pm**   5:43 pm

February 2009						
S	M	T	W	T	F	S
1	2	3	4	5	6	7
8	9	10	11	12	13	14
15	16	17	18	19	20	21
22	23	24	25	26	27	28

March 2009						
S	M	T	W	T	F	S
1	2	3	4	5	6	7
8	9	10	11	12	13	14
15	16	17	18	19	20	21
22	23	24	25	26	27	28
29	30	31				

April 2009						
S	M	T	W	T	F	S
			1	2	3	4
5	6	7	8	9	10	11
12	13	14	15	16	17	18
19	20	21	22	23	24	25
26	27	28	29	30		

16 Monday
3rd ♏
☽ enters ♐ **5:21 am** 2:21 am

17 Tuesday
3rd ♐

St. Patrick's Day

18 Wednesday
3rd ♐
4th quarter **1:47 pm** 10:47 am
☽ V/C **1:47 pm** 10:47 am
☽ enters ♑ **5:18 pm** 2:18 pm

19 Thursday
4th ♑

Eastern time in bold type
Pacific time in medium type

20 Friday
4th ♑
☉ enters ♈ **7:43 am** 4:43 am
☽ V/C **4:06 pm** 1:06 pm

Sun enters Aries • Ostara • Spring Equinox • 7:43 am EDT/ 4:43 am PDT
International Astrology Day

21 Saturday
4th ♑
☽ enters ≈ **6:06 am** 3:06 am

22 Sunday
4th ≈

February 2009						
S	M	T	W	T	F	S
1	2	3	4	5	6	7
8	9	10	11	12	13	14
15	16	17	18	19	20	21
22	23	24	25	26	27	28

March 2009						
S	M	T	W	T	F	S
1	2	3	4	5	6	7
8	9	10	11	12	13	14
15	16	17	18	19	20	21
22	23	24	25	26	27	28
29	30	31				

April 2009						
S	M	T	W	T	F	S
			1	2	3	4
5	6	7	8	9	10	11
12	13	14	15	16	17	18
19	20	21	22	23	24	25
26	27	28	29	30		

Eastern time in bold type
Pacific time in medium type

23 Monday

4th ≈
☽ V/C **8:09 am** 5:09 am
☽ enters ♓ **5:08 pm** 2:08 pm

24 Tuesday

4th ♓

25 Wednesday

4th ♓
☽ V/C **12:53 pm** 9:53 am
☿ enters ♈ **3:55 pm** 12:55 pm
☽ enters ♈ 10:03 pm

26 Thursday

4th ♓
☽ enters ♈ **1:03 am**
New Moon **12:06 pm** 9:06 am

Eastern time in bold type
Pacific time in medium type

27 Friday

1st ♈
☽ V/C   **10:17 pm** 7:17 pm

28 Saturday

1st ♈
☽ enters ♉   **6:09 am** 3:09 am

29 Sunday

1st ♉
☽ V/C   11:00 pm

February 2009						
S	M	T	W	T	F	S
1	2	3	4	5	6	7
8	9	10	11	12	13	14
15	16	17	18	19	20	21
22	23	24	25	26	27	28

March 2009						
S	M	T	W	T	F	S
1	2	3	4	5	6	7
8	9	10	11	12	13	14
15	16	17	18	19	20	21
22	23	24	25	26	27	28
29	30	31				

April 2009						
S	M	T	W	T	F	S
			1	2	3	4
5	6	7	8	9	10	11
12	13	14	15	16	17	18
19	20	21	22	23	24	25
26	27	28	29	30		

Eastern time in bold type
Pacific time in medium type

30 Monday

1st ♉
☽ V/C   **2:00 am**
☽ enters ♊   **9:36 am** 6:36 am

31 Tuesday

1st ♊

1 Wednesday

1st ♊
☽ V/C   **5:03 am** 2:03 am
☽ enters ♋ **12:30 pm** 9:30 am

April Fools' Day (All Fools' Day—Pagan)

2 Thursday

1st ♋
2nd quarter **10:34 am** 7:34 am

Eastern time in bold type
Pacific time in medium type

3 Friday

2nd ♋
☽ V/C   **4:59 am** 1:59 am
☽ enters ♌ **3:32 pm** 12:32 pm

4 Saturday

2nd ♌
♇ Rx   **1:35 pm** 10:35 am
⚹ enters ♓ **3:58 pm** 12:58 pm

5 Sunday

2nd ♌
☽ V/C   **11:38 am** 8:38 am
☽ enters ♍ **7:01 pm** 4:01 pm
♀ enters ♋   11:27 pm

Palm Sunday

March 2009						
S	M	T	W	T	F	S
1	2	3	4	5	6	7
8	9	10	11	12	13	14
15	16	17	18	19	20	21
22	23	24	25	26	27	28
29	30	31				

April 2009						
S	M	T	W	T	F	S
			1	2	3	4
5	6	7	8	9	10	11
12	13	14	15	16	17	18
19	20	21	22	23	24	25
26	27	28	29	30		

May 2009						
S	M	T	W	T	F	S
					1	2
3	4	5	6	7	8	9
10	11	12	13	14	15	16
17	18	19	20	21	22	23
24	25	26	27	28	29	30
31						

Eastern time in bold type
Pacific time in medium type

6 Monday

2nd ♍
☿ enters ⊗   **2:27 am**

7 Tuesday

2nd ♍
☽ V/C   **12:52 pm**   9:52 am
☽ enters ♎ **11:22 pm**   8:22 pm

8 Wednesday

2nd ♎

9 Thursday

2nd ♎
☿ enters ♉ **10:21 am**   7:21 am
Full Moon   **10:56 am**   7:56 am
⚴ enters ♊   **7:19 pm**   4:19 pm
☽ V/C   **9:45 pm**   6:45 pm

Passover begins

Eastern time in bold type
Pacific time in medium type

10 Friday

3rd ♎
☽ enters ♏ **5:23 am** 2:23 am

Good Friday

11 Saturday

3rd ♏
♀ enters ♓ **8:47 am** 5:47 am

12 Sunday

3rd ♏
☽ V/C **1:28 pm** 10:28 am
♄ D **1:42 pm** 10:42 am
☽ enters ♐ **2:00 pm** 11:00 am

Easter

		March 2009				
S	M	T	W	T	F	S
1	2	3	4	5	6	7
8	9	10	11	12	13	14
15	16	17	18	19	20	21
22	23	24	25	26	27	28
29	30	31				

		April 2009				
S	M	T	W	T	F	S
			1	2	3	4
5	6	7	8	9	10	11
12	13	14	15	16	17	18
19	20	21	22	23	24	25
26	27	28	29	30		

		May 2009				
S	M	T	W	T	F	S
					1	2
3	4	5	6	7	8	9
10	11	12	13	14	15	16
17	18	19	20	21	22	23
24	25	26	27	28	29	30
31						

Eastern time in bold type
Pacific time in medium type

13 Monday

3rd ✗

14 Tuesday

3rd ✗
☽ V/C   9:07 pm
☽ enters ♈   10:27 pm

15 Wednesday

3rd ✗
☽ V/C   **12:07 am**
☽ enters ♈   **1:27 am**

16 Thursday

3rd ♈

Passover ends

Eastern time in bold type
Pacific time in medium type

17 Friday

3rd ♑

4th quarter	**9:36 am**	6:36 am
☽ V/C	**12:42 pm**	9:42 am
☽ enters ♒	**2:19 pm**	11:19 am
♀ D	**3:24 pm**	12:24 pm

Orthodox Good Friday

18 Saturday

4th ♒

19 Sunday

4th ♒

☽ V/C	**6:15 pm**	3:15 pm
☉ enters ♉	**6:44 pm**	3:44 pm
☽ enters ♓		10:55 pm

Sun enters Taurus
Orthodox Easter

March 2009						
S	M	T	W	T	F	S
1	2	3	4	5	6	7
8	9	10	11	12	13	14
15	16	17	18	19	20	21
22	23	24	25	26	27	28
29	30	31				

April 2009						
S	M	T	W	T	F	S
			1	2	3	4
5	6	7	8	9	10	11
12	13	14	15	16	17	18
19	20	21	22	23	24	25
26	27	28	29	30		

May 2009						
S	M	T	W	T	F	S
					1	2
3	4	5	6	7	8	9
10	11	12	13	14	15	16
17	18	19	20	21	22	23
24	25	26	27	28	29	30
31						

20 Monday

4th ≈
☽ enters ♓   **1:55 am**

21 Tuesday

4th ♓

22 Wednesday

4th ♓
☽ V/C   **9:29 am**   6:29 am
♂ enters ♈   **9:44 am**   6:44 am
☽ enters ♈   **10:09 am** 7:09 am

Earth Day

23 Thursday

4th ♈

Eastern time in bold type
Pacific time in medium type

24 Friday
4th ♈
♀ enters ♈	**3:18 am**	12:18 am
☽ V/C	**8:11 am**	5:11 am
☽ enters ♉	**2:46 pm**	11:46 am
New Moon	**11:22 pm**	8:22 pm

25 Saturday
1st ♉

26 Sunday
1st ♉
☽ V/C	**11:42 am**	8:42 am
☽ enters ♊	**5:02 pm**	2:02 pm

March 2009						
S	M	T	W	T	F	S
1	2	3	4	5	6	7
8	9	10	11	12	13	14
15	16	17	18	19	20	21
22	23	24	25	26	27	28
29	30	31				

April 2009						
S	M	T	W	T	F	S
			1	2	3	4
5	6	7	8	9	10	11
12	13	14	15	16	17	18
19	20	21	22	23	24	25
26	27	28	29	30		

May 2009						
S	M	T	W	T	F	S
					1	2
3	4	5	6	7	8	9
10	11	12	13	14	15	16
17	18	19	20	21	22	23
24	25	26	27	28	29	30
31						

Eastern time in bold type
Pacific Time in medium type

27 Monday
1st ♊

28 Tuesday
1st ♊
☽ V/C   **12:22 pm**   9:22 am
☽ enters ♋   **6:38 pm**   3:38 pm

29 Wednesday
1st ♋

30 Thursday
1st ♋
☽ V/C   **12:45 pm**   9:45 am
☿ enters ♊   **6:29 pm**   3:29 pm
☽ enters ♌   **8:56 pm**   5:56 pm

1 Friday

1st ♌
2nd quarter **4:44 pm** 1:44 pm

Beltane

2 Saturday

2nd ♌
☽ V/C **6:08 pm** 3:08 pm
☽ enters ♍ 9:37 pm

3 Sunday

2nd ♌
☽ enters ♍ **12:37 am**

April 2009						
S	M	T	W	T	F	S
			1	2	3	4
5	6	7	8	9	10	11
12	13	14	15	16	17	18
19	20	21	22	23	24	25
26	27	28	29	30		

May 2009						
S	M	T	W	T	F	S
					1	2
3	4	5	6	7	8	9
10	11	12	13	14	15	16
17	18	19	20	21	22	23
24	25	26	27	28	29	30
31						

June 2009						
S	M	T	W	T	F	S
	1	2	3	4	5	6
7	8	9	10	11	12	13
14	15	16	17	18	19	20
21	22	23	24	25	26	27
28	29	30				

Eastern time in bold type
Pacific time in medium type

4 Monday

2nd ♍
☽ V/C   **9:31 pm**   6:31 pm

5 Tuesday

2nd ♍
☽ enters ♎   **5:51 am**   2:51 am

Cinco de Mayo

6 Wednesday

2nd ♎
☿ R̟   10:00 pm

7 Thursday

2nd ♎
☿ R̟   **1:00 am**
☽ V/C   **6:00 am**   3:00 am
☽ enters ♏   **12:48 pm**   9:48 am

8 Friday
2nd ♏
Full Moon   9:01 pm

9 Saturday
2nd ♏
Full Moon   **12:01 am**
☽ V/C   **2:48 pm** 11:48 am
☽ enters ♐   **9:49 pm** 6:49 pm

10 Sunday
3rd ♐

Mother's Day

April 2009						
S	M	T	W	T	F	S
			1	2	3	4
5	6	7	8	9	10	11
12	13	14	15	16	17	18
19	20	21	22	23	24	25
26	27	28	29	30		

May 2009						
S	M	T	W	T	F	S
					1	2
3	4	5	6	7	8	9
10	11	12	13	14	15	16
17	18	19	20	21	22	23
24	25	26	27	28	29	30
31						

June 2009						
S	M	T	W	T	F	S
	1	2	3	4	5	6
7	8	9	10	11	12	13
14	15	16	17	18	19	20
21	22	23	24	25	26	27
28	29	30				

Eastern time in bold type
Pacific time in medium type

11 Monday

3rd ♐
☽ V/C   10:55 pm

12 Tuesday

3rd ♐
☽ V/C   **1:55 am**
☽ enters ♑   **9:09 am**   6:09 am

13 Wednesday

3rd ♑
☿ enters ♉   **7:53 pm**   4:53 pm

14 Thursday

3rd ♑
☽ V/C   **8:58 pm**   5:58 pm
☽ enters ≈   **10:01 pm**   7:01 pm

Eastern time in bold type
Pacific time in medium type

15 Friday
3rd ≈

16 Saturday
3rd ≈
ħ D   **10:06 pm**   7:06 pm

17 Sunday
3rd ≈
4th quarter   **3:26 am** 12:26 am
☽ V/C   **6:40 am**   3:40 am
☽ enters ♓ **10:17 am**   7:17 am

April 2009						
S	M	T	W	T	F	S
			1	2	3	4
5	6	7	8	9	10	11
12	13	14	15	16	17	18
19	20	21	22	23	24	25
26	27	28	29	30		

May 2009						
S	M	T	W	T	F	S
					1	2
3	4	5	6	7	8	9
10	11	12	13	14	15	16
17	18	19	20	21	22	23
24	25	26	27	28	29	30
31						

June 2009						
S	M	T	W	T	F	S
	1	2	3	4	5	6
7	8	9	10	11	12	13
14	15	16	17	18	19	20
21	22	23	24	25	26	27
28	29	30				

18 Monday
4th ♓

19 Tuesday
4th ♓
☽ V/C   **5:43 pm**   2:43 pm
☽ enters ♈   **7:30 pm**   4:30 pm

20 Wednesday
4th ♈
☉ enters ♊   **5:51 pm**   2:51 pm

Sun enters Gemini

21 Thursday
4th ♈
☽ V/C   **6:36 pm**   3:36 pm
☽ enters ♉   9:40 pm

Eastern time in bold type
Pacific time in medium type

22 Friday
4th ♈
☽ enters ♉ **12:40 am**

23 Saturday
4th ♉
☽ V/C **8:48 pm** 5:48 pm
☽ enters ♊ 11:34 pm

24 Sunday
4th ♉
☽ enters ♊ **2:34 am**
New Moon **8:11 am** 5:11 am

April 2009						
S	M	T	W	T	F	S
			1	2	3	4
5	6	7	8	9	10	11
12	13	14	15	16	17	18
19	20	21	22	23	24	25
26	27	28	29	30		

May 2009						
S	M	T	W	T	F	S
					1	2
3	4	5	6	7	8	9
10	11	12	13	14	15	16
17	18	19	20	21	22	23
24	25	26	27	28	29	30
31						

June 2009						
S	M	T	W	T	F	S
	1	2	3	4	5	6
7	8	9	10	11	12	13
14	15	16	17	18	19	20
21	22	23	24	25	26	27
28	29	30				

Eastern time in bold type
Pacific time in medium type

25 Monday

1st ♊
☽ V/C   **9:17 pm**   6:17 pm
☽ enters ♋   11:58 pm

Memorial Day (observed)

26 Tuesday

1st ♊
☽ enters ♋   **2:58 am**

27 Wednesday

1st ♋
☽ V/C   **11:06 pm**   8:06 pm

28 Thursday

1st ♋
☽ enters ♌   **3:44 am** 12:44 am
♆ Rℷ   9:30 pm

Eastern time in bold type
Pacific time in medium type

29 Friday

1st ♌
Ψ R_x   **12:30 am**

Shavuot

30 Saturday

1st ♌
☽ V/C   **4:18 am** 1:18 am
☽ enters ♍ **6:17 am** 3:17 am
⚷ R_x   **7:12 am** 4:12 am
☿ D   **9:21 pm** 6:21 pm
2nd quarter **11:22 pm** 8:22 pm

31 Sunday

2nd ♍
♂ enters ♉ **5:18 pm** 2:18 pm

April 2009						
S	M	T	W	T	F	S
			1	2	3	4
5	6	7	8	9	10	11
12	13	14	15	16	17	18
19	20	21	22	23	24	25
26	27	28	29	30		

May 2009						
S	M	T	W	T	F	S
					1	2
3	4	5	6	7	8	9
10	11	12	13	14	15	16
17	18	19	20	21	22	23
24	25	26	27	28	29	30
31						

June 2009						
S	M	T	W	T	F	S
	1	2	3	4	5	6
7	8	9	10	11	12	13
14	15	16	17	18	19	20
21	22	23	24	25	26	27
28	29	30				

Eastern time in bold type
Pacific time in medium type

1 Monday

2nd ♍
☽ V/C   **4:32 am** 1:32 am
☽ enters ♎ **11:17 am** 8:17 am

2 Tuesday

2nd ♎

3 Wednesday

2nd ♎
☽ V/C   **2:00 pm** 11:00 am
☽ enters ♏ **6:43 pm** 3:43 pm
♀ enters ♌ **10:24 pm** 7:24 pm

4 Thursday

2nd ♏

Eastern time in bold type
Pacific time in medium type

5 Friday
2nd ♏
☽ V/C   **10:18 pm**   7:18 pm

6 Saturday
2nd ♏
☽ enters ♐   **4:23 am**   1:23 am
♀ enters ♉   **5:07 am**   2:07 am

7 Sunday
2nd ♐
Full Moon   **2:12 pm**   11:12 am

May 2009						
S	M	T	W	T	F	S
					1	2
3	4	5	6	7	8	9
10	11	12	13	14	15	16
17	18	19	20	21	22	23
24	25	26	27	28	29	30
31						

June 2009						
S	M	T	W	T	F	S
	1	2	3	4	5	6
7	8	9	10	11	12	13
14	15	16	17	18	19	20
21	22	23	24	25	26	27
28	29	30				

July 2009						
S	M	T	W	T	F	S
			1	2	3	4
5	6	7	8	9	10	11
12	13	14	15	16	17	18
19	20	21	22	23	24	25
26	27	28	29	30	31	

Eastern time in bold type
Pacific time in medium type

8 Monday

3rd ♐
☽ V/C   **9:51 am** 6:51 am
☽ enters ♑   **3:59 pm** 12:59 pm

9 Tuesday

3rd ♑

10 Wednesday

3rd ♑
☽ V/C   **11:31 pm** 8:31 pm

11 Thursday

3rd ♑
☽ enters ≈   **4:52 am** 1:52 am

Eastern time in bold type
Pacific time in medium type

12 Friday
3rd ≈

13 Saturday
3rd ≈
☽ V/C   **5:04 pm**   2:04 pm
☽ enters ♓   **5:32 pm**   2:32 pm
☿ enters ♊   **10:47 pm**   7:47 pm

14 Sunday
3rd ♓

Flag Day

		May 2009							June 2009							July 2009			
S	M	T	W	T	F	S	S	M	T	W	T	F	S	S	M	T	W	T	F	S
					1	2		1	2	3	4	5	6				1	2	3	4
3	4	5	6	7	8	9	7	8	9	10	11	12	13	5	6	7	8	9	10	11
10	11	12	13	14	15	16	14	15	16	17	18	19	20	12	13	14	15	16	17	18
17	18	19	20	21	22	23	21	22	23	24	25	26	27	19	20	21	22	23	24	25
24	25	26	27	28	29	30	28	29	30					26	27	28	29	30	31	
31																				

Eastern time in bold type
Pacific time in medium type

15 Monday

3rd ♓
2 R,   **3:50 am** 12:50 am
4th quarter   **6:14 pm** 3:14 pm
☽ V/C   **9:17 pm** 6:17 pm

16 Tuesday

4th ♓
☽ enters ♈ **3:51 am** 12:51 am

17 Wednesday

4th ♈

18 Thursday

4th ♈
☽ V/C   **5:35 am** 2:35 am
☽ enters ♉ **10:20 am** 7:20 am

19 Friday
4th ♉
♀ enters ♋ **2:11 pm** 11:11 am

20 Saturday
4th ♉
☽ V/C · · · · · **8:02 am** 5:02 am
☽ enters ♊ **1:00 pm** 10:00 am
☉ enters ♋ · · · · · 10:45 pm

Sun enters Cancer • Litha • Summer Solstice • 10:45 pm PDT

21 Sunday
4th ♊
☉ enters ♋ **1:45 am**

Father's Day
Sun enters Cancer • Litha • Summer Solstice • 1:45 am EDT

May 2009						
S	M	T	W	T	F	S
					1	2
3	4	5	6	7	8	9
10	11	12	13	14	15	16
17	18	19	20	21	22	23
24	25	26	27	28	29	30
31						

June 2009						
S	M	T	W	T	F	S
	1	2	3	4	5	6
7	8	9	10	11	12	13
14	15	16	17	18	19	20
21	22	23	24	25	26	27
28	29	30				

July 2009						
S	M	T	W	T	F	S
			1	2	3	4
5	6	7	8	9	10	11
12	13	14	15	16	17	18
19	20	21	22	23	24	25
26	27	28	29	30	31	

22 Monday

4th ♊
☽ V/C	**8:20 am**	5:20 am
☽ enters ♋	**1:12 pm**	10:12 am
New Moon	**3:35 pm**	12:35 pm

23 Tuesday

1st ♋

24 Wednesday

1st ♋
| ☽ V/C | **7:24 am** | 4:24 am |
| ☽ enters ♌ | **12:50 pm** | 9:50 am |

25 Thursday

1st ♌

Eastern time in bold type
Pacific time in medium type

26 Friday

1st ♌
☽ V/C   **8:28 am** 5:28 am
☽ enters ♍   **1:46 pm** 10:46 am

27 Saturday

1st ♍

28 Sunday

1st ♍
☽ V/C   **11:26 am** 8:26 am
☽ enters ♎ **5:24 pm** 2:24 pm

		May 2009				
S	M	T	W	T	F	S
					1	2
3	4	5	6	7	8	9
10	11	12	13	14	15	16
17	18	19	20	21	22	23
24	25	26	27	28	29	30
31						

		June 2009				
S	M	T	W	T	F	S
	1	2	3	4	5	6
7	8	9	10	11	12	13
14	15	16	17	18	19	20
21	22	23	24	25	26	27
28	29	30				

		July 2009				
S	M	T	W	T	F	S
			1	2	3	4
5	6	7	8	9	10	11
12	13	14	15	16	17	18
19	20	21	22	23	24	25
26	27	28	29	30	31	

29 Monday

1st ♎︎
2nd quarter **7:28 am** 4:28 am

30 Tuesday

2nd ♎︎
☽ V/C **5:59 pm** 2:59 pm
☽ enters ♏︎ 9:18 pm

1 Wednesday

2nd ♎︎
☽ enters ♏︎ **12:18 am**
♅ R **3:37 am** 12:37 am

2 Thursday

2nd ♏︎
⚸ enters ♈︎ **9:43 pm** 6:43 pm

3 Friday

2nd ♏
☽ V/C **6:03 am** 3:03 am
☽ enters ♐ **10:10 am** 7:10 am
☿ enters ♋ **3:19 pm** 12:19 pm

4 Saturday

2nd ♐

Independence Day

5 Sunday

2nd ♐
♀ enters ♊ **4:22 am** 1:22 am
☽ V/C **3:17 pm** 12:17 pm
☽ enters ♑ **10:07 pm** 7:07 pm

	June 2009					
S	M	T	W	T	F	S
	1	2	3	4	5	6
7	8	9	10	11	12	13
14	15	16	17	18	19	20
21	22	23	24	25	26	27
28	29	30				

	July 2009					
S	M	T	W	T	F	S
			1	2	3	4
5	6	7	8	9	10	11
12	13	14	15	16	17	18
19	20	21	22	23	24	25
26	27	28	29	30	31	

	August 2009					
S	M	T	W	T	F	S
						1
2	3	4	5	6	7	8
9	10	11	12	13	14	15
16	17	18	19	20	21	22
23	24	25	26	27	28	29
30	31					

Eastern time in bold type
Pacific time in medium type

6 Monday
2nd ♑

7 Tuesday
2nd ♑
Full Moon **5:21 am** 2:21 am

Lunar eclipse 15° ♑ 32' • 5:38 am EDT/2:38 am PDT

8 Wednesday
3rd ♑
☽ V/C **5:43 am** 2:43 am
☽ enters ≈ **11:03 am** 8:03 am

9 Thursday
3rd ≈

Eastern time in bold type
Pacific time in medium type

10 Friday

3rd ≈
☽ V/C   **10:17 pm**   7:17 pm
☽ enters ⵍ **11:44 pm**   8:44 pm

11 Saturday

3rd ⵍ
♂ enters ⵠ **10:56 pm**   7:56 pm

12 Sunday

3rd ⵍ

June 2009						
S	M	T	W	T	F	S
	1	2	3	4	5	6
7	8	9	10	11	12	13
14	15	16	17	18	19	20
21	22	23	24	25	26	27
28	29	30				

July 2009						
S	M	T	W	T	F	S
			1	2	3	4
5	6	7	8	9	10	11
12	13	14	15	16	17	18
19	20	21	22	23	24	25
26	27	28	29	30	31	

August 2009						
S	M	T	W	T	F	S
						1
2	3	4	5	6	7	8
9	10	11	12	13	14	15
16	17	18	19	20	21	22
23	24	25	26	27	28	29
30	31					

13 Monday

3rd ♓
D V/C **4:03 am** 1:03 am
D enters ♈ **10:40 am** 7:40 am

14 Tuesday

3rd ♈

15 Wednesday

3rd ♈
4th quarter **5:53 am** 2:53 am
D V/C **11:07 am** 8:07 am
D enters ♉ **6:30 pm** 3:30 pm

16 Thursday

4th ♉

17 Friday
4th ♉
☽ V/C	**4:48 pm**	1:48 pm
☿ enters ♌	**7:07 pm**	4:07 pm
☽ enters ♊	**10:41 pm**	7:41 pm

18 Saturday
4th ♊

19 Sunday
4th ♊
| ☽ V/C | **6:12 pm** | 3:12 pm |
| ☽ enters ♋ | **11:51 pm** | 8:51 pm |

| June 2009 |
| S M T W T F S |
| 1 2 3 4 5 6 |
| 7 8 9 10 11 12 13 |
| 14 15 16 17 18 19 20 |
| 21 22 23 24 25 26 27 |
| 28 29 30 |

| July 2009 |
| S M T W T F S |
| 1 2 3 4 |
| 5 6 7 8 9 10 11 |
| 12 13 14 15 16 17 18 |
| 19 20 21 22 23 24 25 |
| 26 27 28 29 30 31 |

| August 2009 |
| S M T W T F S |
| 1 |
| 2 3 4 5 6 7 8 |
| 9 10 11 12 13 14 15 |
| 16 17 18 19 20 21 22 |
| 23 24 25 26 27 28 29 |
| 30 31 |

Eastern time in bold type
Pacific time in medium type

20 Monday
4th ♋

21 Tuesday
4th ♋
New Moon **10:34 pm** 7:34 pm
☽ V/C **10:34 pm** 7:34 pm
☽ enters ♌ **11:27 pm** 8:27 pm

Solar eclipse 29° ♋ 26' • 10:35 pm EDT/7:35 pm PDT

22 Wednesday
1st ♌
☉ enters ♌ **12:36 pm** 9:36 am

Sun enters Leo

23 Thursday
1st ♌
☽ V/C **4:28 pm** 1:28 pm
☽ enters ♍ **11:22 pm** 8:22 pm

Eastern time in bold type
Pacific time in medium type

24 Friday
1st ♍

25 Saturday
1st ♍
☽ V/C **7:14 pm** 4:14 pm
☽ enters ♎ 10:25 pm

26 Sunday
1st ♍
☽ enters ♎ **1:25 am**

June 2009						
S	M	T	W	T	F	S
	1	2	3	4	5	6
7	8	9	10	11	12	13
14	15	16	17	18	19	20
21	22	23	24	25	26	27
28	29	30				

July 2009						
S	M	T	W	T	F	S
			1	2	3	4
5	6	7	8	9	10	11
12	13	14	15	16	17	18
19	20	21	22	23	24	25
26	27	28	29	30	31	

August 2009						
S	M	T	W	T	F	S
						1
2	3	4	5	6	7	8
9	10	11	12	13	14	15
16	17	18	19	20	21	22
23	24	25	26	27	28	29
30	31					

Eastern time in bold type
Pacific time in medium type

27 Monday

1st ♎︎
☽ V/C   **10:53 pm**   7:53 pm

---

28 Tuesday

1st ♎︎
☽ enters ♏︎   **6:56 am**   3:56 am
2nd quarter   **6:00 pm**   3:00 pm

---

29 Wednesday

2nd ♏︎

---

30 Thursday

2nd ♏︎
☽ V/C   **8:54 am**   5:54 am
☽ enters ♐︎   **4:10 pm**   1:10 pm

Eastern time in bold type
Pacific time in medium type

31 Friday

2nd ♐

♀ enters ♋   **9:28 pm** 6:28 pm

1 Saturday

2nd ♐

♀ enters ♍   10:29 pm
☽ V/C   10:42 pm

Lammas

2 Sunday

2nd ♐

♀ enters ♍   **1:29 am**
☽ V/C   **1:42 am**
☽ enters ♑   **4:08 am** 1:08 am
☿ enters ♍   **7:07 pm** 4:07 pm

July 2009						
S	M	T	W	T	F	S
			1	2	3	4
5	6	7	8	9	10	11
12	13	14	15	16	17	18
19	20	21	22	23	24	25
26	27	28	29	30	31	

August 2009						
S	M	T	W	T	F	S
						1
2	3	4	5	6	7	8
9	10	11	12	13	14	15
16	17	18	19	20	21	22
23	24	25	26	27	28	29
30	31					

September 2009						
S	M	T	W	T	F	S
		1	2	3	4	5
6	7	8	9	10	11	12
13	14	15	16	17	18	19
20	21	22	23	24	25	26
27	28	29	30			

Eastern time in bold type
Pacific time in medium type

3 Monday

2nd ♋
♀ enters ♎   **3:31 pm** 12:31 pm

4 Tuesday

2nd ♋
☽ V/C   **9:21 am** 6:21 am
☽ enters ≈   **5:08 pm** 2:08 pm

5 Wednesday

2nd ≈
Full Moon   **8:55 pm** 5:55 pm

Lunar eclipse 13° ≈ 35' • 8:39 pm EDT/5:39 pm PDT

6 Thursday

3rd ≈
☽ V/C   **8:19 pm** 5:19 pm

Eastern time in bold type
Pacific time in medium type

7 Friday

3rd ♒
☽ enters ♓   **5:34 am**   2:34 am

8 Saturday

3rd ♓

9 Sunday

3rd ♓
☽ V/C   **8:44 am**   5:44 am
☽ enters ♈   **4:23 pm**   1:23 pm
☿ Rx   **8:01 pm**   5:01 pm

July 2009						
S	M	T	W	T	F	S
			1	2	3	4
5	6	7	8	9	10	11
12	13	14	15	16	17	18
19	20	21	22	23	24	25
26	27	28	29	30	31	

August 2009						
S	M	T	W	T	F	S
						1
2	3	4	5	6	7	8
9	10	11	12	13	14	15
16	17	18	19	20	21	22
23	24	25	26	27	28	29
30	31					

September 2009						
S	M	T	W	T	F	S
		1	2	3	4	5
6	7	8	9	10	11	12
13	14	15	16	17	18	19
20	21	22	23	24	25	26
27	28	29	30			

Eastern time in bold type
Pacific time in medium type

10 Monday
3rd ♈

---

11 Tuesday
3rd ♈
☽ V/C   **4:03 pm** 1:03 pm
☽ enters ♉   9:49 pm

---

12 Wednesday
3rd ♈
☽ enters ♉ **12:49 am**

---

13 Thursday
3rd ♉
4th quarter **2:55 pm** 11:55 am
☽ V/C   **11:17 pm** 8:17 pm

Eastern time in bold type
Pacific time in medium type

14 Friday
4th ♉
☽ enters ♊ **6:25 am** 3:25 am

15 Saturday
4th ♊
☽ V/C 11:19 pm

16 Sunday
4th ♊
☽ V/C **2:19 am**
☽ enters ♋ **9:13 am** 6:13 am

July 2009						
S	M	T	W	T	F	S
			1	2	3	4
5	6	7	8	9	10	11
12	13	14	15	16	17	18
19	20	21	22	23	24	25
26	27	28	29	30	31	

August 2009						
S	M	T	W	T	F	S
						1
2	3	4	5	6	7	8
9	10	11	12	13	14	15
16	17	18	19	20	21	22
23	24	25	26	27	28	29
30	31					

September 2009						
S	M	T	W	T	F	S
		1	2	3	4	5
6	7	8	9	10	11	12
13	14	15	16	17	18	19
20	21	22	23	24	25	26
27	28	29	30			

Eastern time in bold type
Pacific time in medium type

17 Monday

4th ⊚

---

18 Tuesday

4th ⊚
☽ V/C   **3:09 am** 12:09 am
☽ enters ♌   **9:56 am** 6:56 am

---

19 Wednesday

4th ♌

---

20 Thursday

4th ♌
New Moon   **6:01 am** 3:01 am
☽ V/C   **6:01 am** 3:01 am
☽ enters ♍ **10:00 am** 7:00 am

---

21 Friday
1st ♍

22 Saturday
1st ♍
☽ V/C **7:44 am** 4:44 am
☽ enters ♎ **11:12 am** 8:12 am
☉ enters ♍ **7:38 pm** 4:38 pm

Sun enters Virgo
Ramadan begins

23 Sunday
1st ♎

July 2009						
S	M	T	W	T	F	S
			1	2	3	4
5	6	7	8	9	10	11
12	13	14	15	16	17	18
19	20	21	22	23	24	25
26	27	28	29	30	31	

August 2009						
S	M	T	W	T	F	S
						1
2	3	4	5	6	7	8
9	10	11	12	13	14	15
16	17	18	19	20	21	22
23	24	25	26	27	28	29
30	31					

September 2009						
S	M	T	W	T	F	S
		1	2	3	4	5
6	7	8	9	10	11	12
13	14	15	16	17	18	19
20	21	22	23	24	25	26
27	28	29	30			

Eastern time in bold type
Pacific time in medium type

24 Monday

1st ♎
☽ V/C **2:10 pm** 11:10 am
☽ enters ♏ **3:16 pm** 12:16 pm

25 Tuesday

1st ♏
♂ enters ♋ **1:15 pm** 10:15 am
☿ enters ♎ **4:18 pm** 1:18 pm

26 Wednesday

1st ♏
♀ enters ♌ **12:11 pm** 9:11 am
☽ V/C **2:34 pm** 11:34 am
☽ enters ♐ **11:16 pm** 8:16 pm

27 Thursday

1st ♐
2nd quarter **7:42 am** 4:42 am

Eastern time in bold type
Pacific time in medium type

```
          TRIPLE SPIRAL
     106-3 FAN TAN ALLEY
          VICTORIA B.C.
     380-7212 FAX 380-7412
        SEE OUR WEBSITE


MISC II              8.95
ITEM CT          1
TXBL-1               8.95
TAX-1 5%             0.45
TXBL-2               8.95
TAX-2 6%             0.54
CHARGE           9.94
    11-29-2008 12:09PM
        2014 CLERK  1
```

```
          TRIPLE SPIRAL
          METAPHYSICAL
          3 FAN TAN ALLEY
          VICTORIA     BC

CARD 5892970000*********
ACCOUNT TYPE     CHEQUING
DATE             2008/11/29
TIME        5054 10:57:56
RECEIPT NUMBER
 S34502720-001-551-001-0
 _____

PURCHASE
TOTAL-CAD

                  $9.94
 _____


APPROVED
AUTH# 144069        00-001
THANK YOU

          CARDHOLDER COPY
```

28 Friday
2nd ♐
⚡ enters ♌ **8:45 am** 5:45 am
☽ V/C 10:26 pm

29 Saturday
2nd ♐
☽ V/C **1:26 am**
☽ enters ♑ **10:44 am** 7:44 am

30 Sunday
2nd ♑

July 2009						
S	M	T	W	T	F	S
			1	2	3	4
5	6	7	8	9	10	11
12	13	14	15	16	17	18
19	20	21	22	23	24	25
26	27	28	29	30	31	

August 2009						
S	M	T	W	T	F	S
						1
2	3	4	5	6	7	8
9	10	11	12	13	14	15
16	17	18	19	20	21	22
23	24	25	26	27	28	29
30	31					

September 2009						
S	M	T	W	T	F	S
		1	2	3	4	5
6	7	8	9	10	11	12
13	14	15	16	17	18	19
20	21	22	23	24	25	26
27	28	29	30			

Eastern time in bold type
Pacific time in medium type

31 Monday

2nd ♑
☽ V/C   **2:09 pm** 11:09 am
☽ enters ≈ **11:43 pm** 8:43 pm

1 Tuesday

2nd ≈

2 Wednesday

2nd ≈
☽ V/C   10:19 pm

3 Thursday

2nd ≈
☽ V/C   **1:19 am**
☽ enters ♓ **11:58 am** 8:58 am

Eastern time in bold type
Pacific time in medium type

4 Friday

2nd ♓
Full Moon **12:02 pm** 9:02 am

5 Saturday

3rd ♓
☽ V/C **12:53 pm** 9:53 am
☽ enters ♈ **10:14 pm** 7:14 pm

6 Sunday

3rd ♈
☿ ℞ 9:45 pm

August 2009
S M T W T F S
1
2 3 4 5 6 7 8
9 10 11 12 13 14 15
16 17 18 19 20 21 22
23 24 25 26 27 28 29
30 31

September 2009
S M T W T F S
1 2 3 4 5
6 7 8 9 10 11 12
13 14 15 16 17 18 19
20 21 22 23 24 25 26
27 28 29 30

October 2009
S M T W T F S
1 2 3
4 5 6 7 8 9 10
11 12 13 14 15 16 17
18 19 20 21 22 23 24
25 26 27 28 29 30 31

Eastern time in bold type
Pacific time in medium type

7 Monday

3rd ♈

☿ ℞   **12:45 am**

☽ V/C   **8:12 pm** 5:12 pm

Labor Day

8 Tuesday

3rd ♈

☽ enters ♉ **6:17 am** 3:17 am

9 Wednesday

3rd ♉

10 Thursday

3rd ♉

☽ V/C   **3:17 am** 12:17 am

☽ enters ♊ **12:17 pm** 9:17 am

Eastern time in bold type
Pacific time in medium type

11 Friday

3rd ♊
♇ D   **12:57 pm** 9:57 am
4th quarter **10:16 pm** 7:16 pm

12 Saturday

4th ♊
☽ V/C   **7:30 am** 4:30 am
☽ enters ♋ **4:19 pm** 1:19 pm

13 Sunday

4th ♋

August 2009						
S	M	T	W	T	F	S
						1
2	3	4	5	6	7	8
9	10	11	12	13	14	15
16	17	18	19	20	21	22
23	24	25	26	27	28	29
30	31					

September 2009						
S	M	T	W	T	F	S
		1	2	3	4	5
6	7	8	9	10	11	12
13	14	15	16	17	18	19
20	21	22	23	24	25	26
27	28	29	30			

October 2009						
S	M	T	W	T	F	S
					1	2	3
4	5	6	7	8	9	10
11	12	13	14	15	16	17
18	19	20	21	22	23	24
25	26	27	28	29	30	31

Eastern time in bold type
Pacific time in medium type

14 Monday

4th ♋
☽ V/C   **9:57 am** 6:57 am
☽ enters ♌ **6:39 pm** 3:39 pm
⚹ enters ♓ **7:00 pm** 4:00 pm

15 Tuesday

4th ♌

16 Wednesday

4th ♌
☽ V/C   **12:10 pm** 9:10 am
☽ enters ♍ **7:56 pm** 4:56 pm

17 Thursday

4th ♍
☿ enters ♍ **11:26 pm** 8:26 pm

Eastern time in bold type
Pacific time in medium type

18 Friday
4th ♍
New Moon	**2:44 pm**	11:44 am
☽ V/C	**7:56 pm**	4:56 pm
☽ enters ♎	**9:26 pm**	6:26 pm

19 Saturday
1st ♎

Rosh Hashanah

20 Sunday
1st ♎
♀ enters ♍	**9:32 am**	6:32 am
☽ V/C	**2:43 pm**	11:43 am
☽ enters ♏		9:52 pm

August 2009						
S	M	T	W	T	F	S
						1
2	3	4	5	6	7	8
9	10	11	12	13	14	15
16	17	18	19	20	21	22
23	24	25	26	27	28	29
30	31					

September 2009						
S	M	T	W	T	F	S
		1	2	3	4	5
6	7	8	9	10	11	12
13	14	15	16	17	18	19
20	21	22	23	24	25	26
27	28	29	30			

October 2009						
S	M	T	W	T	F	S
				1	2	3
4	5	6	7	8	9	10
11	12	13	14	15	16	17
18	19	20	21	22	23	24
25	26	27	28	29	30	31

Eastern time in bold type
Pacific time in medium type

21 Monday

1st ♎︎
☽ enters ♏︎ **12:52 am**

Ramadan ends

---

22 Tuesday

1st ♏︎
☉ enters ♎︎ **5:18 pm**   2:18 pm
☽ V/C   **11:32 pm**   8:32 pm

Sun enters Libra • Mabon • Fall Equinox • 5:18 pm EDT/2:18 am PDT

---

23 Wednesday

1st ♏︎
☽ enters ♐︎ **7:43 am**   4:43 am

---

24 Thursday

1st ♐︎

Eastern time in bold type
Pacific time in medium type

25 Friday

1st ♐

☽ V/C	**10:15 am**	7:15 am
☽ enters ♑	**6:19 pm**	3:19 pm
2nd quarter		9:50 pm

26 Saturday

1st ♑

2nd quarter **12:50 am**

27 Sunday

2nd ♑

☽ V/C   **11:33 pm**   8:33 pm

August 2009						
S	M	T	W	T	F	S
						1
2	3	4	5	6	7	8
9	10	11	12	13	14	15
16	17	18	19	20	21	22
23	24	25	26	27	28	29
30	31					

September 2009						
S	M	T	W	T	F	S
		1	2	3	4	5
6	7	8	9	10	11	12
13	14	15	16	17	18	19
20	21	22	23	24	25	26
27	28	29	30			

October 2009						
S	M	T	W	T	F	S
				1	2	3
4	5	6	7	8	9	10
11	12	13	14	15	16	17
18	19	20	21	22	23	24
25	26	27	28	29	30	31

Eastern time in bold type
Pacific time in medium type

28 Monday

2nd ♑
☽ enters ♒   **7:06 am** 4:06 am

Yom Kippur

29 Tuesday

2nd ♒
☿ D   **9:13 am** 6:13 am

30 Wednesday

2nd ♒
☽ V/C   **7:34 am** 4:34 am
☽ enters ♓ **7:26 pm** 4:26 pm

1 Thursday

2nd ♓

Eastern time in bold type
Pacific time in medium type

2 Friday

2nd ♓

☽ V/C   **11:29 pm** 8:29 pm

3 Saturday

2nd ♓

☽ enters ♈ **5:20 am** 2:20 am
♀ enters ♎ **7:45 am** 4:45 am
Full Moon   11:10 pm

Sukkot begins

4 Sunday

2nd ♈

Full Moon **2:10 am**

☽ V/C   10:46 pm

September 2009						
S	M	T	W	T	F	S
		1	2	3	4	5
6	7	8	9	10	11	12
13	14	15	16	17	18	19
20	21	22	23	24	25	26
27	28	29	30			

October 2009						
S	M	T	W	T	F	S
				1	2	3
4	5	6	7	8	9	10
11	12	13	14	15	16	17
18	19	20	21	22	23	24
25	26	27	28	29	30	31

November 2009						
S	M	T	W	T	F	S
1	2	3	4	5	6	7
8	9	10	11	12	13	14
15	16	17	18	19	20	21
22	23	24	25	26	27	28
29	30					

5 Monday

3rd ♈
☽ V/C   **1:46 am**
☽ enters ♉   **12:33 pm** 9:33 am

6 Tuesday

3rd ♉

7 Wednesday

3rd ♉
☽ V/C   **1:19 pm** 10:19 am
☽ enters ♊   **5:46 pm** 2:46 pm

8 Thursday

3rd ♊

9 Friday
3rd ♊
☽ V/C	**9:35 pm**	6:35 pm
☽ enters ♋	**9:48 pm**	6:48 pm
☿ enters ♎	**11:45 pm**	8:45 pm

Sukkot ends

10 Saturday
3rd ♋

11 Sunday
3rd ♋
4th quarter	**4:56 am**	1:56 am
☽ V/C	**9:37 pm**	6:37 pm
☽ enters ♌		10:02 pm

September 2009						
S	M	T	W	T	F	S
		1	2	3	4	5
6	7	8	9	10	11	12
13	14	15	16	17	18	19
20	21	22	23	24	25	26
27	28	29	30			

October 2009						
S	M	T	W	T	F	S
				1	2	3
4	5	6	7	8	9	10
11	12	13	14	15	16	17
18	19	20	21	22	23	24
25	26	27	28	29	30	31

November 2009						
S	M	T	W	T	F	S
1	2	3	4	5	6	7
8	9	10	11	12	13	14
15	16	17	18	19	20	21
22	23	24	25	26	27	28
29	30					

12 Monday

4th ♋
☽ enters ♌ **1:02 am**
♀ enters ♏ **2:29 pm** 11:29 am
♃ D   9:34 pm

Columbus Day (observed)

13 Tuesday

4th ♌
♃ D   **12:34 am**
☽ V/C   **5:20 pm** 2:20 pm

14 Wednesday

4th ♌
☽ enters ♍ **3:45 am** 12:45 am
♀ enters ♎ **6:46 pm** 3:46 pm

15 Thursday

4th ♍

Eastern time in bold type
Pacific time in medium type

16 Friday

4th ♍
☽ V/C   **6:18 am** 3:18 am
☽ enters ♎ **6:29 am** 3:29 am
♂ enters ♌ **11:32 am** 8:32 am

17 Saturday

4th ♎
New Moon   10:33 pm
☽ V/C   10:33 pm

18 Sunday

4th ♎
New Moon **1:33 am**
☽ V/C   **1:33 am**
☽ enters ♏ **10:22 am** 7:22 am

September 2009						
S	M	T	W	T	F	S
		1	2	3	4	5
6	7	8	9	10	11	12
13	14	15	16	17	18	19
20	21	22	23	24	25	26
27	28	29	30			

October 2009						
S	M	T	W	T	F	S
				1	2	3
4	5	6	7	8	9	10
11	12	13	14	15	16	17
18	19	20	21	22	23	24
25	26	27	28	29	30	31

November 2009						
S	M	T	W	T	F	S
1	2	3	4	5	6	7
8	9	10	11	12	13	14
15	16	17	18	19	20	21
22	23	24	25	26	27	28
29	30					

19 Monday
1st ♏

20 Tuesday
1st ♏
☽ V/C   **2:57 pm** 11:57 am
☽ enters ♐   **4:49 pm** 1:49 pm

21 Wednesday
1st ♐

22 Thursday
1st ♐
☽ V/C   10:13 pm
☽ enters ♑   11:39 pm
☉ enters ♏   11:43 pm

Sun enters Scorpio

Eastern time in bold type
Pacific time in medium type

23 Friday

1st ♐

☽ V/C	**1:13 am**
☽ enters ♑	**2:39 am**
☉ enters ♏	**2:43 am**

Sun enters Scorpio

24 Saturday

1st ♑

25 Sunday

1st ♑

☽ V/C	**2:14 pm**	11:14 am
☽ enters ♒	**3:08 pm**	12:08 pm
2nd quarter	**8:42 pm**	5:42 pm

September 2009						
S	M	T	W	T	F	S
		1	2	3	4	5
6	7	8	9	10	11	12
13	14	15	16	17	18	19
20	21	22	23	24	25	26
27	28	29	30			

October 2009						
S	M	T	W	T	F	S
				1	2	3
4	5	6	7	8	9	10
11	12	13	14	15	16	17
18	19	20	21	22	23	24
25	26	27	28	29	30	31

November 2009						
S	M	T	W	T	F	S
1	2	3	4	5	6	7
8	9	10	11	12	13	14
15	16	17	18	19	20	21
22	23	24	25	26	27	28
29	30					

Eastern time in bold type
Pacific time in medium type

26 Monday

2nd ≈

27 Tuesday

2nd ≈

28 Wednesday

2nd ≈

☽ V/C   **3:22 am** 12:22 am
☽ enters ♓   **3:45 am** 12:45 am

☿ enters ♏   **6:08 am** 3:08 am

29 Thursday

2nd ♓

♄ enters ♎   **1:09 pm** 10:09 am

☽ V/C   9:56 pm

Eastern time in bold type
Pacific time in medium type

30 Friday
2nd ♓
☽ V/C   **12:56 am**
☽ enters ♈   **1:56 pm** 10:56 am
⚷ D   10:45 pm

31 Saturday
2nd ♈
⚷ D   **1:45 am**

Halloween/Samhain

1 Sunday
2nd ♈
☽ V/C   **8:29 am** 5:29 am
☽ enters ♉   **7:44 pm** 4:44 pm

All Saints' Day
Daylight Saving Time ends at 2 am

October 2009						
S	M	T	W	T	F	S
				1	2	3
4	5	6	7	8	9	10
11	12	13	14	15	16	17
18	19	20	21	22	23	24
25	26	27	28	29	30	31

November 2009						
S	M	T	W	T	F	S
1	2	3	4	5	6	7
8	9	10	11	12	13	14
15	16	17	18	19	20	21
22	23	24	25	26	27	28
29	30					

December 2009						
S	M	T	W	T	F	S
		1	2	3	4	5
6	7	8	9	10	11	12
13	14	15	16	17	18	19
20	21	22	23	24	25	26
27	28	29	30	31		

2 Monday

2nd ☿
Full Moon **2:14 pm** 11:14 am

3 Tuesday

3rd ☿
☽ V/C **1:04 pm** 10:04 am
✳ D **4:17 pm** 1:17 pm
☽ enters ♊ **11:53 pm** 8:53 pm

Election Day (general)

4 Wednesday

3rd ♊
♆ D **1:10 pm** 10:10 am

5 Thursday

3rd ♊
☽ V/C **10:47 pm** 7:47 pm
☽ enters ♋ 11:42 pm

6 Friday
3rd ♊
☽ enters ♋ **2:42 am**

7 Saturday
3rd ♋
☽ V/C **5:26 pm** 2:26 pm
♀ enters ♏ **7:23 pm** 4:23 pm

8 Sunday
3rd ♋
☽ enters ♌ **5:23 am** 2:23 am

October 2009						
S	M	T	W	T	F	S
				1	2	3
4	5	6	7	8	9	10
11	12	13	14	15	16	17
18	19	20	21	22	23	24
25	26	27	28	29	30	31

November 2009						
S	M	T	W	T	F	S
1	2	3	4	5	6	7
8	9	10	11	12	13	14
15	16	17	18	19	20	21
22	23	24	25	26	27	28
29	30					

December 2009						
S	M	T	W	T	F	S
		1	2	3	4	5
6	7	8	9	10	11	12
13	14	15	16	17	18	19
20	21	22	23	24	25	26
27	28	29	30	31		

9 Monday

3rd ♌
4th quarter **10:56 am** 7:56 am
☽ V/C **9:43 pm** 6:43 pm

10 Tuesday
4th ♌
☽ enters ♍ **8:30 am** 5:30 am

11 Wednesday
4th ♍
☽ V/C 11:13 pm

Veterans Day

12 Thursday
4th ♍
☽ V/C **2:13 am**
☽ enters ♎ **12:22 pm** 9:22 am

Eastern time in bold type
Pacific time in medium type

13 Friday
4th ♎

14 Saturday
4th ♎
☽ V/C   **6:10 am**   3:10 am
☽ enters ♏ **5:24 pm** 2:24 pm

15 Sunday
4th ♏
☿ enters ♐   **7:28 pm** 4:28 pm

October 2009						
S	M	T	W	T	F	S
				1	2	3
4	5	6	7	8	9	10
11	12	13	14	15	16	17
18	19	20	21	22	23	24
25	26	27	28	29	30	31

November 2009						
S	M	T	W	T	F	S
1	2	3	4	5	6	7
8	9	10	11	12	13	14
15	16	17	18	19	20	21
22	23	24	25	26	27	28
29	30					

December 2009						
S	M	T	W	T	F	S
		1	2	3	4	5
6	7	8	9	10	11	12
13	14	15	16	17	18	19
20	21	22	23	24	25	26
27	28	29	30	31		

16 Monday
4th ♏
New Moon   **2:14 pm** 11:14 am
☽ V/C   **2:14 pm** 11:14 am
☽ enters ♐   9:22 pm

17 Tuesday
1st ♏
☽ enters ♐ **12:22 am**

18 Wednesday
1st ♐
☽ V/C   **9:46 pm** 6:46 pm

19 Thursday
1st ♐
♀ enters ♍ **8:38 am** 5:38 am
☽ enters ♑ **10:00 am** 7:00 am

Eastern time in bold type
Pacific time in medium type

20 Friday
1st ♑

---

21 Saturday
1st ♑
☽ V/C	**10:04 pm**	7:04 pm
☽ enters ♒	**10:11 pm**	7:11 pm
☉ enters ♐	**11:22 pm**	8:22 pm

Sun enters Sagittarius

---

22 Sunday
1st ♒

October 2009	November 2009	December 2009
S M T W T F S	S M T W T F S	S M T W T F S
1 2 3	1 2 3 4 5 6 7	1 2 3 4 5
4 5 6 7 8 9 10	8 9 10 11 12 13 14	6 7 8 9 10 11 12
11 12 13 14 15 16 17	15 16 17 18 19 20 21	13 14 15 16 17 18 19
18 19 20 21 22 23 24	22 23 24 25 26 27 28	20 21 22 23 24 25 26
25 26 27 28 29 30 31	29 30	27 28 29 30 31

Eastern time in bold type
Pacific time in medium type

23 Monday

1st ≈
☽ V/C   **10:35 pm** 7:35 pm

24 Tuesday

1st ≈
☽ enters ✶ **11:07 am** 8:07 am
2nd quarter **4:39 pm** 1:39 pm

25 Wednesday

2nd ✶

26 Thursday

2nd ✶
☽ V/C   **9:17 am** 6:17 am
☽ enters ♈ **10:10 pm** 7:10 pm

Thanksgiving Day

Eastern time in bold type
Pacific time in medium type

27 Friday
2nd ♈

28 Saturday
2nd ♈
☽ V/C   **6:32 pm**   3:32 pm

29 Sunday
2nd ♈
☽ enters ♉   **5:34 am**   2:34 am

October 2009						
S	M	T	W	T	F	S
				1	2	3
4	5	6	7	8	9	10
11	12	13	14	15	16	17
18	19	20	21	22	23	24
25	26	27	28	29	30	31

November 2009						
S	M	T	W	T	F	S
1	2	3	4	5	6	7
8	9	10	11	12	13	14
15	16	17	18	19	20	21
22	23	24	25	26	27	28
29	30					

December 2009						
S	M	T	W	T	F	S
		1	2	3	4	5
6	7	8	9	10	11	12
13	14	15	16	17	18	19
20	21	22	23	24	25	26
27	28	29	30	31		

Eastern time in bold type
Pacific time in medium type

30 Monday
2nd ♉

---

1 Tuesday
2nd ♉
☽ V/C	**8:39 am**	5:39 am
☽ enters ♊	**9:23 am**	6:23 am
♅ D	**3:27 pm**	12:27 pm
♀ enters ♐	**5:03 pm**	2:03 pm
Full Moon		11:30 pm

---

2 Wednesday
2nd ♊
| Full Moon | **2:30 am** |

---

3 Thursday
3rd ♊
| ☽ V/C | **5:27 am** | 2:27 am |
| ☽ enters ♋ | **11:00 am** | 8:00 am |

Eastern time in bold type
Pacific time in medium type

4 Friday
3rd ♋
☽ V/C   9:08 pm

5 Saturday
3rd ♋
☽ V/C   **12:08 am**
☽ enters ♌ **12:07 pm** 9:07 am
☿ enters ♑ **12:24 pm** 9:24 am

6 Sunday
3rd ♌

November 2009						
S	M	T	W	T	F	S
1	2	3	4	5	6	7
8	9	10	11	12	13	14
15	16	17	18	19	20	21
22	23	24	25	26	27	28
29	30					

December 2009						
S	M	T	W	T	F	S
		1	2	3	4	5
6	7	8	9	10	11	12
13	14	15	16	17	18	19
20	21	22	23	24	25	26
27	28	29	30	31		

January 2010						
S	M	T	W	T	F	S
					1	2
3	4	5	6	7	8	9
10	11	12	13	14	15	16
17	18	19	20	21	22	23
24	25	26	27	28	29	30
31						

Eastern time in bold type
Pacific time in medium type

7 Monday
3rd ♌
℞ V/C   **3:57 am** 12:57 am
℞ enters ♍   **2:05 pm** 11:05 am

8 Tuesday
3rd ♍
4th quarter   **7:13 pm** 4:13 pm

9 Wednesday
4th ♍
℞ V/C   **5:04 am** 2:04 am
℞ enters ♎   **5:47 pm** 2:47 pm

10 Thursday
4th ♎
♀ enters ♏   9:57 pm

11 Friday

4th ♎︎
♀ enters ♏︎ **12:57 am**
☽ V/C   **12:44 pm** 9:44 am
☽ enters ♏︎ **11:31 pm** 8:31 pm

12 Saturday

4th ♏︎

Hanukkah begins

13 Sunday

4th ♏︎
☽ V/C   **8:17 pm** 5:17 pm

November 2009						
S	M	T	W	T	F	S
1	2	3	4	5	6	7
8	9	10	11	12	13	14
15	16	17	18	19	20	21
22	23	24	25	26	27	28
29	30					

December 2009						
S	M	T	W	T	F	S
		1	2	3	4	5
6	7	8	9	10	11	12
13	14	15	16	17	18	19
20	21	22	23	24	25	26
27	28	29	30	31		

January 2010						
S	M	T	W	T	F	S
					1	2
3	4	5	6	7	8	9
10	11	12	13	14	15	16
17	18	19	20	21	22	23
24	25	26	27	28	29	30
31						

14 Monday
4th ♏
☽ enters ♐ **7:25 am** 4:25 am

15 Tuesday
4th ♐

16 Wednesday
4th ♐
New Moon **7:02 am** 4:02 am
☽ V/C **7:02 am** 4:02 am
☽ enters ♑ **5:32 pm** 2:32 pm

17 Thursday
1st ♑

Eastern time in bold type
Pacific time in medium type

18 Friday

1st ♑
☽ V/C   **3:07 pm** 12:07 pm

Islamic New Year

19 Saturday

1st ♑
☽ enters ♒   **5:38 am** 2:38 am
♅ enters ♈   **5:09 pm** 2:09 pm

Hanukkah ends

20 Sunday

1st ♒
♂ ℞   **8:26 am** 5:26 am
♀ enters ♐   **3:25 pm** 12:25 pm

November 2009						
S	M	T	W	T	F	S
1	2	3	4	5	6	7
8	9	10	11	12	13	14
15	16	17	18	19	20	21
22	23	24	25	26	27	28
29	30					

December 2009						
S	M	T	W	T	F	S
		1	2	3	4	5
6	7	8	9	10	11	12
13	14	15	16	17	18	19
20	21	22	23	24	25	26
27	28	29	30	31		

January 2010						
S	M	T	W	T	F	S
					1	2
3	4	5	6	7	8	9
10	11	12	13	14	15	16
17	18	19	20	21	22	23
24	25	26	27	28	29	30
31						

Llewellyn's 2009 Pocket Planner and Ephemeris

21 Monday

1st ≈
☽ V/C **7:53 am** 4:53 am
☉ enters ♑ **12:47 pm** 9:47 am
☽ enters ♓ **6:42 pm** 3:42 pm

Sun enters Capricorn • Yule • Winter Solstice • 12:47 pm EST/9:47 am PST

22 Tuesday

1st ♓

23 Wednesday

1st ♓

24 Thursday

1st ♓
☽ V/C **3:09 am** 12:09 am
☽ enters ♈ **6:39 am** 3:39 am
2nd quarter **12:36 pm** 9:36 am

Christmas Eve

Eastern time in bold type
Pacific time in medium type

25 Friday

2nd ♈
♀ enters ♑   **1:17 pm** 10:17 am

Christmas Day

26 Saturday

2nd ♈
☽ V/C   **6:44 am** 3:44 am
☿ ℞   **9:38 am** 6:38 am
☽ enters ♉   **3:26 pm** 12:26 pm

Kwanzaa begins

27 Sunday

2nd ♉

November 2009						
S	M	T	W	T	F	S
1	2	3	4	5	6	7
8	9	10	11	12	13	14
15	16	17	18	19	20	21
22	23	24	25	26	27	28
29	30					

December 2009						
S	M	T	W	T	F	S
		1	2	3	4	5
6	7	8	9	10	11	12
13	14	15	16	17	18	19
20	21	22	23	24	25	26
27	28	29	30	31		

January 2010						
S	M	T	W	T	F	S
					1	2
3	4	5	6	7	8	9
10	11	12	13	14	15	16
17	18	19	20	21	22	23
24	25	26	27	28	29	30
31						

Eastern time in bold type
Pacific time in medium type

28 Monday

2nd ♉
☽ V/C   **12:54 pm** 9:54 am
☽ enters ♊   **8:13 pm** 5:13 pm

29 Tuesday

2nd ♊

30 Wednesday

2nd ♊
☽ V/C   **3:29 pm** 12:29 pm
☽ enters ♋   **9:45 pm** 6:45 pm

31 Thursday

2nd ♋
Full Moon   **2:13 pm** 11:13 am

New Year's Eve
Lunar eclipse 10° ♋ 20' • 2:22 pm EST/11:22 am PST

Eastern time in bold type
Pacific time in medium type

The Year 2010

January
S	M	T	W	T	F	S
					1	2
3	4	5	6	7	8	9
10	11	12	13	14	15	16
17	18	19	20	21	22	23
24	25	26	27	28	29	30
31						

February
S	M	T	W	T	F	S
	1	2	3	4	5	6
7	8	9	10	11	12	13
14	15	16	17	18	19	20
21	22	23	24	25	26	27
28						

March
S	M	T	W	T	F	S
	1	2	3	4	5	6
7	8	9	10	11	12	13
14	15	16	17	18	19	20
21	22	23	24	25	26	27
28	29	30	31			

April
S	M	T	W	T	F	S
				1	2	3
4	5	6	7	8	9	10
11	12	13	14	15	16	17
18	19	20	21	22	23	24
25	26	27	28	29	30	

May
S	M	T	W	T	F	S
						1
2	3	4	5	6	7	8
9	10	11	12	13	14	15
16	17	18	19	20	21	22
23	24	25	26	27	28	29
30	31					

June
S	M	T	W	T	F	S
		1	2	3	4	5
6	7	8	9	10	11	12
13	14	15	16	17	18	19
20	21	22	23	24	25	26
27	28	29	30			

July
S	M	T	W	T	F	S
				1	2	3
4	5	6	7	8	9	10
11	12	13	14	15	16	17
18	19	20	21	22	23	24
25	26	27	28	29	30	31

August
S	M	T	W	T	F	S
1	2	3	4	5	6	7
8	9	10	11	12	13	14
15	16	17	18	19	20	21
22	23	24	25	26	27	28
29	30	31				

September
S	M	T	W	T	F	S
			1	2	3	4
5	6	7	8	9	10	11
12	13	14	15	16	17	18
19	20	21	22	23	24	25
26	27	28	29	30		

October
S	M	T	W	T	F	S
					1	2
3	4	5	6	7	8	9
10	11	12	13	14	15	16
17	18	19	20	21	22	23
24	25	26	27	28	29	30
31						

November
S	M	T	W	T	F	S
	1	2	3	4	5	6
7	8	9	10	11	12	13
14	15	16	17	18	19	20
21	22	23	24	25	26	27
28	29	30				

December
S	M	T	W	T	F	S
			1	2	3	4
5	6	7	8	9	10	11
12	13	14	15	16	17	18
19	20	21	22	23	24	25
26	27	28	29	30	31	

JANUARY 2008

☽ Last Aspect day	ET / hr:mn	PT	asp	☽ Ingress sign	day	ET / hr:mn	PT
1	**7:33 pm**	4:33 pm	△♂	♏	1	**8:32 pm**	5:32 pm
3	**7:30 pm**	4:30 pm	⚹☿	♐	4	**9:13 am**	6:13 am
6	**7:27 pm**	4:27 pm	☌♇	♑	6	**8:43 pm**	5:43 pm
8	**6:37 am**	3:37 am	☌☉	♒	9	**6:13 am**	3:13 am
11	**12:52 pm**	9:52 am	⚹♇	♓	11	**1:44 pm**	10:44 am
13	**6:41 pm**	3:41 pm	□♇	♈	13	**7:23 pm**	4:23 pm
15	**10:39 pm**	7:39 pm	△♇	♉	15	**11:13 pm**	8:13 pm
17	**9:05 pm**	6:05 pm	△☉	♊	17		10:30 pm
17	**9:05 pm**	6:05 pm	△☉	♊	18	**1:30 am**	
19		11:46 pm	☍♇	♋	20	**3:05 am**	12:05 am
20	**2:46 am**		☍♇	♋	20	**3:05 am**	12:05 am
21	**5:56 am**	2:56 am	△♅	♌	22	**5:20 am**	2:20 am
24	**9:43 am**	6:43 am	△♇	♍	24	**9:48 am**	6:48 am
26	**6:32 am**	3:32 am	□♂	♎	26	**5:35 pm**	2:35 pm
28	**4:47 pm**	1:47 pm	△♂	♏	29	**4:35 am**	1:35 am
31	**3:34 am**	12:34 am	□☿	♐	31	**5:08 pm**	2:08 pm

☽ Phases & Eclipses phase	day	ET / hr:mn	PT
New Moon	8	**6:37 am**	3:37 am
2nd Quarter	15	**2:46 pm**	11:46 am
Full Moon	22	**8:35 am**	5:35 am
4th Quarter	29		9:03 pm
4th Quarter	30	**12:03 am**	

Planet Ingress	day	ET / hr:mn	PT
☿ ♒	7	**11:46 pm**	8:46 pm
☉ ♒	20	**11:43 am**	8:43 am
♀ ♑	24	**3:06 am**	12:06 am
♇ ♑	25	**9:37 pm**	6:37 pm

Planetary Motion	day	ET / hr:mn	PT
☿ ℞	28	**3:31 pm**	12:31 pm
♂ D	30	**5:33 pm**	2:33 pm

1 TUESDAY

☽ △ ♆	**12:53 am**	
☽ ⚹ ♇	**6:52 pm**	3:52 pm
☽ △ ♂	**7:33 pm**	4:33 pm
☿ ⊻ ♆		9:47 pm
☽ ⊻ ♀		11:51 pm

2 WEDNESDAY

☿ ⊻ ♆	**12:47 am**	
☽ ⊻ ♀	**2:51 am**	
☽ ⚹ ♃	**3:16 am**	12:16 am
♀ ⊻ ♃	**7:43 am**	4:43 am
☽ ⚹ ♄	**1:31 pm**	10:31 am
♂ ☍ ♇	**4:23 pm**	1:23 pm
☽ ⚹ ☉	**8:57 pm**	5:57 pm

3 THURSDAY

☽ △ ♅	**3:49 am**	12:49 am
☽ □ ♆	**1:44 pm**	10:44 am
☽ ⚹ ☿	**7:30 pm**	4:30 pm

4 FRIDAY

☽ ⚻ ♂	**6:32 am**	3:32 am
☽ ⊻ ♇	**7:45 am**	4:45 am
☽ ⊻ ♃	**5:04 pm**	2:04 pm
☽ ☌ ♀	**10:19 pm**	7:19 pm
☽ □ ♄		10:53 pm

5 SATURDAY

☽ □ ♄	**1:53 am**	
☽ ⊻ ☉	**2:54 pm**	11:54 am
☽ □ ♅	**4:14 pm**	1:14 pm
☽ ⚹ ♆		10:55 pm

6 SUNDAY

☽ ⚹ ♆	**1:55 am**	
☉ ⚹ ♅	**7:18 am**	4:18 am
♀ □ ♄	**8:39 am**	5:39 am
☿ ⚻ ♂	**4:32 pm**	1:32 pm
☽ ☍ ♂	**4:35 pm**	1:35 pm
☽ ⊻ ☿	**4:35 pm**	1:35 pm
☽ ☌ ♇	**7:27 pm**	4:27 pm

7 MONDAY

☽ ☌ ♃	**5:26 am**	2:26 am
☽ △ ♄	**12:42 pm**	9:42 am
☿ ⊻ ♇	**2:39 pm**	11:39 am
☽ ⊻ ♀	**3:50 pm**	12:50 pm
☽ ⚹ ♅		11:54 pm

8 TUESDAY

☽ ⚹ ♅	**2:54 am**	
☽ ☌ ☉	**6:37 am**	3:37 am
☽ ⊻ ♆	**12:14 pm**	9:14 am
☽ ⚻ ♂		9:54 pm

9 WEDNESDAY

☽ ⚻ ♂	**12:54 am**	
☽ ⊻ ♇	**5:10 am**	2:10 am
☽ ☌ ☿	**10:38 am**	7:38 am
☽ ⊻ ♃	**3:40 pm**	12:40 pm
☽ ⚻ ♄	**9:29 pm**	6:29 pm

10 THURSDAY

☽ ⚹ ♀	**6:35 am**	3:35 am
☽ ⊻ ♅	**11:30 am**	8:30 am
☽ ⊻ ☉	**7:43 pm**	4:43 pm
☽ ☌ ♆	**8:30 pm**	5:30 pm

11 FRIDAY

☉ ⊻ ♆	**6:06 am**	3:06 am
☽ △ ♂	**7:29 am**	4:29 am
☿ ⊻ ♃	**8:39 am**	5:39 am
☽ ⚹ ♇	**12:52 pm**	9:52 am
☽ ⚹ ♃	**11:49 pm**	8:49 pm
☽ ⊻ ☿		10:35 pm

12 SATURDAY

☽ ⊻ ☿	**1:35 am**	
☽ ☍ ♄	**4:19 am**	1:19 am
♀ □ ♅	**12:23 pm**	9:23 am
☽ ☌ ♅	**6:12 pm**	3:12 pm
☽ □ ♀	**6:45 pm**	3:45 pm
☿ ⚻ ♄		9:17 pm
☽ ⊻ ♆		11:53 pm

13 SUNDAY

☿ ⚻ ♄	**12:17 am**	
☽ ⊻ ♆	**2:53 am**	
☽ ⚹ ☉	**6:24 am**	3:24 am
☽ □ ♂	**12:24 pm**	9:24 am
☽ □ ♇	**6:41 pm**	3:41 pm

14 MONDAY

☽ □ ♃	**6:01 am**	3:01 am
☽ ⚻ ♄	**9:18 am**	6:18 am
☽ ⚹ ☿	**1:34 pm**	10:34 am
☽ ⊻ ♅	**11:02 pm**	8:02 pm

15 TUESDAY

☽ △ ♀	**4:29 am**	1:29 am
☽ ⚹ ♆	**7:23 am**	4:23 am
☽ □ ☉	**2:46 pm**	11:46 am
☽ ⚹ ♂	**3:40 pm**	12:40 pm
☽ △ ♇	**10:39 pm**	7:39 pm
☉ ⚻ ♂		10:29 pm

16 WEDNESDAY

☉ ⚻ ♂	**1:29 am**	
☽ △ ♃	**10:19 am**	7:19 am
☽ △ ♄	**12:30 pm**	9:30 am
♀ ⚹ ♆	**2:35 pm**	11:35 am
☽ □ ☿	**10:39 pm**	7:39 pm
☽ ⚹ ♅		11:07 pm

17 THURSDAY

☽ ⚹ ♅	**2:07 am**	
☽ □ ♆	**10:13 am**	7:13 am
☽ ⚻ ♀	**11:59 am**	8:59 am
☽ ⊻ ♂	**5:30 pm**	2:30 pm
☽ △ ☉	**9:05 pm**	6:05 pm
☽ ⚻ ♇		10:04 pm

18 FRIDAY

☽ ⚻ ♇	**1:04 am**	
☿ ⊻ ♅	**11:49 am**	8:49 am
☽ ⚻ ♃	**1:08 pm**	10:08 am
☽ □ ♄	**2:19 pm**	11:19 am

19 SATURDAY

☽ □ ♅	**4:02 am**	1:02 am
☽ △ ☿	**5:34 am**	2:34 am
☽ △ ♆	**12:00 pm**	9:00 am
☽ ☍ ♀	**6:13 pm**	3:13 pm
☽ ☌ ♂	**6:35 pm**	3:35 pm
♀ ☍ ♂	**10:10 pm**	7:10 pm
☽ ⚻ ☉		11:25 pm
☽ ☍ ♇		11:46 pm

20 SUNDAY

☽ ⚻ ☉	**2:25 am**	
☽ ☍ ♇	**2:46 am**	
☉ ⊻ ♇	**7:29 am**	4:29 am
☽ ☍ ♃	**3:31 pm**	12:31 pm
☽ ⚹ ♄	**3:45 pm**	12:45 pm

21 MONDAY

♃ △ ♄	**4:14 am**	1:14 am
☽ △ ♅	**5:56 am**	2:56 am
☽ ⚻ ☿	**11:49 am**	8:49 am
☽ ⚻ ♆	**2:01 pm**	11:01 am
☽ ⊻ ♂	**8:09 pm**	5:09 pm
☽ ⚻ ♀		9:58 pm

22 TUESDAY

☽ ⚻ ♀	**12:58 am**	
☽ ⚻ ♇	**5:08 am**	2:08 am
☽ ☍ ☉	**8:35 am**	5:35 am
☽ ⊻ ♄	**6:13 pm**	3:13 pm
☽ ⚻ ♃	**7:00 pm**	4:00 pm
☿ ☌ ♆	**8:15 pm**	5:15 pm

23 WEDNESDAY

☽ ⚻ ♅	**9:22 am**	6:22 am
☽ ☍ ♆	**5:48 pm**	2:48 pm
☽ ☍ ☿	**7:13 pm**	4:13 pm
☽ ⚹ ♂	**11:44 pm**	8:44 pm
♀ ☌ ♇		10:58 pm

24 THURSDAY

♀ ☌ ♇	**1:58 am**	
☽ △ ♇	**9:43 am**	6:43 am
☽ △ ♀	**10:29 am**	7:29 am
☽ ⚻ ☉	**5:37 pm**	2:37 pm
☽ ☌ ♄	**11:13 pm**	8:13 pm
☽ △ ♃		10:10 pm

25 FRIDAY

☽ △ ♃	**1:10 am**	
☽ ☍ ♅	**3:44 pm**	12:44 pm
☽ ⚻ ♆		9:42 pm

26 SATURDAY

☽ ⚻ ♆	**12:42 am**	
☽ ⚻ ☿	**4:53 am**	1:53 am
☽ □ ♂	**6:32 am**	3:32 am
☽ □ ♇	**5:38 pm**	2:38 pm
☽ □ ♀		9:25 pm

27 SUNDAY

☽ □ ♀	**12:25 am**	
☽ △ ☉	**6:56 am**	3:56 am
☽ ⊻ ♄	**7:35 am**	4:35 am
☽ □ ♃	**10:58 am**	7:58 am
☉ ⚻ ♄	**2:20 pm**	11:20 am
☽ ⚻ ♅		10:37 pm

28 MONDAY

☽ ⚻ ♅	**1:37 am**	
☽ △ ♆	**11:02 am**	8:02 am
☽ △ ☿	**4:20 pm**	1:20 pm
☽ △ ♂	**4:47 pm**	1:47 pm

29 TUESDAY

☽ ⚹ ♇	**4:47 am**	1:47 am
☽ ⚹ ♀	**6:32 pm**	3:32 pm
☽ ⚹ ♄	**6:50 pm**	3:50 pm
☉ ⊻ ♃	**7:52 pm**	4:52 pm
♀ △ ♄	**9:19 pm**	6:19 pm
☽ ⚹ ♃	**11:45 pm**	8:45 pm
☽ □ ☉		9:03 pm

30 WEDNESDAY

☽ □ ☉	**12:03 am**	
☽ △ ♅	**1:59 pm**	10:59 am
☽ □ ♆	**11:34 pm**	8:34 pm

31 THURSDAY

☽ □ ☿	**3:34 am**	12:34 am
☽ ⚻ ♂	**5:10 am**	2:10 am
☽ ⊻ ♇	**5:29 pm**	2:29 pm

Eastern time in bold type
Pacific time in medium type

DATE	S.TIME	SUN	MOON	N.NODE	MERCURY	VENUS	MARS	JUPITER	SATURN	URANUS	NEPTUNE	PLUTO	CERES	PALLAS	JUNO	VESTA	CHIRON
1 Tue	6:40:08	09 ♑ 55 38	17 ♎ 28	29 ≈ 04	18 ♑ 52	01 ♐ 31	29 Ⅱ 53	03 ♑ 15	08 ♍ 26	15 ♓ 22	20 ≈ 15	29 ♐ 08	09 ♉ 43	09 ♐ 51	07 ♐ 38	05 ♐ 39	13 ≈ 13
2 Wed	6:44:04	10 56 48	29 15	29 02 D	19 54	02 43	29 31 Rx	03 28	08 24 Rx	15 24	20 17	29 10	09 44	10 07	07 57	06 10	13 17
3 Thu	6:48:01	11 57 58	11 ♏ 05	28 58	21 32	03 56	29 10	03 42	08 23	15 26	20 19	29 13	09 46	10 22	08 16	06 40	13 21
4 Fri	6:51:57	12 59 08	22 57	28 52	23 10	05 09	28 50	03 56	08 21	15 28	20 21	29 15	09 48	10 38	08 35	07 11	13 25
5 Sat	6:55:54	14 00 19	04 ♐ 52	28 44	24 48	06 22	28 29	04 09	08 19	15 30	20 23	29 17	09 51	10 54	08 54	07 41	13 29
6 Sun	6:59:50	15 01 30	16 55	28 35	26 25	07 35	28 10	04 23	08 17	15 32	20 25	29 19	09 54	11 10	09 13	08 12	13 34
7 Mon	7:03:47	16 02 41	29 07	28 26	28 03	08 48	27 51	04 37	08 15	15 34	20 27	29 21	09 57	11 27	09 32	08 42	13 38
8 Tue	7:07:44	17 03 52	11 ♑ 30	28 19	29 41	10 01	27 33	04 50	08 13	15 36	20 29	29 23	10 01	11 43	09 51	09 13	13 42
9 Wed	7:11:40	18 05 03	24 04	28 12	01 ≈ 18	11 14	27 15	05 04	08 11	15 38	20 31	29 26	10 05	12 00	10 10	09 43	13 46
10 Thu	7:15:37	19 06 13	06 ≈ 49	28 08	02 55	12 27	26 58	05 18	08 09	15 40	20 33	29 28	10 09	12 17	10 28	10 14	13 51
11 Fri	7:19:33	20 07 23	19 46	28 06 D	04 31	13 40	26 42	05 31	08 07	15 43	20 35	29 30	10 14	12 34	10 47	10 44	13 55
12 Sat	7:23:30	21 08 33	02 ♓ 54	28 05	06 06	14 54	26 27	05 45	08 04	15 45	20 37	29 32	10 19	12 51	11 06	11 15	13 59
13 Sun	7:27:26	22 09 42	16 14	28 07	07 41	16 07	26 14	05 58	08 02	15 47	20 39	29 34	10 25	13 08	11 24	11 45	14 04
14 Mon	7:31:23	23 10 51	29 47	28 09	09 13	17 20	25 58	06 12	07 59	15 50	20 41	29 36	10 31	13 25	11 42	12 16	14 08
15 Tue	7:35:19	24 11 59	13 ♈ 31	28 10 Rx	10 45	18 33	25 45	06 25	07 56	15 52	20 43	29 38	10 37	13 42	12 01	12 46	14 12
16 Wed	7:39:16	25 13 06	27 31	28 10	12 14	19 47	25 33	06 38	07 53	15 54	20 45	29 40	10 44	14 00	12 19	13 17	14 17
17 Thu	7:43:13	26 14 12	11 ♉ 43	28 09	13 41	21 00	25 21	06 52	07 51	15 57	20 47	29 42	10 51	14 18	12 37	13 47	14 21
18 Fri	7:47:09	27 15 18	26 05	28 07	15 05	22 14	25 11	07 05	07 48	15 59	20 49	29 44	10 58	14 35	12 55	14 18	14 26
19 Sat	7:51:06	28 16 23	10 Ⅱ 35	28 03	16 25	23 27	25 01	07 18	07 44	16 02	20 51	29 46	11 05	14 53	13 13	14 48	14 30
20 Sun	7:55:02	29 17 27	25 07	27 59	17 41	24 41	24 52	07 32	07 41	16 05	20 54	29 48	11 13	15 11	13 31	15 19	14 34
21 Mon	7:58:59	00 ≈ 18 31	09 ♋ 36	27 55	18 52	25 54	24 43	07 45	07 38	16 07	20 56	29 50	11 22	15 30	13 49	15 50	14 39
22 Tue	8:02:55	01 19 33	23 55	27 51	19 58	27 08	24 36	07 58	07 35	16 10	20 58	29 52	11 30	15 48	14 07	16 21	14 43
23 Wed	8:06:52	02 20 35	07 ♌ 58	27 49 D	20 57	28 21	24 29	08 11	07 31	16 12	21 00	29 54	11 39	16 06	14 24	16 51	14 48
24 Thu	8:10:48	03 21 36	21 43	27 47 D	21 49	29 35	24 23	08 24	07 28	16 15	21 02	29 56	11 48	16 25	14 42	17 21	14 52
25 Fri	8:14:45	04 22 37	05 ♍ 09	27 47	22 33	00 ♑ 49	24 18	08 37	07 24	16 18	21 04	29 58	11 58	16 43	14 59	17 52	14 57
26 Sat	8:18:42	05 23 38	18 05	27 47	23 08	02 03	24 14	08 50	07 21	16 21	21 07	00 ♑ 00	12 08	17 02	15 17	18 22	15 02
27 Sun	8:22:38	06 24 36	00 ♎ 44	27 50	23 34	03 16	24 11	09 03	07 17	16 23	21 09	00 02	12 18	17 21	15 34	18 53	15 06
28 Mon	8:26:35	07 25 34	13 06	27 51	23 49 Rx	04 30	24 08	09 16	07 13	16 26	21 11	00 04	12 28	17 40	15 51	19 23	15 11
29 Tue	8:30:31	08 26 32	25 10	27 53	23 53	05 44	24 06	09 29	07 09	16 29	21 13	00 05	12 39	17 59	16 08	19 54	15 15
30 Wed	8:34:28	09 27 30	07 ♏ 12	27 53 D	23 45	06 58	24 05 D	09 42	07 05	16 32	21 16	00 07	12 50	18 18	16 25	20 24	15 20
31 Thu	8:38:24	10 28 26	19 03	27 53	23 27	08 12	24 05	09 42	07 01	16 35	21 18	00 09	13 01	18 37	16 42	20 55	15 24

EPHEMERIS CALCULATED FOR 12 MIDNIGHT GREENWICH MEAN TIME. ALL OTHER DATA AND FACING ASPECTARIAN PAGE IN **EASTERN TIME (BOLD)** AND PACIFIC TIME (REGULAR).

FEBRUARY 2008

☽ Last Aspect day	ET / hr:mn / PT	asp	☽ Ingress sign	day	ET / hr:mn / PT
2	**5:21 pm** 2:21 pm	☍♂	♑	3	**4:52 am** 1:52 am
4	**1:20 pm** 10:20 am	⚹♅	♒	5	**2:10 pm** 11:10 am
7	**10:50 am** 7:50 am	△♂	♓	7	**8:46 pm** 5:46 pm
9	**4:05 pm** 1:05 pm	□♂	♈	9	10:17 pm
9	**4:05 pm** 1:05 pm	□♂	♈	10	**1:17 am**
11	**8:00 pm** 5:00 pm	⚹♂	♉	12	**4:34 am** 1:34 am
13	9:05 pm	△♀	♊	14	**7:19 am** 4:19 am
14	**12:05 am**	△♀	♊	14	**7:19 am** 4:19 am
16	**5:17 am** 2:17 am	△☉	♋	16	**10:12 am** 7:12 am
17	**4:13 pm** 1:13 pm	△♅	♌	18	**1:51 pm** 10:51 am
20	**12:52 pm** 9:52 am	⚹♂	♍	20	**7:06 pm** 4:06 pm
22	**9:14 pm** 6:14 pm	□♂	♎	22	11:44 pm
22	**9:14 pm** 6:14 pm	□♂	♎	23	**2:44 am**
25	**8:35 am** 5:35 am	△♂	♏	25	**1:05 pm** 10:05 am
27	**9:53 am** 6:53 am	□♆	♐	27	10:22 pm
27	**9:53 am** 6:53 am	□♆	♐	28	**1:22 am**

☽ Phases & Eclipses phase	day	ET / hr:mn / PT
New Moon	6	**10:44 pm** 7:44 pm
(eclipse)	6	17° ♒ 44'
2nd Quarter	13	**10:33 pm** 7:33 pm
Full Moon	20	**10:30 pm** 7:30 pm
(eclipse)	20	1° ♍ 53'
4th Quarter	28	**9:18 pm** 6:18 pm

Planet Ingress	day	ET / hr:mn / PT
♀ ♒	17	**11:22 am** 8:22 am
⚶ ♓	17	**5:22 pm** 2:22 pm
☉ ♓	18	10:49 pm
☉ ♓	19	**1:49 am**

Planetary Motion	day	ET / hr:mn / PT
☿ D	18	**9:57 pm** 6:57 pm

1 FRIDAY
♀ ☌ ♃ **6:33 am** 3:33 am
☽ □ ♄ **7:03 am** 4:03 am
☽ ⚺ ♃ **1:24 pm** 10:24 am
☽ ⚺ ♀ **2:03 pm** 11:03 am
☽ ⚹ ☉ **6:11 pm** 3:11 pm
☽ □ ♅ 11:37 pm

2 SATURDAY
☽ □ ♅ **2:37 am**
☽ ⚹ ♆ **11:57 am** 8:57 am
☽ ⚹ ☿ **12:31 pm** 9:31 am
☽ ☍ ♂ **5:21 pm** 2:21 pm
☿ ☌ ♆ **7:55 pm** 4:55 pm

3 SUNDAY
☽ ☌ ♇ **5:21 am** 2:21 am
☽ △ ♄ **5:59 pm** 2:59 pm
☽ ☌ ♃ 10:26 pm

4 MONDAY
☽ ☌ ♃ **1:26 am**
☽ ☌ ♀ **7:29 am** 4:29 am
☽ ⚺ ☉ **10:12 am** 7:12 am
☽ ⚹ ♅ **1:20 pm** 10:20 am
☽ ⚺ ☿ **6:18 pm** 3:18 pm
☽ ⚺ ♆ **10:12 pm** 7:12 pm

5 TUESDAY
☽ ⚻ ♂ **3:25 am** 12:25 am
☽ ⚺ ♇ **2:45 pm** 11:45 am
☽ ⚻ ♄ 11:21 pm
☉ ⚺ ♅ 11:57 pm

6 WEDNESDAY
☽ ⚻ ♄ **2:21 am**
☉ ⚺ ♅ **2:57 am**
☽ ⚺ ♃ **10:39 am** 7:39 am
☉ ☌ ☿ **1:19 pm** 10:19 am
☿ ⚺ ♅ **9:14 pm** 6:14 pm
☽ ☌ ☿ **9:17 pm** 6:17 pm
☽ ⚺ ♀ **9:17 pm** 6:17 pm
☿ ⚺ ♀ **9:18 pm** 6:18 pm
☽ ⚺ ♅ **9:18 pm** 6:18 pm
♀ ⚹ ♅ **9:22 pm** 6:22 pm
☽ ☌ ☉ **10:44 pm** 7:44 pm

7 THURSDAY
☽ ☌ ♆ **5:41 am** 2:41 am
☽ △ ♂ **10:50 am** 7:50 am
☽ ⚹ ♇ **9:27 pm** 6:27 pm

8 FRIDAY
☽ ☍ ♄ **8:08 am** 5:08 am
☽ ⚹ ♃ **5:13 pm** 2:13 pm
☽ ⚺ ☿ **10:21 pm** 7:21 pm
☽ ☌ ♅ 11:49 pm

9 SATURDAY
☽ ☌ ♅ **2:49 am**
☽ ⚹ ♀ **7:52 am** 4:52 am
☽ ⚺ ☉ **8:15 am** 5:15 am
☽ ⚺ ♆ **10:51 am** 7:51 am
☽ □ ♂ **4:05 pm** 1:05 pm
☽ □ ♇ 11:03 pm

10 SUNDAY
☽ □ ♇ **2:03 am**
☉ ⚺ ♀ **5:49 am** 2:49 am

☽ ⚻ ♄ **12:02 pm** 9:02 am
♀ ⚺ ♆ **6:14 pm** 3:14 pm
☉ ☌ ♆ **9:03 pm** 6:03 pm
☽ □ ♃ **9:56 pm** 6:56 pm
☽ ⚹ ☿ **10:28 pm** 7:28 pm

11 MONDAY
☿ ⚺ ♃ **4:45 am** 1:45 am
☽ ⚺ ♅ **6:44 am** 3:44 am
☽ ⚹ ♆ **2:32 pm** 11:32 am
☽ ⚹ ☉ **3:50 pm** 12:50 pm
☽ □ ♀ **4:25 pm** 1:25 pm
☽ ⚹ ♂ **8:00 pm** 5:00 pm

12 TUESDAY
☽ △ ♇ **5:24 am** 2:24 am
☽ △ ♄ **2:52 pm** 11:52 am
☽ □ ☿ **10:28 pm** 7:28 pm
☽ △ ♃ 10:39 pm

13 WEDNESDAY
☽ △ ♃ **1:39 am**
☽ ⚹ ♅ **9:49 am** 6:49 am
♀ ⚻ ♂ **2:29 pm** 11:29 am
☽ □ ♆ **5:30 pm** 2:30 pm
☽ □ ☉ **10:33 pm** 7:33 pm
☽ ⚺ ♂ **11:21 pm** 8:21 pm
☽ △ ♀ 9:05 pm

14 THURSDAY
☽ △ ♀ **12:05 am**
☽ ⚻ ♇ **8:15 am** 5:15 am
☉ △ ♂ **11:39 am** 8:39 am
☽ □ ♄ **5:20 pm** 2:20 pm
☽ △ ☿ **11:02 pm** 8:02 pm

15 FRIDAY
☽ ⚻ ♃ **5:06 am** 2:06 am
☽ □ ♅ **12:46 pm** 9:46 am
☽ △ ♆ **8:25 pm** 5:25 pm
☽ ☌ ♂ 11:47 pm

16 SATURDAY
☽ ☌ ♂ **2:47 am**
☽ △ ☉ **5:17 am** 2:17 am
☽ ⚻ ♀ **7:47 am** 4:47 am
☽ ☍ ♇ **11:13 am** 8:13 am
☽ ⚹ ♄ **8:01 pm** 5:01 pm
☽ ⚻ ☿ 9:47 pm

17 SUNDAY
☽ ⚻ ☿ **12:47 am**
☽ ☍ ♃ **8:57 am** 5:57 am
☽ △ ♅ **4:13 pm** 1:13 pm
♀ ⚺ ♇ **11:39 pm** 8:39 pm
☽ ⚻ ♆ **11:56 pm** 8:56 pm

18 MONDAY
☽ ⚺ ♂ **7:01 am** 4:01 am
☽ ⚻ ☉ **12:54 pm** 9:54 am
☽ ⚻ ♇ **2:59 pm** 11:59 am
☽ ☍ ♀ **4:28 pm** 1:28 pm
☽ ⚺ ♄ **11:37 pm** 8:37 pm

19 TUESDAY
☽ ☍ ☿ **4:26 am** 1:26 am
☽ ⚻ ♃ **1:58 pm** 10:58 am
☉ ⚹ ♇ **5:48 pm** 2:48 pm
☽ ⚻ ♅ **8:55 pm** 5:55 pm

20 WEDNESDAY
☽ ☍ ♆ **4:49 am** 1:49 am
☽ ⚹ ♂ **12:52 pm** 9:52 am
☽ △ ♇ **8:22 pm** 5:22 pm
☽ ☍ ☉ **10:30 pm** 7:30 pm

21 THURSDAY
☽ ⚻ ♀ **3:20 am** 12:20 am
☽ ☌ ♄ **4:56 am** 1:56 am
☽ ⚻ ☿ **10:55 am** 7:55 am
♀ ⚻ ♄ **7:23 pm** 4:23 pm
☽ △ ♃ **9:01 pm** 6:01 pm

22 FRIDAY
☽ ☍ ♅ **3:43 am** 12:43 am
☽ ⚻ ♆ **11:56 am** 8:56 am
☽ □ ♂ **9:14 pm** 6:14 pm

23 SATURDAY
☽ □ ♇ **4:09 am** 1:09 am
☽ ⚻ ☉ **11:10 am** 8:10 am
☽ ⚺ ♄ **12:42 pm** 9:42 am
☽ △ ♀ **5:31 pm** 2:31 pm
☽ △ ☿ **9:09 pm** 6:09 pm

24 SUNDAY
☉ ☍ ♄ **4:48 am** 1:48 am
☽ □ ♃ **6:49 am** 3:49 am
☽ ⚻ ♅ **1:15 pm** 10:15 am
☽ △ ♆ **9:46 pm** 6:46 pm

25 MONDAY
☽ △ ♂ **8:35 am** 5:35 am
☽ ⚹ ♇ **2:40 pm** 11:40 am
☽ ⚹ ♄ **11:05 pm** 8:05 pm

26 TUESDAY
☽ △ ☉ **3:15 am** 12:15 am
☽ □ ♀ **11:17 am** 8:17 am
☽ □ ☿ **11:22 am** 8:22 am
☿ ☌ ♀ **12:51 pm** 9:51 am
☽ ⚹ ♃ **7:13 pm** 4:13 pm
☽ △ ♅ 10:13 pm

27 WEDNESDAY
☽ △ ♅ **1:13 am**
☽ □ ♆ **9:53 am** 6:53 am
☽ ⚻ ♂ **10:10 pm** 7:10 pm

28 THURSDAY
☽ ⚺ ♇ **3:04 am** 12:04 am
☽ □ ♄ **11:06 am** 8:06 am
☽ □ ☉ **9:18 pm** 6:18 pm

29 FRIDAY
☽ ⚹ ☿ **4:05 am** 1:05 am
☽ ⚹ ♀ **6:48 am** 3:48 am
☽ ⚺ ♃ **8:40 am** 5:40 am
☽ □ ♅ **2:01 pm** 11:01 am
☽ ⚹ ♆ **10:30 pm** 7:30 pm

Eastern time in bold type
Pacific time in medium type

FEBRUARY 2008

DATE	S.TIME	SUN	MOON	N.NODE	MERCURY	VENUS	MARS	JUPITER	SATURN	URANUS	NEPTUNE	PLUTO	CERES	PALLAS	JUNO	VESTA	CHIRON
1 Fri	08:42:21	11≈29 22	00 ♐ 56	27 ≈ 52	22 ≈ 57	09 ♑ 25	24 ♊ 05	09 ♑ 55	06 ♍ 57	16 ♓ 38	21 ≈ 20	00 ♑ 11	13 ♉ 13	18 ♓ 56	16 ♐ 59	21 ≈ 25	15 ≈ 29
2 Sat	08:46:17	12 30 17	12 53	27 50 R	22 17 R	10 39	24 06	10 08	06 53 R	16 41	21 23	00 13	13 25	19 16	17 15	21 56	15 34
3 Sun	08:50:14	13 31 12	24 58	27 48	21 27	11 53	24 08	10 20	06 49	16 44	21 25	00 14	13 37	19 35	17 32	22 26	15 38
4 Mon	08:54:11	14 32 05	07 ♑ 16	27 46	20 29	13 07	24 11	10 33	06 45	16 47	21 27	00 16	13 49	19 55	17 48	22 57	15 43
5 Tue	08:58:07	15 32 58	19 48	27 43	19 24	14 21	24 14	10 45	06 40	16 50	21 29	00 17	14 02	20 15	18 05	23 27	15 47
6 Wed	09:02:04	16 33 49	02 ≈ 36	27 42 D	18 15	15 35	24 18	10 58	06 36	16 53	21 31	00 19	14 15	20 34	18 21	23 58	15 52
7 Thu	09:06:00	17 34 40	15 40	27 42	17 03	16 49	24 23	11 10	06 31	16 56	21 34	00 21	14 28	20 54	18 37	24 28	15 56
8 Fri	09:09:57	18 35 29	29 01	27 42	15 40	18 03	24 29	11 23	06 27	16 59	21 36	00 23	14 41	21 14	18 53	24 59	16 01
9 Sat	09:13:53	19 36 17	12 ♓ 35	27 42	14 40	19 17	24 35	11 35	06 23	17 02	21 38	00 24	14 55	21 34	19 09	25 29	16 06
10 Sun	09:17:50	20 37 03	26 22	27 42	13 32	20 31	24 41	11 47	06 18	17 06	21 41	00 26	15 09	21 54	19 24	25 59	16 10
11 Mon	09:21:46	21 37 48	10 ♈ 18	27 43	12 28	21 45	24 49	11 59	06 13	17 09	21 43	00 27	15 23	22 15	19 40	26 30	16 15
12 Tue	09:25:43	22 38 31	24 22	27 44	11 31	22 59	24 57	12 12	06 09	17 12	21 45	00 29	15 37	22 35	19 55	27 00	16 19
13 Wed	09:29:40	23 39 13	08 ♉ 31	27 44	10 41	24 13	25 06	12 24	06 04	17 15	21 47	00 30	15 52	22 55	20 10	27 30	16 24
14 Thu	09:33:36	24 39 53	22 43	27 44 R	09 58	25 27	25 15	12 36	05 59	17 18	21 50	00 32	16 06	23 16	20 26	28 01	16 28
15 Fri	09:37:33	25 40 31	06 ♊ 54	27 44	09 25	26 41	25 25	12 47	05 55	17 21	21 52	00 33	16 22	23 36	20 41	28 31	16 33
16 Sat	09:41:29	26 41 08	21 04	27 44	08 55	27 55	25 36	12 59	05 50	17 25	21 54	00 35	16 37	23 57	20 55	29 01	16 37
17 Sun	09:45:26	27 41 43	05 ♋ 09	27 44 D	08 36	29 09	25 47	13 11	05 45	17 28	21 56	00 36	16 52	24 18	21 10	29 32	16 42
18 Mon	09:49:22	28 42 16	19 08	27 44	08 24	00 ≈ 24	25 58	13 23	05 41	17 31	21 59	00 38	17 08	24 38	21 25	00 ♓ 02	16 46
19 Tue	09:53:19	29 42 48	02 ♌ 57	27 44 R	08 19 D	01 38	26 11	13 34	05 36	17 35	22 01	00 40	17 24	24 59	21 39	00 33	16 51
20 Wed	09:57:15	00 ♓ 43 18	16 34	27 44	08 22	02 52	26 23	13 46	05 31	17 38	22 03	00 42	17 40	25 20	21 53	01 03	16 55
21 Thu	10:01:12	01 43 46	29 57	27 44	08 31	04 06	26 37	13 57	05 26	17 41	22 06	00 43	17 56	25 41	22 07	01 33	17 00
22 Fri	10:05:09	02 44 12	13 ♍ 04	27 44	08 46	05 20	26 50	14 08	05 21	17 45	22 08	00 44	18 13	26 02	22 21	02 03	17 04
23 Sat	10:09:05	03 44 37	25 55	27 44	09 08	06 34	27 05	14 20	05 16	17 48	22 10	00 45	18 29	26 23	22 35	02 33	17 09
24 Sun	10:13:02	04 45 00	08 ♎ 30	27 43	09 34	07 48	27 19	14 31	05 12	17 51	22 12	00 45	18 46	26 44	22 49	03 03	17 13
25 Mon	10:16:58	05 45 22	20 50	27 42	10 06	09 02	27 35	14 42	05 07	17 55	22 15	00 47	19 03	27 06	23 02	03 33	17 18
26 Tue	10:20:55	06 45 42	02 ♏ 58	27 41	10 42	10 17	27 50	14 53	05 02	17 58	22 17	00 48	19 20	27 27	23 16	04 03	17 22
27 Wed	10:24:51	07 46 01	14 57	27 39	11 22	11 31	28 06	15 04	04 57	18 01	22 19	00 49	19 38	27 48	23 29	04 34	17 26
28 Thu	10:28:48	08 46 19	26 51	27 39	12 07	12 45	28 23	15 15	04 52	18 05	22 21	00 50	19 55	28 10	23 42	05 04	17 31
29 Fri	10:32:44	09 46 35	08 ♐ 44	27 38	12 55	13 59	28 40	15 25	04 47	18 08	22 23	00 51	20 13	28 31	23 54	05 34	17 35

EPHEMERIS CALCULATED FOR 12 MIDNIGHT GREENWICH MEAN TIME. ALL OTHER DATA AND FACING ASPECTARIAN PAGE IN **EASTERN TIME (BOLD)** AND PACIFIC TIME (REGULAR).

MARCH 2008

☽ Last Aspect day	ET / hr:mn / PT	asp	☽ Ingress sign	day	ET / hr:mn / PT
1	**11:54 am** 8:54 am	☍♂	♑	1	**1:33 pm** 10:33 am
2	10:16 pm	⚹♅	♒	3	**11:24 pm** 8:24 pm
3	**1:16 am**	⚹♅	♒	3	**11:24 pm** 8:24 pm
5	**4:46 pm** 1:46 pm	☌♆	♓	6	**5:53 am** 2:53 am
7	**2:04 pm** 11:04 am	☌♅	♈	8	**9:23 am** 6:23 am
10	**7:09 am** 4:09 am	⚹♀	♉	10	**12:13 pm** 9:13 am
12	**1:26 pm** 10:26 am	□♀	♊	12	**1:54 pm** 10:54 am
14	**4:23 pm** 1:23 pm	△☿	♋	14	**4:37 pm** 1:37 pm
16	**2:58 pm** 11:58 am	△☉	♌	16	**9:04 pm** 6:04 pm
18	**2:38 pm** 11:38 am	☍♆	♍	19	**3:25 am** 12:25 am
20	**3:28 pm** 12:28 pm	☍♅	♎	21	**11:45 am** 8:45 am
23	**8:41 am** 5:41 am	△♆	♏	23	**10:06 pm** 7:06 pm
25	**8:36 pm** 5:36 pm	□♆	♐	26	**10:11 am** 7:11 am
28	**9:21 am** 6:21 am	⚹♆	♑	28	**10:43 pm** 7:43 pm
30	9:54 pm	⚹☿	♒	31	**9:34 am** 6:34 am
31	**12:54 am**	⚹☿	♒	31	**9:34 am** 6:34 am

☽ Phases & Eclipses phase	day	ET / hr:mn / PT
New Moon	7	**12:14 pm** 9:14 am
2nd Quarter	14	**6:45 am** 3:45 am
Full Moon	21	**2:40 pm** 11:40 am
4th Quarter	29	**5:47 pm** 2:47 pm

Planet Ingress		day	ET / hr:mn / PT
♀	♈	3	**9:21 pm** 6:21 pm
♂	♋	4	**5:01 am** 2:01 am
♀	♓	12	**6:51 pm** 3:51 pm
☿	♓	14	**6:46 pm** 3:46 pm
☉	♈	19	10:48 pm
☉	♈	20	**1:48 am**
?	♊	29	**5:21 am** 2:21 am

Planetary Motion
day ET / hr:mn / PT

1 SATURDAY
♀ ⚺ ♃ **3:32 am** 12:32 am
☽ ☍ ♂ **11:54 am** 8:54 am
☽ ☌ ♇ **3:17 pm** 12:17 pm
☽ △ ♄ **10:39 pm** 7:39 pm

2 SUNDAY
☽ ⚹ ☉ **2:12 pm** 11:12 am
☽ ⚺ ☿ **8:13 pm** 5:13 pm
☽ ☌ ♃ **8:43 pm** 5:43 pm
☽ ⚺ ♀ 9:37 pm
☽ ⚹ ♅ 10:16 pm

3 MONDAY
☽ ⚺ ♀ **12:37 am**
☽ ⚹ ♅ **1:16 am**
☿ ⚺ ♃ **3:46 am** 12:46 am
♀ ⚺ ♅ **7:30 am** 4:30 am
☽ ⚺ ♆ **9:17 am** 6:17 am
☽ ⚻ ♂ **11:16 pm** 8:16 pm
☽ ⚺ ♇ 10:08 pm

4 TUESDAY
☽ ⚺ ♇ **1:08 am**
☽ ⚻ ♄ **7:40 am** 4:40 am

5 WEDNESDAY
☽ ⚺ ☉ **3:19 am** 12:19 am
☽ ⚺ ♃ **5:32 am** 2:32 am
☽ ☌ ☿ **9:06 am** 6:06 am
☽ ⚺ ♅ **9:19 am** 6:19 am
☿ ⚺ ♅ **11:51 am** 8:51 am

☽ ☌ ♀ **2:10 pm** 11:10 am
☽ ☌ ♆ **4:46 pm** 1:46 pm

6 THURSDAY
☽ △ ♂ **7:04 am** 4:04 am
☽ ⚹ ♇ **7:33 am** 4:33 am
☽ ☍ ♄ **1:20 pm** 10:20 am
☉ ⚹ ♃ **2:04 pm** 11:04 am
♀ ☌ ♆ **7:02 pm** 4:02 pm

7 FRIDAY
♂ ☍ ♇ **4:11 am** 1:11 am
☽ ⚹ ♃ **10:54 am** 7:54 am
☽ ☌ ☉ **12:14 pm** 9:14 am
☽ ☌ ♅ **2:04 pm** 11:04 am
☽ ⚺ ☿ **6:15 pm** 3:15 pm
☽ ⚺ ♆ **9:02 pm** 6:02 pm
☽ ⚺ ♀ **11:27 pm** 8:27 pm

8 SATURDAY
☽ □ ♇ **11:02 am** 8:02 am
☽ □ ♂ **11:45 am** 8:45 am
☉ ☌ ♅ **3:19 pm** 12:19 pm
☽ ⚻ ♄ **4:15 pm** 1:15 pm

9 SUNDAY
☿ ☌ ♆ **4:52 am** 12:52 am
☽ □ ♃ **2:52 pm** 11:52 am
☽ ⚺ ♅ **5:33 pm** 2:33 pm
☽ ⚺ ☉ **7:19 pm** 4:19 pm
☽ ⚹ ♆ 9:15 pm
☽ ⚹ ☿ 11:01 pm

10 MONDAY
☽ ⚹ ♆ **12:15 am**
☽ ⚹ ☿ **2:01 am**
☽ ⚹ ♀ **7:09 am** 4:09 am
☽ △ ♇ **1:54 pm** 10:54 am
☽ ⚹ ♂ **3:47 pm** 12:47 pm
☽ △ ♄ **6:43 pm** 3:43 pm

11 TUESDAY
☽ △ ♃ **4:59 pm** 1:59 pm
☽ ⚹ ♅ **7:19 pm** 4:19 pm
☽ ⚹ ☉ 9:34 pm
☽ □ ♆ 10:58 pm

12 WEDNESDAY
☽ ⚹ ☉ **12:34 am**
☽ □ ♆ **1:58 am**
☽ □ ☿ **8:27 am** 5:27 am
☽ □ ♀ **1:26 pm** 10:26 am
☽ ⚻ ♇ **3:38 pm** 12:38 pm
☽ ⚺ ♂ **6:47 pm** 3:47 pm
☽ □ ♄ **8:13 pm** 5:13 pm
☉ ⚺ ♆ **9:27 pm** 6:27 pm

13 THURSDAY
♀ ⚹ ♇ **3:09 pm** 12:09 pm
☽ ⚻ ♃ **7:42 pm** 4:42 pm
☽ □ ♅ **9:45 pm** 6:45 pm

14 FRIDAY
☽ △ ♆ **4:28 am** 1:28 am
☽ □ ☉ **6:45 am** 3:45 am
☽ △ ☿ **4:23 pm** 1:23 pm
♂ ⚹ ♄ **5:24 pm** 2:24 pm

☽ ☍ ♇ **6:26 pm** 3:26 pm
☽ △ ♀ **9:04 pm** 6:04 pm
☽ ⚹ ♄ **10:52 pm** 7:52 pm
☽ ☌ ♂ **11:03 pm** 8:03 pm

15 SATURDAY
☿ ⚹ ♇ **1:10 pm** 10:10 am
♀ ☍ ♄ **4:16 pm** 1:16 pm
☽ ☍ ♃ **11:58 pm** 8:58 pm
☽ △ ♅ 10:44 pm

16 SUNDAY
☽ △ ♅ **1:44 am**
♀ △ ♂ **4:21 am** 1:21 am
☽ ⚻ ♆ **8:36 am** 5:36 am
☽ △ ☉ **2:58 pm** 11:58 am
☽ ⚻ ♇ **10:59 pm** 7:59 pm
☽ ⚻ ☿ 11:56 pm

17 MONDAY
☽ ⚻ ☿ **2:56 am**
☽ ⚺ ♄ **3:15 am** 12:15 am
☽ ⚺ ♂ **5:16 am** 2:16 am
☿ ☍ ♄ **5:47 am** 2:47 am
☽ ⚻ ♀ **7:00 am** 4:00 am

18 TUESDAY
☽ ⚻ ♃ **6:09 am** 3:09 am
☽ ⚻ ♅ **7:37 am** 4:37 am
☿ △ ♂ **7:37 am** 4:37 am
☽ ☍ ♆ **2:38 pm** 11:38 am
☽ ⚻ ☉ 10:34 pm

19 WEDNESDAY
☽ ⚻ ☉ **1:34 am**
☽ △ ♇ **5:26 am** 2:26 am
☽ ☌ ♄ **9:33 am** 6:33 am
☽ ⚹ ♂ **1:38 pm** 10:38 am
☽ ☍ ☿ **4:29 pm** 1:29 pm
☽ ☍ ♀ **7:31 pm** 4:31 pm

20 THURSDAY
☽ △ ♃ **2:20 pm** 11:20 am
☽ ☍ ♅ **3:28 pm** 12:28 pm
☽ ⚻ ♆ **10:39 pm** 7:39 pm

21 FRIDAY
☉ □ ♇ **4:38 am** 1:38 am
☽ □ ♇ **1:52 pm** 10:52 am
☽ ☍ ☉ **2:40 pm** 11:40 am
☽ ⚺ ♄ **5:48 pm** 2:48 pm
☽ □ ♂ 9:14 pm

22 SATURDAY
☽ □ ♂ **12:14 am**
☽ ⚻ ☿ **9:15 am** 6:15 am
☽ ⚻ ♀ **10:44 am** 7:44 am
☽ □ ♃ 9:34 pm
☽ ⚻ ♅ 10:22 pm

23 SUNDAY
☽ □ ♃ **12:34 am**
☽ ⚻ ♅ **1:22 am**
☉ ⚻ ♄ **4:01 am** 1:01 am
☽ △ ♆ **8:41 am** 5:41 am
☽ ⚹ ♇ 9:20 pm

24 MONDAY
☽ ⚹ ♇ **12:20 am**
☽ ⚹ ♄ **4:03 am** 1:03 am
☽ ⚻ ☉ **6:20 am** 3:20 am
☿ ☌ ♀ **9:29 am** 6:29 am
☽ △ ♂ **1:07 pm** 10:07 am

25 TUESDAY
☽ △ ♀ **4:39 am** 1:39 am
☽ △ ☿ **5:21 am** 2:21 am
☽ ⚹ ♃ **12:45 pm** 9:45 am
☽ △ ♅ **1:13 pm** 10:13 am
☽ □ ♆ **8:36 pm** 5:36 pm

26 WEDNESDAY
☽ ⚺ ♇ **12:29 pm** 9:29 am
☽ □ ♄ **3:57 pm** 12:57 pm
☽ △ ☉ 9:04 pm

27 THURSDAY
☽ △ ☉ **12:04 am**
☽ ⚻ ♂ **3:43 am** 12:43 am
☿ ⚹ ♃ **2:56 pm** 11:56 am
☿ ☌ ♅ **4:07 pm** 1:07 pm
☽ □ ♀ 9:13 pm
☽ ⚺ ♃ 10:59 pm
☽ □ ♅ 11:05 pm

28 FRIDAY
☽ □ ♀ **12:13 am**
☽ ⚺ ♃ **1:59 am**
☽ □ ♅ **2:05 am**
☽ □ ☿ **3:40 am** 12:40 am

☽ ⚹ ♆ **9:21 am** 6:21 am
♀ ⚹ ♃ **6:54 pm** 3:54 pm
♀ ☌ ♅ **6:58 pm** 3:58 pm
♃ ⚹ ♅ **8:16 pm** 5:16 pm
☽ ☌ ♇ 10:00 pm

29 SATURDAY
☽ ☌ ♇ **1:00 am**
☽ △ ♄ **4:08 am** 1:08 am
☽ □ ☉ **5:47 pm** 2:47 pm
☽ ☍ ♂ **6:14 pm** 3:14 pm
☿ ⚺ ♆ **7:54 pm** 4:54 pm

30 SUNDAY
☉ □ ♂ **3:20 am** 12:20 am
☽ ⚹ ♅ **2:02 pm** 11:02 am
☽ ☌ ♃ **2:15 pm** 11:15 am
☽ ⚹ ♀ **6:36 pm** 3:36 pm
☽ ⚺ ♆ **8:54 pm** 5:54 pm
☽ ⚹ ☿ 9:54 pm

31 MONDAY
☽ ⚹ ☿ **12:54 am**
☽ ⚺ ♇ **11:45 am** 8:45 am
☽ ⚻ ♄ **2:28 pm** 11:28 am
♀ ⚺ ♆ **6:04 pm** 3:04 pm

Eastern time in bold type
Pacific time in medium type

MARCH 2008

DATE	S.TIME	SUN	MOON	N.NODE	MERCURY	VENUS	MARS	JUPITER	SATURN	URANUS	NEPTUNE	PLUTO	CERES	PALLAS	JUNO	VESTA	CHIRON
1 Sat	10:36:41	10♓46'49	20♐41	27♒39	13♒47	15♒13	28♊57	15♑36	04♍38℞	18♓15	22♒26	00♑52	20♉49	28♓53	24♐07	06♓04	17♒39
2 Sun	10:40:38	11 47'02	01♑46	27 39	14 41	16 27	29 15	15 46	04 33	18 18	22 28	00 53	21 06	29 14	24 19	06 34	17 44
3 Mon	10:44:34	12 47'14	14 43	27 41	15 39	17 42	29 33	15 57	04 28	18 21	22 30	00 54	21 23	29 36	24 32	07 04	17 48
4 Tue	10:48:31	13 47'24	27 39	27 42	16 39	18 56	29 52	16 07	04 24	18 25	22 32	00 55	21 40	29 58	24 44	07 34	17 52
5 Wed	10:52:27	14 47'32	10♒35	27 43	17 42	20 10	00♋11	16 17	04 19	18 28	22 34	00 56	21 58	00♈20	24 56	08 04	17 56
6 Thu	10:56:24	15 47'38	23 52	27 44℞	18 47	21 24	00 31	16 27	04 14	18 32	22 36	00 57	22 15	00 42	25 07	08 33	18 00
7 Fri	11:00:20	16 47'43	07♓30	27 44	19 55	22 38	00 50	16 37	04 10	18 36	22 39	00 58	22 33	01 03	25 19	09 03	18 05
8 Sat	11:04:17	17 47'46	21 29	27 42	21 05	23 53	01 11	16 47	04 05	18 39	22 41	00 59	22 51	01 25	25 30	09 33	18 09
9 Sun	11:08:13	18 47'47	05♈44	27 40	22 17	25 07	01 31	16 57	04 00	18 43	22 43	00 59	23 09	01 47	25 41	10 03	18 13
10 Mon	11:12:10	19 47'46	20 11	27 37	23 30	26 21	01 52	17 07	03 56	18 46	22 45	01 00	23 27	02 09	25 52	10 33	18 17
11 Tue	11:16:07	20 47'43	04♉43	27 34	24 46	27 35	02 13	17 16	03 51	18 49	22 47	01 01	23 46	02 32	26 02	11 02	18 21
12 Wed	11:20:03	21 47'38	19 14	27 31	26 03	28 49	02 35	17 26	03 47	18 53	22 49	01 01	24 04	02 54	26 13	11 32	18 25
13 Thu	11:24:00	22 47'30	03♊39	27 29	27 22	00♓04	02 56	17 35	03 43	18 56	22 51	01 02	24 23	03 16	26 23	12 02	18 29
14 Fri	11:27:56	23 47'21	17 55	27 28 D	28 42	01 18	03 19	17 44	03 38	19 00	22 53	01 03	24 42	03 38	26 33	12 31	18 33
15 Sat	11:31:53	24 47'09	01♋58	27 28	00♓04	02 32	03 41	17 53	03 34	19 03	22 55	01 03	25 01	04 01	26 43	13 01	18 37
16 Sun	11:35:49	25 46'55	15 48	27 29	01 28	03 46	04 04	18 02	03 30	19 07	22 57	01 04	25 20	04 23	26 52	13 30	18 41
17 Mon	11:39:46	26 46'38	29 24	27 30	02 53	05 00	04 27	18 11	03 25	19 10	22 59	01 04	25 40	04 45	27 02	14 00	18 44
18 Tue	11:43:42	27 46'20	12♌48	27 32	04 19	06 14	04 50	18 20	03 21	19 13	23 01	01 05	26 00	05 08	27 11	14 30	18 48
19 Wed	11:47:39	28 45'59	26 03	27 32℞	05 47	07 29	05 14	18 28	03 17	19 16	23 03	01 05	26 20	05 30	27 20	14 59	18 52
20 Thu	11:51:36	29 45'36	08♍57	27 30	07 16	08 43	05 38	18 37	03 13	19 20	23 05	01 06	26 40	05 53	27 28	15 28	18 56
21 Fri	11:55:32	00♈45'10	21 43	27 28	08 47	09 57	06 02	18 45	03 09	19 23	23 07	01 06	27 00	06 15	27 37	15 58	18 59
22 Sat	11:59:29	01 44'43	04♎18	27 26	10 19	11 11	06 26	18 53	03 05	19 27	23 09	01 06	27 21	06 38	27 45	16 27	19 03
23 Sun	12:03:25	02 44'13	16 42	27 20	11 52	12 25	06 51	19 01	03 02	19 30	23 11	01 07	27 42	07 01	27 53	16 56	19 07
24 Mon	12:07:22	03 43'42	28 56	27 14	13 27	13 39	07 16	19 09	02 58	19 34	23 12	01 07	28 03	07 23	28 00	17 26	19 10
25 Tue	12:11:18	04 43'09	11♏01	27 07	15 01	14 53	07 41	19 17	02 54	19 37	23 14	01 08	28 24	07 46	28 08	17 55	19 14
26 Wed	12:15:15	05 42'34	22 58	27 00	16 41	16 08	08 06	19 25	02 51	19 40	23 16	01 08	28 45	08 09	28 15	18 24	19 17
27 Thu	12:19:11	06 41'57	04♐52	26 55	18 19	17 22	08 32	19 32	02 47	19 44	23 18	01 08	29 07	08 32	28 22	18 53	19 21
28 Fri	12:23:08	07 41'18	16 44	26 50	19 59	18 36	08 58	19 40	02 44	19 47	23 20	01 08	29 29	08 55	28 28	19 22	19 24
29 Sat	12:27:04	08 40'38	28 39	26 48 D	21 41	19 50	09 24	19 47	02 41	19 50	23 21	01 09	29 51	09 18	28 34	19 51	19 27
30 Sun	12:31:01	09 39'56	10♑42	26 47	23 23	21 04	09 50	19 54	02 40	19 50	23 23	01 09	00♊13	09 41	28 41	20 20	19 31
31 Mon	12:34:58	10 39'12	22 57	26 48	25 08	22 18	10 16	20 01	02 37	19 53	23 25	01 09	00 35	10 04	28 46	20 49	19 34

EPHEMERIS CALCULATED FOR 12 MIDNIGHT GREENWICH MEAN TIME. ALL OTHER DATA AND FACING ASPECTARIAN PAGE IN **EASTERN TIME (BOLD)** AND PACIFIC TIME (REGULAR).

APRIL 2008

☽ Last Aspect day	ET / hr:mn / PT		asp	☽ Ingress sign	day	ET / hr:mn / PT	
2	**5:13 am**	2:13 am	☌ ♆	♓	2	**4:55 pm**	1:55 pm
4	**5:43 pm**	2:43 pm	☌ ♀	♈	4	**8:27 pm**	5:27 pm
6	**11:01 am**	8:01 am	⚹ ♆	♉	6	**9:19 pm**	6:19 pm
8	**11:12 am**	8:12 am	□ ♆	♊	8	**9:27 pm**	6:27 pm
10	**12:11 pm**	9:11 am	△ ♆	♋	10	**10:43 pm**	7:43 pm
12	**2:32 pm**	11:32 am	□ ☉	♌	12		11:29 pm
12	**2:32 pm**	11:32 am	□ ☉	♌	13	**2:29 am**	
14		9:56 pm	△ ☉	♍	15	**9:06 am**	6:06 am
15	**12:56 am**		△ ☉	♍	15	**9:06 am**	6:06 am
16		10:59 pm	△ ♃	♎	17	**6:10 pm**	3:10 pm
17	**1:59 am**		△ ♃	♎	17	**6:10 pm**	3:10 pm
19	**4:54 pm**	1:54 pm	△ ♆	♏	20	**5:00 am**	2:00 am
22	**4:53 am**	1:53 am	□ ♆	♐	22	**5:07 pm**	2:07 pm
24	**5:37 pm**	2:37 pm	⚹ ♆	♑	25	**5:47 am**	2:47 am
27	**10:18 am**	7:18 am	□ ♀	♒	27	**5:27 pm**	2:27 pm
29		10:25 pm	⚹ ♀	♓	29		11:11 pm
30	**1:25 am**		⚹ ♀	♓	30	**2:11 am**	

☽ Phases & Eclipses phase	day	ET / hr:mn / PT	
New Moon	5	**11:55 pm**	8:55 pm
2nd Quarter	12	**2:32 pm**	11:32 am
Full Moon	20	**6:25 am**	3:25 am
4th Quarter	28	**10:12 am**	7:12 am

Planet Ingress		day	ET / hr:mn / PT	
☿	♈	2	**1:44 pm**	10:44 am
♀	♈	5		10:35 pm
♀	♈	6	**1:35 am**	
☿	♉	17	**5:07 pm**	2:07 pm
⚶	♈	19	**4:07 am**	1:07 am
☉	♉	19	**12:51 pm**	9:51 am
♀	♉	30	**9:34 am**	6:34 am

Planetary Motion	day	ET / hr:mn / PT	
♇ ℞	2	**5:23 am**	2:23 am
⚵ ℞	18	**8:48 am**	5:48 am

1 TUESDAY
☽ ⚻ ♂ **6:09 am** 3:09 am
☽ ⚹ ☉ **8:28 am** 5:28 am
☽ ⚺ ♅ **10:55 pm** 7:55 pm
☽ ⚺ ♃ **11:22 pm** 8:22 pm

2 WEDNESDAY
☽ ☌ ♆ **5:13 am** 2:13 am
☽ ⚺ ♀ **8:44 am** 5:44 am
☽ ⚺ ☿ **5:25 pm** 2:25 pm
☽ ⚹ ♇ **6:57 pm** 3:57 pm
☽ ☍ ♄ **9:16 pm** 6:16 pm

3 THURSDAY
☿ □ ♇ **4:54 am** 1:54 am
☽ △ ♂ **1:52 pm** 10:52 am
☽ ⚺ ☉ **6:18 pm** 3:18 pm
☿ ⚻ ♄ **9:21 pm** 6:21 pm

4 FRIDAY
☽ ☌ ♅ **3:51 am** 12:51 am
☽ ⚹ ♃ **4:29 am** 1:29 am
☽ ⚺ ♆ **9:38 am** 6:38 am
☽ ☌ ♀ **5:43 pm** 2:43 pm
☽ □ ♇ **10:21 pm** 7:21 pm
☽ ⚻ ♄ 9:21 pm

5 SATURDAY
☽ ⚻ ♄ **12:21 am**
☽ ☌ ☿ **4:25 am** 1:25 am
☽ □ ♂ **5:46 pm** 2:46 pm
☽ ☌ ☉ **11:55 pm** 8:55 pm

6 SUNDAY
☽ ⚺ ♅ **5:36 am** 2:36 am
☽ □ ♃ **6:21 am** 3:21 am
☽ ⚹ ♆ **11:01 am** 8:01 am
☽ ⚺ ♀ **11:06 pm** 8:06 pm
☽ △ ♇ **11:10 pm** 8:10 pm
♀ □ ♇ **11:48 pm** 8:48 pm
☽ △ ♄ 9:57 pm

7 MONDAY
☽ △ ♄ **12:57 am**
☽ ⚺ ☿ **12:06 pm** 9:06 am
☽ ⚹ ♂ **7:37 pm** 4:37 pm
♀ ⚻ ♄ **8:49 pm** 5:49 pm

8 TUESDAY
☽ ⚺ ☉ **3:31 am** 12:31 am
☽ ⚹ ♅ **5:54 am** 2:54 am
☽ △ ♃ **6:47 am** 3:47 am
☽ □ ♆ **11:12 am** 8:12 am
☽ ⚻ ♇ **11:17 pm** 8:17 pm
☽ □ ♄ 9:57 pm

9 WEDNESDAY
☽ □ ♄ **12:57 am**
☽ ⚹ ♀ **3:36 am** 12:36 am
☉ ⚺ ♅ **5:54 pm** 2:54 pm
☽ ⚹ ☿ **7:48 pm** 4:48 pm
☽ ⚺ ♂ **9:39 pm** 6:39 pm

10 THURSDAY
☽ □ ♅ **6:48 am** 3:48 am
☽ ⚹ ☉ **7:41 am** 4:41 am
☽ ⚻ ♃ **7:50 am** 4:50 am
☉ □ ♃ **10:11 am** 7:11 am
☽ △ ♆ **12:11 pm** 9:11 am
☿ □ ♂ **1:13 pm** 10:13 am
☽ ☍ ♇ 9:37 pm
☽ ⚹ ♄ 11:14 pm

11 FRIDAY
☽ ☍ ♇ **12:37 am**
☽ ⚹ ♄ **2:14 am**
☽ □ ♀ **9:51 am** 6:51 am
☽ ☌ ♂ 10:50 pm

12 SATURDAY
☽ ☌ ♂ **1:50 am**
☽ □ ☿ **6:36 am** 3:36 am
☽ △ ♅ **9:52 am** 6:52 am
☽ ☍ ♃ **11:05 am** 8:05 am
☽ □ ☉ **2:32 pm** 11:32 am
☽ ⚻ ♆ **3:26 pm** 12:26 pm

13 SUNDAY
☉ ⚹ ♆ **3:30 am** 12:30 am
☽ ⚻ ♇ **4:28 am** 1:28 am
☿ ⚺ ♅ **5:04 am** 2:04 am
☽ ⚺ ♄ **6:04 am** 3:04 am
☿ □ ♃ **1:49 pm** 10:49 am
☽ △ ♀ **7:35 pm** 4:35 pm

14 MONDAY
☽ ⚺ ♂ **9:11 am** 6:11 am
☽ ⚻ ♅ **3:49 pm** 12:49 pm
☽ ⚻ ♃ **5:13 pm** 2:13 pm
☿ ⚹ ♆ **6:09 pm** 3:09 pm
☽ ☍ ♆ **9:35 pm** 6:35 pm
☽ △ ☿ **10:13 pm** 7:13 pm
☽ △ ☉ 9:56 pm

15 TUESDAY
☽ △ ☉ **12:56 am**
☽ △ ♇ **11:10 am** 8:10 am
☽ ☌ ♄ **12:44 pm** 9:44 am

16 WEDNESDAY
☉ ☌ ☿ **3:24 am** 12:24 am
☽ ⚻ ♀ **9:03 am** 6:03 am
☽ ⚹ ♂ **7:32 pm** 4:32 pm
☽ ☍ ♅ 9:25 pm
☽ △ ♃ 10:59 pm

17 THURSDAY
☽ ☍ ♅ **12:25 am**
☽ △ ♃ **1:59 am**
☽ ⚻ ♆ **6:17 am** 3:17 am
☽ ⚻ ☉ **2:31 pm** 11:31 am
☽ ⚻ ☿ **6:23 pm** 3:23 pm
☽ □ ♇ **8:16 pm** 5:16 pm
☽ ⚺ ♄ **9:48 pm** 6:48 pm

18 FRIDAY
☿ △ ♇ **5:22 am** 2:22 am
☿ △ ♄ **2:10 pm** 11:10 am
☽ ☍ ♀ 10:25 pm

19 SATURDAY
☽ ☍ ♀ **1:25 am**
☽ □ ♂ **8:12 am** 5:12 am
☽ ⚻ ♅ **10:59 am** 7:59 am
☽ □ ♃ **12:41 pm** 9:41 am
☽ △ ♆ **4:54 pm** 1:54 pm

20 SUNDAY
☽ ☍ ☉ **6:25 am** 3:25 am
☽ ⚹ ♇ **7:07 am** 4:07 am
☽ ⚹ ♄ **8:37 am** 5:37 am
☉ △ ♇ **2:56 pm** 11:56 am
☽ ☍ ☿ **5:48 pm** 2:48 pm

21 MONDAY
☉ △ ♄ **9:05 am** 6:05 am
☽ ⚻ ♀ **7:51 pm** 4:51 pm
☽ △ ♂ **10:32 pm** 7:32 pm
☽ △ ♅ **11:00 pm** 8:00 pm
☽ ⚹ ♃ 9:47 pm

22 TUESDAY
☽ ⚹ ♃ **12:47 am**
☽ □ ♆ **4:53 am** 1:53 am
♂ △ ♅ **10:47 am** 7:47 am
☽ ⚺ ♇ **7:13 pm** 4:13 pm
☽ □ ♄ **8:41 pm** 5:41 pm
☽ ⚻ ☉ **11:56 pm** 8:56 pm

23 WEDNESDAY
♀ ⚺ ♅ **3:32 am** 12:32 am
♀ □ ♂ **2:07 pm** 11:07 am
☽ ⚻ ☿ **7:09 pm** 4:09 pm
♀ □ ♃ **9:35 pm** 6:35 pm

24 THURSDAY
♂ ☍ ♃ **9:23 am** 6:23 am
☽ □ ♅ **11:51 am** 8:51 am
☽ ⚺ ♃ **1:40 pm** 10:40 am
☽ ⚻ ♂ **1:51 pm** 10:51 am
☽ △ ♀ **3:28 pm** 12:28 pm
☽ ⚹ ♆ **5:37 pm** 2:37 pm

25 FRIDAY
☽ ☌ ♇ **7:49 am** 4:49 am
☽ △ ♄ **9:16 am** 6:16 am
♀ ⚹ ♆ **12:33 pm** 9:33 am
☽ △ ☉ **5:58 pm** 2:58 pm

26 SATURDAY
☽ △ ☿ **7:59 pm** 4:59 pm
☽ ⚹ ♅ 9:15 pm
☽ ☌ ♃ 11:00 pm

27 SUNDAY
☽ ⚹ ♅ **12:15 am**
☽ ☌ ♃ **2:00 am**
☽ ☍ ♂ **4:36 am** 1:36 am
☽ ⚺ ♆ **5:44 am** 2:44 am
☽ □ ♀ **10:18 am** 7:18 am
☽ ⚺ ♇ **7:22 pm** 4:22 pm
☽ ⚻ ♄ **8:46 pm** 5:46 pm
☿ ⚹ ♅ **10:36 pm** 7:36 pm

28 MONDAY
♂ ⚻ ♆ **8:14 am** 5:14 am
☿ △ ♃ **9:41 am** 6:41 am
☽ □ ☉ **10:12 am** 7:12 am

29 TUESDAY
☿ □ ♆ **9:10 am** 6:10 am
☽ ⚺ ♅ **10:12 am** 7:12 am
☽ ⚺ ♃ **11:50 am** 8:50 am
☽ ☌ ♆ **3:15 pm** 12:15 pm
☽ □ ☿ **4:17 pm** 1:17 pm
☽ ⚻ ♂ **4:30 pm** 1:30 pm
☿ ⚹ ♂ **6:19 pm** 3:19 pm
☽ ⚹ ♀ 10:25 pm

30 WEDNESDAY
☽ ⚹ ♀ **1:25 am**
☽ ⚹ ♇ **3:55 am** 12:55 am
☽ ☍ ♄ **5:15 am** 2:15 am
☽ ⚹ ☉ **10:07 pm** 7:07 pm

Eastern time in bold type
Pacific time in medium type

APRIL 2008

EPHEMERIS CALCULATED FOR 12 MIDNIGHT GREENWICH MEAN TIME. ALL OTHER DATA AND FACING ASPECTARIAN PAGE IN **EASTERN TIME (BOLD)** AND PACIFIC TIME (REGULAR).

DATE	S.TIME	SUN	MOON	N.NODE	MERCURY	VENUS	MARS	JUPITER	SATURN	URANUS	NEPTUNE	PLUTO	CERES	PALLAS	JUNO	VESTA	CHIRON
1 Tue	12:38:54	11♈38 26	05♒30	26♒49	26♓53	23♓32	10♋43	20♑08	02♍34	19♓57	23♒26	01♑09	00♑57	10♑27	28♐52	21♓18	19♒37
2 Wed	12:42:51	12 37 38	18♒24	26 51R.	28 40	24 46	11 10	20 14	02 31R.	20 00	23 28	01 09R.	01 19	10 50	28 57	21 47	19 40
3 Thu	12:46:47	13 36 49	01♓44	26 51	00♈28	26 00	11 37	20 21	02 27	20 03	23 30	01 09	01 41	11 13	29 02	22 16	19 44
4 Fri	12:50:44	14 35 57	14♓19	26 46	02 18	27 15	12 04	20 27	02 25	20 06	23 31	01 09	02 04	11 36	29 07	22 45	19 47
5 Sat	12:54:40	15 35 04	26♓57	26 46	04 09	28 29	12 32	20 33	02 22	20 10	23 33	01 09	02 26	11 59	29 11	23 13	19 50
6 Sun	12:58:37	16 34 09	09♈28	26 40	06 02	29 43	12 59	20 39	02 19	20 13	23 34	01 09	02 48	12 22	29 15	23 42	19 53
7 Mon	13:02:33	17 33 11	21♈52	26 32	07 56	00♈57	13 27	20 45	02 16	20 16	23 36	01 09	03 11	12 45	29 19	24 11	19 56
8 Tue	13:06:30	18 32 12	04♉09	26 24	09 51	02 11	13 55	20 51	02 14	20 19	23 38	01 09	03 33	13 09	29 22	24 39	19 58
9 Wed	13:10:27	19 31 11	16♉21	26 17	11 48	03 25	14 23	20 56	02 11	20 22	23 39	01 08	03 56	13 32	29 25	25 08	20 01
10 Thu	13:14:23	20 30 07	28♉28	26 10	13 46	04 39	14 52	21 02	02 09	20 25	23 40	01 08	04 19	13 55	29 28	25 36	20 04
11 Fri	13:18:20	21 29 02	10♊32	26 06	15 46	05 53	15 20	21 07	02 06	20 28	23 42	01 08	04 42	14 19	29 31	26 05	20 07
12 Sat	13:22:16	22 27 53	22♊37	26 03D	17 47	07 07	15 49	21 12	02 04	20 31	23 43	01 08	05 05	14 42	29 33	26 33	20 09
13 Sun	13:26:13	23 26 43	04♋46	26 03	19 49	08 21	16 18	21 17	02 02	20 34	23 45	01 07	05 28	15 05	29 35	27 02	20 12
14 Mon	13:30:09	24 25 30	17♋03	26 04	21 52	09 35	16 47	21 22	01 58	20 37	23 46	01 07	05 51	15 29	29 37	27 30	20 15
15 Tue	13:34:06	25 24 15	29♋31	26 04R.	23 57	10 49	17 16	21 26	01 56	20 40	23 47	01 07	06 14	15 52	29 39	27 58	20 17
16 Wed	13:38:02	26 22 58	12♌14	26 04	26 02	12 03	17 45	21 31	01 54	20 43	23 49	01 06	06 37	16 16	29 40	28 26	20 20
17 Thu	13:41:59	27 21 38	25♌16	26 02	28 08	13 17	18 14	21 35	01 53	20 46	23 50	01 06	07 01	16 39	29 40R.	28 54	20 22
18 Fri	13:45:56	28 20 16	08♍40	25 57	00♉15	14 31	18 44	21 39	01 51	20 49	23 51	01 05	07 24	17 03	29 40	29 23	20 24
19 Sat	13:49:52	29 18 53	22♍28	25 49	02 23	15 45	19 14	21 43	01 50	20 52	23 52	01 05	07 47	17 26	29 40	29 51	20 27
20 Sun	13:53:49	00♉17 27	06♎41	25 39	04 30	16 59	19 43	21 46	01 49	20 55	23 54	01 04	08 11	17 50	29 39	00♈18	20 29
21 Mon	13:57:45	01 15 59	21♎15	25 27	06 38	18 13	20 13	21 50	01 47	20 58	23 55	01 04	08 35	18 13	29 38	00 46	20 31
22 Tue	14:01:42	02 14 30	06♏06	25 15	08 45	19 27	20 44	21 53	01 45	21 01	23 56	01 03	08 58	18 37	29 37	01 14	20 33
23 Wed	14:05:38	03 12 58	21♏04	25 03	10 51	20 41	21 14	21 56	01 44	21 03	23 57	01 02	09 22	19 01	29 35	01 42	20 35
24 Thu	14:09:35	04 11 25	06♐00	24 52	12 57	21 55	21 44	21 59	01 44	21 06	23 58	01 01	09 46	19 24	29 33	02 10	20 37
25 Fri	14:13:31	05 09 50	20♐42	24 43	15 01	23 09	22 15	22 02	01 43	21 09	23 59	01 01	10 10	19 48	29 31	02 37	20 39
26 Sat	14:17:28	06 08 14	05♑01	24 37	17 04	24 23	22 45	22 05	01 43	21 11	24 00	01 00	10 33	20 12	29 28	03 05	20 41
27 Sun	14:21:25	07 06 36	18♑53	24 33	19 05	25 37	23 16	22 07	01 42	21 14	24 01	01 00	10 57	20 36	29 25	03 32	20 43
28 Mon	14:25:21	08 04 56	02♒17	24 32D	21 04	26 50	23 47	22 10	01 42	21 17	24 02	00 59	11 21	20 59	29 22	04 00	20 45
29 Tue	14:29:18	09 03 15	15♒16	24 32R.	23 01	28 04	24 18	22 12	01 42	21 19	24 03	00 58	11 46	21 23	29 18	04 27	20 47
30 Wed	14:33:14	10 01 33	27♒51	24 32	24 54	29 18	24 49	22 14	01 41	21 22	24 04	00 57	12 10	21 47	29 13	04 55	20 48

MAY 2008

☽ Last Aspect day	ET / hr:mn	PT	asp	☽ Ingress sign day	ET / hr:mn	PT
2	5:34 am	2:34 am	✶☿	♈ 2	6:51 am	3:51 am
4	3:16 am	12:16 am	□♂	♉ 4	7:58 am	4:58 am
6	4:21 am	1:21 am	✶♂	♊ 6	7:17 am	4:17 am
7	9:36 pm	6:36 pm	△♆	♋ 8	7:02 am	4:02 am
9	8:06 pm	5:06 pm	☍♃	♌ 10	9:10 am	6:10 am
12	4:09 am	1:09 am	☍♆	♍ 12	2:48 pm	11:48 am
14	12:38 pm	9:38 am	△☉	♎ 14	11:46 pm	8:46 pm
16	11:29 pm	8:29 pm	△♆	♏ 17	10:59 am	7:59 am
19	10:11 pm	7:11 pm	☍☉	♐ 19	11:18 pm	8:18 pm
21		9:19 pm	✶♆	♑ 22	11:55 am	8:55 am
22	12:19 am		✶♆	♑ 22	11:55 am	8:55 am
24	8:26 am	5:26 am	✶♅	♒ 24	11:51 pm	8:51 pm
26	10:49 pm	7:49 pm	☌♆	♓ 27	9:38 am	6:38 am
28		11:23 pm	☌♅	♈ 29	3:52 pm	12:52 pm
29	2:23 am		☌♅	♈ 29	3:52 pm	12:52 pm
31	8:54 am	5:54 am	✶♆	♉ 31	6:18 pm	3:18 pm

☽ Phases & Eclipses phase	day	ET / hr:mn	PT
New Moon	5	8:18 am	5:18 am
2nd Quarter	11	11:47 pm	8:47 pm
Full Moon	19	10:11 pm	7:11 pm
4th Quarter	27	10:56 pm	7:56 pm

Planet Ingress	day	ET / hr:mn	PT
☿ ♊	2	4:00 pm	1:00 pm
♂ ♌	9	4:20 pm	1:20 pm
♀ ♉	20	9:54 am	6:54 am
☉ ♊	20	12:01 pm	9:01 am
♀ ♊	24	6:52 pm	3:52 pm

Planetary Motion	day	ET / hr:mn	PT
♄ D	2	11:07 pm	8:07 pm
♃ ℞	9	8:11 am	5:11 am
⚷ ℞	25	7:42 am	4:42 am
☿ ℞	26	11:48 am	8:48 am
♆ ℞	26	12:14 pm	9:14 am

1 THURSDAY
♀ △ ♇ **3:48 am** 12:48 am
☽ ☌ ♅ **4:14 pm** 1:14 pm
☽ ✶ ♃ **5:41 pm** 2:41 pm
♀ △ ♄ **6:20 pm** 3:20 pm
☽ ⚺ ♆ **8:47 pm** 5:47 pm
☽ △ ♂ **11:57 pm** 8:57 pm

2 FRIDAY
☽ ✶ ☿ **5:34 am** 2:34 am
☽ □ ♇ **8:24 am** 5:24 am
☽ ⚻ ♄ **9:41 am** 6:41 am
☽ ⚺ ♀ **11:08 am** 8:08 am

3 SATURDAY
☿ ⚻ ♇ **4:45 am** 1:45 am
☽ ⚺ ☉ **4:59 am** 1:59 am
☿ □ ♄ **3:50 pm** 12:50 pm
☽ ⚺ ♅ **6:21 pm** 3:21 pm
☽ □ ♃ **7:39 pm** 4:39 pm
☽ ✶ ♆ **10:32 pm** 7:32 pm

4 SUNDAY
☽ □ ♂ **3:16 am** 12:16 am
☽ △ ♇ **9:23 am** 6:23 am
☽ △ ♄ **10:39 am** 7:39 am
☽ ⚺ ☿ **12:56 pm** 9:56 am
☽ ☌ ♀ **4:21 pm** 1:21 pm

5 MONDAY
☽ ☌ ☉ **8:18 am** 5:18 am
☽ ✶ ♅ **6:05 pm** 3:05 pm

Eastern time in bold type
Pacific time in medium type

☽ △ ♃ **7:16 pm** 4:16 pm
☽ □ ♆ **10:05 pm** 7:05 pm

6 TUESDAY
☽ ✶ ♂ **4:21 am** 1:21 am
☽ ⚻ ♇ **8:38 am** 5:38 am
☽ □ ♄ **9:57 am** 6:57 am
☽ ☌ ☿ **5:31 pm** 2:31 pm
☽ ⚺ ♀ **7:45 pm** 4:45 pm

7 WEDNESDAY
☽ ⚺ ☉ **10:48 am** 7:48 am
☽ □ ♅ **5:37 pm** 2:37 pm
☽ ⚻ ♃ **6:43 pm** 3:43 pm
☽ △ ♆ **9:36 pm** 6:36 pm

8 THURSDAY
☽ ⚺ ♂ **5:47 am** 2:47 am
☽ ☍ ♇ **8:22 am** 5:22 am
☽ ✶ ♄ **9:48 am** 6:48 am
☽ ⚺ ☿ **10:44 pm** 7:44 pm
☽ ✶ ♀ 9:24 pm

9 FRIDAY
☽ ✶ ♀ **12:24 am**
☽ ✶ ☉ **3:18 pm** 12:18 pm
☽ △ ♅ **7:03 pm** 4:03 pm
☽ ☍ ♃ **8:06 pm** 5:06 pm
☽ ⚻ ♆ **11:11 pm** 8:11 pm

10 SATURDAY
☽ ☌ ♂ **9:50 am** 6:50 am
☽ ⚻ ♇ **10:31 am** 7:31 am

☽ ⚺ ♄ **12:10 pm** 9:10 am
♂ ⚻ ♇ 11:55 pm

11 SUNDAY
♂ ⚻ ♇ **2:55 am**
☽ ✶ ☿ **7:06 am** 4:06 am
☽ □ ♀ **8:51 am** 5:51 am
☽ □ ☉ **11:47 pm** 8:47 pm
☽ ⚻ ♅ **11:50 pm** 8:50 pm
☉ ✶ ♅ 9:32 pm
☽ ⚻ ♃ 9:47 pm

12 MONDAY
☉ ✶ ♅ **12:32 am**
☽ ⚻ ♃ **12:47 am**
☽ ☍ ♆ **4:09 am** 1:09 am
☉ △ ♃ **1:29 pm** 10:29 am
☽ △ ♇ **4:11 pm** 1:11 pm
☽ ⚺ ♂ **5:51 pm** 2:51 pm
☽ ☌ ♄ **6:04 pm** 3:04 pm
♂ ⚺ ♄ **11:16 pm** 8:16 pm

13 TUESDAY
☽ □ ☿ **7:20 pm** 4:20 pm
☽ △ ♀ **10:03 pm** 7:03 pm

14 WEDNESDAY
☽ ☍ ♅ **8:08 am** 5:08 am
☽ △ ♃ **8:56 am** 5:56 am
☉ □ ♆ **11:50 am** 8:50 am
☽ ⚻ ♆ **12:34 pm** 9:34 am
☽ △ ☉ **12:38 pm** 9:38 am
☽ □ ♇ 10:08 pm

15 THURSDAY
☽ □ ♇ **1:08 am**
☽ ⚺ ♄ **3:18 am** 12:18 am
☽ ✶ ♂ **5:36 am** 2:36 am

16 FRIDAY
☽ △ ☿ **10:12 am** 7:12 am
☽ ⚻ ♀ **3:01 pm** 12:01 pm
☽ ⚻ ♅ **7:01 pm** 4:01 pm
☽ □ ♃ **7:36 pm** 4:36 pm
☽ △ ♆ **11:29 pm** 8:29 pm

17 SATURDAY
☽ ⚻ ☉ **4:38 am** 1:38 am
☽ ✶ ♇ **12:17 pm** 9:17 am
☽ ✶ ♄ **2:43 pm** 11:43 am
☽ □ ♂ **7:48 pm** 4:48 pm

18 SUNDAY
♀ ✶ ♅ **7:23 am** 4:23 am
♀ △ ♃ **11:17 am** 8:17 am
☽ ⚻ ☿ 10:51 pm

19 MONDAY
☽ ⚻ ☿ **1:51 am**
☽ △ ♅ **7:18 am** 4:18 am
☽ ✶ ♃ **7:35 am** 4:35 am
☽ ☍ ♀ **9:59 am** 6:59 am
☽ □ ♆ **11:41 am** 8:41 am
☽ ☍ ☉ **10:11 pm** 7:11 pm
☽ ⚺ ♇ 9:31 pm
♀ □ ♆ 11:28 pm

20 TUESDAY
☽ ⚺ ♇ **12:31 am**
♀ □ ♆ **2:28 am**
☽ □ ♄ **3:14 am** 12:14 am
☽ △ ♂ **11:09 am** 8:09 am
☉ ⚻ ♇ 11:22 pm

21 WEDNESDAY
☉ ⚻ ♇ **2:22 am**
♃ ✶ ♅ **2:04 pm** 11:04 am
☽ ☍ ☿ **5:01 pm** 2:01 pm
☽ ⚺ ♃ **8:01 pm** 5:01 pm
☽ □ ♅ **8:03 pm** 5:03 pm
☽ ✶ ♆ 9:19 pm

22 THURSDAY
☽ ✶ ♆ **12:19 am**
☽ ⚻ ♀ **5:35 am** 2:35 am
☽ ☌ ♇ **1:01 pm** 10:01 am
☉ □ ♄ **2:25 pm** 11:25 am
☽ △ ♄ **4:00 pm** 1:00 pm
☽ ⚻ ☉ **4:08 pm** 1:08 pm
☽ ⚻ ♂ 11:39 pm

23 FRIDAY
☽ ⚻ ♂ **2:39 am**

24 SATURDAY
☽ ⚻ ☿ **6:43 am** 3:43 am
☽ ☌ ♃ **8:03 am** 5:03 am
☽ ✶ ♅ **8:26 am** 5:26 am
☽ ⚺ ♆ **12:30 pm** 9:30 am
☽ △ ♀ 9:25 pm
☽ ⚺ ♇ 9:49 pm

25 SUNDAY
☽ △ ♀ **12:25 am**
☽ ⚺ ♇ **12:49 am**
☽ ⚻ ♄ **4:01 am** 1:01 am
♀ ⚻ ♇ **4:20 am** 1:20 am
☽ △ ☉ **9:04 am** 6:04 am
☽ ☍ ♂ **5:02 pm** 2:02 pm

26 MONDAY
♀ □ ♄ **1:10 pm** 10:10 am
☽ △ ☿ **5:39 pm** 2:39 pm
☽ ⚺ ♃ **6:20 pm** 3:20 pm
☽ ⚺ ♅ **7:03 pm** 4:03 pm
☽ ☌ ♆ **10:49 pm** 7:49 pm

27 TUESDAY
☽ ✶ ♇ **10:27 am** 7:27 am
☽ ☍ ♄ **1:46 pm** 10:46 am
☽ □ ♀ **4:16 pm** 1:16 pm
☽ □ ☉ **10:56 pm** 7:56 pm

28 WEDNESDAY
☽ ⚻ ♂ **4:25 am** 1:25 am
☽ □ ☿ 9:33 pm
☽ ✶ ♃ 10:23 pm
☽ ☌ ♅ 11:23 pm

29 THURSDAY
☽ □ ☿ **12:33 am**
☽ ✶ ♃ **1:23 am**
☽ ☌ ♅ **2:23 am**
☽ ⚺ ♆ **5:47 am** 2:47 am
☽ □ ♇ **4:32 pm** 1:32 pm
☽ ⚻ ♄ **7:53 pm** 4:53 pm

30 FRIDAY
☽ ✶ ♀ **3:14 am** 12:14 am
☽ ✶ ☉ **8:08 am** 5:08 am
☽ △ ♂ **11:30 am** 8:30 am

31 SATURDAY
☽ ✶ ☿ **3:08 am** 12:08 am
☽ □ ♃ **4:34 am** 1:34 am
☽ ⚺ ♅ **5:48 am** 2:48 am
☽ ✶ ♆ **8:54 am** 5:54 am
☽ △ ♇ **6:51 pm** 3:51 pm
☽ △ ♄ **10:13 pm** 7:13 pm

MAY 2008

DATE	S.TIME	SUN	MOON	N.NODE	MERCURY	VENUS	MARS	JUPITER	SATURN	URANUS	NEPTUNE	PLUTO	CERES	PALLAS	JUNO	VESTA	CHIRON
1 Thu	14:37:11	10♉59 48	09♓53	24≈31	26♉45	00♉32	25♋50	22♑15	01♍41	21♓27	24≈05	00♑56	12♊34	22♈11	29♈14	05♈22	20≈50
2 Fri	14:41:07	11 58 03	23 38	24 28R.	28 33	01 46	25 51	22 17	01 41R.	21 29	24 06	00 56	12 58	22 34	29 10R.	05 49	20 51
3 Sat	14:45:04	12 56 15	07♈51	24 23	00♊17	03 00	26 22	22 18	01 41 D	21 32	24 07	00 55	13 22	22 58	29 05	06 16	20 53
4 Sun	14:49:00	13 54 26	22 32	24 15	01 58	04 14	26 54	22 19	01 41	21 34	24 08	00 54	13 47	23 22	29 00	06 43	20 54
5 Mon	14:52:57	14 52 36	07♉35	24 05	03 35	05 28	27 25	22 20	01 41	21 36	24 08	00 53	14 11	23 46	28 55	07 10	20 56
6 Tue	14:56:54	15 50 44	22 49	23 54	05 09	06 42	27 57	22 21	01 41	21 39	24 09	00 52	14 36	24 10	28 49	07 37	20 57
7 Wed	15:00:50	16 48 51	08♊04	23 44	06 39	07 55	28 29	22 22	01 42	21 41	24 10	00 51	15 00	24 34	28 43	08 04	20 58
8 Thu	15:04:47	17 46 55	23 10	23 36	08 05	09 09	29 01	22 22	01 42	21 43	24 10	00 50	15 24	24 58	28 37	08 31	20 59
9 Fri	15:08:43	18 44 58	07♋56	23 28	09 27	10 23	29 33	22 22	01 43	21 45	24 11	00 50	15 49	25 22	28 30	08 58	21 00
10 Sat	15:12:40	19 42 59	22 19	23 24	10 45	11 37	00♌05	22 22	01 43	21 47	24 12	00 49	16 14	25 46	28 23	09 24	21 01
11 Sun	15:16:36	20 40 58	06♌14	23 22	11 58	12 51	00 37	22 22	01 44	21 49	24 12	00 48	16 39	26 10	28 16	09 51	21 02
12 Mon	15:20:33	21 38 55	19 43	23 22	13 08	14 05	01 09	22 21	01 45	21 52	24 13	00 47	17 04	26 34	28 08	10 17	21 03
13 Tue	15:24:29	22 36 51	02♍48	23 22	14 13	15 18	01 42	22 21	01 46	21 54	24 13	00 46	17 28	26 58	28 01	10 44	21 04
14 Wed	15:28:26	23 34 44	15 34	23 20	15 15	16 32	02 14	22 20	01 47	21 56	24 14	00 45	17 53	27 22	27 52	11 10	21 05
15 Thu	15:32:23	24 32 36	28 03	23 17	16 11	17 46	02 47	22 19	01 48	21 58	24 14	00 43	18 18	27 46	27 44	11 37	21 06
16 Fri	15:36:19	25 30 26	10♎21	23 12	17 04	19 00	03 19	22 18	01 50	21 59	24 14	00 42	18 43	28 10	27 35	12 03	21 07
17 Sat	15:40:16	26 28 14	22 29	23 03	17 51	20 13	03 52	22 17	01 51	22 01	24 15	00 41	19 08	28 34	27 26	12 29	21 07
18 Sun	15:44:12	27 26 01	04♏31	22 52	18 35	21 27	04 25	22 15	01 53	22 03	24 15	00 40	19 33	28 58	27 17	12 55	21 08
19 Mon	15:48:09	28 23 46	16 28	22 39	19 13	22 41	04 58	22 14	01 54	22 05	24 15R.	00 39	19 58	29 22	27 07	13 20	21 08
20 Tue	15:52:05	29 21 30	28 22	22 25	19 47	23 55	05 31	22 12	01 56	22 07	24 15	00 37	20 23	29 46	26 57	13 46	21 08
21 Wed	15:56:02	00♊19 12	10♐22	21 59	20 17	25 09	06 04	22 10	01 58	22 08	24 15	00 36	20 48	00♉10	26 47	14 12	21 09
22 Thu	15:59:58	01 16 54	22 07	21 49	20 41	26 22	06 37	22♑22R.	02 00	22 10	24 15	00 35	21 13	00 34	26 36	14 38	21 09
23 Fri	16:03:55	02 14 34	04♑14	21 42	21 01	27 36	07 10	22 05	02 02	22 12	24 15	00 34	21 38	00 58	26 26	15 03	21 09R.
24 Sat	16:07:52	03 12 13	16 54	21 37	21 16	28 50	07 43	22 02	02 04	22 13	24 15	00 32	22 04	01 22	26 15	15 29	21 09
25 Sun	16:11:48	04 09 50	28 03	21 35	21 26	00♊03	08 16	22 00	02 06	22 15	24 15	00 31	22 29	01 47	26 04	15 54	21 09
26 Mon	16:15:45	05 07 27	10♒17	21 35 D	21 31R.	01 17	08 50	21 57	02 09	22 16	24 15	00 30	22 54	02 11	25 52	16 19	21 09
27 Tue	16:19:41	06 05 03	22 46	21 35	21 32	02 31	09 23	21 53	02 11	22 18	24 15	00 28	23 20	02 35	25 41	16 45	21 09
28 Wed	16:23:38	07 02 38	05♓34	21 33	21 28	03 45	09 57	21 50	02 13	22 19	24 15	00 27	23 45	02 59	25 29	17 10	21 09
29 Thu	16:27:34	08 00 12	18 45	21 33	21 20	04 58	10 30	21 47	02 16	22 20	24 15	00 25	24 10	03 23	25 17	17 35	21 08
30 Fri	16:31:31	08 57 45	02♈23	21 29	21 08	06 12	11 04	21 43	02 18	22 22	24 15	00 24	24 36	03 47	25 04	18 00	21 08
31 Sat	16:35:27	09 55 17	16 29	21 29	20 51	07 26	11 38	21 39	02 21	22 23	24 15	00 23	25 01	04 11	24 52	18 25	21 08

EPHEMERIS CALCULATED FOR 12 MIDNIGHT GREENWICH MEAN TIME. ALL OTHER DATA AND FACING ASPECTARIAN PAGE IN **EASTERN TIME (BOLD)** AND PACIFIC TIME (REGULAR).

JUNE 2008

☽ Last Aspect day	ET / hr:mn / PT	asp	☽ Ingress sign	day	ET / hr:mn / PT
2	**9:02 am** 6:02 am	□ ♆	♊	2	**6:06 pm** 3:06 pm
4	**8:08 am** 5:08 am	△ ♆	♋	4	**5:16 pm** 2:16 pm
6	**5:32 am** 2:32 am	△ ♅	♌	6	**6:00 pm** 3:00 pm
8	**11:40 am** 8:40 am	☍ ♆	♍	8	**10:01 pm** 7:01 pm
10	**3:42 pm** 12:42 pm	☍ ♅	♎	11	**5:55 am** 2:55 am
13	**5:15 am** 2:15 am	△ ♆	♏	13	**4:53 pm** 1:53 pm
15	**5:29 pm** 2:29 pm	□ ♆	♐	16	**5:19 am** 2:19 am
18	**5:37 pm** 2:37 pm	☌ ♇	♑	18	**5:51 pm** 2:51 pm
20	**3:02 pm** 12:02 pm	✶ ♅	♒	21	**5:33 am** 2:33 am
23	**3:04 pm** 12:04 pm	✶ ♇	♓	23	**3:32 pm** 12:32 pm

☽ Last Aspect day	ET / hr:mn / PT	asp	☽ Ingress sign	day	ET / hr:mn / PT
25	**10:16 pm** 7:16 pm	□ ♇	♈	25	**10:49 pm** 7:49 pm
27	11:14 pm	△ ♇	♉	27	11:50 pm
28	**2:14 am**	△ ♇	♉	28	**2:50 am**
29	11:43 pm	□ ♂	♊	30	**4:03 am** 1:03 am
30	**2:43 am**	□ ♂	♊	30	**4:03 am** 1:03 am

☽ Phases & Eclipses phase	day	ET / hr:mn / PT
New Moon	3	**3:22 pm** 12:22 pm
2nd Quarter	10	**11:03 am** 8:03 am
Full Moon	18	**1:30 pm** 10:30 am
4th Quarter	26	**8:10 am** 5:10 am

Planet Ingress	day	ET / hr:mn / PT
⚳ ♋	11	**11:56 am** 8:56 am
♇ ♐	13	10:13 pm
♇ ♐	14	**1:13 am**
♀ ♋	18	**4:48 am** 1:48 am
☉ ♋	20	**7:59 pm** 4:59 pm
⚵ ♉	29	9:56 pm
⚵ ♉	30	**12:56 am**

Planetary Motion	day	ET / hr:mn / PT
☿ D	19	**10:31 am** 7:31 am
♅ R℞	26	**8:01 pm** 5:01 pm

1 SUNDAY
☽ ⚺ ♀ **9:24 am** 6:24 am
☽ ⚺ ☉ **12:56 pm** 9:56 am
☽ □ ♂ **2:39 pm** 11:39 am
☽ ⚺ ☿ 11:22 pm

2 MONDAY
☽ ⚺ ☿ **2:22 am**
☽ △ ♃ **4:42 am** 1:42 am
☽ ✶ ♅ **6:09 am** 3:09 am
☽ □ ♆ **9:02 am** 6:02 am
☽ ⚻ ♇ **6:32 pm** 3:32 pm
☽ □ ♄ **10:02 pm** 7:02 pm

3 TUESDAY
☽ ☌ ♀ **12:53 pm** 9:53 am
☽ ☌ ☉ **3:22 pm** 12:22 pm
☽ ✶ ♂ **3:43 pm** 12:43 pm
☽ ☌ ☿ 9:05 pm

4 WEDNESDAY
☽ ☌ ☿ **12:05 am**
☽ ⚻ ♃ **3:35 am** 12:35 am
☉ ✶ ♂ **4:34 am** 1:34 am
☽ □ ♅ **5:20 am** 2:20 am
☽ △ ♆ **8:08 am** 5:08 am
☽ ☍ ♇ **5:38 pm** 2:38 pm
☽ ✶ ♄ **9:25 pm** 6:25 pm

5 THURSDAY
☽ ⚺ ♀ **4:43 pm** 1:43 pm
☽ ⚺ ♂ **5:15 pm** 2:15 pm
☽ ⚺ ☉ **6:17 pm** 3:17 pm
☽ ⚺ ☿ **10:21 pm** 7:21 pm

6 FRIDAY
☽ ☍ ♃ **3:24 am** 12:24 am
♀ ✶ ♂ **4:16 am** 1:16 am
☽ △ ♅ **5:32 am** 2:32 am
☽ ⚻ ♆ **8:24 am** 5:24 am
☽ ⚻ ♇ **6:18 pm** 3:18 pm
☽ ⚺ ♄ **10:35 pm** 7:35 pm

7 SATURDAY
☉ ☌ ☿ **11:27 am** 8:27 am
☿ ☌ ♀ **5:03 pm** 2:03 pm
☽ ☌ ♂ **9:38 pm** 6:38 pm
☽ ✶ ☿ **10:57 pm** 7:57 pm
☽ ✶ ♀ **11:48 pm** 8:48 pm
☽ ✶ ☉ 9:19 pm

8 SUNDAY
☽ ✶ ☉ **12:19 am**
☽ ⚻ ♃ **6:01 am** 3:01 am
☽ ⚻ ♅ **8:41 am** 5:41 am
☽ ☍ ♆ **11:40 am** 8:40 am
☿ ✶ ♂ **2:28 pm** 11:28 am
☽ △ ♇ **10:15 pm** 7:15 pm
☉ ☌ ♀ 9:18 pm

9 MONDAY
☉ ☌ ♀ **12:18 am**
☽ ☌ ♄ **3:11 am** 12:11 am
☽ □ ☿ 11:59 pm

10 TUESDAY
☽ □ ☿ **2:59 am**
☽ ⚺ ♂ **6:18 am** 3:18 am
☽ □ ☉ **11:03 am** 8:03 am
☽ □ ♀ **11:53 am** 8:53 am
☽ △ ♃ **12:23 pm** 9:23 am
☽ ☍ ♅ **3:42 pm** 12:42 pm
♀ ⚻ ♃ **4:46 pm** 1:46 pm
☽ ⚻ ♆ **6:49 pm** 3:49 pm

11 WEDNESDAY
☉ ⚻ ♃ **3:17 am** 12:17 am
☽ □ ♇ **6:03 am** 3:03 am
☽ ⚺ ♄ **11:43 am** 8:43 am

12 THURSDAY
♀ □ ♅ **3:38 am** 12:38 am
☽ △ ☿ **10:27 am** 7:27 am
☽ ✶ ♂ **7:03 pm** 4:03 pm
☽ □ ♃ **10:06 pm** 7:06 pm
☉ □ ♅ 10:24 pm
☽ ⚻ ♅ 11:05 pm
☽ △ ☉ 11:09 pm

13 FRIDAY
☉ □ ♅ **1:24 am**
☽ ⚻ ♅ **2:05 am**
☽ △ ☉ **2:09 am**
☽ △ ♀ **4:37 am** 1:37 am
☽ △ ♆ **5:15 am** 2:15 am
♀ △ ♆ **10:53 am** 7:53 am
☽ ✶ ♇ **4:54 pm** 1:54 pm
☽ ✶ ♄ **11:14 pm** 8:14 pm

14 SATURDAY
☉ △ ♆ **5:02 pm** 2:02 pm
☽ ⚻ ☿ **8:28 pm** 5:28 pm
♂ ⚻ ♃ 11:06 pm

15 SUNDAY
♂ ⚻ ♃ **2:06 am**
☽ ✶ ♃ **9:45 am** 6:45 am
☽ □ ♂ **10:13 am** 7:13 am
☽ △ ♅ **2:22 pm** 11:22 am
☽ □ ♆ **5:29 pm** 2:29 pm
☽ ⚻ ☉ **7:39 pm** 4:39 pm
☽ ⚻ ♀ **11:50 pm** 8:50 pm

16 MONDAY
☽ ⚺ ♇ **5:13 am** 2:13 am
☽ □ ♄ **12:06 pm** 9:06 am

17 TUESDAY
☽ ☍ ☿ **7:54 am** 4:54 am
☽ ⚺ ♃ **9:51 pm** 6:51 pm
☽ △ ♂ 10:57 pm
♀ ☍ ♇ 11:46 pm

18 WEDNESDAY
☽ △ ♂ **1:57 am**
♀ ☍ ♇ **2:46 am**
☽ □ ♅ **3:01 am** 12:01 am
☽ ✶ ♆ **6:02 am** 3:02 am
☽ ☍ ☉ **1:30 pm** 10:30 am
☽ ☌ ♇ **5:37 pm** 2:37 pm
☽ ☍ ♀ **7:21 pm** 4:21 pm
♂ ⚻ ♅ 9:08 pm
☽ △ ♄ 9:58 pm

19 THURSDAY
♂ ⚻ ♅ **12:08 am**
☽ △ ♄ **12:58 am**
☽ ⚻ ☿ **7:51 pm** 4:51 pm

20 FRIDAY
☽ ☌ ♃ **9:22 am** 6:22 am
☽ ✶ ♅ **3:02 pm** 12:02 pm
☉ ☍ ♇ **3:42 pm** 12:42 pm
☽ ⚻ ♂ **4:59 pm** 1:59 pm
☽ ⚺ ♆ **5:54 pm** 2:54 pm

21 SATURDAY
☽ ⚺ ♇ **5:12 am** 2:12 am
♀ ✶ ♄ **5:14 am** 2:14 am
☽ ⚻ ☉ **6:22 am** 3:22 am
♂ ☍ ♆ **11:32 am** 8:32 am
☽ ⚻ ♄ **12:53 pm** 9:53 am
☽ ⚻ ♀ **1:41 pm** 10:41 am

22 SUNDAY
☽ △ ☿ **7:32 am** 4:32 am
☽ ⚺ ♃ **7:31 pm** 4:31 pm
☽ ⚺ ♅ 10:33 pm

23 MONDAY
☽ ⚺ ♅ **1:33 am**
☽ ☌ ♆ **4:14 am** 1:14 am
☽ ☍ ♂ **6:16 am** 3:16 am
☽ ✶ ♇ **3:04 pm** 12:04 pm
☽ △ ☉ **9:01 pm** 6:01 pm
☽ ☍ ♄ **10:57 pm** 7:57 pm

24 TUESDAY
☽ △ ♀ **5:28 am** 2:28 am
☽ □ ☿ **5:51 pm** 2:51 pm
☉ ✶ ♄ 10:00 pm

25 WEDNESDAY
☉ ✶ ♄ **1:00 am**
☽ ✶ ♃ **3:20 am** 12:20 am
☽ ☌ ♅ **9:35 am** 6:35 am
☽ ⚺ ♆ **12:03 pm** 9:03 am
☽ ⚻ ♂ **4:38 pm** 1:38 pm
☽ □ ♇ **10:16 pm** 7:16 pm

26 THURSDAY
☽ ⚻ ♄ **6:09 am** 3:09 am
☽ □ ☉ **8:10 am** 5:10 am
☽ □ ♀ **5:21 pm** 2:21 pm
☽ ✶ ☿ 10:39 pm

27 FRIDAY
☽ ✶ ☿ **1:39 am**
☽ □ ♃ **8:05 am** 5:05 am
☽ ⚺ ♅ **2:24 pm** 11:24 am
☽ ✶ ♆ **4:40 pm** 1:40 pm
☽ △ ♂ **11:18 pm** 8:18 pm
☽ △ ♇ 11:14 pm

28 SATURDAY
☽ △ ♇ **2:14 am**
☽ △ ♄ **10:02 am** 7:02 am
☽ ✶ ☉ **3:16 pm** 12:16 pm
☽ ✶ ♀ 9:58 pm

29 SUNDAY
☽ ✶ ♀ **12:58 am**
☽ ⚺ ☿ **6:34 am** 3:34 am
☽ △ ♃ **9:47 am** 6:47 am
☽ ✶ ♅ **4:12 pm** 1:12 pm
☽ □ ♆ **6:18 pm** 3:18 pm
☽ □ ♂ 11:43 pm

30 MONDAY
☽ □ ♂ **2:43 am**
☽ ⚻ ♇ **3:23 am** 12:23 am
☽ □ ♄ **11:14 am** 8:14 am
♂ △ ♇ **6:56 pm** 3:56 pm
☽ ⚺ ☉ **7:16 pm** 4:16 pm

Eastern time in bold type
Pacific time in medium type

JUNE 2008

DATE	S.TIME	SUN	MOON	N.NODE	MERCURY	VENUS	MARS	JUPITER	SATURN	URANUS	NEPTUNE	PLUTO	CERES	PALLAS	JUNO	VESTA	CHIRON
1 Sun	16:39:24	10♊52 49	01♉03	21♒22	20♊31	08♊40	12♌12	21♑35	02♍24	22♓23	24♒15	00♑20	25♑27	04♉36	24♐39	18♈49	21♒08
2 Mon	16:43:21	11 50 20	16 00	21 13 R	20 08 R	09 53	12 46	21 31 R	02 27	22 25	24 15 R	00 18 R	25 52	05 00	24 27 R	19 14	21 07 R
3 Tue	16:47:17	12 47 49	01♊13	21 04	19 41	11 07	13 20	21 27	02 30	22 26	24 14	00 17	26 18	05 24	24 14	19 38	21 07
4 Wed	16:51:14	13 45 19	16 31	20 46	19 12	12 21	13 54	21 22	02 33	22 28	24 14	00 15	26 43	05 48	24 01	20 03	21 06
5 Thu	16:55:10	14 42 47	01♋43	20 40	18 42	13 35	14 28	21 17	02 37	22 29	24 14	00 14	27 09	06 12	23 48	20 27	21 05
6 Fri	16:59:07	15 40 14	16 39	20 36	18 09	14 48	15 02	21 13	02 40	22 31	24 14	00 12	27 34	06 36	23 34	20 51	21 05
7 Sat	17:03:03	16 37 40	01♌12	20 35	17 36	16 02	15 36	21 08	02 43	22 32	24 13	00 11	28 00	07 01	23 21	21 16	21 04
8 Sun	17:07:00	17 35 05	15 16	20 34 D	17 03	17 16	16 11	21 02	02 47	22 33	24 13	00 09	28 26	07 25	23 08	21 40	21 03
9 Mon	17:10:57	18 32 29	28 53	20 35	16 29	18 30	16 45	20 57	02 51	22 34	24 12	00 08	28 51	07 49	22 54	22 03	21 02
10 Tue	17:14:53	19 29 51	12♍09	20 35 R	15 57	19 43	17 19	20 51	02 54	22 34	24 12	00 06	29 17	08 13	22 41	22 27	21 01
11 Wed	17:18:50	20 27 13	24 49	20 34	15 26	20 57	17 54	20 46	02 58	22 35	24 12	00 05	29 43	08 37	22 27	22 51	21 00
12 Thu	17:22:46	21 24 33	07♎13	20 31	14 56	22 11	18 28	20 40	03 02	22 36	24 11	00 03	00♒09	09 01	22 13	23 14	20 59
13 Fri	17:26:43	22 21 53	19 30	20 28	14 29	23 24	19 03	20 35	03 06	22 36	24 11	00 02	00 34	09 25	22 00	23 38	20 58
14 Sat	17:30:39	23 19 11	01♏34	20 25	14 05	24 38	19 38	20 29	03 10	22 37	24 10	00 00	01 00	09 50	21 46	24 01	20 57
15 Sun	17:34:36	24 16 29	13 30	20 17	13 44	25 52	20 12	20 23	03 14	22 37	24 09	29♐59	01 26	10 14	21 32	24 24	20 56
16 Mon	17:38:32	25 13 46	25 23	20 08	13 27	27 06	20 47	20 17	03 18	22 38	24 09	29 57	01 52	10 38	21 19	24 47	20 54
17 Tue	17:42:29	26 11 02	07♐15	19 57	13 14	28 19	21 22	20 10	03 23	22 38	24 08	29 56	02 18	11 02	21 05	25 10	20 53
18 Wed	17:46:26	27 08 18	19 08	19 48	13 05	29 33	21 57	20 04	03 27	22 38	24 07	29 54	02 44	11 26	20 51	25 33	20 52
19 Thu	17:50:22	28 05 33	01♑04	19 39	13 00 D	00♋47	22 32	19 57	03 32	22 38	24 07	29 53	03 09	11 50	20 38	25 55	20 50
20 Fri	17:54:19	29 02 48	13 04	19 31	12 59	02 00	23 07	19 51	03 36	22 38	24 06	29 51	03 35	12 14	20 24	26 18	20 49
21 Sat	17:58:15	00♋00 02	25 09	19 26	13 03	03 14	23 42	19 44	03 41	22 39	24 05	29 49	04 01	12 38	20 11	26 40	20 47
22 Sun	18:02:12	00 57 16	07♒22	19 24 D	13 12	04 28	24 17	19 37	03 45	22 39	24 04	29 48	04 27	13 02	19 58	27 03	20 45
23 Mon	18:06:08	01 54 29	19 46	19 23	13 25	05 42	24 52	19 30	03 50	22 39	24 04	29 46	04 53	13 26	19 44	27 25	20 44
24 Tue	18:10:05	02 51 43	02♓30	19 24	13 44	06 55	25 27	19 23	03 55	22 39	24 03	29 45	05 19	13 50	19 31	27 47	20 42
25 Wed	18:14:01	03 48 56	15 34	19 25	14 07	08 09	26 03	19 16	04 00	22 39	24 02	29 43	05 45	14 14	19 18	28 09	20 40
26 Thu	18:17:58	04 46 09	28 58	19 26 R	14 34	09 23	26 38	19 09	04 05	22 39 R	24 01	29 42	06 11	14 38	19 06	28 30	20 38
27 Fri	18:21:55	05 43 22	11♈59	19 24	15 06	10 36	27 14	19 02	04 10	22 39	24 00	29 40	06 37	15 02	18 53	28 52	20 36
28 Sat	18:25:51	06 40 36	25 37	19 21	15 43	11 50	27 49	18 54	04 15	22 39	23 59	29 39	07 03	15 26	18 40	29 13	20 34
29 Sun	18:29:48	07 37 49	09♉18	19 21	16 25	13 04	28 24	18 47	04 20	22 39	23 58	29 37	07 29	15 50	18 28	29 35	20 32
30 Mon	18:33:44	08 35 03	23 00	19 16	17 10	14 18	29 00	18 39	04 25	22 39	23 57	29 36	07 55	16 14	18 16	29 56	20 30

EPHEMERIS CALCULATED FOR 12 MIDNIGHT GREENWICH MEAN TIME. ALL OTHER DATA AND FACING ASPECTARIAN PAGE IN EASTERN TIME (BOLD) AND PACIFIC TIME (REGULAR).

JULY 2008

☽ Last Aspect day	ET / hr:mn / PT		asp	☽ Ingress sign	day	ET / hr:mn / PT	
2	**3:08 am**	12:08 am	☍ ♇	♋	2	**3:53 am**	12:53 am
3	**4:13 pm**	1:13 pm	△ ♅	♌	4	**4:15 am**	1:15 am
6	**6:04 am**	3:04 am	△ ♇	♍	6	**7:04 am**	4:04 am
8	**12:21 pm**	9:21 am	□ ♇	♎	8	**1:31 pm**	10:31 am
10	**10:14 pm**	7:14 pm	✶ ♇	♏	10	**11:35 pm**	8:35 pm
12	**11:05 pm**	8:05 pm	□ ♆	♐	13	**11:50 am**	8:50 am
15	**10:44 pm**	7:44 pm	☌ ♇	♑	15		9:20 pm
15	**10:44 pm**	7:44 pm	☌ ♇	♑	16	**12:20 am**	
18	**3:59 am**	12:59 am	☍ ☉	♒	18	**11:40 am**	8:40 am
20	**7:25 pm**	4:25 pm	✶ ♇	♓	20	**9:07 pm**	6:07 pm
22		11:39 pm	□ ♇	♈	23	**4:22 am**	1:22 am
23	**2:39 am**		□ ♇	♈	23	**4:22 am**	1:22 am
25	**7:30 am**	4:30 am	△ ♇	♉	25	**9:14 am**	6:14 am
26		9:52 pm	□ ♆	♊	27	**11:55 am**	8:55 am
27	**12:52 am**		□ ♆	♊	27	**11:55 am**	8:55 pm
29	**11:25 am**	8:25 am	☍ ♇	♋	29	**1:11 pm**	10:11 am
30		10:31 pm	△ ♅	♌	31	**2:21 pm**	11:21 am
31	**1:31 am**		△ ♅	♌	31	**2:21 pm**	11:21 am

☽ Phases & Eclipses phase	day	ET / hr:mn / PT	
New Moon	2	**10:18 pm**	7:18 pm
2nd Quarter	9		9:35 pm
2nd Quarter	10	**12:35 am**	
Full Moon	18	**3:59 am**	12:59 am
4th Quarter	25	**2:41 pm**	11:41 am

Planet Ingress		day	ET / hr:mn / PT	
♂	♍	1	**12:21 pm**	9:21 am
☿	♋	10	**4:17 pm**	1:17 pm
♀	♌	12	**2:39 pm**	11:39 am
☉	♌	22	**6:55 am**	3:55 am
☿	♌	26	**7:48 am**	4:48 am

Planetary Motion	day	ET / hr:mn / PT

1 TUESDAY
☽ ⊻ ♀ **5:38 am** 2:38 am
☿ ⊼ ♃ **8:15 am** 5:15 am
☽ ⊼ ♃ **9:32 am** 6:32 am
☽ ☌ ☿ **9:37 am** 6:37 am
☽ □ ♅ **4:11 pm** 1:11 pm
☽ △ ♆ **6:12 pm** 3:12 pm

2 WEDNESDAY
☽ ☍ ♇ **3:08 am** 12:08 am
☽ ✶ ♂ **4:31 am** 1:31 am
☽ ✶ ♄ **11:18 am** 8:18 am
☽ ☌ ☉ **10:18 pm** 7:18 pm
♀ ☍ ♃ 10:18 pm

3 THURSDAY
♀ ☍ ♃ **1:18 am**
☽ ☍ ♃ **9:03 am** 6:03 am
☽ ☌ ♀ **9:49 am** 6:49 am
☽ ⊻ ☿ **12:59 pm** 9:59 am
☽ △ ♅ **4:13 pm** 1:13 pm
☽ ⊼ ♆ **6:15 pm** 3:15 pm

4 FRIDAY
☽ ⊼ ♇ **3:24 am** 12:24 am
☽ ⊻ ♂ **6:59 am** 3:59 am
☽ ⊻ ♄ **12:15 pm** 9:15 am
☽ ⊻ ☉ 11:56 pm

5 SATURDAY
☽ ⊻ ☉ **2:56 am**
☿ □ ♅ **7:07 am** 4:07 am
☽ ⊼ ♃ **10:16 am** 7:16 am
☽ ⊻ ♀ **4:18 pm** 1:18 pm
☽ ⊼ ♅ **6:16 pm** 3:16 pm
☽ ✶ ☿ **7:19 pm** 4:19 pm
☽ ☍ ♆ **8:21 pm** 5:21 pm

6 SUNDAY
☽ △ ♇ **6:04 am** 3:04 am
☿ △ ♆ **6:46 am** 3:46 am
☽ ☌ ♂ **12:18 pm** 9:18 am
♀ △ ♅ **2:32 pm** 11:32 am
☽ ☌ ♄ **3:58 pm** 12:58 pm

7 MONDAY
☽ ✶ ☉ **11:23 am** 8:23 am
♀ ⊼ ♆ **1:46 pm** 10:46 am
☽ △ ♃ **2:40 pm** 11:40 am
☽ ☍ ♅ **11:44 pm** 8:44 pm
☽ ⊼ ♆ 10:56 pm

8 TUESDAY
☽ ⊼ ♆ **1:56 am**
☽ ✶ ♀ **3:14 am** 12:14 am
☽ □ ☿ **6:57 am** 3:57 am
☽ □ ♇ **12:21 pm** 9:21 am
☽ ⊻ ♂ **9:53 pm** 6:53 pm
☽ ⊻ ♄ **11:30 pm** 8:30 pm

9 WEDNESDAY
☉ ☍ ♃ **3:39 am** 12:39 am
☽ □ ♃ **10:46 pm** 7:46 pm
☽ □ ☉ 9:35 pm

10 THURSDAY
☽ □ ☉ **12:35 am**
☿ ☍ ♇ **5:50 am** 2:50 am
☽ ⊼ ♅ **8:57 am** 5:57 am
☽ △ ♆ **11:14 am** 8:14 am
♂ ☌ ♄ **2:11 pm** 11:11 am
☽ □ ♀ **7:10 pm** 4:10 pm
☽ ✶ ♇ **10:14 pm** 7:14 pm
☽ △ ☿ 9:39 pm

11 FRIDAY
☽ △ ☿ **12:39 am**
☽ ✶ ♄ **10:34 am** 7:34 am
☽ ✶ ♂ **11:27 am** 8:27 am
♀ ⊼ ♇ 9:48 pm

12 SATURDAY
♀ ⊼ ♇ **12:48 am**
☽ ✶ ♃ **9:41 am** 6:41 am
☽ △ ☉ **5:24 pm** 2:24 pm
☽ △ ♅ **8:47 pm** 5:47 pm
☽ □ ♆ **11:05 pm** 8:05 pm

13 SUNDAY
☽ ⊻ ♇ **10:20 am** 7:20 am
☽ △ ♀ **2:16 pm** 11:16 am
☽ ⊼ ☿ **10:41 pm** 7:41 pm
☽ □ ♄ **11:31 pm** 8:31 pm

14 MONDAY
☽ □ ♂ **3:09 am** 12:09 am
☿ ✶ ♄ **4:36 am** 1:36 am
☉ △ ♅ **11:03 am** 8:03 am
☽ ⊻ ♃ **9:39 pm** 6:39 pm

15 TUESDAY
☽ □ ♅ **9:19 am** 6:19 am
☽ ⊼ ☉ **11:16 am** 8:16 am
☽ ✶ ♆ **11:34 am** 8:34 am
☉ ⊼ ♆ **2:50 pm** 11:50 am
☿ ✶ ♂ **5:11 pm** 2:11 pm
☽ ☌ ♇ **10:44 pm** 7:44 pm

16 WEDNESDAY
☽ ⊼ ♀ **9:39 am** 6:39 am
☽ △ ♄ **12:24 pm** 9:24 am
☽ △ ♂ **6:39 pm** 3:39 pm
☽ ☍ ☿ **9:48 pm** 6:48 pm

17 THURSDAY
☽ ☌ ♃ **9:01 am** 6:01 am
♀ ⊻ ♄ **2:53 pm** 11:53 am
☽ ✶ ♅ **8:57 pm** 5:57 pm
☽ ⊻ ♆ **11:07 pm** 8:07 pm

18 FRIDAY
☽ ☍ ☉ **3:59 am** 12:59 am
☽ ⊻ ♇ **10:00 am** 7:00 am
☽ ⊼ ♄ **11:55 pm** 8:55 pm

19 SATURDAY
☽ ☍ ♀ **3:14 am** 12:14 am
☽ ⊼ ♂ **8:30 am** 5:30 am
☿ ☍ ♃ **3:54 pm** 12:54 pm
☽ ⊻ ♃ **6:48 pm** 3:48 pm
☽ ⊼ ☿ **7:23 pm** 4:23 pm

20 SUNDAY
☽ ⊻ ♅ **6:51 am** 3:51 am
☽ ☌ ♆ **8:54 am** 5:54 am
☽ ⊼ ☉ **6:24 pm** 3:24 pm
☽ ✶ ♇ **7:25 pm** 4:25 pm

21 MONDAY
☉ ⊼ ♇ **7:48 am** 4:48 am
☽ ☍ ♄ **9:25 am** 6:25 am
☽ ⊼ ♀ **6:06 pm** 3:06 pm
☽ ☍ ♂ **8:00 pm** 5:00 pm
☽ ✶ ♃ 11:35 pm

22 TUESDAY
☽ ✶ ♃ **2:35 am**
☽ △ ☿ **2:06 pm** 11:06 am
☽ ☌ ♅ **2:35 pm** 11:35 am
☽ ⊻ ♆ **4:33 pm** 1:33 pm
☿ △ ♅ **5:10 pm** 2:10 pm
☽ □ ♇ 11:39 pm

23 WEDNESDAY
☽ □ ♇ **2:39 am**
☿ ⊼ ♆ **5:22 am** 2:22 am
☽ △ ☉ **6:01 am** 3:01 am
♀ ⊻ ♂ **8:09 am** 5:09 am
☽ ⊼ ♄ **4:35 pm** 1:35 pm

24 THURSDAY
☽ ⊼ ♂ **4:50 am** 1:50 am
☽ △ ♀ **5:52 am** 2:52 am
☽ □ ♃ **8:06 am** 5:06 am
☽ ⊻ ♅ **7:59 pm** 4:59 pm
☽ ✶ ♆ **9:50 pm** 6:50 pm

25 FRIDAY
♀ ⊼ ♃ **4:39 am** 1:39 am
☽ □ ☿ **5:11 am** 2:11 am
☽ △ ♇ **7:30 am** 4:30 am
☽ □ ☉ **2:41 pm** 11:41 am
☿ ⊼ ♇ **8:19 pm** 5:19 pm
☽ △ ♄ **9:20 pm** 6:20 pm

26 SATURDAY
☽ △ ♂ **10:59 am** 7:59 am
☽ △ ♃ **11:21 am** 8:21 am
☽ □ ♀ **2:32 pm** 11:32 am
♂ △ ♃ **6:04 pm** 3:04 pm
☽ ✶ ♅ **11:05 pm** 8:05 pm
☽ □ ♆ 9:52 pm

27 SUNDAY
☽ □ ♆ **12:52 am**
☽ ⊼ ♇ **10:11 am** 7:11 am
☽ ✶ ☿ **4:44 pm** 1:44 pm
☽ ✶ ☉ **8:44 pm** 5:44 pm
☽ □ ♄ **11:59 pm** 8:59 pm

28 MONDAY
☽ ⊼ ♃ **12:48 pm** 9:48 am
☽ □ ♂ **3:01 pm** 12:01 pm
☽ ✶ ♀ **8:50 pm** 5:50 pm
☽ □ ♅ 9:32 pm
☽ △ ♆ 11:16 pm

29 TUESDAY
☽ □ ♅ **12:32 am**
☽ △ ♆ **2:16 am**
☽ ☍ ♇ **11:25 am** 8:25 am
☉ ☌ ☿ **4:04 pm** 1:04 pm
☿ ⊻ ♄ **9:21 pm** 6:21 pm
☽ ⊻ ☉ 10:18 pm
☽ ✶ ♄ 10:29 pm
☽ ⊻ ☿ 11:08 pm

30 WEDNESDAY
☽ ⊻ ☉ **1:18 am**
☽ ✶ ♄ **1:29 am**
☽ ⊻ ☿ **2:08 am**
☉ ⊻ ♄ **4:29 am** 1:29 am
☽ ☍ ♃ **1:28 pm** 10:28 am
♀ ⊼ ♅ **4:22 pm** 1:22 pm
☽ ✶ ♂ **6:13 pm** 3:13 pm
☽ △ ♅ 10:31 pm
☽ ⊻ ♀ 11:22 pm

31 THURSDAY
☽ △ ♅ **1:31 am**
☽ ⊻ ♀ **2:22 am**
☽ ⊼ ♆ **3:14 am** 12:14 am
♀ ☍ ♆ **12:29 pm** 9:29 am
☽ ⊼ ♇ **12:30 pm** 9:30 am

Eastern time in bold type
Pacific time in medium type

JULY 2008

DATE	S.TIME	SUN	MOON	N.NODE	MERCURY	VENUS	MARS	JUPITER	SATURN	URANUS	NEPTUNE	PLUTO	CERES	PALLAS	JUNO	VESTA	CHIRON
1 Tue	18:37:41	09♋32 16	09♊58	19♒11	18♊21	15♋31	29♌36	18♑32 R	04♍31	22♓39	23♒56	29♐34 R	08♑21	16♉38	18♐04 R	00♊17	20♒28 R
2 Wed	18:41:37	10 29 30	25 03	19 05	18 55	16 45	00♍11	18 24	04 36	22 39	23 55	29 33	08 47	17 02	17 52	00 37	20 26
3 Thu	18:45:34	11 26 44	10♋06	19 00	19 54	17 59	00 47	18 17	04 42	22 38	23 54	29 31	09 13	17 26	17 40	00 58	20 24
4 Fri	18:49:31	12 23 58	24 57	18 57	20 58	19 13	01 23	18 09	04 47	22 38	23 53	29 30	09 39	17 50	17 29	01 19	20 22
5 Sat	18:53:27	13 21 11	09♌30	18 55 D	22 05	20 26	01 59	18 02	04 53	22 37	23 52	29 28	10 05	18 14	17 18	01 39	20 19
6 Sun	18:57:24	14 18 25	23 38	18 55	23 17	21 40	02 35	17 54	04 58	22 37	23 51	29 27	10 32	18 38	17 07	01 59	20 17
7 Mon	19:01:20	15 15 38	07♍20	18 56	24 32	22 54	03 11	17 46	05 04	22 36	23 49	29 25	10 58	19 02	16 57	02 19	20 15
8 Tue	19:05:17	16 12 51	20 35	18 57	25 52	24 08	03 47	17 38	05 10	22 36	23 48	29 24	11 24	19 25	16 46	02 39	20 12
9 Wed	19:09:13	17 10 03	03♎26	18 59 R	27 16	25 21	04 23	17 31	05 16	22 35	23 47	29 22	11 50	19 49	16 36	02 58	20 10
10 Thu	19:13:10	18 07 16	15 57	18 59	28 43	26 35	04 59	17 23	05 22	22 35	23 46	29 21	12 16	20 13	16 26	03 18	20 07
11 Fri	19:17:06	19 04 29	28 12	18 59	00♋14	27 49	05 35	17 15	05 28	22 34	23 44	29 19	12 42	20 37	16 17	03 37	20 05
12 Sat	19:21:03	20 01 41	10♏15	18 55	01 50	29 03	06 11	17 08	05 34	22 34	23 43	29 18	13 08	21 00	16 07	03 56	20 02
13 Sun	19:25:00	20 58 54	22 10	18 54	03 28	00♌16	06 47	17 00	05 40	22 33	23 42	29 16	13 34	21 24	15 58	04 15	19 59
14 Mon	19:28:56	21 56 07	04♐02	18 51	05 11	01 30	07 24	16 52	05 46	22 33	23 41	29 15	14 00	21 47	15 50	04 34	19 57
15 Tue	19:32:53	22 53 19	15 55	18 46	06 56	02 44	08 00	16 45	05 52	22 32	23 39	29 14	14 26	22 11	15 41	04 52	19 54
16 Wed	19:36:49	23 50 32	27 50	18 42	08 45	03 58	08 36	16 37	05 59	22 31	23 38	29 12	14 52	22 34	15 33	05 10	19 51
17 Thu	19:40:46	24 47 46	09♑51	18 38	10 37	05 11	09 13	16 29	06 05	22 30	23 37	29 11	15 19	22 58	15 26	05 28	19 49
18 Fri	19:44:42	25 44 59	22 00	18 35	12 32	06 25	09 49	16 22	06 11	22 30	23 35	29 09	15 45	23 21	15 18	05 46	19 46
19 Sat	19:48:39	26 42 13	04♒17	18 34	14 29	07 39	10 26	16 14	06 17	22 29	23 34	29 08	16 11	23 45	15 11	06 04	19 43
20 Sun	19:52:35	27 39 28	16 45	18 33 D	16 29	08 53	11 03	16 07	06 24	22 28	23 32	29 07	16 37	24 08	15 04	06 22	19 40
21 Mon	19:56:32	28 36 42	29 24	18 33	18 30	10 06	11 39	16 00	06 30	22 26	23 31	29 05	17 03	24 32	14 58	06 39	19 37
22 Tue	20:00:29	29 33 58	12♓16	18 34	20 34	11 20	12 16	15 52	06 37	22 25	23 29	29 03	17 29	24 55	14 52	06 56	19 34
23 Wed	20:04:25	00♌31 14	25 22	18 37	22 38	12 34	12 53	15 45	06 43	22 24	23 28	29 02	17 55	25 18	14 46	07 13	19 32
24 Thu	20:08:22	01 28 31	08♈44	18 38 R	24 44	13 48	13 29	15 38	06 50	22 23	23 27	29 00	18 22	25 41	14 41	07 29	19 29
25 Fri	20:12:18	02 25 49	22 22	18 37	26 51	15 02	14 06	15 31	06 57	22 21	23 25	28 59	18 48	26 04	14 35	07 46	19 26
26 Sat	20:16:15	03 23 08	06♉17	18 36	28 58	16 15	14 43	15 24	07 03	22 20	23 24	28 58	19 14	26 28	14 31	08 02	19 23
27 Sun	20:20:11	04 20 28	20 28	18 37	01♌05	17 29	15 20	15 17	07 10	22 18	23 22	28 58	19 40	26 51	14 26	08 18	19 20
28 Mon	20:24:08	05 17 49	04♊53	18 36	03 11	18 43	15 57	15 10	07 17	22 16	23 21	28 57	20 06	27 14	14 22	08 33	19 17
29 Tue	20:28:04	06 15 12	19 29	18 35	05 18	19 57	16 34	15 03	07 24	22 15	23 19	28 56	20 32	27 37	14 18	08 49	19 14
30 Wed	20:32:01	07 12 35	04♋10	18 34	07 24	21 10	17 11	14 56	07 30	22 14	23 17	28 55	20 58	27 59	14 15	09 04	19 10
31 Thu	20:35:58	08 09 59	18 51	18 32	09 29	22 24	17 49	14 50	07 37	22 13	23 16	28 53	21 24	28 22	14 12	09 19	19 07

EPHEMERIS CALCULATED FOR 12 MIDNIGHT GREENWICH MEAN TIME. ALL OTHER DATA AND FACING ASPECTARIAN PAGE IN **EASTERN TIME (BOLD)** AND PACIFIC TIME (REGULAR).

AUGUST 2008

☽ Last Aspect day	ET / hr:mn	PT	asp	☽ Ingress sign	day	ET / hr:mn	PT
2	2:59 pm	11:59 am	△♇	♍	2	4:59 pm	1:59 pm
4	8:16 pm	5:16 pm	□♇	♎	4	10:28 pm	7:28 pm
7	5:01 am	2:01 am	✶♇	♏	7	7:26 am	4:26 am
9	5:02 pm	2:02 pm	□☿	♐	9	7:10 pm	4:10 pm
12	5:04 am	2:04 am	☌♇	♑	12	7:42 am	4:42 am
14	1:09 pm	10:09 am	△♂	♒	14	6:56 pm	3:56 pm
16		10:14 pm	✶♇	♓	17	3:46 am	12:46 am
17	1:14 am		✶♇	♓	17	3:46 am	12:46 am
19	7:41 am	4:41 am	□♇	♈	19	10:10 am	7:10 am
21	12:53 pm	9:53 am	△☉	♉	21	2:38 pm	11:38 am
23	5:19 am	2:19 am	□♆	♊	23	5:48 pm	2:48 pm
25	5:52 pm	2:52 pm	☍♇	♋	25	8:18 pm	5:18 pm
27	8:13 pm	5:13 pm	✶☿	♌	27	10:51 pm	7:51 pm
29	11:44 pm	8:44 pm	△♇	♍	29		11:18 pm
29	11:44 pm	8:44 pm	△♇	♍	30	2:18 am	

☽ Phases & Eclipses phase	day	ET / hr:mn	PT
New Moon	1	6:12 am	3:12 am
	1	9° ♌ 32'	
2nd Quarter	8	4:20 pm	1:20 pm
Full Moon	16	5:16 pm	2:16 pm
	16	24° ♒ 21'	
4th Quarter	23	7:49 pm	4:49 am
New Moon	30	3:58 pm	12:58 pm

Planet Ingress		day	ET / hr:mn	PT
♀	♊	4	3:30 am	12:30 am
♀	♍	5		9:20 pm
♀	♍	6	12:20 am	
☿	♍	10	6:51 am	3:51 am
♂	♎	19	6:03 am	3:03 am
⚷	♌	19	5:25 pm	2:25 pm
☉	♍	22	2:02 pm	11:02 am
☿	♎	28	10:50 pm	7:50 pm
♀	♎	30	10:41 am	7:41 am

Planetary Motion		day	ET / hr:mn	PT
⚵	D	8	5:40 am	2:40 am

1 FRIDAY
☽ ⚺ ♄ 3:16 am 12:16 am
☽ ☌ ☉ 6:12 am 3:12 am
☽ ☌ ☿ 11:52 am 8:52 am
☽ ⚻ ♃ 2:47 pm 11:47 am
☽ ⚺ ♂ 10:20 pm 7:20 pm

2 SATURDAY
☽ ⚻ ♅ 3:31 am 12:31 am
☽ ☍ ♆ 5:18 am 2:18 am
☿ ⚻ ♃ 7:27 am 4:27 am
☽ ☌ ♀ 9:18 am 6:18 am
☽ △ ♇ 2:59 pm 11:59 am

3 SUNDAY
☽ ☌ ♄ 6:58 am 3:58 am
☽ ⚺ ☉ 1:30 pm 10:30 am
☽ △ ♃ 6:16 pm 3:16 pm
☽ ⚺ ☿ 9:42 pm

4 MONDAY
☽ ⚺ ☿ 12:42 am
☽ ☌ ♂ 5:13 am 2:13 am
☽ ☍ ♅ 8:02 am 5:02 am
☽ ⚻ ♆ 9:56 am 6:56 am
☽ ⚺ ♀ 7:46 pm 4:46 pm
☽ □ ♇ 8:16 pm 5:16 pm
♀ △ ♇ 9:53 pm

5 TUESDAY
♀ △ ♇ 12:53 am
☽ ⚺ ♄ 1:52 pm 10:52 am

☿ ⚺ ♂ 7:23 pm 4:23 pm
☽ ✶ ☉ 9:49 pm
☽ □ ♃ 10:00 pm
☿ ⚻ ♅ 10:46 pm
☉ ⚻ ♃ 11:56 pm

6 WEDNESDAY
☽ ✶ ☉ 12:49 am
☽ □ ♃ 1:00 am
☿ ⚻ ♅ 1:46 am
☉ ⚻ ♃ 2:56 am
♂ ☍ ♅ 2:37 pm 11:37 am
☿ ☍ ♆ 2:40 pm 11:40 am
☽ ⚻ ♅ 3:58 pm 12:58 pm
☽ ⚺ ♂ 4:02 pm 1:02 pm
☽ △ ♆ 6:00 pm 3:00 pm
☽ ✶ ☿ 6:37 pm 3:37 pm

7 THURSDAY
☽ ✶ ♇ 5:01 am 2:01 am
☽ ✶ ♀ 10:54 am 7:54 am
☽ ✶ ♄ 9:19 pm

8 FRIDAY
☽ ✶ ♄ 12:19 am
♂ ⚻ ♆ 5:27 am 2:27 am
☽ ✶ ♃ 11:01 am 8:01 am
☽ □ ☉ 4:20 pm 1:20 pm
☽ △ ♅ 11:58 pm

9 SATURDAY
☽ △ ♅ 2:58 am
☽ □ ♆ 5:06 am 2:06 am

☽ ✶ ♂ 6:28 am 3:28 am
☿ △ ♇ 2:17 pm 11:17 am
☽ ⚺ ♇ 4:36 pm 1:36 pm
☽ □ ☿ 5:02 pm 2:02 pm

10 SUNDAY
☽ □ ♀ 5:39 am 2:39 am
☽ □ ♄ 1:08 pm 10:08 am
☽ ⚺ ♃ 10:58 pm 7:58 pm

11 MONDAY
☽ △ ☉ 10:06 am 7:06 am
☽ □ ♅ 3:21 pm 12:21 pm
☽ ✶ ♆ 5:31 pm 2:31 pm
☽ □ ♂ 10:24 pm 7:24 pm

12 TUESDAY
☽ ☌ ♇ 5:04 am 2:04 am
☽ △ ☿ 4:21 pm 1:21 pm
☽ △ ♀ 9:57 pm
☽ △ ♄ 11:04 pm

13 WEDNESDAY
☽ △ ♀ 12:57 am
☽ △ ♄ 2:04 am
☽ ☌ ♃ 10:43 am 7:43 am
♀ ☌ ♄ 1:03 pm 10:03 am
☉ ⚻ ♅ 10:20 pm
☽ ✶ ♅ 11:57 pm

14 THURSDAY
☉ ⚻ ♅ 1:20 am
☽ ✶ ♅ 2:57 am
☽ ⚻ ☉ 3:05 am 12:05 am
☽ ⚺ ♆ 5:04 am 2:04 am

☽ △ ♂ 1:09 pm 10:09 am
☽ ⚺ ♇ 4:20 pm 1:20 pm

15 FRIDAY
☉ ☍ ♆ 3:43 am 12:43 am
☽ ⚻ ☿ 12:48 pm 9:48 am
☽ ⚻ ♄ 1:12 pm 10:12 am
☿ ☌ ♄ 3:59 pm 12:59 pm
☽ ⚻ ♀ 5:54 pm 2:54 pm
☽ ⚺ ♃ 8:35 pm 5:35 pm

16 SATURDAY
☽ ⚺ ♅ 12:20 pm 9:20 am
☽ ☌ ♆ 2:23 pm 11:23 am
☽ ☍ ☉ 5:16 pm 2:16 pm
♀ △ ♃ 8:16 pm 5:16 pm
☽ ⚻ ♂ 10:10 pm
☽ ✶ ♇ 10:14 pm
♂ □ ♇ 11:15 pm

17 SUNDAY
☽ ⚻ ♂ 1:10 am
☽ ✶ ♇ 1:14 am
♂ □ ♇ 2:15 am
☿ △ ♃ 9:23 pm 6:23 pm
☽ ☍ ♄ 9:46 pm 6:46 pm

18 MONDAY
☽ ✶ ♃ 4:01 am 1:01 am
☽ ☍ ☿ 5:00 am 2:00 am
☽ ☍ ♀ 7:26 am 4:26 am
☽ ☌ ♅ 7:13 pm 4:13 pm
☽ ⚺ ♆ 9:13 pm 6:13 pm

19 TUESDAY
☽ ⚻ ☉ 4:19 am 1:19 am
☽ □ ♇ 7:41 am 4:41 am
☽ ☍ ♂ 10:22 am 7:22 am

20 WEDNESDAY
☽ ⚻ ♄ 3:57 am 12:57 am
☽ □ ♃ 9:15 am 6:15 am
☽ ⚻ ☿ 5:31 pm 2:31 pm
☽ ⚻ ♀ 6:01 pm 3:01 pm
☽ ⚺ ♅ 9:01 pm
☽ ✶ ♆ 10:59 pm
☉ △ ♇ 11:51 pm

21 THURSDAY
☽ ⚺ ♅ 12:01 am
☽ ✶ ♆ 1:59 am
☉ △ ♇ 2:51 am
☿ ☌ ♀ 11:44 am 8:44 am
☽ △ ♇ 12:11 pm 9:11 am
☽ △ ☉ 12:53 pm 9:53 am
☽ ⚻ ♂ 5:20 pm 2:20 pm

22 FRIDAY
☽ △ ♄ 8:23 am 5:23 am
☽ △ ♃ 12:52 pm 9:52 am
☿ ☍ ♅ 11:13 pm
☽ △ ♀ 11:32 pm

23 SATURDAY
☿ ☍ ♅ 2:13 am
☽ △ ♀ 2:32 am
☽ ✶ ♅ 3:22 am 12:22 am
☽ △ ☿ 3:30 am 12:30 am

☽ □ ♆ 5:19 am 2:19 am
♀ ☍ ♅ 11:49 am 8:49 am
☽ ⚻ ♇ 3:22 pm 12:22 pm
☽ □ ☉ 7:49 pm 4:49 pm
☿ ⚻ ♆ 8:11 pm 5:11 pm
☽ △ ♂ 10:52 pm 7:52 pm

24 SUNDAY
♀ ⚻ ♆ 9:58 am 6:58 am
☽ □ ♄ 11:42 am 8:42 am
☽ ⚻ ♃ 3:30 pm 12:30 pm

25 MONDAY
☽ □ ♅ 5:52 am 2:52 am
☽ △ ♆ 7:50 am 4:50 am
☽ □ ♀ 9:56 am 6:56 am
☽ □ ☿ 12:03 pm 9:03 am
☽ ☍ ♇ 5:52 pm 2:52 pm
☽ ✶ ☉ 10:58 pm

26 TUESDAY
☽ ✶ ☉ 1:58 am
☽ □ ♂ 3:43 am 12:43 am
☽ ✶ ♄ 2:35 pm 11:35 am
☽ ☍ ♃ 5:47 pm 2:47 pm

27 WEDNESDAY
☽ △ ♅ 8:11 am 5:11 am
☽ ⚻ ♆ 10:12 am 7:12 am
☽ ✶ ♀ 5:10 pm 2:10 pm
☽ ✶ ☿ 8:13 pm 5:13 pm
☽ ⚻ ♇ 8:22 pm 5:22 pm
☿ □ ♇ 9:37 pm 6:37 pm

28 THURSDAY
☽ ⚺ ☉ 8:17 am 5:17 am
☽ ✶ ♂ 8:44 am 5:44 am
☽ ⚺ ♄ 5:47 pm 2:47 pm
☽ ⚻ ♃ 8:27 pm 5:27 pm

29 FRIDAY
☉ ⚺ ♂ 3:24 am 12:24 am
♀ □ ♇ 5:51 am 2:51 am
☽ ⚻ ♅ 11:08 am 8:08 am
☽ ☍ ♆ 1:14 pm 10:14 am
☽ △ ♇ 11:44 pm 8:44 pm
☽ ⚺ ♀ 10:29 pm

30 SATURDAY
☽ ⚺ ♀ 1:29 am
☽ ⚺ ☿ 5:20 am 2:20 am
☽ ⚺ ♂ 3:03 pm 12:03 pm
☽ ☌ ☉ 3:58 pm 12:58 pm
☽ ☌ ♄ 10:21 pm 7:21 pm
☽ △ ♃ 9:30 pm

31 SUNDAY
☽ △ ♃ 12:30 am
☽ ☍ ♅ 3:44 pm 12:44 pm
☽ ⚻ ♆ 5:58 pm 2:58 pm

Eastern time in bold type
Pacific time in medium type

AUGUST 2008

DATE	S.TIME	SUN	MOON	N.NODE	MERCURY	VENUS	MARS	JUPITER	SATURN	URANUS	NEPTUNE	PLUTO	CERES	PALLAS	JUNO	VESTA	CHIRON
1 Fri	20:39:54	09 ♋ 07 24	03 ♌ 24	18 ♒ 32 ℞	11 ♌ 33	26 ♋ 38	18 ♍ 26	14 ♑ 43	07 ♍ 44	22 ♓ 11	23 ♒ 14	28 ♐ 52	21 ♋ 50	28 ♋ 45	14 ♐ 09	09 ♒ 34	19 ≈ 04
2 Sat	20:43:51	10 04 50	17 44	18 31 ℞	13 36	24 52	19 03	14 37 ℞	07 51	22 10 ℞	23 13 ℞	28 51 ℞	22 16	29 08	14 07 ℞	09 48	19 01 ℞
3 Sun	20:47:47	11 02 16	01 ♍ 45	18 32	15 38	26 05	19 40	14 31	07 58	22 08	23 11	28 50	22 42	29 30	14 05	10 02	18 58
4 Mon	20:51:44	11 59 44	15 24	18 33	17 38	27 19	20 18	14 25	08 05	22 06	23 08	28 49	23 08	29 53	14 03	10 16	18 55
5 Tue	20:55:40	12 57 12	28 40	18 33	19 37	28 33	20 55	14 19	08 12	22 05	23 06	28 48	23 34	00 ♌ 15	14 02	10 30	18 52
6 Wed	20:59:37	13 54 41	11 ♎ 33	18 33	21 35	29 47	21 33	14 13	08 19	22 03	23 06	28 47	24 00	00 38	14 01	10 43	18 49
7 Thu	21:03:33	14 52 10	24 07	18 34	23 31	01 ♍ 00	22 10	14 07	08 27	22 01	23 05	28 46	24 26	01 00	14 00 D	10 56	18 45
8 Fri	21:07:30	15 49 41	06 ♏ 24	18 34 ℞	25 25	02 14	22 48	14 02	08 34	22 00	23 03	28 45	24 52	01 22	14 00	11 09	18 42
9 Sat	21:11:27	16 47 12	18 28	18 34	27 18	03 28	23 25	13 56	08 41	21 58	23 01	28 44	25 18	01 45	14 00	11 21	18 39
10 Sun	21:15:23	17 44 44	00 ♐ 25	18 34 D	29 10	04 42	24 03	13 51	08 48	21 56	23 00	28 43	25 44	02 07	14 00	11 33	18 36
11 Mon	21:19:20	18 42 17	12 17	18 34	00 ♍ 59	05 55	24 41	13 46	08 55	21 54	22 58	28 43	26 10	02 29	14 01	11 45	18 33
12 Tue	21:23:16	19 39 51	24 06	18 33	02 49	07 09	25 18	13 41	09 03	21 52	22 56	28 42	26 36	02 51	14 02	11 57	18 30
13 Wed	21:27:13	20 37 26	06 ♑ 09	18 33	04 36	08 23	25 56	13 36	09 10	21 50	22 55	28 41	27 02	03 13	14 03	12 08	18 27
14 Thu	21:31:09	21 35 02	18 16	18 33	06 21	09 37	26 34	13 31	09 17	21 48	22 53	28 40	27 28	03 34	14 05	12 19	18 23
15 Fri	21:35:06	22 32 39	00 ≈ 33	18 33	08 05	10 50	27 12	13 27	09 25	21 46	22 51	28 39	27 54	03 56	14 07	12 30	18 20
16 Sat	21:39:02	23 30 17	13 04	18 33	09 48	12 04	27 50	13 23	09 32	21 44	22 50	28 39	28 20	04 18	14 09	12 40	18 17
17 Sun	21:42:59	24 27 57	25 49	18 35	11 29	13 18	28 28	13 18	09 39	21 42	22 48	28 38	28 45	04 39	14 12	12 50	18 14
18 Mon	21:46:56	25 25 37	08 ♓ 49	18 34	13 09	14 31	29 06	13 14	09 47	21 40	22 47	28 37	29 11	05 00	14 15	12 59	18 11
19 Tue	21:50:52	26 23 19	22 05	18 33	14 47	15 45	29 44	13 11	09 54	21 38	22 45	28 36	29 37	05 22	14 18	13 09	18 08
20 Wed	21:54:49	27 21 02	05 ♈ 33	18 32	16 24	16 59	00 ♎ 22	13 07	10 02	21 36	22 44	28 36	00 ♌ 03	05 43	14 22	13 18	18 05
21 Thu	21:58:45	28 18 47	19 15	18 32	17 59	18 12	01 00	13 03	10 09	21 34	22 42	28 35	00 29	06 04	14 26	13 26	18 02
22 Fri	22:02:42	29 16 34	03 ♉ 07	18 31	19 33	19 26	01 39	13 00	10 17	21 32	22 40	28 34	00 54	06 25	14 30	13 35	17 58
23 Sat	22:06:38	00 ♍ 14 22	17 09	18 30	21 05	20 40	02 17	12 57	10 24	21 30	22 39	28 34	01 20	06 45	14 35	13 43	17 55
24 Sun	22:10:35	01 12 12	01 ♊ 18	18 29 D	22 36	21 53	02 55	12 54	10 32	21 29	22 37	28 34	01 46	07 06	14 39	13 50	17 52
25 Mon	22:14:31	02 10 04	15 32	18 30	24 06	23 07	03 34	12 51	10 39	21 27	22 35	28 33	02 11	07 27	14 45	13 57	17 49
26 Tue	22:18:28	03 07 58	29 49	18 31	25 34	24 21	04 12	12 49	10 47	21 25	22 34	28 33	02 37	07 47	14 50	14 04	17 46
27 Wed	22:22:25	04 05 54	14 ♋ 06	18 32	27 01	25 34	04 51	12 46	10 54	21 23	22 32	28 32	03 02	08 07	14 56	14 11	17 43
28 Thu	22:26:21	05 03 51	28 26	18 33	28 26	26 48	05 29	12 44	11 02	21 21	22 31	28 32	03 28	08 26	15 02	14 17	17 40
29 Fri	22:30:18	06 01 50	12 ♌ 36	18 33 ℞	29 50	28 01	06 08	12 42	11 09	21 19	22 29	28 32	03 53	08 48	15 08	14 22	17 37
30 Sat	22:34:14	06 59 51	26 23	18 33	01 ♎ 13	29 15	06 46	12 40	11 17	21 17	22 27	28 31	04 19	09 07	15 15	14 27	17 35
31 Sun	22:38:11	07 57 53	10 ♍ 05	18 32	02 33	00 ♎ 29	07 25	12 38	11 24	21 15	22 26	28 31	04 44	09 27	15 22	14 32	17 32

EPHEMERIS CALCULATED FOR 12 MIDNIGHT GREENWICH MEAN TIME. ALL OTHER DATA AND FACING ASPECTARIAN PAGE IN **EASTERN TIME (BOLD)** AND PACIFIC TIME (REGULAR).

SEPTEMBER 2008

☽ Last Aspect day	ET / hr:mn / PT	asp	☽ Ingress sign	day	ET / hr:mn / PT
1	**5:01 am** 2:01 am	□ ♇	♎	1	**7:44 am** 4:44 am
3	**1:09 pm** 10:09 am	⚹ ♇	♏	3	**4:02 pm** 1:02 pm
5	**11:45 am** 8:45 am	□ ♆	♐	6	**3:11 am** 12:11 am
8	**12:43 pm** 9:43 am	☌ ♇	♑	8	**3:45 pm** 12:45 pm
10	**9:15 am** 6:15 am	⚹ ♅	♒	11	**3:19 am** 12:19 am
13	**9:19 am** 6:19 am	⚹ ♇	♓	13	**12:04 pm** 9:04 am
15	**3:03 pm** 12:03 pm	□ ♇	♈	15	**5:39 pm** 2:39 pm
17	**6:26 pm** 3:26 pm	△ ♇	♉	17	**8:56 pm** 5:56 pm
19	**6:51 pm** 3:51 pm	△ ☉	♊	19	**11:17 pm** 8:17 pm
21	10:04 pm	□ ☉	♋	21	10:48 pm
22	**1:04 am**	□ ☉	♋	22	**1:48 am**
23	**5:16 pm** 2:16 pm	□ ♂	♌	24	**5:13 am** 2:13 am
26	**7:20 am** 4:20 am	△ ♇	♍	26	**9:52 am** 6:52 am
28	**1:31 pm** 10:31 am	□ ♇	♎	28	**4:05 pm** 1:05 pm
30	**9:47 pm** 6:47 pm	⚹ ♇	♏	30	9:26 pm
30	**9:47 pm** 6:47 pm	⚹ ♇	♏	10/1	**12:26 am**

☽ Phases & Eclipses phase	day	ET / hr:mn / PT
2nd Quarter	7	**10:04 am** 7:04 am
Full Moon	15	**5:13 am** 2:13 am
4th Quarter	21	10:04 pm
4th Quarter	22	**1:04 am**
New Moon	29	**4:12 am** 1:12 am

Planet Ingress	day	ET / hr:mn / PT
☉ ♎	22	**11:44 am** 8:44 am
♀ ♏	23	**10:59 pm** 7:59 pm

Planetary Motion	day	ET / hr:mn / PT
♃ D	7	9:16 pm
♃ D	8	**12:16 am**
♇ D	8	**11:14 pm** 8:14 pm
⚵ ℞	10	**7:47 pm** 4:47 pm
☿ ℞	24	**3:17 am** 12:17 am

1 MONDAY
☽ □ ♇ **5:01 am** 2:01 am
☽ ☌ ♀ **12:23 pm** 9:23 am
☽ ☌ ☿ **4:55 pm** 1:55 pm
☽ ☌ ♂ **11:58 pm** 8:58 pm
☽ ⚺ ☉ 11:27 pm

2 TUESDAY
☽ ⚺ ☉ **2:27 am**
☽ ⚺ ♄ **5:20 am** 2:20 am
☽ □ ♃ **6:59 am** 3:59 am
☽ ⚻ ♅ **10:57 pm** 7:57 pm
☽ △ ♆ 10:23 pm

3 WEDNESDAY
☽ △ ♆ **1:23 am**
☽ ⚹ ♇ **1:09 pm** 10:09 am
☉ ☌ ♄ **9:59 pm** 6:59 pm

4 THURSDAY
☽ ⚺ ♀ **3:10 am** 12:10 am
☽ ⚺ ☿ **8:06 am** 5:06 am
☽ ⚺ ♂ **12:21 pm** 9:21 am
☉ △ ♃ **1:41 pm** 10:41 am
☽ ⚹ ♄ **3:25 pm** 12:25 pm
☽ ⚹ ♃ **4:28 pm** 1:28 pm
☽ ⚹ ☉ **4:43 pm** 1:43 pm

5 FRIDAY
☽ △ ♅ **9:08 am** 6:08 am
☽ □ ♆ **11:45 am** 8:45 am
☽ ⚺ ♇ 9:10 pm

Eastern time in bold type
Pacific time in medium type

6 SATURDAY
☽ ⚺ ♇ **12:10 am**
☽ ⚹ ♀ **9:35 pm** 6:35 pm
☽ ⚹ ☿ 11:20 pm

7 SUNDAY
☽ ⚹ ☿ **2:20 am**
☽ ⚹ ♂ **3:42 am** 12:42 am
☽ □ ♄ **4:01 am** 1:01 am
☽ ⚺ ♃ **4:26 am** 1:26 am
☽ □ ☉ **10:04 am** 7:04 am
♂ ⚺ ♄ **10:51 am** 7:51 am
♂ □ ♃ **5:05 pm** 2:05 pm
☽ □ ♅ **9:19 pm** 6:19 pm
☿ ⚺ ♄ **10:47 pm** 7:47 pm
☽ ⚹ ♆ 9:02 pm
☿ □ ♃ 10:09 pm

8 MONDAY
☽ ⚹ ♆ **12:02 am**
☿ □ ♃ **1:09 am**
☽ ☌ ♇ **12:43 pm** 9:43 am
☿ ☌ ♂ **1:44 pm** 10:44 am
♃ △ ♄ **7:18 pm** 4:18 pm

9 TUESDAY
♀ □ ♃ **4:12 pm** 1:12 pm
☽ ☌ ♃ **4:54 pm** 1:54 pm
☽ □ ♀ **4:59 pm** 1:59 pm
☽ △ ♄ **5:07 pm** 2:07 pm
♀ ⚺ ♄ **6:31 pm** 3:31 pm
☽ □ ♂ **7:38 pm** 4:38 pm
☽ □ ☿ **8:40 pm** 5:40 pm

10 WEDNESDAY
☽ △ ☉ **3:42 am** 12:42 am
☽ ⚹ ♅ **9:15 am** 6:15 am
☽ ⚺ ♆ **11:59 am** 8:59 am
☽ ⚺ ♇ 9:24 pm

11 THURSDAY
☽ ⚺ ♇ **12:24 am**
♀ ☌ ♂ **10:06 pm** 7:06 pm

12 FRIDAY
☽ ⚺ ♃ **3:29 am** 12:29 am
☽ ⚻ ♄ **4:14 am** 1:14 am
☽ △ ♂ **9:14 am** 6:14 am
☽ △ ♀ **9:47 am** 6:47 am
☽ △ ☿ **11:46 am** 8:46 am
☽ ⚻ ☉ **6:30 pm** 3:30 pm
☽ ⚺ ♅ **6:48 pm** 3:48 pm
☽ ☌ ♆ **9:28 pm** 6:28 pm
☉ ☍ ♅ **10:21 pm** 7:21 pm

13 SATURDAY
☽ ⚹ ♇ **9:19 am** 6:19 am

14 SUNDAY
☉ ⚻ ♆ **8:54 am** 5:54 am
☽ ⚹ ♃ **10:56 am** 7:56 am
☽ ☍ ♄ **12:05 pm** 9:05 am
☽ ⚻ ♂ **7:06 pm** 4:06 pm
☿ ☌ ♀ **9:37 pm** 6:37 pm
☽ ⚻ ☿ **10:15 pm** 7:15 pm
☽ ⚻ ♀ **10:16 pm** 7:16 pm
☽ ☌ ♅ 10:09 pm

15 MONDAY
☽ ☌ ♅ **1:09 am**
☽ ⚺ ♆ **3:44 am** 12:44 am
☽ ☍ ☉ **5:13 am** 2:13 am
☽ □ ♇ **3:03 pm** 12:03 pm

16 TUESDAY
♀ ⚻ ♅ **5:13 am** 2:13 am
☽ □ ♃ **3:29 pm** 12:29 pm
☽ ⚻ ♄ **4:59 pm** 1:59 pm
☽ ☍ ♂ 10:46 pm

17 WEDNESDAY
☽ ☍ ♂ **1:46 am**
☿ ⚻ ♅ **4:02 am** 1:02 am
☽ ⚺ ♅ **4:52 am** 1:52 am
☽ ☍ ☿ **4:55 am** 1:55 am
☽ ☍ ♀ **7:11 am** 4:11 am
☽ ⚹ ♆ **7:26 am** 4:26 am
♀ △ ♆ **9:58 am** 6:58 am
☽ ⚻ ☉ **12:45 pm** 9:45 am
☽ △ ♇ **6:26 pm** 3:26 pm

18 THURSDAY
☽ △ ♃ **6:19 pm** 3:19 pm
☽ △ ♄ **8:07 pm** 5:07 pm

19 FRIDAY
☽ ⚻ ♂ **6:45 am** 3:45 am
☽ ⚹ ♅ **7:14 am** 4:14 am
☽ ⚻ ☿ **9:23 am** 6:23 am
☽ □ ♆ **9:49 am** 6:49 am
☽ ⚻ ♀ **2:21 pm** 11:21 am
♂ ⚻ ♅ **4:26 pm** 1:26 pm
☽ △ ☉ **6:51 pm** 3:51 pm
☽ ⚻ ♇ **8:49 pm** 5:49 pm
☿ △ ♆ **11:21 pm** 8:21 pm

20 SATURDAY
☽ ⚻ ♃ **8:45 pm** 5:45 pm
☽ □ ♄ **10:52 pm** 7:52 pm
☉ □ ♇ **11:46 pm** 8:46 pm

21 SUNDAY
☽ □ ♅ **9:28 am** 6:28 am
☽ △ ♂ **11:35 am** 8:35 am
☽ △ ♆ **12:08 pm** 9:08 am
☽ △ ☿ **1:05 pm** 10:05 am
☽ △ ♀ **9:33 pm** 6:33 pm
♂ △ ♆ **10:57 pm** 7:57 pm
☽ ☍ ♇ **11:20 pm** 8:20 pm
☽ □ ☉ 10:04 pm

22 MONDAY
☽ □ ☉ **1:04 am**
♀ ⚹ ♇ **6:24 pm** 3:24 pm
☽ ☍ ♃ **11:46 pm** 8:46 pm
☽ ⚹ ♄ 11:12 pm

23 TUESDAY
☽ ⚹ ♄ **2:12 am**
☿ ☌ ♂ **6:51 am** 3:51 am
☽ △ ♅ **12:24 pm** 9:24 am
☽ ⚻ ♆ **3:12 pm** 12:12 pm
☽ □ ☿ **4:50 pm** 1:50 pm
☽ □ ♂ **5:16 pm** 2:16 pm
☽ ⚻ ♇ 11:43 pm

24 WEDNESDAY
☽ ⚻ ♇ **2:43 am**
☽ □ ♀ **5:50 am** 2:50 am
☽ ⚹ ☉ **8:23 am** 5:23 am

25 THURSDAY
☽ ⚻ ♃ **3:52 am** 12:52 am
☽ ⚺ ♄ **6:38 am** 3:38 am
☽ ⚻ ♅ **4:28 pm** 1:28 pm
☽ ☍ ♆ **7:24 pm** 4:24 pm
☽ ⚹ ☿ **8:52 pm** 5:52 pm
☽ ⚹ ♂ 9:19 pm

26 FRIDAY
☽ ⚹ ♂ **12:19 am**
☽ △ ♇ **7:20 am** 4:20 am
☽ ⚹ ♀ **3:44 pm** 12:44 pm
☽ ⚺ ☉ **5:15 pm** 2:15 pm

27 SATURDAY
☽ △ ♃ **9:22 am** 6:22 am
☽ ☌ ♄ **12:29 pm** 9:29 am
☽ ☍ ♅ **9:58 pm** 6:58 pm
☽ ⚻ ♆ 10:04 pm
☽ ⚺ ☿ 10:20 pm

28 SUNDAY
☽ ⚻ ♆ **1:04 am**
☽ ⚺ ☿ **1:20 am**
☿ △ ♆ **8:25 am** 5:25 am
☽ ⚺ ♂ **9:07 am** 6:07 am
☽ □ ♇ **1:31 pm** 10:31 am

29 MONDAY
☽ ⚺ ♀ **3:49 am** 12:49 am
☽ ☌ ☉ **4:12 am** 1:12 am
☽ □ ♃ **4:43 pm** 1:43 pm
☽ ⚺ ♄ **8:13 pm** 5:13 pm
☉ ⚺ ♀ **11:24 pm** 8:24 pm

30 TUESDAY
☽ ⚻ ♅ **5:23 am** 2:23 am
☽ ☌ ☿ **6:30 am** 3:30 am
☽ △ ♆ **8:42 am** 5:42 am
☽ ☌ ♂ **8:20 pm** 5:20 pm
☽ ⚹ ♇ **9:47 pm** 6:47 pm
☿ ⚻ ♅ 10:26 pm

SEPTEMBER 2008

DATE	S.TIME	SUN	MOON	N.NODE	MERCURY	VENUS	MARS	JUPITER	SATURN	URANUS	NEPTUNE	PLUTO	CERES	PALLAS	JUNO	VESTA	CHIRON
1 Mon	22:42:07	08♍55 57	23♍32	18♒30	03♎53	01♎42	08♎43	12♑37 R	11♍32	21♓09 R	22♒24 R	28♐31 R	05♌31	09♊47	15♐29	14♋37	17♒29 R
2 Tue	22:46:04	09 54 22	06♎41	18 27 R	05 10	02 56	09 22	12 36 R	11 39	21 07 R	22 23 R	28 31 R	05 56	10 06	15 36	14 41	17 26 R
3 Wed	22:50:00	10 52 49	19 31	18 24	06 26	04 09	10 01	12 35	11 47	21 05	22 21	28 30	06 01	10 25	15 44	14 44	17 23
4 Thu	22:53:57	11 51 18	02♏03	18 21	07 40	05 23	10 41	12 34	11 54	21 02	22 20	28 30	06 26	10 44	15 52	14 48	17 20
5 Fri	22:57:54	12 49 48	14 21	18 17	08 50	06 36	11 19	12 33	12 02	21 00	22 18	28 30	06 51	11 03	16 01	14 50	17 18
6 Sat	23:01:50	13 48 20	26 25	18 15	10 03	07 50	11 58	12 32	12 10	20 57	22 17	28 30	07 16	11 22	16 09	14 53	17 15
7 Sun	23:05:47	14 46 54	08♐32	18 14 D	11 12	09 03	12 37	12 32	12 17	20 55	22 15	28 30	07 42	11 40	16 18	14 55	17 12
8 Mon	23:09:43	15 45 29	20 14	18 14	12 18	10 17	13 16	12 32 D	12 25	20 53	22 14	28 30 D	08 07	11 59	16 27	14 56	17 10
9 Tue	23:13:40	16 44 07	02♑07	18 15	13 22	11 30	13 55	12 32	12 32	20 50	22 12	28 30	08 32	12 17	16 36	14 57	17 07
10 Wed	23:17:36	17 42 46	14 06	18 16	14 24	12 44	14 34	12 32	12 40	20 48	22 11	28 30	08 57	12 35	16 46	14 58 R	17 04
11 Thu	23:21:33	18 41 27	26 15	18 18	15 24	13 57	15 14	12 33	12 47	20 45	22 09	28 30	09 22	12 52	16 56	14 58	17 02
12 Fri	23:25:29	19 40 10	08♒38	18 19 R	16 20	15 11	15 53	12 33	12 55	20 43	22 08	28 30	09 47	13 10	17 06	14 58	16 59
13 Sat	23:29:26	20 38 54	21 19	18 19	17 14	16 24	16 33	12 34	13 02	20 41	22 07	28 30	10 12	13 27	17 16	14 57	16 57
14 Sun	23:33:23	21 37 41	04♓32	18 19	18 05	17 38	16 33	12 35	13 10	20 38	22 05	28 30	10 37	13 44	17 27	14 56	16 55
15 Mon	23:37:19	22 36 29	17 41	18 16	18 53	18 51	17 12	12 36	13 17	20 36	22 04	28 30	11 01	14 01	17 37	14 55	16 52
16 Tue	23:41:16	23 35 19	01♈21	18 12	19 37	20 04	17 52	12 38	13 25	20 33	22 03	28 30	11 26	14 18	17 48	14 53	16 50
17 Wed	23:45:12	24 34 11	15 18	18 08	20 18	21 18	18 31	12 39	13 32	20 31	22 01	28 31	11 51	14 34	18 00	14 50	16 48
18 Thu	23:49:09	25 33 05	29 27	18 04	20 54	22 31	19 11	12 41	13 40	20 28	21 59	28 31	12 16	14 50	18 11	14 47	16 45
19 Fri	23:53:05	26 32 00	13♉43	18 01	21 26	23 44	19 50	12 43	13 47	20 26	21 57	28 31	12 40	15 06	18 23	14 44	16 43
20 Sat	23:57:02	27 30 58	28 03	17 55	21 54	24 58	20 30	12 45	13 55	20 24	21 56	28 32	13 05	15 22	18 35	14 40	16 41
21 Sun	00:00:58	28 29 57	12♊30	17 48	22 16	26 11	21 10	12 48	14 02	20 22	21 56	28 32	13 29	15 37	18 47	14 36	16 39
22 Mon	00:04:55	29 28 58	26 34	17 47 D	22 33	27 24	21 50	12 50	14 10	20 19	21 55	28 32	13 54	15 52	18 59	14 31	16 37
23 Tue	00:08:51	00♎28 01	10♋40	17 47	22 45	28 38	22 30	12 53	14 17	20 17	21 53	28 33	14 18	16 07	19 12	14 26	16 35
24 Wed	00:12:48	01 27 06	24 40	17 48	22 50 R	29 51	23 10	12 56	14 24	20 14	21 52	28 33	14 43	16 21	19 25	14 20	16 33
25 Thu	00:16:45	02 26 13	08♌30	17 49 R	22 49	01♏04	23 50	12 59	14 32	20 12	21 51	28 34	15 07	16 36	19 38	14 14	16 31
26 Fri	00:20:41	03 25 22	22 11	17 50	22 40	02 17	24 30	13 02	14 39	20 10	21 50	28 34	15 31	16 50	19 51	14 08	16 29
27 Sat	00:24:38	04 24 32	05♍41	17 48	22 25	03 31	25 10	13 06	14 46	20 08	21 49	28 35	15 55	17 03	20 04	14 01	16 28
28 Sun	00:28:34	05 23 45	19 00	17 44	22 02	04 44	25 50	13 09	14 54	20 05	21 48	28 35	16 19	17 16	20 18	13 53	16 26
29 Mon	00:32:31	06 22 59	02♎07	17 38	21 32	05 57	26 30	13 13	15 01	20 03	21 47	28 36	16 43	17 29	20 32	13 46	16 24
30 Tue	00:36:27	07 22 15	15 05	17 31	20 54	07 10	27 11	13 17	15 08	20 01	21 46	28 37	17 07	17 42	20 46	13 37	16 23

EPHEMERIS CALCULATED FOR 12 MIDNIGHT GREENWICH MEAN TIME. ALL OTHER DATA AND FACING ASPECTARIAN PAGE IN **EASTERN TIME (BOLD)** AND PACIFIC TIME (REGULAR).

OCTOBER 2008

☽ Last Aspect day	ET / hr:mn / PT		asp	☽ Ingress sign	day	ET / hr:mn / PT	
9/30	**9:47 pm**	6:47 pm	⚹ ♇	♏	1	**12:26 am**	
2	**6:46 pm**	3:46 pm	□ ♆	♐	3	**11:14 am**	8:14 am
5	**9:08 pm**	6:08 pm	☌ ♇	♑	5	**11:48 pm**	8:48 pm
7	**3:37 pm**	12:37 pm	⚹ ♅	♒	8	**12:03 pm**	9:03 am
10	**7:13 pm**	4:13 pm	⚹ ♇	♓	10	**9:31 pm**	6:31 pm
12		10:02 pm	□ ♇	♈	13	**3:07 am**	12:07 am
13	**1:02 am**		□ ♇	♈	13	**3:07 am**	12:07 am
15	**3:36 am**	12:36 am	△ ♇	♉	15	**5:31 am**	2:31 am
17	**3:33 am**	12:33 am	☍ ♀	♊	17	**6:25 am**	3:25 am
19	**5:52 am**	2:52 am	☍ ♇	♋	19	**7:40 am**	4:40 am

☽ Last Aspect day	ET / hr:mn / PT		asp	☽ Ingress sign	day	ET / hr:mn / PT	
21	**7:54 am**	4:54 am	□ ☉	♌	21	**10:35 am**	7:35 am
23	**1:53 pm**	10:53 am	△ ♇	♍	23	**3:40 pm**	12:40 pm
25	**9:02 pm**	6:02 pm	□ ♇	♎	25	**10:47 pm**	7:47 pm
28	**6:05 am**	3:05 am	⚹ ♇	♏	28	**7:47 am**	4:47 am
29		10:45 pm	□ ♆	♐	30	**6:41 pm**	3:41 pm
30	**1:45 am**		□ ♆	♐	30	**6:41 pm**	3:41 pm

☽ Phases & Eclipses phase	day	ET / hr:mn / PT	
2nd Quarter	7	**5:04 am**	2:04 am
Full Moon	14	**4:02 pm**	1:02 pm
4th Quarter	21	**7:54 am**	4:54 am
New Moon	28	**7:14 pm**	4:14 pm

Planet Ingress	day	ET / hr:mn / PT	
♂ ♏	3		9:34 pm
♂ ♏	4	**12:34 am**	
♀ ♐	18	**2:31 pm**	11:31 am
☉ ♏	22	**9:08 pm**	6:08 pm

Planetary Motion	day	ET / hr:mn / PT	
☿ D	15	**4:06 pm**	1:06 pm
⚷ D	25	**4:13 am**	1:13 am
♀ ℞	25		10:55 pm
♀ ℞	26	**1:55 am**	

1 WEDNESDAY
☿ ⊼ ♅ **1:26 am**
☽ ⊻ ☉ **5:59 pm** 2:59 pm
☽ ☌ ♀ **6:54 pm** 3:54 pm
♂ ⚹ ♇ 9:01 pm
☽ ⚹ ♃ 11:29 pm

2 THURSDAY
♂ ⚹ ♇ **12:01 am**
☽ ⚹ ♃ **2:29 am**
☽ ⚹ ♄ **6:22 am** 3:22 am
☽ ⊻ ☿ **12:40 pm** 9:40 am
☽ △ ♅ **3:11 pm** 12:11 pm
☽ □ ♆ **6:46 pm** 3:46 pm

3 FRIDAY
☽ ⊻ ♇ **8:33 am** 5:33 am
☽ ⊻ ♂ **10:26 am** 7:26 am

4 SATURDAY
☽ ⚹ ☉ **10:50 am** 7:50 am
☽ ⊻ ♀ **1:12 pm** 10:12 am
☽ ⊻ ♃ **2:39 pm** 11:39 am
☽ □ ♄ **6:52 pm** 3:52 pm
☽ ⚹ ☿ **7:45 pm** 4:45 pm

5 SUNDAY
☽ □ ♅ **3:09 am** 12:09 am
☿ ⊻ ♄ **3:56 am** 12:56 am
♀ ⚹ ♃ **4:22 am** 1:22 am
☽ ⚹ ♆ **6:56 am** 3:56 am
☽ ☌ ♇ **9:08 pm** 6:08 pm
☿ ⊻ ♀ 10:05 pm
☽ ⚹ ♂ 11:40 pm

6 MONDAY
☿ ⊻ ♀ **1:05 am**
☽ ⚹ ♂ **2:40 am**
☉ □ ♃ **12:52 pm** 9:52 am
☉ ☌ ☿ **4:53 pm** 1:53 pm
☿ □ ♃ **7:46 pm** 4:46 pm
♀ ⚹ ♄ 10:42 pm

7 TUESDAY
♀ ⚹ ♄ **1:42 am**
☽ □ ☿ **3:04 am** 12:04 am
☽ ☌ ♃ **3:50 am** 12:50 am
☽ □ ☉ **5:04 am** 2:04 am
☽ △ ♄ **8:11 am** 5:11 am
☽ ⚹ ♀ **8:51 am** 5:51 am
☽ ⚹ ♅ **3:37 pm** 12:37 pm
☽ ⊻ ♆ **7:27 pm** 4:27 pm

8 WEDNESDAY
☽ ⊻ ♇ **9:31 am** 6:31 am
☽ □ ♂ **6:22 pm** 3:22 pm
☉ ⊻ ♄ **11:18 pm** 8:18 pm

9 THURSDAY
☽ △ ☿ **9:31 am** 6:31 am
☽ ⊻ ♃ **3:30 pm** 12:30 pm
☽ ⊼ ♄ **7:44 pm** 4:44 pm
☽ △ ☉ **9:17 pm** 6:17 pm
♀ △ ♅ 10:48 pm
☽ ⊻ ♅ 11:06 pm
☽ □ ♀ 11:08 pm

10 FRIDAY
♀ △ ♅ **1:48 am**
☽ ⊻ ♅ **2:06 am**
☽ □ ♀ **2:08 am**
☽ ☌ ♆ **5:50 am** 2:50 am
☽ ⚹ ♇ **7:13 pm** 4:13 pm

11 SATURDAY
☽ △ ♂ **6:35 am** 3:35 am
☽ ⊼ ☿ **2:09 pm** 11:09 am
♀ □ ♆ **4:20 pm** 1:20 pm
☽ ⚹ ♃ **11:35 pm** 8:35 pm

12 SUNDAY
☽ ☍ ♄ **3:35 am** 12:35 am
☉ ⊼ ♅ **8:51 am** 5:51 am
☽ ⊼ ☉ **8:54 am** 5:54 am
☽ ☌ ♅ **8:54 am** 5:54 am
☽ ⊻ ♆ **12:28 pm** 9:28 am
☽ △ ♀ **2:26 pm** 11:26 am
☽ □ ♇ 10:02 pm

13 MONDAY
☽ □ ♇ **1:02 am**
☽ ⊼ ♂ **2:16 pm** 11:16 am
☽ ☍ ☿ **4:41 pm** 1:41 pm

14 TUESDAY
☽ □ ♃ **3:52 am** 12:52 am
☽ ⊼ ♄ **7:39 am** 4:39 am
☉ △ ♆ **9:19 am** 6:19 am
☽ ⊻ ♅ **12:08 pm** 9:08 am
☽ ⚹ ♆ **3:34 pm** 12:34 pm
☽ ☍ ☉ **4:02 pm** 1:02 pm
☽ ⊼ ♀ **10:09 pm** 7:09 pm

15 WEDNESDAY
☽ △ ♇ **3:36 am** 12:36 am
☿ ⊻ ♂ **4:12 am** 1:12 am
☽ ⊼ ☿ **5:55 pm** 2:55 pm
☽ ☍ ♂ **6:37 pm** 3:37 pm

16 THURSDAY
☽ △ ♃ **5:40 am** 2:40 am
☽ △ ♄ **9:21 am** 6:21 am
☽ ⚹ ♅ **1:15 pm** 10:15 am
☽ □ ♆ **4:40 pm** 1:40 pm
☽ ⊼ ☉ **8:42 pm** 5:42 pm

17 FRIDAY
☽ ☍ ♀ **3:33 am** 12:33 am
☽ ⊼ ♇ **4:36 am** 1:36 am
♀ ⊻ ♇ **4:28 pm** 1:28 pm
☽ △ ☿ **7:25 pm** 4:25 pm
☽ ⊼ ♂ **9:51 pm** 6:51 pm

18 SATURDAY
☽ ⊼ ♃ **6:56 am** 3:56 am
☽ □ ♄ **10:37 am** 7:37 am
☽ □ ♅ **2:05 pm** 11:05 am
☽ △ ♆ **5:38 pm** 2:38 pm
☽ △ ☉ 10:21 pm

19 SUNDAY
☽ △ ☉ **1:21 am**
☽ ☍ ♇ **5:52 am** 2:52 am
☽ ⊼ ♀ **9:15 am** 6:15 am
☽ □ ☿ **11:00 pm** 8:00 pm
☽ △ ♂ 11:02 pm

20 MONDAY
☽ △ ♂ **2:02 am**
☽ ☍ ♃ **9:19 am** 6:19 am
☽ ⚹ ♄ **1:06 pm** 10:06 am
☽ △ ♅ **4:12 pm** 1:12 pm
☽ ⊼ ♆ **7:58 pm** 4:58 pm

21 TUESDAY
☽ □ ☉ **7:54 am** 4:54 am
☽ ⊼ ♇ **8:47 am** 5:47 am
☽ △ ♀ **5:08 pm** 2:08 pm
☉ ⚹ ♇ **8:23 pm** 5:23 pm

22 WEDNESDAY
☽ ⚹ ☿ **6:04 am** 3:04 am
☽ □ ♂ **8:29 am** 5:29 am
☽ ⊼ ♃ **1:49 pm** 10:49 am
☽ ⊻ ♄ **5:40 pm** 2:40 pm
☽ ⊼ ♅ **8:24 pm** 5:24 pm
☽ ☍ ♆ 9:24 pm

23 THURSDAY
☽ ☍ ♆ **12:24 am**
☽ △ ♇ **1:53 pm** 10:53 am
☽ ⚹ ☉ **5:10 pm** 2:10 pm

24 FRIDAY
☽ □ ♀ **3:52 am** 12:52 am
☽ ⊻ ☿ **5:01 pm** 2:01 pm
☽ ⚹ ♂ **5:29 pm** 2:29 pm
☽ △ ♃ **8:33 pm** 5:33 pm
☽ ☌ ♄ 9:26 pm
☽ ☍ ♅ 11:42 pm

25 SATURDAY
☽ ☌ ♄ **12:26 am**
☽ ☍ ♅ **2:42 am**
☿ ⊻ ♂ **3:11 am** 12:11 am
☽ ⊼ ♆ **6:57 am** 3:57 am
☽ □ ♇ **9:02 pm** 6:02 pm

26 SUNDAY
☽ ⊻ ☉ **5:00 am** 2:00 am
☿ □ ♃ **8:14 am** 5:14 am
☽ ⚹ ♀ **5:15 pm** 2:15 pm

27 MONDAY
☽ ⊻ ♂ **4:46 am** 1:46 am
☽ □ ♃ **5:17 am** 2:17 am
☽ ☌ ☿ **7:37 am** 4:37 am
☽ ⊻ ♄ **9:08 am** 6:08 am
☽ ⊼ ♅ **10:55 am** 7:55 am
☽ △ ♆ **3:24 pm** 12:24 pm
♂ ⚹ ♃ **4:29 pm** 1:29 pm
☿ ⊻ ♄ **9:58 pm** 6:58 pm

28 TUESDAY
☽ ⚹ ♇ **6:05 am** 3:05 am
☿ ⊼ ♅ **12:11 pm** 9:11 am
☽ ☌ ☉ **7:14 pm** 4:14 pm

29 WEDNESDAY
☽ ⊻ ♀ **9:09 am** 6:09 am
☽ ⚹ ♃ **3:59 pm** 12:59 pm
☽ ☌ ♂ **6:17 pm** 3:17 pm
☽ ⚹ ♄ **7:45 pm** 4:45 pm
☽ △ ♅ **9:01 pm** 6:01 pm
☽ ⊻ ☿ 10:41 pm
☽ □ ♆ 10:45 pm
☿ △ ♆ 11:11 pm

30 THURSDAY
☽ ⊻ ☿ **1:41 am**
☽ □ ♆ **1:45 am**
☿ △ ♆ **2:11 am**
☽ ⊻ ♇ **5:03 pm** 2:03 pm
♂ ⚹ ♄ **11:51 pm** 8:51 pm

31 FRIDAY
☽ ⊻ ☉ **11:54 am** 8:54 am
♂ △ ♅ **4:32 pm** 1:32 pm

Eastern time in bold type
Pacific time in medium type

OCTOBER 2008

DATE	S.TIME	SUN	MOON	N.NODE	MERCURY	VENUS	MARS	JUPITER	SATURN	URANUS	NEPTUNE	PLUTO	CERES	PALLAS	JUNO	VESTA	CHIRON
1 Wed	00:40:24	08≏11 13	27≏41	17≈22	20≏41	08♏23	27♏51	13♑26	15♍17	19♓58	21≈45	28♐37	17♌37	17♊54	21♐00	13♐29	16≈21
2 Thu	00:44:20	09 10 15	10♏07	17 12R.	19 17R.	09 37	28 31	13 30	15 25	19 56R.	21 44R.	28 38	17 56	18 06	21 14	13 20R.	16 20R.
3 Fri	00:48:17	10 09 19	22 20	17 03	18 19	10 50	29 12	13 35	15 29	19 54	21 43	28 39	18 19	18 17	21 29	13 10	16 18
4 Sat	00:52:14	11 08 24	04♐23	16 55	17 16	12 03	29 52	13 40	15 37	19 52	21 42	28 39	18 42	18 28	21 43	13 00	16 17
5 Sun	00:56:10	12 07 32	16 17	16 49	16 09	13 16	00♏33	13 45	15 44	19 50	21 41	28 40	19 06	18 39	21 58	12 50	16 15
6 Mon	01:00:07	13 06 41	28 07	16 46	14 59	14 29	01 14	13 50	15 51	19 48	21 40	28 41	19 30	18 50	22 13	12 39	16 14
7 Tue	01:04:03	14 05 52	09♑58	16 44 D	13 49	15 42	01 54	13 55	15 58	19 45	21 39	28 42	19 53	18 59	22 29	12 28	16 13
8 Wed	01:08:00	15 05 05	21 55	16 44	12 40	16 55	02 35	14 01	16 05	19 43	21 38	28 43	20 16	19 09	22 44	12 17	16 12
9 Thu	01:11:56	16 04 20	04≈03	16 46R.	11 34	18 08	03 16	14 06	16 12	19 41	21 37	28 44	20 39	19 18	23 00	12 05	16 11
10 Fri	01:15:53	17 03 36	16 26	16 45	10 34	19 21	03 56	14 12	16 18	19 39	21 37	28 45	21 02	19 27	23 15	11 53	16 10
11 Sat	01:19:49	18 02 54	29 11	16 42	09 40	20 34	04 37	14 18	16 25	19 37	21 36	28 46	21 25	19 35	23 31	11 40	16 09
12 Sun	01:23:46	19 02 14	12♓19	16 37	08 54	21 47	05 18	14 25	16 32	19 35	21 36	28 47	21 48	19 43	23 47	11 28	16 08
13 Mon	01:27:43	20 01 35	25 38	16 29	08 18	23 00	05 59	14 31	16 39	19 33	21 35	28 48	22 11	19 50	24 04	11 14	16 07
14 Tue	01:31:39	21 00 59	09♈14	16 20	07 53	24 13	06 40	14 37	16 46	19 31	21 34	28 49	22 34	19 57	24 20	11 01	16 06
15 Wed	01:35:36	22 00 25	23 03	16 09	07 38 D	25 25	07 21	14 44	16 52	19 29	21 33	28 50	22 56	20 03	24 37	10 48	16 06
16 Thu	01:39:32	22 59 52	06♉54	15 59	07 34	26 38	08 02	14 51	16 59	19 27	21 33	28 51	23 19	20 09	24 53	10 34	16 05
17 Fri	01:43:29	23 59 22	20 45	15 55	07 41	27 51	08 44	14 58	17 05	19 25	21 32	28 52	23 41	20 15	25 10	10 20	16 04
18 Sat	01:47:25	24 58 54	04♊36	15 50	07 59	29 04	09 25	15 05	17 12	19 24	21 32	28 53	24 04	20 20	25 27	10 05	16 04
19 Sun	01:51:22	25 58 29	18 30	15 44	08 27	00♐17	10 06	15 12	17 18	19 22	21 32	28 55	24 26	20 24	25 45	09 51	16 03
20 Mon	01:55:19	26 58 07	02♋36	15 40	09 05	01 29	10 47	15 20	17 25	19 20	21 31	28 56	24 48	20 28	26 02	09 36	16 03
21 Tue	01:59:15	27 57 45	16 42	15 39 D	09 51	02 42	11 29	15 27	17 31	19 18	21 31	28 57	25 10	20 31	26 19	09 21	16 03
22 Wed	02:03:12	28 57 26	00♌48	15 39	10 45	03 55	12 10	15 35	17 38	19 17	21 30	28 58	25 32	20 34	26 37	09 06	16 03
23 Thu	02:07:08	29 57 09	14 54	15 38	11 45	05 07	12 52	15 43	17 44	19 15	21 30	29 00	25 54	20 36	26 55	08 51	16 03
24 Fri	02:11:05	00♏56 56	29 00	15 35	12 52	06 20	13 33	15 51	17 50	19 13	21 29	29 01	26 16	20 38	27 13	08 35	16 02
25 Sat	02:15:01	01 56 45	13 06	15 35	14 05	07 33	14 15	15 59	17 56	19 12	21 29	29 02	26 37	20 39R.	27 31	08 20	16 02 D
26 Sun	02:18:58	02 56 37	27 12	15 29	15 22	08 45	14 57	16 07	18 02	19 10	21 29	29 04	26 59	20 39	27 49	08 04	16 02
27 Mon	02:22:54	03 56 31	11♎18	15 25	16 43	09 58	15 39	16 15	18 08	19 09	21 29	29 05	27 20	20 38	28 07	07 49	16 02
28 Tue	02:26:51	04 56 27	23 54	15 18	18 08	11 10	16 20	16 24	18 14	19 07	21 28	29 07	27 41	20 37	28 25	07 33	16 02
29 Wed	02:30:47	05 56 26	06♏14	14 54	19 35	12 23	17 02	16 33	18 20	19 06	21 28	29 08	28 02	20 35	28 44	07 17	16 03
30 Thu	02:34:44	06 56 27	18 34	14 44	21 05	13 35	17 44	16 41	18 26	19 05	21 28	29 10	28 23	20 33	29 03	07 02	16 03
31 Fri	02:38:41	07 56 30	00♐17	14 26	22 36	14 48	18 26	16 50	18 32	19 03	21 28	29 11	28 44	20 32	29 21	06 46	16 03

EPHEMERIS CALCULATED FOR 12 MIDNIGHT GREENWICH MEAN TIME. ALL OTHER DATA AND FACING ASPECTARIAN PAGE IN **EASTERN TIME (BOLD)** AND PACIFIC TIME (REGULAR).

NOVEMBER 2008

☽ Last Aspect day	ET / hr:mn / PT		asp	☽ Ingress sign	day	ET / hr:mn / PT	
2	**4:41 am**	1:41 am	☌ ♇	♑	2	**6:13 am**	3:13 am
3		10:47 pm	⚹ ♂	♒	4	**7:01 pm**	4:01 pm
4	**1:47 am**		⚹ ♂	♒	4	**7:01 pm**	4:01 pm
7	**4:33 am**	1:33 am	⚹ ♇	♓	7	**5:43 am**	2:43 am
9	**11:28 am**	8:28 am	□ ♇	♈	9	**12:26 pm**	9:26 am
11	**2:17 pm**	11:17 am	△ ♇	♉	11	**3:05 pm**	12:05 pm
13	**12:12 pm**	9:12 am	☍ ♂	♊	13	**3:11 pm**	12:11 pm
15	**2:17 pm**	11:17 am	☍ ♇	♋	15	**2:52 pm**	11:52 am
17	**8:43 am**	5:43 am	△ ☉	♌	17	**4:07 pm**	1:07 pm
19	**7:48 pm**	4:48 pm	△ ♇	♍	19	**8:12 pm**	5:12 pm
22	**3:02 am**	12:02 am	□ ♇	♎	22	**3:20 am**	12:20 am
24	**12:45 pm**	9:45 am	⚹ ♇	♏	24	**12:54 pm**	9:54 am
26	**7:32 am**	4:32 am	□ ♆	♐	26		9:14 pm
26	**7:32 am**	4:32 am	□ ♆	♐	27	**12:14 am**	
28	**7:53 pm**	4:53 pm	⚹ ♆	♑	29	**12:48 pm**	9:48 am

☽ Phases & Eclipses phase	day	ET / hr:mn / PT	
2nd Quarter	5	**11:03 pm**	8:03 pm
Full Moon	12		10:17 pm
Full Moon	13	**1:17 am**	
4th Quarter	19	**4:31 pm**	1:31 pm
New Moon	27	**11:54 am**	8:54 am

Planet Ingress		day	ET / hr:mn / PT	
⚵	♑	1	**8:46 pm**	5:46 pm
⚳	♍	3	**12:22 pm**	9:22 am
☿	♏	4	**11:00 am**	8:00 am
♀	♑	12	**10:25 am**	7:25 am
♂	♐	16	**3:26 am**	12:26 am
☉	♐	21	**5:44 pm**	2:44 pm
☿	♐	22		11:09 pm
☿	♐	23	**2:09 am**	
♇	♑	26	**8:03 pm**	5:03 pm

Planetary Motion		day	ET / hr:mn / PT	
♆	D	1		11:38 pm
♆	D	2	**1:38 am**	
♅	D	27	**11:08 am**	8:08 am

1 SATURDAY
☽ ☌ ♀ **3:36 am** 12:36 am
☽ ⚺ ♃ **4:38 am** 1:38 am
☽ □ ♄ **8:14 am** 5:14 am
☽ □ ♅ **8:56 am** 5:56 am
☽ ⚺ ♂ **9:59 am** 6:59 am
☽ ⚹ ♆ **1:53 pm** 10:53 am
♀ ⚺ ♃ **3:04 pm** 12:04 pm
☽ ⚹ ☿ **10:56 pm** 7:56 pm

2 SUNDAY
☽ ☌ ♇ **4:41 am** 1:41 am

3 MONDAY
♀ □ ♄ **3:41 am** 12:41 am
☽ ⚹ ☉ **5:21 am** 2:21 am
♀ □ ♅ **6:18 am** 3:18 am
☽ ☌ ♃ **5:22 pm** 2:22 pm
☽ △ ♄ **8:40 pm** 5:40 pm
☽ ⚹ ♅ **8:47 pm** 5:47 pm
☽ ⚺ ♀ **10:26 pm** 7:26 pm
☿ ⚹ ♇ 9:31 pm
☽ ⚹ ♂ 10:47 pm
☽ ⚺ ♆ 10:50 pm
♂ □ ♆ 11:44 pm

4 TUESDAY
☿ ⚹ ♇ **12:31 am**
☽ ⚹ ♂ **1:47 am**
☽ ⚺ ♆ **1:50 am**
♂ □ ♆ **2:44 am**

♄ ☍ ♅ **8:35 am** 5:35 am
☽ ⚺ ♇ **5:39 pm** 2:39 pm
☽ □ ☿ **8:16 pm** 5:16 pm

5 WEDNESDAY
♀ ⚹ ♆ **7:56 am** 4:56 am
☽ □ ☉ **11:03 pm** 8:03 pm

6 THURSDAY
☽ ⚺ ♃ **6:03 am** 3:03 am
☽ ⚺ ♅ **8:27 am** 5:27 am
☽ ⚻ ♄ **8:52 am** 5:52 am
☽ ☌ ♆ **1:23 pm** 10:23 am
☽ ⚹ ♀ **4:32 pm** 1:32 pm
☽ □ ♂ **4:54 pm** 1:54 pm
♀ ⚺ ♂ 10:13 pm

7 FRIDAY
♀ ⚺ ♂ **1:13 am**
☽ ⚹ ♇ **4:33 am** 1:33 am
☽ △ ☿ **3:27 pm** 12:27 pm

8 SATURDAY
☽ △ ☉ **12:43 pm** 9:43 am
☽ ⚹ ♃ **3:13 pm** 12:13 pm
☽ ☌ ♅ **4:40 pm** 1:40 pm
☽ ☍ ♄ **5:30 pm** 2:30 pm
☽ ⚺ ♆ **9:21 pm** 6:21 pm

9 SUNDAY
☽ △ ♂ **3:40 am** 12:40 am
☽ □ ♀ **5:41 am** 2:41 am
☽ □ ♇ **11:28 am** 8:28 am

10 MONDAY
☉ ⚹ ♃ **3:54 am** 12:54 am
☽ ⚻ ☿ **4:31 am** 1:31 am
☉ △ ♅ **4:21 pm** 1:21 pm
☽ □ ♃ **8:00 pm** 5:00 pm
☽ ⚺ ♅ **8:40 pm** 5:40 pm
☽ ⚻ ☉ **9:00 pm** 6:00 pm
☽ ⚻ ♄ **9:48 pm** 6:48 pm
☽ ⚹ ♆ 10:04 pm

11 TUESDAY
☽ ⚹ ♆ **1:04 am**
☉ ⚹ ♄ **9:24 am** 6:24 am
☽ ⚻ ♂ **9:33 am** 6:33 am
☽ △ ♀ **1:22 pm** 10:22 am
☽ △ ♇ **2:17 pm** 11:17 am
♀ ☌ ♇ 9:55 pm

12 WEDNESDAY
♀ ☌ ♇ **12:55 am**
☽ ☍ ☿ **12:14 pm** 9:14 am
☽ △ ♃ **9:24 pm** 6:24 pm
☽ ⚹ ♅ **9:26 pm** 6:26 pm
☽ △ ♄ **10:50 pm** 7:50 pm
♃ ⚹ ♅ 9:40 pm
☽ ☍ ☉ 10:17 pm
☽ □ ♆ 10:42 pm

13 THURSDAY
♃ ⚹ ♅ **12:40 am**
☽ ☍ ☉ **1:17 am**
☽ □ ♆ **1:42 am**
☉ □ ♆ **7:31 am** 4:31 am
☽ ☍ ♂ **12:12 pm** 9:12 am

☽ ⚻ ♇ **2:31 pm** 11:31 am
☽ ⚻ ♀ **5:39 pm** 2:39 pm

14 FRIDAY
☽ ⚻ ☿ **5:34 pm** 2:34 pm
☽ □ ♅ **8:59 pm** 5:59 pm
☽ ⚻ ♃ **9:33 pm** 6:33 pm
☽ □ ♄ **10:39 pm** 7:39 pm
☽ △ ♆ 10:18 pm

15 SATURDAY
☽ △ ♆ **1:18 am**
☽ ⚻ ☉ **4:16 am** 1:16 am
☽ ⚻ ♂ **2:14 pm** 11:14 am
☽ ☍ ♇ **2:17 pm** 11:17 am
♂ ⚺ ♇ **3:12 pm** 12:12 pm
☽ ☍ ♀ **9:32 pm** 6:32 pm
☿ △ ♅ 10:26 pm

16 SUNDAY
☿ △ ♅ **1:26 am**
☿ ⚹ ♃ **11:00 am** 8:00 am
☿ ⚹ ♄ **7:28 pm** 4:28 pm
☽ △ ♅ **9:26 pm** 6:26 pm
☽ ☍ ♃ **10:38 pm** 7:38 pm
☽ ⚹ ♄ **11:27 pm** 8:27 pm
☽ △ ☿ **11:55 pm** 8:55 pm
☽ ⚻ ♆ 10:58 pm

17 MONDAY
☽ ⚻ ♆ **1:58 am**
☽ △ ☉ **8:43 am** 5:43 am
☽ ⚻ ♇ **3:37 pm** 12:37 pm
☽ △ ♂ **6:04 pm** 3:04 pm
☿ □ ♆ **6:30 pm** 3:30 pm

18 TUESDAY
☽ ⚻ ♀ **3:43 am** 12:43 am
☽ ⚻ ♅ 9:20 pm
☽ ⚻ ♃ 11:21 pm
☽ ⚺ ♄ 11:48 pm

19 WEDNESDAY
☽ ⚻ ♅ **12:20 am**
☽ ⚻ ♃ **2:21 am**
☽ ⚺ ♄ **2:48 am**
☽ ☍ ♆ **5:13 am** 2:13 am
☽ □ ☿ **9:49 am** 6:49 am
☽ □ ☉ **4:31 pm** 1:31 pm
☽ △ ♇ **7:48 pm** 4:48 pm
☽ □ ♂ 10:14 pm

20 THURSDAY
☽ □ ♂ **1:14 am**
☽ △ ♀ **1:45 pm** 10:45 am

21 FRIDAY
☽ ☍ ♅ **6:20 am** 3:20 am
♃ △ ♄ **7:12 am** 4:12 am
☽ ☌ ♄ **9:15 am** 6:15 am
☽ △ ♃ **9:16 am** 6:16 am
☽ ⚻ ♆ **11:34 am** 8:34 am
☉ ⚺ ♇ **1:34 pm** 10:34 am
☽ ⚹ ☿ 9:06 pm

22 SATURDAY
☽ ⚹ ☿ **12:06 am**
☽ □ ♇ **3:02 am** 12:02 am
☽ ⚹ ☉ **4:09 am** 1:09 am

☽ ⚹ ♂ **11:56 am** 8:56 am
☿ ⚺ ♇ 9:12 pm

23 SUNDAY
☿ ⚺ ♇ **12:12 am**
☽ □ ♀ **3:36 am** 12:36 am
☽ ⚻ ♅ **3:04 pm** 12:04 pm
☽ ⚺ ♄ **6:26 pm** 3:26 pm
☽ □ ♃ **7:01 pm** 4:01 pm
☽ △ ♆ **8:35 pm** 5:35 pm

24 MONDAY
☽ ⚹ ♇ **12:45 pm** 9:45 am
☽ ⚺ ☿ **6:02 pm** 3:02 pm
☽ ⚺ ☉ **6:55 pm** 3:55 pm
☽ ⚺ ♂ 10:27 pm

25 TUESDAY
☽ ⚺ ♂ **1:27 am**
☉ ☌ ☿ **11:52 am** 8:52 am
☽ ⚹ ♀ **8:19 pm** 5:19 pm
☽ △ ♅ 10:47 pm

26 WEDNESDAY
☽ △ ♅ **1:47 am**
☽ ⚹ ♄ **5:34 am** 2:34 am
☽ ⚹ ♃ **6:50 am** 3:50 am
☽ □ ♆ **7:32 am** 4:32 am
☽ ⚺ ♇ 9:14 pm

27 THURSDAY
☽ ⚺ ♇ **12:14 am**
☽ ☌ ☉ **11:54 am** 8:54 am
☽ ☌ ☿ **2:30 pm** 11:30 am
☽ ☌ ♂ **4:56 pm** 1:56 pm

28 FRIDAY
♀ ⚹ ♅ **4:20 am** 1:20 am
♃ ⚺ ♆ **5:35 am** 2:35 am
☽ □ ♅ **1:57 pm** 10:57 am
☽ ⚺ ♀ **3:01 pm** 12:01 pm
☽ □ ♄ **6:07 pm** 3:07 pm
☽ ⚹ ♆ **7:53 pm** 4:53 pm
☽ ⚺ ♃ **8:07 pm** 5:07 pm
☿ ☌ ♂ **10:39 pm** 7:39 pm

29 SATURDAY
☽ ☌ ♇ **12:59 pm** 9:59 am
♀ △ ♄ **11:36 pm** 8:36 pm

30 SUNDAY
☽ ⚺ ☉ **6:21 am** 3:21 am
☽ ⚺ ♂ **9:42 am** 6:42 am
☽ ⚺ ☿ **12:36 pm** 9:36 am
♀ ⚺ ♆ **4:35 pm** 1:35 pm
☽ ⚹ ♅ 11:55 pm

Eastern time in bold type
Pacific time in medium type

NOVEMBER 2008

DATE	S.TIME	SUN	MOON	N.NODE	MERCURY	VENUS	MARS	JUPITER	SATURN	URANUS	NEPTUNE	PLUTO	CERES	PALLAS	JUNO	VESTA	CHIRON
1 Sat	02:42:37	08♏56 17	12♐37	14♒14℞	24♎10	16♐00	19♏08	16♑50	18♍38	19♓01℞	21♒28 D	29♐13	29♌05	20♉29℞	29♐40	06♉30℞	16♒04
2 Sun	02:46:34	09 56 20	24 29	14 04℞	25 44	17 12	19 50	16 59	18 43	18 59	21 28	29 14	29 25	20 25	29 59	06 15	16 04
3 Mon	02:50:30	10 56 26	06♑17	13 57	27 19	18 25	20 32	17 09	18 49	18 58	21 28	29 16	29 45	20 21	00♑19	05 59	16 05
4 Tue	02:54:27	11 56 33	18 06	13 53	28 56	19 37	21 15	17 18	18 55	18 57	21 28	29 17	00♍06	20 15	00 38	05 44	16 05
5 Wed	02:58:23	12 56 42	29 59	13 52	00♏32	20 49	21 57	17 27	19 00	18 56	21 28	29 19	00 26	20 10	00 57	05 28	16 06
6 Thu	03:02:20	13 56 52	12♒03	13 51	02 09	22 02	22 39	17 37	19 05	18 55	21 29	29 21	00 45	20 04	01 17	05 13	16 06
7 Fri	03:06:16	14 57 03	24 23	13 51	03 47	23 14	23 21	17 47	19 11	18 54	21 29	29 22	01 05	19 56	01 36	04 58	16 07
8 Sat	03:10:13	15 57 17	07♓17	13 50	05 24	24 26	24 04	17 56	19 16	18 53	21 29	29 24	01 25	19 48	01 56	04 44	16 08
9 Sun	03:14:10	16 57 31	20 11	13 47	07 02	25 38	24 46	18 06	19 21	18 52	21 30	29 26	01 44	19 40	02 16	04 29	16 09
10 Mon	03:18:06	17 57 47	03♈46	13 42	08 39	26 50	25 29	18 16	19 26	18 51	21 30	29 28	02 03	19 31	02 36	04 15	16 10
11 Tue	03:22:03	18 58 05	17 51	13 33	10 17	28 02	26 11	18 27	19 31	18 50	21 30	29 29	02 22	19 21	02 56	04 00	16 11
12 Wed	03:25:59	19 58 24	02♉24	13 23	11 54	29 14	26 54	18 37	19 36	18 49	21 31	29 31	02 41	19 11	03 16	03 46	16 12
13 Thu	03:29:56	20 58 45	17 18	13 11	13 31	00♑26	27 37	18 47	19 41	18 48	21 31	29 33	03 00	19 00	03 36	03 33	16 14
14 Fri	03:33:52	21 59 07	02♊25	12 59	15 08	01 38	28 20	18 58	19 46	18 47	21 31	29 35	03 19	18 49	03 57	03 19	16 15
15 Sat	03:37:49	22 59 32	17 33	12 50	16 45	02 49	29 02	19 08	19 51	18 46	21 31	29 37	03 37	18 36	04 17	03 06	16 16
16 Sun	03:41:45	23 59 58	02♋34	12 42	18 22	04 01	29 45	19 19	19 55	18 48	21 32	29 38	03 55	18 24	04 38	02 53	16 18
17 Mon	03:45:42	25 00 26	17 19	12 38	19 58	05 13	00♐28	19 30	20 00	18 47	21 32	29 40	04 13	18 10	04 58	02 41	16 19
18 Tue	03:49:39	26 00 55	01♌42	12 36 D	21 34	06 24	01 11	19 41	20 04	18 47	21 32	29 42	04 31	17 56	05 19	02 29	16 21
19 Wed	03:53:35	27 01 27	15 42	12 35℞	23 10	07 36	01 54	19 51	20 09	18 46	21 33	29 44	04 48	17 42	05 40	02 17	16 22
20 Thu	03:57:32	28 02 00	29 19	12 35	24 46	08 47	02 37	20 03	20 13	18 46	21 33	29 46	05 06	17 27	06 01	02 05	16 24
21 Fri	04:01:28	29 02 35	12♍36	12 32	26 21	09 59	03 20	20 14	20 17	18 45	21 34	29 48	05 23	17 11	06 22	01 54	16 26
22 Sat	04:05:25	00♐03 12	25 34	12 32	27 57	11 10	04 03	20 25	20 21	18 45	21 35	29 50	05 40	16 55	06 43	01 43	16 27
23 Sun	04:09:21	01 03 50	08♎17	12 27	29 32	12 21	04 46	20 36	20 26	18 45	21 35	29 52	05 57	16 39	07 04	01 33	16 29
24 Mon	04:13:18	02 04 30	20 47	12 18	01♐07	13 33	05 30	20 48	20 29	18 45	21 36	29 54	06 13	16 21	07 25	01 23	16 31
25 Tue	04:17:14	03 05 12	03♏08	12 07	02 41	14 44	06 13	20 59	20 33	18 45	21 37	29 56	06 30	16 04	07 47	01 14	16 33
26 Wed	04:21:11	04 05 55	14 44	11 55	04 16	15 55	06 56	21 11	20 37	18 45	21 38	29 58	06 46	15 46	08 08	01 04	16 35
27 Thu	04:25:08	05 06 40	26 47	11 42	05 50	17 06	07 40	21 23	20 40	18 44 D	21 39	00♑00	07 01	15 28	08 29	00 56	16 37
28 Fri	04:29:04	06 07 26	09♐21	11 29	07 23	18 17	08 23	21 34	20 44	18 44	21 39	00 02	07 17	15 09	08 51	00 47	16 39
29 Sat	04:33:01	07 08 13	21 14	11 17	08 59	19 28	09 07	21 46	20 48	18 44	21 40	00 04	07 32	14 50	09 13	00 39	16 41
30 Sun	04:36:57	08 09 02	03♑03	11 08	10 33	20 38	09 50	21 58	20 51	18 44	21 41	00 06	07 48	14 30	09 35	00 32	16 43

EPHEMERIS CALCULATED FOR 12 MIDNIGHT GREENWICH MEAN TIME. ALL OTHER DATA AND FACING ASPECTARIAN PAGE IN **EASTERN TIME (BOLD)** AND PACIFIC TIME (REGULAR).

DECEMBER 2008

☽ Last Aspect day	ET / hr:mn / PT		asp	☽ Ingress sign day	ET / hr:mn / PT	
1	**10:44 am**	7:44 am	☌ ♀	≈ 1		10:44 pm
1	**10:44 am**	7:44 am	☌ ♀	≈ 2	**1:44 am**	
3	**9:14 pm**	6:14 pm	☌ ♆	♓ 4	**1:23 pm**	10:23 am
6	**7:43 pm**	4:43 pm	✶ ♀	♈ 6	**9:44 pm**	6:44 pm
8	**4:35 pm**	1:35 pm	△ ☿	♉ 8		10:52 pm
8	**4:35 pm**	1:35 pm	△ ☿	♉ 9	**1:52 am**	
10	**5:23 pm**	2:23 pm	△ ♃	♊ 10		11:33 pm
10	**5:23 pm**	2:23 pm	△ ♃	♊ 11	**2:33 am**	
12	**1:01 pm**	10:01 am	△ ♆	♋ 12		10:39 pm
12	**1:01 pm**	10:01 am	△ ♆	♋ 13	**1:39 am**	
14	**5:27 pm**	2:27 pm	☍ ♃	♌ 14		10:22 pm
14	**5:27 pm**	2:27 pm	☍ ♃	♌ 15	**1:22 am**	
16	**7:45 pm**	4:45 pm	△ ☉	♍ 17	**3:35 am**	12:35 am
19	**5:29 am**	2:29 am	□ ☉	♎ 19	**9:23 am**	6:23 am
21	**11:57 am**	8:57 am	□ ♃	♏ 21	**6:36 pm**	3:36 pm
23		9:29 pm	✶ ♃	♐ 24	**6:13 am**	3:13 am
24	**12:29 am**		✶ ♃	♐ 24	**6:13 am**	3:13 am
26	**6:25 pm**	3:25 pm	☌ ♂	♑ 26	**6:56 pm**	3:56 pm
29	**4:20 am**	1:20 am	☌ ♃	≈ 29	**7:42 am**	4:42 am
31	**1:34 pm**	10:34 am	☌ ♀	♓ 31	**7:27 pm**	4:27 pm

☽ Phases & Eclipses phase	day	ET / hr:mn / PT	
2nd Quarter	5	**4:25 pm**	1:25 pm
Full Moon	12	**11:37 am**	8:37 am
4th Quarter	19	**5:29 am**	2:29 am
New Moon	27	**7:22 am**	4:22 am

Planet Ingress	day	ET / hr:mn / PT	
⚶ ♈	4		9:01 pm
⚶ ♈	5	**12:01 am**	
♀ ≈	7	**6:36 pm**	3:36 pm
☿ ♑	12	**5:12 am**	2:12 am
☉ ♑	21	**7:04 am**	4:04 am
♂ ♑	26		11:30 pm
♂ ♑	27	**2:30 am**	
⚶ ♉	27	**4:47 am**	1:47 am

Planetary Motion	day	ET / hr:mn / PT	
⚶ D	15	**11:33 pm**	8:33 pm
♄ R	31	**1:08 pm**	10:08 am

1 MONDAY
☽ ✶ ♅ **2:55 am**
♀ ☌ ♃ **3:44 am** 12:44 am
☽ △ ♄ **7:23 am** 4:23 am
☽ ⚺ ♆ **8:57 am** 5:57 am
☽ ☌ ♃ **10:08 am** 7:08 am
☽ ☌ ♀ **10:44 am** 7:44 am
☽ ⚺ ♇ 11:06 pm

2 TUESDAY
☽ ⚺ ♇ **2:06 am**
☽ ✶ ☉ 9:45 pm
☽ ✶ ♂ 11:22 pm

3 WEDNESDAY
☉ ✶ ☽ **12:45 am**
☽ ✶ ♂ **2:22 am**
☽ ✶ ☿ **10:21 am** 7:21 am
☽ ⚺ ♅ **3:19 pm** 12:19 pm
☽ ⚻ ♄ **7:53 pm** 4:53 pm
☽ ☌ ♆ **9:14 pm** 6:14 pm
☽ ⚺ ♃ **11:21 pm** 8:21 pm

4 THURSDAY
☽ ⚺ ♀ **5:17 am** 2:17 am
☽ ✶ ♇ **1:54 pm** 10:54 am
☿ □ ♅ 9:52 pm

5 FRIDAY
☿ □ ♅ **12:52 am**
☽ □ ☉ **4:25 pm** 1:25 pm
☽ □ ♂ **4:26 pm** 1:26 pm
☉ ☌ ♂ **5:04 pm** 2:04 pm
☽ ☌ ♅ 10:07 pm

6 SATURDAY
☽ ☌ ♅ **1:07 am**
☽ □ ☿ **4:27 am** 1:27 am
☽ ☍ ♄ **5:36 am** 2:36 am
☽ ⚺ ♆ **6:44 am** 3:44 am
☽ ✶ ♃ **9:33 am** 6:33 am
☿ □ ♄ **2:14 pm** 11:14 am
☽ ✶ ♀ **7:43 pm** 4:43 pm
☽ □ ♇ **10:22 pm** 7:22 pm
☿ ✶ ♆ **11:37 pm** 8:37 pm

7 SUNDAY
☽ △ ♂ 10:51 pm
♀ ⚺ ♇ 11:43 pm

8 MONDAY
☽ △ ♂ **1:51 am**
♀ ⚺ ♇ **2:43 am**
☽ △ ☉ **3:06 am** 12:06 am
☿ ⚺ ♃ **4:35 am** 1:35 am
☽ ⚺ ♅ **6:52 am** 3:52 am
☽ ⚻ ♄ **11:08 am** 8:08 am
☽ ✶ ♆ **12:05 pm** 9:05 am
☽ □ ♃ **3:25 pm** 12:25 pm
☽ △ ☿ **4:35 pm** 1:35 pm
☽ △ ♇ 11:35 pm

9 TUESDAY
☽ △ ♇ **2:35 am**
☽ □ ♀ **4:37 am** 1:37 am

10 WEDNESDAY
☽ ⚻ ♂ **6:35 am** 3:35 am
☉ □ ♅ **7:03 am** 4:03 am
☽ ✶ ♅ **8:42 am** 5:42 am
☽ ⚻ ☉ **8:49 am** 5:49 am
☽ △ ♄ **12:47 pm** 9:47 am
☽ □ ♆ **1:38 pm** 10:38 am
☽ △ ♃ **5:23 pm** 2:23 pm
☽ ⚻ ☿ **11:29 pm** 8:29 pm

11 THURSDAY
☽ ⚻ ♇ **3:21 am** 12:21 am
☽ △ ♀ **9:11 am** 6:11 am
♂ □ ♅ 10:50 pm

12 FRIDAY
♂ □ ♅ **1:50 am**
☽ □ ♅ **8:10 am** 5:10 am
☽ ☍ ♂ **8:29 am** 5:29 am
☽ ☍ ☉ **11:37 am** 8:37 am
☽ □ ♄ **12:14 pm** 9:14 am
☽ △ ♆ **1:01 pm** 10:01 am
☿ ☌ ♇ **1:42 pm** 10:42 am
☽ ⚻ ♃ **5:18 pm** 2:18 pm
☉ □ ♄ **9:20 pm** 6:20 pm
☽ ☍ ♇ 11:33 pm

13 SATURDAY
☽ ☍ ♇ **2:33 am**
☽ ☍ ☿ **3:59 am** 12:59 am
☉ ✶ ♆ **9:05 am** 6:05 am
☽ ⚻ ♀ **12:06 pm** 9:06 am

14 SUNDAY
☽ △ ♅ **7:27 am** 4:27 am
☽ ⚻ ♂ **10:10 am** 7:10 am
☽ ✶ ♄ **11:40 am** 8:40 am
☽ ⚻ ♆ **12:25 pm** 9:25 am
☽ ⚻ ☉ **2:22 pm** 11:22 am
☽ ☍ ♃ **5:27 pm** 2:27 pm
☽ ⚻ ♇ 11:25 pm

15 MONDAY
☽ ⚻ ♇ **2:25 am**
☽ ⚻ ☿ **9:29 am** 6:29 am
☽ ☍ ♀ **4:21 pm** 1:21 pm
♂ □ ♄ **5:46 pm** 2:46 pm

16 TUESDAY
☽ ⚻ ♅ **8:37 am** 5:37 am
♂ ✶ ♆ **9:16 am** 6:16 am
☽ ⚺ ♄ **1:08 pm** 10:08 am
☽ ☍ ♆ **1:54 pm** 10:54 am
☽ △ ♂ **2:09 pm** 11:09 am
☽ △ ☉ **7:45 pm** 4:45 pm
☽ ⚻ ♃ **7:56 pm** 4:56 pm
☉ ⚺ ♃ **10:56 pm** 7:56 pm

17 WEDNESDAY
☽ △ ♇ **4:51 am** 1:51 am
☽ △ ☿ **6:49 pm** 3:49 pm
☽ ⚻ ♀ 9:20 pm

18 THURSDAY
☽ ⚻ ♀ **12:20 am**
☽ ☍ ♅ **1:06 pm** 10:06 am
☽ ☌ ♄ **5:58 pm** 2:58 pm
☽ ⚻ ♆ **6:48 pm** 3:48 pm
☽ □ ♂ **10:08 pm** 7:08 pm
☽ △ ♃ 11:05 pm

19 FRIDAY
☽ △ ♃ **2:05 am**
☽ □ ☉ **5:29 am** 2:29 am
☽ □ ♇ **10:52 am** 7:52 am

20 SATURDAY
☽ □ ☿ **9:21 am** 6:21 am
☽ △ ♀ **1:02 pm** 10:02 am
☽ ⚻ ♅ **9:13 pm** 6:13 pm
☽ ⚺ ♄ 11:25 pm

21 SUNDAY
☽ ⚺ ♄ **2:25 am**
☽ △ ♆ **3:19 am** 12:19 am
☽ ✶ ♂ **10:21 am** 7:21 am
☽ □ ♃ **11:57 am** 8:57 am
☽ ✶ ☉ **7:39 pm** 4:39 pm
☽ ✶ ♇ **8:21 pm** 5:21 pm

22 MONDAY
☉ ☌ ♇ **4:23 am** 1:23 am
♂ ⚺ ♃ **11:41 pm** 8:41 pm

23 TUESDAY
☽ ✶ ☿ **4:19 am** 1:19 am
☽ □ ♀ **5:39 am** 2:39 am
☽ △ ♅ **8:13 am** 5:13 am
☽ ✶ ♄ **1:34 pm** 10:34 am
☽ □ ♆ **2:33 pm** 11:33 am
☽ ✶ ♃ 9:29 pm
☽ ⚺ ♂ 10:39 pm

24 WEDNESDAY
☽ ✶ ♃ **12:29 am**
☽ ⚺ ♂ **1:39 am**
☽ ⚺ ♇ **8:12 am** 5:12 am
♀ ⚺ ♅ **9:38 am** 6:38 am
☿ ✶ ♅ **11:33 am** 8:33 am
☽ ⚺ ☉ **12:52 pm** 9:52 am
☿ ⚺ ♀ **4:57 pm** 1:57 pm

25 THURSDAY
☽ □ ♅ **8:46 pm** 5:46 pm
☽ ✶ ♀ 9:22 pm
☽ ⚺ ☿ 10:32 pm
☽ □ ♄ 11:10 pm

26 FRIDAY
☽ ✶ ♀ **12:22 am**
☽ ⚺ ☿ **1:32 am**
☽ □ ♄ **2:10 am**
☽ ✶ ♆ **3:14 am** 12:14 am
☿ △ ♄ **6:37 am** 3:37 am
☽ ⚺ ♃ **2:20 pm** 11:20 am
☿ ⚺ ♆ **3:24 pm** 12:24 pm
☽ ☌ ♂ **6:25 pm** 3:25 pm
♀ ⚻ ♄ **7:31 pm** 4:31 pm
☽ ☌ ♇ **9:07 pm** 6:07 pm

27 SATURDAY
☽ ☌ ☉ **7:22 am** 4:22 am
♀ ☌ ♆ **7:28 am** 4:28 am

28 SUNDAY
☽ ✶ ♅ **9:46 am** 6:46 am
♂ ☌ ♇ **3:02 pm** 12:02 pm
☽ △ ♄ **3:04 pm** 12:04 pm
☽ ⚺ ♆ **4:14 pm** 1:14 pm
☽ ⚺ ♀ **7:32 pm** 4:32 pm
☽ ☌ ☿ **10:53 pm** 7:53 pm

29 MONDAY
☽ ☌ ♃ **4:20 am** 1:20 am
☽ ⚺ ♇ **10:04 am** 7:04 am
☽ ⚺ ♂ **11:17 am** 8:17 am
☽ ⚺ ☉ 10:41 pm

30 TUESDAY
☽ ⚺ ☉ **1:41 am**
☽ ⚺ ♅ **10:10 pm** 7:10 pm

31 WEDNESDAY
☽ ⚻ ♄ **3:14 am** 12:14 am
☽ ☌ ♆ **4:31 am** 1:31 am
☿ ☌ ♃ **6:40 am** 3:40 am
☽ ☌ ♀ **1:34 pm** 10:34 am
☽ ⚺ ♃ **5:18 pm** 2:18 pm
☽ ⚺ ☿ **6:21 pm** 3:21 pm
☽ ✶ ♇ **9:55 pm** 6:55 pm
☽ ✶ ♂ 11:49 pm

Eastern time in bold type
Pacific time in medium type

DECEMBER 2008

DATE	S.TIME	SUN	MOON	N.NODE	MERCURY	VENUS	MARS	JUPITER	SATURN	URANUS	NEPTUNE	PLUTO	CERES	PALLAS	JUNO	VESTA	CHIRON
1 Mon	04:40:54	09♐09'51	14♑51	11≈02	12♐47	21♑49	10♐34	22♑30	20♍55	18♓45	21≈42	00♑08	08♍02	14♊11	09♍57	00≈25	16≈46
2 Tue	04:44:50	10 10 42	26 40	10 58R	13 41	23 00	11 18	22 35	20 58	18 45	21 43	00 10	08 17	13 51R	10 19	00 18R	16 48
3 Wed	04:48:47	11 11 34	08≈34	10 57	15 15	24 10	12 01	22 47	21 01	18 45	21 44	00 12	08 31	13 31	10 41	00 12	16 50
4 Thu	04:52:43	12 12 26	20 37	10 57	16 49	25 21	12 45	22 59	21 04	18 46	21 45	00 14	08 45	13 11	11 03	00 06	16 53
5 Fri	04:56:40	13 13 20	02♓54	10D 58	18 23	26 31	13 29	23 12	21 07	18 46	21 46	00 17	08 59	12 51	11 25	00 01	16 56
6 Sat	05:00:37	14 14 14	15 30	10 59	19 57	27 41	14 13	23 24	21 10	18 46	21 47	00 19	09 13	12 30	11 47	29♑56	16 58
7 Sun	05:04:33	15 15 08	28 30	10 58	21 31	28 51	14 57	23 37	21 12	18 47	21 48	00 21	09 26	12 10	12 09	29 52	17 01
8 Mon	05:08:30	16 16 04	11♈57	10 55	23 04	00≈01	15 41	23 49	21 15	18 47	21 50	00 23	09 39	11 49	12 32	29 48	17 03
9 Tue	05:12:26	17 17 00	25 55	10 50	24 38	01 11	16 25	24 02	21 18	18 48	21 51	00 25	09 52	11 29	12 54	29 45	17 06
10 Wed	05:16:23	18 17 57	10♉22	10 42	26 12	02 21	17 09	24 15	21 20	18 48	21 52	00 27	10 04	11 09	13 17	29 42	17 09
11 Thu	05:20:19	19 18 55	25 15	10 34	27 46	03 30	17 53	24 28	21 22	18 49	21 53	00 30	10 16	10 49	13 39	29 39	17 12
12 Fri	05:24:16	20 19 53	10♊26	10 26	29 20	04 40	18 37	24 41	21 24	18 50	21 55	00 32	10 28	10 28	14 02	29 37	17 14
13 Sat	05:28:13	21 20 53	25 45	10 19	00♑54	05 49	19 21	24 54	21 27	18 50	21 56	00 34	10 39	10 09	14 25	29 35	17 17
14 Sun	05:32:09	22 21 53	11♋04	10 14	02 28	06 58	20 06	25 07	21 29	18 51	21 57	00 36	10 50	09 49	14 47	29 34	17 20
15 Mon	05:36:06	23 22 54	26 04	10 11D	04 02	08 07	20 50	25 20	21 30	18 52	21 59	00 38	11 01	09 30	15 10	29 33D	17 23
16 Tue	05:40:02	24 23 55	10♌37	10 11	05 36	09 16	21 34	25 33	21 32	18 53	22 00	00 40	11 12	09 11	15 33	29 33	17 26
17 Wed	05:43:59	25 24 58	25 00	10 11	07 10	10 25	22 19	25 46	21 34	18 54	22 01	00 42	11 22	08 52	15 56	29 33	17 29
18 Thu	05:47:55	26 26 00	08♍49	10 12	08 43	11 34	23 03	25 59	21 36	18 55	22 03	00 45	11 32	08 33	16 19	29 34	17 33
19 Fri	05:51:52	27 27 03	22 11	10 13R	10 17	12 42	23 48	26 13	21 37	18 56	22 04	00 47	11 41	08 15	16 42	29 35	17 36
20 Sat	05:55:48	28 28 11	05♎10	10 13	11 50	13 50	24 32	26 26	21 38	18 57	22 06	00 49	11 51	07 58	17 05	29 36	17 39
21 Sun	05:59:45	29 29 18	17 49	10 11	13 23	14 58	25 17	26 39	21 40	18 58	22 07	00 51	11 59	07 41	17 28	29 38	17 42
22 Mon	06:03:42	00♑30 24	00♏30	10 07	14 56	16 06	26 02	26 53	21 41	18 59	22 09	00 53	12 08	07 24	17 51	29 40	17 46
23 Tue	06:07:38	01 31 32	12 23	09 55	16 28	17 14	26 47	27 06	21 42	19 01	22 11	00 56	12 16	07 08	18 15	29 43	17 49
24 Wed	06:11:35	02 32 40	24 25	09 48	18 00	18 22	27 31	27 20	21 43	19 02	22 12	00 58	12 24	06 52	18 38	29 46	17 52
25 Thu	06:15:31	03 33 49	06♐21	09 41	19 31	19 29	28 16	27 33	21 44	19 03	22 14	01 00	12 31	06 37	19 01	29 50	17 56
26 Fri	06:19:28	04 34 59	18 12	09 35	21 01	20 36	29 01	27 47	21 45	19 05	22 15	01 02	12 38	06 23	19 25	29 54	17 59
27 Sat	06:23:24	05 36 09	00♑02	09 30	22 30	21 43	29 46	28 00	21 45	19 06	22 17	01 04	12 45	06 09	19 48	29 58	18 03
28 Sun	06:27:21	06 37 19	11 51	09 27	23 58	22 50	00♑31	28 14	21 45	19 08	22 19	01 07	12 51	05 56	20 12	00≈03	18 06
29 Mon	06:31:17	07 38 29	23 42	09 27	25 24	23 57	01 16	28 28	21 46	19 09	22 21	01 09	12 57	05 44	20 35	00 08	18 10
30 Tue	06:35:14	08 39 40	05≈37	09 26D	26 48	25 03	02 01	28 42	21 46	19 11	22 22	01 11	13 02	05 32	20 59	00 14	18 14
31 Wed	06:39:11	09 40 50	17 37	09 26	28 10	26 09	02 46	28 57	21 46R	19 13	22 24	01 13	13 07	05 20	21 23	00 20	18 17

EPHEMERIS CALCULATED FOR 12 MIDNIGHT GREENWICH MEAN TIME. ALL OTHER DATA AND FACING ASPECTARIAN PAGE IN **EASTERN TIME (BOLD)** AND PACIFIC TIME (REGULAR).

JANUARY 2009

☽ Last Aspect day	ET / hr:mn / PT	asp	☽ Ingress sign day	ET / hr:mn / PT
3	**3:50 am** 12:50 am	✶♃	♈ 3	**4:50 am** 1:50 am
4	**9:44 pm** 6:44 pm	✶♆	♉ 5	**10:46 am** 7:46 am
6	10:05 pm	□♆	♊ 7	**1:11 pm** 10:11 am
7	**1:05 am**	□♆	♊ 7	**1:11 pm** 10:11 am
8	10:39 pm	△♆	♋ 9	**1:14 pm** 10:14 am
9	**1:39 am**	△♆	♋ 9	**1:14 pm** 10:14 am
10	**11:26 pm** 8:26 pm	✶♄	♌ 11	**12:41 pm** 9:41 am
12	10:38 pm	☍♆	♍ 13	**1:33 pm** 10:33 am
13	**1:38 am**	☍♆	♍ 13	**1:33 pm** 10:33 am
15	**9:37 am** 6:37 am	△☉	♎ 15	**5:30 pm** 2:30 pm

☽ Last Aspect day	ET / hr:mn / PT	asp	☽ Ingress sign day	ET / hr:mn / PT
17	**9:46 pm** 6:46 pm	□☉	♏ 17	10:20 pm
17	**9:46 pm** 6:46 pm	□☉	♏ 18	**1:20 am**
19	**10:36 pm** 7:36 pm	□♆	♐ 20	**12:30 pm** 9:30 am
22	**11:23 am** 8:23 am	✶♆	♑ 22	10:18 pm
22	**11:23 am** 8:23 am	✶♆	♑ 23	**1:18 am**
25	**4:08 am** 1:08 am	☌☿	♒ 25	**1:56 pm** 10:56 am
27	**12:12 pm** 9:12 am	☌♆	♓ 27	10:12 pm
27	**12:12 pm** 9:12 am	☌♆	♓ 28	**1:12 am**
30	**4:23 am** 1:23 am	☌♀	♈ 30	**10:25 am** 7:25 am

☽ Phases & Eclipses phase	day	ET / hr:mn / PT
2nd Quarter	4	**6:56 am** 3:56 am
Full Moon	10	**10:27 pm** 7:27 pm
4th Quarter	17	**9:46 pm** 6:46 pm
New Moon	25	11:55 pm
New Moon	26	**2:55 am**
☄	26	6° ♒ 30'

Planet Ingress		day	ET / hr:mn / PT
☿	♒	1	**4:51 am** 1:51 am
♀	♓	3	**7:35 am** 4:35 am
♃	♒	5	**10:41 am** 7:41 am
☉	♒	19	**5:40 pm** 2:40 pm
☿	♑	20	9:36 pm
☿	♑	21	**12:36 am**
⚵	♒	21	**6:58 am** 3:58 am

Planetary Motion		day	ET / hr:mn / PT
⚳	℞	11	**8:06 am** 5:06 am
☿	℞	11	**11:43 am** 8:43 am
♀	D	14	**2:51 pm** 11:51 am
☿	D	31	11:10 pm

1 THURSDAY
☽✶♂ **2:49 am**
☽✶☉ **6:09 pm** 3:09 pm

2 FRIDAY
☿⚺♇ **6:19 am** 3:19 am
☽☌♅ **8:41 am** 5:41 am
☽☍♄ **1:23 pm** 10:23 am
☽⚺♆ **2:45 pm** 11:45 am
♀⚺♃ **5:43 pm** 2:43 pm

3 SATURDAY
☽✶♃ **3:50 am** 12:50 am
☽⚺♀ **4:34 am** 1:34 am
☽□♇ **7:20 am** 4:20 am
☽✶☿ **9:42 am** 6:42 am
☽□♂ **3:18 pm** 12:18 pm

4 SUNDAY
☽□☉ **6:56 am** 3:56 am
♀✶♇ **2:32 pm** 11:32 am
☽⚺♅ **4:03 pm** 1:03 pm
☽⚻♄ **8:18 pm** 5:18 pm
☽✶♆ **9:44 pm** 6:44 pm

5 MONDAY
☽□♃ **10:46 am** 7:46 am
☽△♇ **1:14 pm** 10:14 am
☽✶♀ **3:05 pm** 12:05 pm
☽□☿ **7:28 pm** 4:28 pm
☽△♂ **11:34 pm** 8:34 pm

Eastern time in bold type
Pacific time in medium type

6 TUESDAY
☽△☉ **3:08 pm** 12:08 pm
☽✶♅ **7:46 pm** 4:46 pm
☽△♄ **11:35 pm** 8:35 pm
☽□♆ 10:05 pm

7 WEDNESDAY
☽□♆ **1:05 am**
☽△♃ **2:00 pm** 11:00 am
☽⚻♇ **3:38 pm** 12:38 pm
☽□♀ **9:09 pm** 6:09 pm
☽△☿ 9:02 pm

8 THURSDAY
☽△☿ **12:02 am**
☽⚻♂ **3:55 am** 12:55 am
☽⚻☉ **7:36 pm** 4:36 pm
☽□♅ **8:34 pm** 5:34 pm
☽□♄ 9:05 pm
☽△♆ 10:39 pm

9 FRIDAY
☽□♄ **12:05 am**
☽△♆ **1:39 am**
☉✶♅ **10:28 am** 7:28 am
☽⚻♃ **2:46 pm** 11:46 am
☽☍♇ **3:43 pm** 12:43 pm
☽△♀ 9:31 pm
☽⚻☿ 10:10 pm

10 SATURDAY
☽△♀ **12:31 am**
☽⚻☿ **1:10 am**
☽☍♂ **6:04 am** 3:04 am
☿⚺♀ **12:14 pm** 9:14 am
☽△♅ **8:06 pm** 5:06 pm
☽☍☉ **10:27 pm** 7:27 pm
☽✶♄ **11:26 pm** 8:26 pm
☽⚻♆ 10:10 pm

11 SUNDAY
☽⚻♆ **1:10 am**
☉△♄ **1:02 pm** 10:02 am
☽☍♃ **2:59 pm** 11:59 am
☽⚻♇ **3:18 pm** 12:18 pm
☽☍☿ 10:03 pm

12 MONDAY
☽☍☿ **1:03 am**
☽⚻♀ **3:43 am** 12:43 am
☽⚻♂ **8:23 am** 5:23 am
♃⚺♇ **2:51 pm** 11:51 am
☉⚺♆ **4:18 pm** 1:18 pm
☽⚻♅ **8:23 pm** 5:23 pm
☽⚺♄ **11:39 pm** 8:39 pm
☽☍♆ 10:38 pm
☽⚻☉ 11:19 pm

13 TUESDAY
☽☍♆ **1:38 am**
☽⚻☉ **2:19 am**
☽△♇ **4:25 pm** 1:25 pm

☽⚻♃ **4:47 pm** 1:47 pm
☽⚻☿ 10:32 pm

14 WEDNESDAY
☽⚻☿ **1:32 am**
☽☍♀ **9:20 am** 6:20 am
☽△♂ **1:14 pm** 10:14 am
☽☍♅ **11:15 pm** 8:15 pm
☽☌♄ 11:31 pm

15 THURSDAY
☽☌♄ **2:31 am**
☽⚻♆ **4:52 am** 1:52 am
☽△☉ **9:37 am** 6:37 am
☽□♇ **8:43 pm** 5:43 pm
☽△♃ **9:55 pm** 6:55 pm

16 FRIDAY
☽△☿ **3:43 am** 12:43 am
☽⚻♀ **7:18 pm** 4:18 pm
☽□♂ **10:21 pm** 7:21 pm

17 SATURDAY
☽⚻♅ **5:55 am** 2:55 am
☽⚺♄ **9:09 am** 6:09 am
☽△♆ **11:56 am** 8:56 am
☽□☉ **9:46 pm** 6:46 pm

18 SUNDAY
☽✶♇ **4:56 am** 1:56 am
☽□♃ **7:09 am** 4:09 am
☽□☿ **7:53 am** 4:53 am
☿☌♃ **2:07 pm** 11:07 am

19 MONDAY
☽△♀ **9:59 am** 6:59 am
☽✶♂ **11:58 am** 8:58 am
☿⚺♇ **12:55 pm** 9:55 am
☽△♅ **4:18 pm** 1:18 pm
☽✶♄ **7:21 pm** 4:21 pm
☽□♆ **10:36 pm** 7:36 pm

20 TUESDAY
☉☌☿ **10:59 am** 7:59 am
☽✶☿ **1:41 pm** 10:41 am
☽✶☉ **2:15 pm** 11:15 am
☽⚺♇ **4:25 pm** 1:25 pm
☽✶♃ **7:46 pm** 4:46 pm

21 WEDNESDAY
☉⚺♇ **4:25 pm** 1:25 pm

22 THURSDAY
☽□♀ **3:43 am** 12:43 am
☽⚺♂ **4:31 am** 1:31 am
☽□♅ **4:59 am** 1:59 am
☽□♄ **7:42 am** 4:42 am
☽✶♆ **11:23 am** 8:23 am
♂✶♅ **11:59 am** 8:59 am
♀☌♅ **8:01 pm** 5:01 pm
☽⚺☿ **8:35 pm** 5:35 pm

23 FRIDAY
☽☌♇ **5:26 am** 2:26 am
☽⚺☉ **8:49 am** 5:49 am

☽⚺♃ **9:53 am** 6:53 am
☉☌♃ 9:44 pm

24 SATURDAY
☉☌♃ **12:44 am**
♂△♄ **3:04 am** 12:04 am
♀☍♄ **3:15 am** 12:15 am
♀✶♂ **4:05 am** 1:05 am
☽✶♅ **6:04 pm** 3:04 pm
☽△♄ **8:20 pm** 5:20 pm
☽☌♂ **9:35 pm** 6:35 pm
☽✶♀ **9:51 pm** 6:51 pm
☽⚺♆ 9:23 pm

25 SUNDAY
☽⚺♆ **12:23 am**
☽☌☿ **4:08 am** 1:08 am
☽⚺♇ **6:10 pm** 3:10 pm
☽☌♃ **11:36 pm** 8:36 pm
☽☌☉ 11:55 pm

26 MONDAY
☽☌☉ **2:55 am**
♀⚺♆ **7:29 am** 4:29 am
☿✶♀ **6:31 pm** 3:31 pm
♂⚺♆ **6:58 pm** 3:58 pm
☿☌♂ 10:11 pm

27 TUESDAY
☿☌♂ **1:11 am**
☽⚺♅ **6:06 am** 3:06 am
☿⚺♆ **7:22 am** 4:22 am

☽⚻♄ **7:52 am** 4:52 am
☽⚺☿ **11:57 am** 8:57 am
☽☌♆ **12:12 pm** 9:12 am
☽⚺♂ **1:18 pm** 10:18 am
☽⚺♀ **2:26 pm** 11:26 am

28 WEDNESDAY
☽✶♇ **5:27 am** 2:27 am
☽⚺♃ **11:43 am** 8:43 am
☽⚺☉ **7:01 pm** 4:01 pm

29 THURSDAY
☽☌♅ **4:15 pm** 1:15 pm
☽☍♄ **5:31 pm** 2:31 pm
☽✶☿ **7:33 pm** 4:33 pm
☽⚺♆ **10:05 pm** 7:05 pm
☽✶♂ 11:41 pm

30 FRIDAY
☽✶♂ **2:41 am**
☽☌♀ **4:23 am** 1:23 am
☽□♇ **2:38 pm** 11:38 am
☽✶♃ **9:33 pm** 6:33 pm

31 SATURDAY
☽✶☉ **8:16 am** 5:16 am
☽⚺♅ 9:00 pm
☽⚻♄ 9:48 pm
☽□☿ 11:21 pm

JANUARY 2009

DATE	S.TIME	SUN	MOON	N.NODE	MERCURY	VENUS	MARS	JUPITER	SATURN	URANUS	NEPTUNE	PLUTO	CERES	PALLAS	JUNO	VESTA	CHIRON
1 Thu	06:43:07	10♑42 11	29 ≈ 46	09 ≈ 27	29 ♑ 29	27 ≈ 15	03 ♑ 39	28 ♑ 55	21 ♍ 46	19 ♓ 14	22 ≈ 26	01 ♑ 15	13 ♍ 12	05 ♊ 10	21 ♑ 46	00 ♑ 26	18 ≈ 21
2 Fri	06:47:04	11 43 11	12 ♓ 08	09 29	00 ≈ 44	28 21	04 16	29 09	21 46 R	19 16	22 28	01 18	13 16	05 00 R	22 10	00 33	18 25
3 Sat	06:51:00	12 44 21	24 45	09 31	01 56	29 26	05 02	29 23	21 46	19 18	22 30	01 20	13 20	04 51	22 34	00 40	18 29
4 Sun	06:54:57	13 45 31	07 ♈ 41	09 32 R	03 03	00 ♓ 31	05 47	29 37	21 45	19 19	22 33	01 22	13 24	04 43	22 58	00 47	18 32
5 Mon	06:58:53	14 46 40	21 01	09 32	04 06	01 36	06 32	29 51	21 45	19 21	22 35	01 24	13 27	04 35	23 22	00 55	18 36
6 Tue	07:02:50	15 47 49	04 ♉ 43	09 31	05 02	02 40	07 18	00 ≈ 05	21 44	19 23	22 37	01 26	13 29	04 28	23 45	01 03	18 40
7 Wed	07:06:46	16 48 58	18 58	09 28	05 51	03 44	08 03	00 19	21 43	19 25	22 39	01 28	13 31	04 22	24 09	01 11	18 44
8 Thu	07:10:43	17 50 06	03 ♊ 34	09 26	06 33	04 48	08 48	00 33	21 42	19 27	22 41	01 30	13 33	04 17	24 33	01 20	18 48
9 Fri	07:14:40	18 51 14	18 30	09 23	07 06	05 52	09 34	00 47	21 41	19 29	22 43	01 33	13 34	04 12	24 57	01 30	18 52
10 Sat	07:18:36	19 52 22	03 ♋ 39	09 20	07 29	06 55	10 19	01 01	21 40	19 31	22 45	01 35	13 35	04 09	25 21	01 39	18 56
11 Sun	07:22:33	20 53 30	18 52	09 18	07 43 R	07 58	11 05	01 15	21 39	19 33	22 47	01 37	13 36 R	04 05	25 45	01 49	19 00
12 Mon	07:26:29	21 54 37	03 ♌ 47	09 17 D	07 45	09 00	11 50	01 29	21 38	19 36	22 49	01 39	13 36	04 03	26 10	01 59	19 04
13 Tue	07:30:26	22 55 43	18 47	09 17	07 36	10 02	12 36	01 43	21 36	19 38	22 51	01 41	13 35	04 01	26 34	02 10	19 08
14 Wed	07:34:22	23 56 50	03 ♍ 15	09 18	07 14	11 04	13 22	01 57	21 35	19 40	22 53	01 43	13 35	04 00 D	26 58	02 20	19 12
15 Thu	07:38:19	24 57 56	17 16	09 19	06 42	12 05	14 07	02 11	21 33	19 42	22 55	01 45	13 33	04 00	27 22	02 31	19 16
16 Fri	07:42:16	25 59 02	00 ♎ 50	09 21	05 58	13 06	14 53	02 25	21 32	19 45	22 57	01 47	13 32	04 01	27 46	02 43	19 20
17 Sat	07:46:12	27 00 07	13 58	09 22	05 03	14 07	15 39	02 40	21 30	19 47	22 59	01 49	13 29	04 02	28 11	02 54	19 25
18 Sun	07:50:09	28 01 13	26 42	09 22 R	04 00	15 07	16 25	02 54	21 28	19 49	23 02	01 51	13 27	04 04	28 35	03 06	19 29
19 Mon	07:54:05	29 02 18	09 ♏ 06	09 22	02 50	16 06	17 11	03 08	21 26	19 52	23 04	01 53	13 24	04 06	28 59	03 19	19 33
20 Tue	07:58:02	00 ≈ 03 22	21 15	09 21	01 35	17 05	17 57	03 22	21 24	19 54	23 06	01 55	13 20	04 10	29 23	03 31	19 37
21 Wed	08:01:58	01 04 26	03 ♐ 12	09 20	00 18	18 04	18 43	03 36	21 22	19 57	23 08	01 57	13 16	04 14	29 48	03 44	19 41
22 Thu	08:05:55	02 05 32	15 05	09 20	29 ♑ 03	19 02	19 29	03 50	21 19	19 59	23 10	01 59	13 12	04 18	00 ≈ 12	03 57	19 46
23 Fri	08:09:51	03 06 36	26 54	09 19	27 46	20 00	20 15	04 05	21 17	20 02	23 12	02 01	13 07	04 24	00 37	04 11	19 50
24 Sat	08:13:48	04 07 40	08 ♑ 43	09 17	26 35	20 57	21 01	04 19	21 14	20 04	23 15	02 03	13 02	04 30	01 01	04 24	19 54
25 Sun	08:17:45	05 08 42	20 35	09 17	25 30	21 53	21 47	04 33	21 14	20 07	23 17	02 05	12 56	04 36	01 26	04 38	19 58
26 Mon	08:21:41	06 09 43	02 ≈ 32	09 16 D	24 32	22 49	22 33	04 47	21 12	20 10	23 19	02 07	12 50	04 43	01 50	04 52	20 03
27 Tue	08:25:38	07 10 44	14 36	09 16	23 42	23 44	23 19	05 01	21 09	20 12	23 21	02 09	12 43	04 51	02 15	05 07	20 07
28 Wed	08:29:34	08 11 44	26 49	09 16	23 01	24 39	24 05	05 16	21 06	20 15	23 23	02 11	12 36	05 00	02 39	05 21	20 11
29 Thu	08:33:31	09 12 43	09 ♓ 14	09 17 R	22 29	25 33	24 51	05 30	21 04	20 18	23 26	02 12	12 29	05 09	03 04	05 36	20 16
30 Fri	08:37:27	10 13 41	21 48	09 17	22 05	26 26	25 38	05 44	21 01	20 21	23 28	02 14	12 21	05 19	03 28	05 51	20 20
31 Sat	08:41:24	11 14 39	04 ♈ 37	09 16	21 51	27 19	26 24	05 58	20 58	20 24	23 30	02 16	12 13	05 29	03 53	06 07	20 25

EPHEMERIS CALCULATED FOR 12 MIDNIGHT GREENWICH MEAN TIME. ALL OTHER DATA AND FACING ASPECTARIAN PAGE IN EASTERN TIME (BOLD) AND PACIFIC TIME (REGULAR).

FEBRUARY 2009

☽ Last Aspect day	ET / hr:mn / PT	asp	☽ Ingress sign day	ET / hr:mn / PT
1	**1:08 pm** 10:08 am	□♂	♉ 1	**5:08 pm** 2:08 pm
3	**8:27 pm** 5:27 pm	△♂	♊ 3	**9:14 pm** 6:14 pm
5	**12:44 pm** 9:44 am	△♆	♋ 5	**11:05 pm** 8:05 pm
7	**2:07 pm** 11:07 am	☍☿	♌ 7	**11:43 pm** 8:43 pm
9	**2:28 pm** 11:28 am	☍♆	♍ 9	9:38 pm
9	**2:28 pm** 11:28 am	☍♆	♍ 10	**12:38 am**
11	**11:17 pm** 8:17 pm	△☿	♎ 12	**3:33 am** 12:33 am
14	**9:46 am** 6:46 am	□☿	♏ 14	**9:50 am** 6:50 am
16	**4:37 pm** 1:37 pm	□☉	♐ 16	**7:53 pm** 4:53 pm
18	**8:36 pm** 5:36 pm	⚹♆	♑ 19	**8:25 am** 5:25 am

☽ Last Aspect day	ET / hr:mn / PT	asp	☽ Ingress sign day	ET / hr:mn / PT
21	**4:01 am** 1:01 am	⚹♅	♒ 21	**9:06 pm** 6:06 pm
23	**9:08 pm** 6:08 pm	☌♆	♓ 24	**7:59 am** 4:59 am
25	10:09 pm	☌♅	♈ 26	**4:24 pm** 1:24 pm
26	**1:09 am**	☌♅	♈ 26	**4:24 pm** 1:24 pm
28	**12:51 pm** 9:51 am	⚹♆	♉ 28	**10:33 pm** 7:33 pm

☽ Phases & Eclipses phase	day	ET / hr:mn / PT
2nd Quarter	2	**6:13 pm** 3:13 pm
Full Moon	9	**9:49 am** 6:49 am
●	9	20° ♌ 52'
4th Quarter	16	**4:37 pm** 1:37 pm
New Moon	24	**8:35 pm** 5:35 pm

Planet Ingress	day	ET / hr:mn / PT
♀ ♈	2	**10:41 pm** 7:41 pm
♂ ♒	4	**10:55 am** 7:55 am
☿ ♒	14	**10:39 am** 7:39 am
☉ ♓	18	**7:46 am** 4:46 am

Planetary Motion	day	ET / hr:mn / PT
☿ D	1	**2:10 am**

1 SUNDAY
☽⚺♅ **12:00 am**
☽⚻♄ **12:48 am**
☽□☿ **2:21 am**
☽⚹♆ **5:32 am** 2:32 am
☽□♂ **1:08 pm** 10:08 am
☽⚺♀ **3:11 pm** 12:11 pm
☽△♇ **9:17 pm** 6:17 pm

2 MONDAY
☽□♃ **4:43 am** 1:43 am
☽□☉ **6:13 pm** 3:13 pm

3 TUESDAY
☽⚹♅ **5:07 am** 2:07 am
☽△♄ **5:29 am** 2:29 am
☽△☿ **7:41 am** 4:41 am
☽□♆ **10:20 am** 7:20 am
☽△♂ **8:27 pm** 5:27 pm
☽⚹♀ **10:38 pm** 7:38 pm
☽⚻♇ 10:17 pm

4 WEDNESDAY
☽⚻♇ **1:17 am**
☽△♃ **9:08 am** 6:08 am
☽△☉ 10:00 pm

5 THURSDAY
☽△☉ **1:00 am**
♄☍♅ **5:56 am** 2:56 am
☽□♄ **7:45 am** 4:45 am
☽□♅ **7:46 am** 4:46 am

☽⚻☿ **11:23 am** 8:23 am
☽△♆ **12:44 pm** 9:44 am
♀□♇ **11:25 pm** 8:25 pm
☽⚻♂ 10:06 pm

6 FRIDAY
☽⚻♂ **1:06 am**
☽☍♇ **3:06 am** 12:06 am
☽□♀ **3:18 am** 12:18 am
☽⚻♃ **11:23 am** 8:23 am
☿⚺♆ 11:02 pm

7 SATURDAY
☿⚺♆ **2:02 am**
☽⚻☉ **5:36 am** 2:36 am
☽⚹♄ **8:25 am** 5:25 am
☽△♅ **8:48 am** 5:48 am
☽⚻♆ **1:38 pm** 10:38 am
☽☍☿ **2:07 pm** 11:07 am
♂⚺♇ **4:17 pm** 1:17 pm

8 SUNDAY
☽⚻♇ **3:46 am** 12:46 am
☽☍♂ **4:23 am** 1:23 am
☽△♀ **6:31 am** 3:31 am
☽☍♃ **12:42 pm** 9:42 am
☉⚻♄ **8:38 pm** 5:38 pm

9 MONDAY
☉⚺♅ **6:41 am** 3:41 am
☽⚺♄ **8:51 am** 5:51 am
☽⚻♅ **9:37 am** 6:37 am

☽☍☉ **9:49 am** 6:49 am
☽☍♆ **2:28 pm** 11:28 am
☽⚻☿ **5:24 pm** 2:24 pm

10 TUESDAY
☽△♇ **4:53 am** 1:53 am
☽⚻♂ **8:12 am** 5:12 am
☽⚻♀ **10:14 am** 7:14 am
☽⚻♃ **2:49 pm** 11:49 am

11 WEDNESDAY
☽☌♄ **10:43 am** 7:43 am
☽☍♅ **11:55 am** 8:55 am
☽⚻☉ **3:52 pm** 12:52 pm
☽⚻♆ **4:59 pm** 1:59 pm
☽△☿ **11:17 pm** 8:17 pm

12 THURSDAY
☉☌♆ **7:40 am** 4:40 am
☽□♇ **8:08 am** 5:08 am
☽△♂ **2:40 pm** 11:40 am
☽☍♀ **4:28 pm** 1:28 pm
☽△♃ **7:29 pm** 4:29 pm

13 FRIDAY
☽⚺♄ **3:32 pm** 12:32 pm
☽⚻♅ **5:19 pm** 2:19 pm
☽△♆ **10:40 pm** 7:40 pm
☽△☉ 10:51 pm

14 SATURDAY
☽△☉ **1:51 am**
☽□☿ **9:46 am** 6:46 am
☽⚹♇ **2:52 pm** 11:52 am

☽□♂ 10:24 pm
☽⚻♀ 11:39 pm

15 SUNDAY
☽□♂ **1:24 am**
☽⚻♀ **2:39 am**
☽□♃ **3:59 am** 12:59 am
☽⚹♄ 9:05 pm
☽△♅ 11:33 pm

16 MONDAY
☽⚹♄ **12:05 am**
☽△♅ **2:33 am**
☽□♆ **8:11 am** 5:11 am
☽□☉ **4:37 pm** 1:37 pm
☿⚺♇ **10:43 pm** 7:43 pm
♀⚹♃ **11:47 pm** 8:47 pm
☽⚺♇ 10:20 pm
☽⚹☿ 10:36 pm

17 TUESDAY
☽⚺♇ **1:20 am**
☽⚹☿ **1:36 am**
♂☌♃ **11:27 am** 8:27 am
☽⚹♃ **4:12 pm** 1:12 pm
☽⚹♂ **4:26 pm** 1:26 pm
☽△♀ **4:41 pm** 1:41 pm

18 WEDNESDAY
♀⚹♂ **4:31 am** 1:31 am
☽□♄ **11:40 am** 8:40 am
☽□♅ **2:51 pm** 11:51 am
☽⚹♆ **8:36 pm** 5:36 pm

19 THURSDAY
☽⚹☉ **10:43 am** 7:43 am
☽☌♇ **2:06 pm** 11:06 am
☽⚺☿ **9:03 pm** 6:03 pm

20 FRIDAY
☽⚺♃ **6:16 am** 3:16 am
☽□♀ **8:21 am** 5:21 am
☽⚺♂ **9:35 am** 6:35 am
☽△♄ 9:11 pm

21 SATURDAY
☽△♄ **12:11 am**
☉⚹♇ **3:03 am** 12:03 am
☽⚹♅ **4:01 am** 1:01 am
☽⚺♆ **9:38 am** 6:38 am
☽⚺♇ 11:47 pm

22 SUNDAY
☽⚺♇ **2:47 am**
☽⚺☉ **4:55 am** 1:55 am
☽☌☿ **4:33 pm** 1:33 pm
☽☌♃ **7:37 pm** 4:37 pm
☽⚹♀ **10:48 pm** 7:48 pm
☽☌♂ 10:48 pm

23 MONDAY
☽☌♂ **1:48 am**
☽⚻♄ **11:29 am** 8:29 am
☽⚺♅ **3:48 pm** 12:48 pm
☽☌♆ **9:08 pm** 6:08 pm
☿☌♃ 10:52 pm

24 TUESDAY
☿☌♃ **1:52 am**
☽⚹♇ **1:33 pm** 10:33 am
☽☌☉ **8:35 pm** 5:35 pm

25 WEDNESDAY
☽⚺♃ **6:38 am** 3:38 am
☽⚺☿ **9:30 am** 6:30 am
☽⚺♀ **10:23 am** 7:23 am
☽⚺♂ **3:16 pm** 12:16 pm
☿⚹♀ **7:59 pm** 4:59 pm
☽☍♄ **8:26 pm** 5:26 pm
☽☌♅ 10:09 pm

26 THURSDAY
☽☌♅ **1:09 am**
☽⚺♆ **6:10 am** 3:10 am
☽□♇ **9:48 pm** 6:48 pm

27 FRIDAY
☽⚺☉ **9:04 am** 6:04 am
☽⚹♃ **3:03 pm** 12:03 pm
☽☌♀ **6:57 pm** 3:57 pm
☽⚹☿ **11:20 pm** 8:20 pm
☽⚹♂ 10:48 pm

28 SATURDAY
☽⚹♂ **1:48 am**
☽⚻♄ **3:01 am** 12:01 am
☽⚺♅ **8:07 am** 5:07 am
☽⚹♆ **12:51 pm** 9:51 am
♂⚻♄ **8:47 pm** 5:47 pm

Eastern time in bold type
Pacific time in medium type

FEBRUARY 2009

DATE	S.TIME	SUN	MOON	N.NODE	MERCURY	VENUS	MARS	JUPITER	SATURN	URANUS	NEPTUNE	PLUTO	CERES	PALLAS	JUNO	VESTA	CHIRON
1 Sun	08:45:20	12♒15 33	17♈41	09♒16R	21♑45 D	28♓11	27♑10	06♒12	20♍54	20♓26	23♒30	02♑18	12♍04	05♊40	04♋17	06♉22	20♒29
2 Mon	08:49:17	13 16 27	01♉03	09 16 D	21 47	29 02	27 56	06 27	20 51R	20 29	23 32	02 20	11 55R	05 51	04 42	06 38	20 33
3 Tue	08:53:14	14 17 20	14 42	09 16	21 55	29 52	28 43	06 41	20 48	20 32	23 35	02 21	11 46	06 03	05 06	06 54	20 38
4 Wed	08:57:10	15 18 11	28 41	09 16	22 11	00♈42	29 29	06 55	20 45	20 35	23 37	02 23	11 36	06 16	05 31	07 10	20 42
5 Thu	09:01:07	16 19 01	12♊57	09 17	22 33	01 31	29 29	07 09	20 41	20 38	23 39	02 25	11 26	06 29	05 56	07 27	20 46
6 Fri	09:05:03	17 19 50	27 30	09 17	23 01	02 18	01♒02	07 23	20 38	20 41	23 41	02 27	11 16	06 43	06 21	07 44	20 51
7 Sat	09:09:00	18 20 37	12♋14	09 18	23 34	03 05	01 49	07 37	20 34	20 44	23 44	02 28	11 05	06 57	06 45	08 00	20 55
8 Sun	09:12:56	19 21 23	27 05	09 18R	24 12	03 51	02 35	07 51	20 30	20 47	23 46	02 30	10 54	07 11	07 10	08 18	21 00
9 Mon	09:16:53	20 22 07	11♌54	09 18	24 54	04 36	03 22	08 05	20 27	20 50	23 48	02 31	10 43	07 26	07 35	08 35	21 04
10 Tue	09:20:49	21 22 50	26 35	09 18	25 40	05 19	04 08	08 19	20 23	20 53	23 50	02 33	10 32	07 42	07 59	08 52	21 08
11 Wed	09:24:46	22 23 31	11♍01	09 17	26 30	06 02	04 55	08 33	20 19	20 56	23 53	02 35	10 20	07 58	08 24	09 10	21 13
12 Thu	09:28:43	23 24 11	25 05	09 15	27 24	06 44	05 41	08 47	20 15	20 59	23 55	02 36	10 08	08 14	08 49	09 28	21 17
13 Fri	09:32:39	24 24 50	08♎45	09 13	28 20	07 24	06 28	09 01	20 11	21 03	23 57	02 38	09 55	08 31	09 13	09 46	21 22
14 Sat	09:36:36	25 25 28	22 01	09 11	29 20	08 03	07 14	09 15	20 07	21 06	24 00	02 39	09 43	08 49	09 38	10 04	21 26
15 Sun	09:40:32	26 26 05	04♏52	09 09	00♒22	08 41	08 01	09 29	20 03	21 09	24 02	02 41	09 30	09 06	10 03	10 22	21 30
16 Mon	09:44:29	27 26 41	17 21	09 09 D	01 27	09 18	08 48	09 43	19 58	21 12	24 04	02 42	09 17	09 25	10 28	10 41	21 35
17 Tue	09:48:25	28 27 16	29 33	09 08	02 33	09 53	09 34	09 57	19 54	21 15	24 06	02 44	09 04	09 43	10 52	11 00	21 39
18 Wed	09:52:22	29 27 48	11♐41	09 08	03 42	10 27	10 21	10 11	19 50	21 19	24 09	02 45	08 50	10 02	11 17	11 18	21 43
19 Thu	09:56:18	00♓28 20	23 42	09 09	04 53	10 59	11 08	10 25	19 46	21 22	24 11	02 46	08 37	10 21	11 42	11 38	21 48
20 Fri	10:00:15	01 28 50	05♑52	09 11	06 06	11 30	11 55	10 38	19 41	21 25	24 13	02 48	08 23	10 41	12 07	11 57	21 52
21 Sat	10:04:12	02 29 20	17 02	09 13	07 21	11 59	12 41	10 52	19 37	21 28	24 16	02 49	08 09	11 01	12 31	12 16	21 56
22 Sun	10:08:08	03 29 47	28 57	09 14R	08 37	12 27	13 28	11 06	19 32	21 32	24 18	02 50	07 55	11 22	12 56	12 36	22 01
23 Mon	10:12:05	04 30 14	11♒11	09 15	09 55	12 53	14 15	11 19	19 28	21 35	24 20	02 52	07 42	11 42	13 21	12 55	22 05
24 Tue	10:16:01	05 30 38	23 16	09 14	11 14	13 17	15 02	11 33	19 23	21 38	24 22	02 53	07 28	12 04	13 46	13 15	22 09
25 Wed	10:19:58	06 31 01	05♓16	09 11	12 35	13 39	15 49	11 47	19 19	21 42	24 25	02 54	07 14	12 25	14 10	13 35	22 14
26 Thu	10:23:54	07 31 23	17 16	09 08	13 57	13 59	16 36	12 00	19 14	21 45	24 27	02 55	06 59	12 47	14 35	13 55	22 18
27 Fri	10:27:51	08 31 42	00♈07	09 03	15 20	14 18	17 22	12 14	19 09	21 48	24 29	02 57	06 45	13 09	15 00	14 15	22 22
28 Sat	10:31:47	09 32 00	14 36	08 58	16 45	14 34	18 09	12 27	19 05	21 52	24 31	02 58	06 31	13 31	15 25	14 36	22 27

EPHEMERIS CALCULATED FOR 12 MIDNIGHT GREENWICH MEAN TIME. ALL OTHER DATA AND FACING ASPECTARIAN PAGE IN **EASTERN TIME (BOLD)** AND PACIFIC TIME (REGULAR).

MARCH 2009

☽ Last Aspect day	ET / hr:mn / PT	asp	☽ Ingress sign	day	ET / hr:mn / PT
2	**5:42 pm** 2:42 pm	□ ♆	♊	2	11:59 pm
2	**5:42 pm** 2:42 pm	□ ♆	♊	3	**2:59 am**
4	**9:10 pm** 6:10 pm	△ ♆	♋	5	**6:07 am** 3:07 am
6	**7:29 pm** 4:29 pm	△ ♅	♌	7	**8:24 am** 5:24 am
9	**3:56 am** 12:56 am	☍ ♂	♍	9	**11:34 am** 8:34 am
10	10:48 pm	☍ ♅	♎	11	**2:46 pm** 11:46 am
11	**1:48 am**	☍ ♅	♎	11	**2:46 pm** 11:46 am
13	**6:39 pm** 3:39 pm	△ ♂	♏	13	**8:22 pm** 5:22 pm
15	**8:43 pm** 5:43 pm	△ ☉	♐	16	**5:21 am** 2:21 am
18	**1:47 pm** 10:47 am	□ ☉	♑	18	**5:18 pm** 2:18 pm

☽ Last Aspect day	ET / hr:mn / PT	asp	☽ Ingress sign	day	ET / hr:mn / PT
20	**4:06 pm** 1:06 pm	✶ ♅	♒	21	**6:06 am** 3:06 am
23	**8:09 am** 5:09 am	☌ ♆	♓	23	**5:08 pm** 2:08 pm
25	**12:53 pm** 9:53 am	☌ ♅	♈	25	10:03 pm
25	**12:53 pm** 9:53 am	☌ ♅	♈	26	**1:03 am**
27	**10:17 pm** 7:17 pm	✶ ♆	♉	28	**6:09 am** 3:09 am
29	11:00 pm	□ ♆	♊	30	**9:36 am** 6:36 am
30	**2:00 am**	□ ♆	♊	30	**9:36 pm** 6:36 am

☽ Phases & Eclipses phase	day	ET / hr:mn / PT
2nd Quarter	3	11:46 pm
2nd Quarter	4	**2:46 am**
Full Moon	10	**10:38 pm** 7:38 pm
4th Quarter	18	**1:47 pm** 10:47 am
New Moon	26	**12:06 pm** 9:06 am

Planet Ingress		day	ET / hr:mn / PT
☿	♓	8	**2:56 pm** 11:56 am
♂	♓	14	**11:20 pm** 8:20 pm
☉	♈	20	**7:43 am** 4:43 am
☿	♈	25	**3:55 pm** 12:55 pm

Planetary Motion	day	ET / hr:mn / PT
♀ ℞	6	**12:17 pm** 9:17 am

1 SUNDAY
☽ △ ♇ **3:50 am** 12:50 am
☿ ⚻ ♄ **7:56 am** 4:56 am
☽ ✶ ☉ **6:54 pm** 3:54 pm
☽ □ ♃ **9:19 pm** 6:19 pm
☿ ☌ ♂ **10:05 pm** 7:05 pm
☽ ⚺ ♀ 10:03 pm

2 MONDAY
☽ ⚺ ♀ **1:03 am**
☽ △ ♄ **7:43 am** 4:43 am
☽ □ ♂ **10:02 am** 7:02 am
☽ □ ☿ **10:42 am** 7:42 am
☽ ✶ ♅ **1:10 pm** 10:10 am
☽ □ ♆ **5:42 pm** 2:42 pm

3 TUESDAY
☽ ⚻ ♇ **8:11 am** 5:11 am
☿ ⚺ ♅ **10:35 am** 7:35 am
☉ ⚺ ♃ **12:42 pm** 9:42 am
☽ △ ♃ 10:58 pm
☉ □ ☽ 11:46 pm

4 WEDNESDAY
☽ △ ♃ **1:58 am**
☽ □ ☉ **2:46 am**
☽ ✶ ♀ **5:17 am** 2:17 am
☽ □ ♄ **11:00 am** 8:00 am
☽ △ ♂ **4:33 pm** 1:33 pm
☽ □ ♅ **4:49 pm** 1:49 pm
☽ △ ☿ **8:17 pm** 5:17 pm

☽ △ ♆ **9:10 pm** 6:10 pm
♂ ⚺ ♅ **9:41 pm** 6:41 pm

5 THURSDAY
☿ ☌ ♆ **4:39 am** 1:39 am
☽ ☍ ♇ **11:16 am** 8:16 am
☉ ⚺ ♀ **4:25 pm** 1:25 pm

6 FRIDAY
☽ ⚻ ♃ **5:27 am** 2:27 am
☽ □ ♀ **8:06 am** 5:06 am
☽ △ ☉ **9:15 am** 6:15 am
☽ ✶ ♄ **1:16 pm** 10:16 am
☽ △ ♅ **7:29 pm** 4:29 pm
☽ ⚻ ♂ **9:55 pm** 6:55 pm
☽ ⚻ ♆ **11:41 pm** 8:41 pm

7 SATURDAY
☽ ⚻ ☿ **4:46 am** 1:46 am
☽ ⚻ ♇ **1:34 pm** 10:34 am

8 SUNDAY
♂ ☌ ♆ **8:50 am** 5:50 am
☽ ☍ ♃ **9:20 am** 6:20 am
☽ △ ♀ **11:04 am** 8:04 am
☉ ☍ ♄ **3:53 pm** 12:53 pm
☽ ⚺ ♄ **4:05 pm** 1:05 pm
☽ ⚻ ☉ **4:06 pm** 1:06 pm
☽ ⚻ ♅ **10:47 pm** 7:47 pm
☽ ☍ ♆ 11:56 pm

9 MONDAY
☽ ☍ ♆ **2:56 am**
☽ ☍ ♂ **3:56 am** 12:56 am
☽ ☍ ☿ **2:10 pm** 11:10 am
☽ △ ♇ **4:49 pm** 1:49 pm

10 TUESDAY
☽ ⚻ ♃ **12:36 pm** 9:36 am
☽ ⚻ ♀ **1:10 pm** 10:10 am
☿ ✶ ♇ **1:38 pm** 10:38 am
☽ ☌ ♄ **6:26 pm** 3:26 pm
☽ ☍ ☉ **10:38 pm** 7:38 pm
☽ ☍ ♅ 10:48 pm

11 WEDNESDAY
☽ ☍ ♅ **1:48 am**
☽ ⚻ ♆ **5:59 am** 2:59 am
♀ ✶ ♃ **8:34 am** 5:34 am
☽ ⚻ ♂ **9:56 am** 6:56 am
☽ □ ♇ **8:15 pm** 5:15 pm
☽ ⚻ ☿ 9:24 pm

12 THURSDAY
☽ ⚻ ☿ **12:24 am**
☽ ☍ ♀ **4:36 pm** 1:36 pm
☽ △ ♃ **5:40 pm** 2:40 pm
☉ ☌ ♅ **9:27 pm** 6:27 pm
☽ ⚺ ♄ **10:38 pm** 7:38 pm

13 FRIDAY
☽ ⚻ ♅ **6:54 am** 3:54 am
☽ ⚻ ☉ **7:38 am** 4:38 am
☽ △ ♆ **11:14 am** 8:14 am

☽ △ ♂ **6:39 pm** 3:39 pm
☽ ✶ ♇ 11:14 pm

14 SATURDAY
☽ ✶ ♇ **2:14 am**
☽ △ ☿ **2:45 pm** 11:45 am
☽ ⚻ ♀ **10:31 pm** 7:31 pm
☽ □ ♃ 10:53 pm

15 SUNDAY
☽ □ ♃ **1:53 am**
☽ ✶ ♄ **5:52 am** 2:52 am
☉ ⚺ ♆ **8:53 am** 5:53 am
☽ △ ♅ **3:17 pm** 12:17 pm
☽ □ ♆ **7:47 pm** 4:47 pm
☽ △ ☉ **8:43 pm** 5:43 pm

16 MONDAY
☽ □ ♂ **7:24 am** 4:24 am
☽ ⚺ ♇ **11:38 am** 8:38 am
☿ ⚺ ♀ **3:00 pm** 12:00 pm

17 TUESDAY
☽ △ ♀ **7:12 am** 4:12 am
☽ □ ☿ **10:39 am** 7:39 am
☽ ✶ ♃ **1:38 pm** 10:38 am
☽ □ ♄ **4:24 pm** 1:24 pm
☽ □ ♅ 11:57 pm

18 WEDNESDAY
☽ □ ♅ **2:57 am**
☽ ✶ ♆ **7:32 am** 4:32 am
☿ ⚺ ♃ **9:03 am** 6:03 am
☽ □ ☉ **1:47 pm** 10:47 am

☽ ✶ ♂ **11:41 pm** 8:41 pm
☽ ☌ ♇ **11:51 pm** 8:51 pm
☿ ☍ ♄ 9:00 pm
♂ ✶ ♇ 11:15 pm

19 THURSDAY
☿ ☍ ♄ **12:00 am**
♂ ✶ ♇ **2:15 am**
☽ □ ♀ **5:32 pm** 2:32 pm

20 FRIDAY
☽ ⚺ ♃ **3:27 am** 12:27 am
☽ △ ♄ **4:48 am** 1:48 am
☽ ✶ ☿ **10:13 am** 7:13 am
☽ ✶ ♅ **4:06 pm** 1:06 pm
☽ ⚺ ♆ **8:33 pm** 5:33 pm

21 SATURDAY
☽ ✶ ☉ **8:08 am** 5:08 am
☽ ⚺ ♇ **12:37 pm** 9:37 am
☽ ⚺ ♂ **4:39 pm** 1:39 pm
☿ ☌ ♅ 10:02 pm

22 SUNDAY
☿ ☌ ♅ **1:02 am**
☽ ✶ ♀ **3:18 am** 12:18 pm
♃ ⚻ ♄ **12:46 pm** 9:46 am
☽ ⚻ ♄ **4:27 pm** 1:27 pm
☽ ☌ ♃ **4:32 pm** 1:32 pm

23 MONDAY
☽ ⚺ ♅ **3:59 am** 12:59 am
☿ ⚺ ♆ **5:16 am** 2:16 am
☽ ☌ ♆ **8:09 am** 5:09 am

☽ ⚺ ☿ **8:39 am** 5:39 am
☉ □ ♇ **2:35 pm** 11:35 am
☽ ✶ ♇ **11:22 pm** 8:22 pm
☽ ⚺ ☉ 9:07 pm

24 TUESDAY
☽ ⚺ ☉ **12:07 am**
☽ ☌ ♂ **7:02 am** 4:02 am
☽ ⚺ ♀ **10:43 am** 7:43 am
☽ ☍ ♄ 10:24 pm
☽ ⚺ ♃ 11:42 pm

25 WEDNESDAY
☽ ☍ ♄ **1:24 am**
☽ ⚺ ♃ **2:42 am**
☽ ☌ ♅ **12:53 pm** 9:53 am
☽ ⚺ ♆ **4:42 pm** 1:42 pm
♀ ⚺ ♂ **6:05 pm** 3:05 pm
☽ ☌ ☿ 11:36 pm

26 THURSDAY
☽ ☌ ☿ **2:36 am**
☽ □ ♇ **6:58 am** 3:58 am
☽ ☌ ☉ **12:06 pm** 9:06 am
☽ ☌ ♀ **3:15 pm** 12:15 pm
☽ ⚺ ♂ **5:36 pm** 2:36 pm

27 FRIDAY
☽ ⚻ ♄ **7:19 am** 4:19 am
☿ □ ♇ **8:16 am** 5:16 am
☽ ✶ ♃ **9:38 am** 6:38 am
☉ ☌ ♀ **3:24 pm** 12:24 pm
☽ ⚺ ♅ **6:44 pm** 3:44 pm
☽ ✶ ♆ **10:17 pm** 7:17 pm

28 SATURDAY
☽ △ ♇ **11:51 am** 8:51 am
☽ ⚺ ☿ **4:25 pm** 1:25 pm
☽ ⚺ ♀ **5:31 pm** 2:31 pm
☽ ⚺ ☉ **8:47 pm** 5:47 pm
☿ ☌ ♀ **10:31 pm** 7:31 pm
☽ ✶ ♂ 10:10 pm

29 SUNDAY
☽ ✶ ♂ **1:10 am**
☽ △ ♄ **11:03 am** 8:03 am
☽ □ ♃ **2:18 pm** 11:18 am
☽ ✶ ♅ **10:39 pm** 7:39 pm
☽ □ ♆ 11:00 pm

30 MONDAY
☽ □ ♆ **2:00 am**
☽ ⚻ ♇ **3:12 pm** 12:12 pm
☽ ✶ ♀ **6:37 pm** 3:37 pm
☉ ☌ ☿ **11:29 pm** 8:29 pm

31 TUESDAY
☽ ✶ ☉ **3:50 am** 12:50 am
☽ ✶ ☿ **4:12 am** 1:12 am
☽ □ ♂ **7:18 am** 4:18 am
☽ □ ♄ **1:51 pm** 10:51 am
☽ △ ♃ **5:59 pm** 2:59 pm
☽ □ ♅ 10:48 pm

Eastern time in bold type
Pacific time in medium type

MARCH 2009

DATE	S.TIME	SUN	MOON	N.NODE	MERCURY	VENUS	MARS	JUPITER	SATURN	URANUS	NEPTUNE	PLUTO	CERES	PALLAS	JUNO	VESTA	CHIRON
1 Sun	10:35:44	10♓32 16	28♈49	08♒53	18♒11	14♈56	18♒56	12♒41	19♍00	21♓55	24♒33	02♑59	06♍17	13♊54	15♒49	14♉56	22♒31
2 Mon	10:39:41	11 32 29	11♉36	08 49℞	19 38	15 11	19 43	12 54	18 55℞	21 59	24 36	03 00	06 04℞	14 17	16 14	15 17	22 35
3 Tue	10:43:37	12 32 41	23 23	08 46	21 06	15 18	20 30	13 07	18 51	22 02	24 38	03 01	05 52	14 40	16 39	15 38	22 39
4 Wed	10:47:34	13 32 51	05♊09	08 45 D	22 36	15 24	21 17	13 21	18 46	22 05	24 40	03 02	05 36	15 04	17 03	15 59	22 43
5 Thu	10:51:30	14 32 59	17 08	08 45	24 06	15 27	22 04	13 34	18 41	22 09	24 42	03 03	05 22	15 28	17 28	16 20	22 47
6 Fri	10:55:27	15 33 04	29 26	08 46	25 38	15 27℞	22 51	13 47	18 36	22 12	24 44	03 04	05 09	15 52	17 53	16 41	22 52
7 Sat	10:59:23	16 33 08	12♋08	08 48	27 11	15 27	23 38	14 00	18 32	22 16	24 47	03 05	04 56	16 16	18 18	17 02	22 56
8 Sun	11:03:20	17 33 09	25 21	08 49℞	28 45	15 25	24 25	14 13	18 27	22 19	24 49	03 06	04 43	16 41	18 42	17 23	23 00
9 Mon	11:07:16	18 33 08	09♌06	08 48	00♓21	15 21	25 12	14 26	18 22	22 22	24 51	03 07	04 30	17 05	19 07	17 45	23 04
10 Tue	11:11:13	19 33 05	23 20	08 46	01 57	15 14	25 59	14 39	18 17	22 26	24 53	03 07	04 17	17 30	19 31	18 06	23 08
11 Wed	11:15:10	20 33 00	07♍59	08 41	03 34	15 05	26 46	14 52	18 12	22 29	24 55	03 08	04 04	17 56	19 56	18 28	23 12
12 Thu	11:19:06	21 32 53	23 08	08 35	05 13	14 53	27 33	15 05	18 08	22 33	24 57	03 09	03 52	18 21	20 21	18 50	23 16
13 Fri	11:23:03	22 32 44	08♎34	08 27	06 52	14 38	28 20	15 17	18 03	22 36	24 59	03 10	03 40	18 47	20 45	19 12	23 20
14 Sat	11:26:59	23 32 33	24 08	08 20	08 33	14 21	29 06	15 30	17 58	22 40	25 01	03 10	03 28	19 13	21 10	19 34	23 24
15 Sun	11:30:56	24 32 20	09♏40	08 12	10 15	14 02	29 53	15 43	17 53	22 43	25 03	03 11	03 17	19 39	21 34	19 56	23 28
16 Mon	11:34:52	25 32 06	25 12	08 02	11 59	13 40	00♓40	15 55	17 49	22 46	25 05	03 12	03 05	20 05	21 59	20 18	23 32
17 Tue	11:38:49	26 31 50	10♐27	08 00 D	13 43	13 16	01 27	16 08	17 44	22 50	25 07	03 12	02 55	20 31	22 23	20 40	23 35
18 Wed	11:42:45	27 31 33	25 12	08 00	15 29	12 50	02 14	16 20	17 39	22 53	25 09	03 13	02 44	20 58	22 48	21 03	23 39
19 Thu	11:46:42	28 31 13	09♑27	08 00	17 16	12 22	03 01	16 33	17 35	22 57	25 11	03 14	02 34	21 25	23 12	21 25	23 43
20 Fri	11:50:38	29 30 52	23 08	08 00	19 04	11 52	03 48	16 45	17 30	23 00	25 13	03 14	02 24	21 52	23 37	21 48	23 47
21 Sat	11:54:35	00♈30 29	06♒12	08 00	20 54	11 21	04 35	16 57	17 25	23 04	25 15	03 15	02 14	22 19	24 01	22 11	23 51
22 Sun	11:58:32	01 30 05	18 57	08 02℞	22 44	10 47	05 22	17 09	17 21	23 07	25 17	03 15	02 05	22 46	24 26	22 33	23 54
23 Mon	12:02:28	02 29 38	01♓20	08 02	24 36	10 13	06 09	17 21	17 16	23 10	25 19	03 15	01 56	23 14	24 50	22 56	23 58
24 Tue	12:06:25	03 29 10	14 12	07 59	26 30	09 37	06 56	17 33	17 12	23 14	25 21	03 16	01 47	23 41	25 14	23 19	24 02
25 Wed	12:10:21	04 28 40	26 09	07 46	28♓25	09 01	07 43	17 45	17 07	23 17	25 23	03 16	01 39	24 09	25 39	23 42	24 05
26 Thu	12:14:18	05 28 07	08♈01	07 37	00♈20	08 24	08 30	17 57	17 03	23 21	25 25	03 17	01 32	24 37	26 03	24 05	24 09
27 Fri	12:18:14	06 27 33	20 10	07 37	02 17	07 46	09 17	18 09	16 59	23 24	25 27	03 17	01 24	25 05	26 27	24 29	24 12
28 Sat	12:22:11	07 26 57	02♉18	07 27	04 15	07 08	10 04	18 20	16 54	23 27	25 28	03 17	01 17	25 33	26 51	24 52	24 16
29 Sun	12:26:07	08 26 18	14 20	07 18	06 14	06 31	10 51	18 32	16 50	23 31	25 30	03 17	01 11	26 01	27 16	25 15	24 19
30 Mon	12:30:04	09 25 38	26 18	07 08	08 14	05 53	11 38	18 43	16 46	23 34	25 32	03 18	01 05	26 30	27 40	25 39	24 23
31 Tue	12:34:01	10 24 55	08♊14	07 01	10 16	05 17	12 25	18 55	16 41	23 37	25 34	03 18	00 59	26 58	28 04	26 02	24 26

EPHEMERIS CALCULATED FOR 12 MIDNIGHT GREENWICH MEAN TIME. ALL OTHER DATA AND FACING ASPECTARIAN PAGE IN **EASTERN TIME (BOLD)** AND PACIFIC TIME (REGULAR).

APRIL 2009

Phases & Eclipses

phase	day	ET / hr:mn / PT	
2nd Quarter	2	10:34 am	7:34 am
Full Moon	9	10:56 am	7:56 am
4th Quarter	17	9:36 am	6:36 am
New Moon	24	11:22 pm	8:22 pm

Planet Ingress

	day	ET / hr:mn / PT	
♀	4	3:58 pm	12:58 pm
	5		11:27 pm
	6	2:27 am	
	9	10:21 am	7:21 am
	11	7:19 pm	4:19 pm
	18	8:47 am	5:47 am
	22	6:44 pm	3:44 pm
	22	9:44 am	6:44 am
	24	3:18 pm	12:18 pm
	30	6:29 pm	3:29 pm

Planetary Motion

	day	ET / hr:mn / PT	
♀ R.	4	1:35 pm	10:35 am
♀ D	12	1:42 pm	10:42 am
♀ D	17	3:24 pm	12:24 pm

---

1 WEDNESDAY

2 THURSDAY

3 FRIDAY

4 SATURDAY

5 SUNDAY

6 MONDAY

7 TUESDAY

8 WEDNESDAY

9 THURSDAY

10 FRIDAY

11 SATURDAY

12 SUNDAY

13 MONDAY

14 TUESDAY

15 WEDNESDAY

16 THURSDAY

17 FRIDAY

18 SATURDAY

19 SUNDAY

20 MONDAY

21 TUESDAY

22 WEDNESDAY

23 THURSDAY

24 FRIDAY

25 SATURDAY

26 SUNDAY

27 MONDAY

28 TUESDAY

29 WEDNESDAY

30 THURSDAY

Eastern time in **bold type**
Pacific time in medium type

APRIL 2009

DATE	S.TIME	SUN	MOON	N.NODE	MERCURY	VENUS	MARS	JUPITER	SATURN	URANUS	NEPTUNE	PLUTO	CERES	PALLAS	JUNO	VESTA	CHIRON
1 Wed	12:37:57	11♈24 10	20Ⅱ16	06♒57 R	14♈17	04♈41 R	13♓45	19♒26	16♍37 R	23♓41	25♒36	03♑18	00♉54 R	27Ⅱ27	28♒28	26♓26	24♒29
2 Thu	12:41:54	12 23 33	04♋25	06 55	16 25	04 06 R	14 31	19 39	16 33 R	23 44	25 39	03 18	00 51 R	27 56	28 52	26 49	24 32
3 Fri	12:45:50	13 22 53	18 32	06 55	18 29	03 32	15 16	19 50	16 29	23 47	25 41	03 18	00 49	28 25	29 16	27 13	24 36
4 Sat	12:49:47	14 21 41	02♌37	06 55 R	20 33	03 00	16 02	20 01	16 25	23 50	25 42	03 18 R	00 47	28 54	29 40	27 37	24 39
5 Sun	12:53:43	15 20 47	16 38	06 55	22 37	02 29	16 47	20 12	16 21	23 54	25 44	03 18	00 45	29 23	00♓04	28 01	24 42
6 Mon	12:57:40	16 19 50	00♍34	06 48	24 41	02 01	17 33	20 23	16 18	23 57	25 45	03 18	00 41	29 52	00 28	28 25	24 45
7 Tue	13:01:36	17 18 51	14 24	06 41	26 45	01 34	18 18	20 33	16 14	24 00	25 47	03 18	00 37	00♋21	00 52	28 48	24 48
8 Wed	13:05:33	18 17 49	28 06	06 31	28 47	01 09	19 04	20 43	16 10	24 03	25 49	03 18	00 34	00 51	01 16	29 12	24 51
9 Thu	13:09:30	19 16 46	11♎36	06 19	00♉48	00 47	19 49	20 54	16 07	24 07	25 50	03 18	00 31	01 20	01 40	29 37	24 54
10 Fri	13:13:26	20 15 40	24 53	06 06	02 48	00 26	20 35	21 04	16 03	24 10	25 52	03 18	00 27	01 50	02 03	00♈01	24 57
11 Sat	13:17:23	21 14 33	07♏33	06 06	04 46	00 09	21 20	21 14	16 00	24 13	25 53	03 17	00 26	02 19	02 27	00 25	25 00
12 Sun	13:21:19	22 13 23	20 38	05 54	06 42	29♓54	22 06	21 24	15 56	24 16	25 55	03 17	00 25	02 49	02 51	00 49	25 03
13 Mon	13:25:16	23 12 12	03♐05	05 45	08 35	29 40	22 51	21 34	15 53	24 19	25 56	03 17	00 24 D	03 19	03 14	01 13	25 06
14 Tue	13:29:12	24 10 59	15 17	05 36	10 25	29 30	23 37	21 44	15 50	24 22	25 57	03 17	00 24	03 49	03 38	01 38	25 08
15 Wed	13:33:09	25 09 45	27 18	05 30	12 11	29 21	24 22	21 53	15 46	24 25	25 59	03 16	00 25	04 19	04 01	02 02	25 11
16 Thu	13:37:05	26 08 28	09♑10	05 27	13 55	29 16	25 08	22 03	15 43	24 28	26 00	03 16	00 27	04 49	04 25	02 27	25 14
17 Fri	13:41:02	27 07 10	20 58	05 26 D	15 34	29 13 D	25 53	22 12	15 40	24 31	26 01	03 16	00 28	05 19	04 48	02 51	25 16
18 Sat	13:44:59	28 05 50	02♒50	05 26 R	17 09	29 12	26 39	22 22	15 38	24 34	26 03	03 15	00 30	05 49	05 11	03 16	25 19
19 Sun	13:48:55	29 04 28	14 47	05 26	18 40	29 14	27 24	22 31	15 35	24 37	26 04	03 15	00 33	06 19	05 35	03 40	25 21
20 Mon	13:52:52	00♉03 05	26 57	05 25	20 07	29 18	28 10	22 40	15 32	24 40	26 05	03 14	00 35	06 49	05 58	04 05	25 24
21 Tue	13:56:48	01 01 40	09♓15	05 21	21 29	29 24	28 55	22 49	15 29	24 43	26 06	03 14	00 39	07 19	06 21	04 30	25 26
22 Wed	14:00:45	02 00 13	22 15	05 15	22 46	29 32	29 41	22 57	15 27	24 46	26 07	03 13	00 42	07 50	06 44	04 54	25 28
23 Thu	14:04:41	02 58 45	05♈29	05 06	23 59	29 43	00♈26	23 06	15 24	24 49	26 09	03 13	00 46	08 20	07 07	05 19	25 31
24 Fri	14:08:38	03 57 14	19 06	04 56	25 06	29 56	01 12	23 15	15 22	24 52	26 10	03 12	00 51	08 51	07 31	05 44	25 33
25 Sat	14:12:34	04 55 42	03♉00	04 44	26 09	00♈11	01 57	23 23	15 20	24 55	26 11	03 12	00 55	09 21	07 53	06 09	25 35
26 Sun	14:16:31	05 54 09	17 20	04 32	27 06	00 27	02 43	23 31	15 17	24 58	26 12	03 11	01 01	09 52	08 16	06 34	25 37
27 Mon	14:20:28	06 52 33	01Ⅱ48	04 21	27 58	00 46	03 28	23 39	15 15	25 00	26 13	03 10	01 06	10 22	08 39	06 59	25 39
28 Tue	14:24:24	07 50 56	16 19	04 13	28 45	01 06	04 14	23 43	15 13	25 03	26 14	03 10	01 12	10 53	09 02	07 24	25 41
29 Wed	14:28:21	08 49 16	00♋50	04 07	29 26	01 29	04 59	23 47	15 11	25 06	26 15	03 09	01 18	11 23	09 25	07 49	25 43
30 Thu	14:32:17	09 47 35	15 13	04 05	00♊01	01 53	05 45	24 01	15 10	25 08	26 15	03 08	01 25	11 54	09 47	08 14	25 45

EPHEMERIS CALCULATED FOR 12 MIDNIGHT GREENWICH MEAN TIME. ALL OTHER DATA AND FACING ASPECTARIAN PAGE IN **EASTERN TIME (BOLD)** AND PACIFIC TIME (REGULAR).

☽ Last Aspect day	ET / hr:mn	PT	asp	☽ Ingress sign	day	ET / hr:mn	PT
2	**6:08 pm**	3:08 pm	☍♆	♍	2		9:37 pm
2	**6:08 pm**	3:08 pm	☍♆	♍	3	**12:37 am**	
4	**9:31 pm**	6:31 pm	☍♅	♎	5	**5:51 am**	2:51 am
7	**6:00 am**	3:00 am	△♆	♏	7	**12:48 pm**	9:48 am
9	**2:48 pm**	11:48 am	□♆	♐	9	**9:49 pm**	6:49 pm
11		10:55 pm	✶♆	♑	12	**9:09 am**	6:09 am
12	**1:55 am**		✶♆	♑	12	**9:09 am**	6:09 am
14	**8:58 pm**	5:58 pm	△☿	♒	14	**10:01 pm**	7:01 pm
17	**6:40 am**	3:40 am	□☿	♓	17	**10:17 am**	7:17 am
19	**5:43 pm**	2:43 pm	✶☉	♈	19	**7:30 pm**	4:30 pm
21	**6:36 pm**	3:36 pm	✶♆	♉	21		9:40 pm
21	**6:36 pm**	3:36 pm	✶♆	♉	22	**12:40 am**	
23	**8:48 pm**	5:48 pm	□♆	♊	23		11:34 pm
23	**8:48 pm**	5:48 pm	□♆	♊	24	**2:34 am**	
25	**9:17 pm**	6:17 pm	△♆	♋	25		11:58 pm
25	**9:17 pm**	6:17 pm	△♆	♋	26	**2:58 am**	
27	**11:06 pm**	8:06 pm	□♂	♌	28	**3:44 am**	12:44 am
30	**4:18 am**	1:18 am	△♂	♍	30	**6:17 am**	3:17 am

☽ Phases & Eclipses phase	day	ET / hr:mn	PT
2nd Quarter	1	**4:44 pm**	1:44 pm
Full Moon	8		9:01 pm
Full Moon	9	**12:01 am**	
4th Quarter	17	**3:26 am**	12:26 am
New Moon	24	**8:11 am**	5:11 am
2nd Quarter	30	**11:22 pm**	8:22 pm

Planet Ingress		day	ET / hr:mn	PT
☿	♉	13	**7:53 pm**	4:53 pm
☉	♊	20	**5:51 pm**	2:51 pm
♂	♉	31	**5:18 pm**	2:18 pm

Planetary Motion		day	ET / hr:mn	PT
☿	℞	6		10:00 pm
☿	℞	7	**1:00 am**	
♄	D	16	**10:06 pm**	7:06 pm
♆	℞	28		9:30 pm
♆	℞	29	**12:30 am**	
⚷	℞	30	**7:12 am**	4:12 am
☿	D	30	**9:21 pm**	6:21 pm

1 FRIDAY
- ☽△♀ **1:00 am**
- ☽⚻♇ **2:14 am**
- ☽△♂ **8:43 am** 5:43 am
- ☽□☉ **4:44 pm** 1:44 pm
- ☽⚺♄ **10:45 pm** 7:45 pm

2 SATURDAY
- ♀□♇ **1:10 pm** 10:10 am
- ☽☍♃ **2:24 pm** 11:24 am
- ☽⚻♅ **4:21 pm** 1:21 pm
- ☽☍♆ **6:08 pm** 3:08 pm
- ☽□☿ 11:28 pm

3 SUNDAY
- ☽□☿ **2:28 am**
- ☽△♇ **6:01 am** 3:01 am
- ☽⚻♀ **6:40 am** 3:40 am
- ☽⚻♂ **3:52 pm** 12:52 pm
- ☽△☉ 10:02 pm

4 MONDAY
- ☽△☉ **1:02 am**
- ☽☌♄ **3:07 am** 12:07 am
- ☽⚻♃ **7:50 pm** 4:50 pm
- ☽☍♅ **9:31 pm** 6:31 pm
- ☽⚻♆ **11:14 pm** 8:14 pm

5 TUESDAY
- ☉△♄ **5:34 am** 2:34 am
- ☽△☿ **8:46 am** 5:46 am
- ☽□♇ **11:22 am** 8:22 am
- ☽☍♀ **2:20 pm** 11:20 am
- ☽☍♂ 9:54 pm

6 WEDNESDAY
- ☽☍♂ **12:54 am**
- ☽⚺♄ **9:06 am** 6:06 am
- ☽⚻☉ **11:21 am** 8:21 am
- ☽△♃ 11:56 pm

7 THURSDAY
- ☽△♃ **2:56 am**
- ☽⚻♅ **4:21 am** 1:21 am
- ☽△♆ **6:00 am** 3:00 am
- ☽⚻☿ **4:01 pm** 1:01 pm
- ☽✶♇ **6:27 pm** 3:27 pm
- ☽⚻♀ 9:12 pm

8 FRIDAY
- ☽⚻♀ **12:12 am**
- ☽⚻♂ **12:06 pm** 9:06 am
- ☽✶♄ **4:58 pm** 1:58 pm
- ☽☍☉ 9:01 pm

9 SATURDAY
- ☽☍☉ **12:01 am**
- ☽□♃ **12:04 pm** 9:04 am
- ☽△♅ **1:12 pm** 10:12 am
- ☽□♆ **2:48 pm** 11:48 am
- ☽☍☿ 9:30 pm

10 SUNDAY
- ☽☍☿ **12:30 am**
- ☽⚺♇ **3:37 am** 12:37 am
- ☽△♀ **12:50 pm** 9:50 am
- ☽△♂ 10:59 pm

11 MONDAY
- ☽△♂ **1:59 am**
- ☽□♄ **3:05 am** 12:05 am
- ☽⚻☉ **3:35 pm** 12:35 pm
- ♂⚻♄ **7:23 pm** 4:23 pm
- ☽✶♃ **11:33 pm** 8:33 pm
- ☽□♅ 9:24 pm
- ☽✶♆ 10:55 pm

12 TUESDAY
- ☽□♅ **12:24 am**
- ☽✶♆ **1:55 am**
- ☽⚻☿ **10:22 am** 7:22 am
- ☽☌♇ **3:05 pm** 12:05 pm

13 WEDNESDAY
- ☽□♀ **4:21 am** 1:21 am
- ☽△♄ **3:20 pm** 12:20 pm
- ☽□♂ **6:24 pm** 3:24 pm

14 THURSDAY
- ☽△☉ **9:35 am** 6:35 am
- ☽⚺♃ **12:48 pm** 9:48 am
- ☽✶♅ **1:20 pm** 10:20 am
- ☽⚺♆ **2:44 pm** 11:44 am
- ☽△☿ **8:58 pm** 5:58 pm

15 FRIDAY
- ☽⚺♇ **3:54 am** 12:54 am
- ☽✶♀ **9:17 pm** 6:17 pm

16 SATURDAY
- ☽⚻♄ **4:13 am** 1:13 am
- ☉□♃ **4:45 am** 1:45 am
- ☉✶♅ **9:09 am** 6:09 am
- ☽✶♂ **11:24 am** 8:24 am
- ☉□♆ 10:05 pm
- ☽☌♃ 10:47 pm
- ☽⚺♅ 11:01 pm

17 SUNDAY
- ☉□♆ **1:05 am**
- ☽☌♃ **1:47 am**
- ☽⚺♅ **2:01 am**
- ☽☌♆ **3:15 am** 12:15 am
- ☽□☉ **3:26 am** 12:26 am
- ☽□☿ **6:40 am** 3:40 am
- ☽✶♇ **3:52 pm** 12:52 pm

18 MONDAY
- ☉☌☿ **6:02 am** 3:02 am
- ☽⚺♀ **12:29 pm** 9:29 am
- ☽☍♄ **3:13 pm** 12:13 pm
- ☽⚺♂ 10:45 pm

19 TUESDAY
- ☽⚺♂ **1:45 am**
- ♃⚺♅ **10:25 am** 7:25 am
- ☽☌♅ **11:55 am** 8:55 am
- ☽⚺♃ **11:56 am** 8:56 am
- ☽⚺♆ **12:57 pm** 9:57 am
- ☽✶☿ **1:39 pm** 10:39 am
- ☽✶☉ **5:43 pm** 2:43 pm
- ☽□♇ 9:38 pm

20 WEDNESDAY
- ☽□♇ **12:38 am**
- ☿□♆ **5:21 am** 2:21 am
- ♀⚻♄ **7:43 am** 4:43 am
- ☽⚻♄ **10:27 pm** 7:27 pm
- ☽☌♀ **11:22 pm** 8:22 pm
- ☿□♃ **11:44 pm** 8:44 pm
- ☿✶♅ 11:46 pm

21 THURSDAY
- ☿✶♅ **2:46 am**
- ☽☌♂ **11:22 am** 8:22 am
- ☽⚺☿ **5:09 pm** 2:09 pm
- ☽⚺♅ **5:45 pm** 2:45 pm
- ☽✶♃ **5:56 pm** 2:56 pm
- ☽✶♆ **6:36 pm** 3:36 pm
- ☽⚺☉ 11:56 pm

22 FRIDAY
- ☽⚺☉ **2:56 am**
- ☽△♇ **5:22 am** 2:22 am
- ☽△♄ 10:50 pm

23 SATURDAY
- ☽△♄ **1:50 am**
- ☽⚺♀ **5:47 am** 2:47 am
- ☉⚻♇ **1:55 pm** 10:55 am
- ☽⚺♂ **4:42 pm** 1:42 pm
- ☽☌☿ **5:47 pm** 2:47 pm
- ☽✶♅ **8:06 pm** 5:06 pm
- ☽□♃ **8:25 pm** 5:25 pm
- ☽□♆ **8:48 pm** 5:48 pm

24 SUNDAY
- ☿⚺♂ **6:08 am** 3:08 am
- ☽⚻♇ **6:58 am** 3:58 am
- ☽☌☉ **8:11 am** 5:11 am
- ☽□♄ 11:47 pm

25 MONDAY
- ☽□♄ **2:47 am**
- ☽✶♀ **9:32 am** 6:32 am
- ☽⚺☿ **5:01 pm** 2:01 pm
- ☽✶♂ **7:50 pm** 4:50 pm
- ☽□♅ **8:41 pm** 5:41 pm
- ☽△♃ **9:07 pm** 6:07 pm
- ☽△♆ **9:17 pm** 6:17 pm

26 TUESDAY
- ☽☍♇ **7:16 am** 4:16 am
- ☽⚺☉ **11:52 am** 8:52 am
- ♂⚺♅ **1:09 pm** 10:09 am
- ♂✶♃ **11:19 pm** 8:19 pm
- ♂✶♆ 9:37 pm

27 WEDNESDAY
- ♂✶♆ **12:37 am**
- ☽✶♄ **3:12 am** 12:12 am
- ☽□♀ **1:03 pm** 10:03 am
- ♃☌♆ **4:06 pm** 1:06 pm
- ☽✶☿ **4:38 pm** 1:38 pm
- ☽△♅ **9:24 pm** 6:24 pm
- ☽⚻♆ **9:56 pm** 6:56 pm
- ☽⚻♃ **9:58 pm** 6:58 pm
- ☽□♂ **11:06 pm** 8:06 pm

28 THURSDAY
- ☽⚻♇ **8:04 am** 5:04 am
- ☽✶☉ **4:23 pm** 1:23 pm

29 FRIDAY
- ☽⚺♄ **4:48 am** 1:48 am
- ☿⚺♀ **3:23 pm** 12:23 pm
- ☽□☿ **6:09 pm** 3:09 pm
- ☽△♀ **6:21 pm** 3:21 pm
- ☽⚻♅ **11:46 pm** 8:46 pm
- ☽☍♆ 9:14 pm
- ☽☍♃ 9:27 pm

30 SATURDAY
- ☽☍♆ **12:14 am**
- ☽☍♃ **12:27 am**
- ☽△♂ **4:18 am** 1:18 am
- ☽△♇ **10:44 am** 7:44 am
- ☽□☉ **11:22 pm** 8:22 pm

31 SUNDAY
- ☽☌♄ **8:38 am** 5:38 am
- ☽△☿ **10:31 pm** 7:31 pm
- ☽⚻♀ 11:36 pm

Eastern time in bold type
Pacific time in medium type

MAY 2009

DATE	S.TIME	SUN	MOON	N.NODE	MERCURY	VENUS	MARS	JUPITER	SATURN	URANUS	NEPTUNE	PLUTO	CERES	PALLAS	JUNO	VESTA	CHIRON
1 Fri	14:36:14	10♉45 51	29♋27	04♒04 R	00♊33	02♈18	06♈31	23♒55	15♍08	25♓11	26♒16	03♑08	01♍32	12♋25	10♓10	08♊39	25♒47
2 Sat	14:40:10	11 44 05	13♌30	04 04 R	00 58	02 46	07 17	24 03	15 06 R	25 14	26 17	03 07 R	01 40	12 55	10 32	09 04	25 49
3 Sun	14:44:07	12 42 17	27 22	04 03	01 18	03 14	08 03	24 11	15 05	25 16	26 17	03 06	01 47	13 26	10 55	09 30	25 50
4 Mon	14:48:03	13 40 27	11♍22	04 01	01 32	03 45	08 49	24 18	15 04	25 19	26 18	03 05	01 56	13 57	11 17	09 55	25 52
5 Tue	14:52:00	14 38 35	24 31	03 56	01 41	04 16	09 35	24 25	15 02	25 21	26 19	03 04	02 04	14 28	11 39	10 20	25 54
6 Wed	14:55:57	15 36 41	07♎49	03 49	01♊44 R	04 50	10 22	24 32	15 01	25 24	26 20	03 03	02 13	14 59	12 01	10 45	25 55
7 Thu	14:59:53	16 34 45	20 56	03 39	01 43	05 24	11 08	24 39	15 00	25 26	26 21	03 02	02 22	15 29	12 24	11 11	25 57
8 Fri	15:03:50	17 32 48	03♏51	03 27	01 37	06 00	11 54	24 46	14 59	25 29	26 22	03 01	02 31	16 00	12 46	11 36	25 58
9 Sat	15:07:46	18 30 49	16 34	03 14	01 27	06 37	12 40	24 53	14 58	25 31	26 22	03 00	02 41	16 31	13 08	12 01	25 59
10 Sun	15:11:43	19 28 48	29♏04	03 02	01 13	07 15	13 25	24 59	14 57	25 33	26 23	02 59	02 51	17 02	13 29	12 27	26 01
11 Mon	15:15:39	20 26 46	11♐21	02 51	00 56	07 54	14 11	25 06	14 57	25 36	26 23	02 58	03 02	17 33	13 51	12 52	26 02
12 Tue	15:19:36	21 24 42	23 27	02 43	00 37	08 34	14 57	25 12	14 56	25 38	26 24	02 57	03 12	18 04	14 13	13 18	26 03
13 Wed	15:23:32	22 22 37	05♑23	02 37	00 18	09 16	15 43	25 18	14 56	25 40	26 24	02 56	03 23	18 35	14 34	13 43	26 04
14 Thu	15:27:29	23 20 31	17 13	02 34	00 00	09 58	16 29	25 24	14 55	25 42	26 25	02 55	03 35	19 06	14 56	14 09	26 05
15 Fri	15:31:26	24 18 23	29 00	02 33 D	29♉50	10 42	17 15	25 30	14 55	25 45	26 25	02 54	03 46	19 37	15 17	14 34	26 06
16 Sat	15:35:22	25 16 14	10♒50	02 33	28 59	11 26	18 00	25 35	14 55	25 47	26 26	02 53	03 58	20 08	15 39	15 00	26 07
17 Sun	15:39:19	26 14 03	22 48	02 33 R	28 25	12 11	18 46	25 41	14 55 D	25 49	26 26	02 52	04 11	20 39	16 00	15 26	26 08
18 Mon	15:43:15	27 11 52	04♓58	02 31	27 51	12 57	19 31	25 46	14 55	25 51	26 27	02 51	04 23	21 10	16 21	15 51	26 09
19 Tue	15:47:12	28 09 39	17 26	02 23	27 16	13 44	20 17	25 51	14 55	25 53	26 27	02 50	04 36	21 41	16 42	16 17	26 10
20 Wed	15:51:08	29 07 25	00♈16	02 15	26 41	14 32	21 03	25 56	14 55	25 55	26 27	02 48	04 49	22 12	17 03	16 43	26 10
21 Thu	15:55:05	00♊05 10	13 33	02 13	26 07	15 20	21 48	26 01	14 55	25 57	26 28	02 47	05 02	22 43	17 24	17 08	26 11
22 Fri	15:59:01	01 02 54	27 17	02 13	25 34	16 09	22 33	26 05	14 56	25 59	26 28	02 46	05 16	23 14	17 44	17 34	26 12
23 Sat	16:02:58	02 00 37	11♉48	02 04	25 03	16 59	23 19	26 10	14 57	26 01	26 28	02 45	05 29	23 45	18 05	18 00	26 12
24 Sun	16:06:55	02 58 19	25 59	01 55	24 35	17 50	24 04	26 14	14 57	26 02	26 28	02 43	05 43	24 16	18 25	18 25	26 12
25 Mon	16:10:51	03 56 00	10♊18	01 46	24 09	18 41	24 49	26 18	14 58	26 04	26 28	02 42	05 58	24 47	18 46	18 51	26 13
26 Tue	16:14:48	04 53 39	24 09	01 40	23 46	19 33	25 35	26 22	14 59	26 06	26 29	02 41	06 12	25 18	19 06	19 17	26 13
27 Wed	16:18:44	05 51 17	07♋10	01 36	23 27	20 25	26 20	26 26	15 00	26 07	26 29	02 39	06 27	25 49	19 26	19 43	26 13
28 Thu	16:22:41	06 48 54	21 18	01 34 D	23 12	21 18	27 05	26 30	15 01	26 09	26 29	02 38	06 42	26 20	19 46	20 09	26 14
29 Fri	16:26:37	07 46 29	04♌48	01 34	23 01	22 12	27 50	26 33	15 02	26 11	26 29 R	02 37	06 57	26 51	20 06	20 35	26 14
30 Sat	16:30:34	08 44 03	18 00	01 35	22 55	23 06	28 35	26 36	15 03	26 12	26 29	02 35	07 13	27 22	20 26	21 00	26 14 R
31 Sun	16:34:30	09 41 35	00♍54	01 36 R	22♉52 D	24 01	29 20	26 39	15 05	26 14	26 29	02 34	07 29	27 53	20 45	21 26	26 14

EPHEMERIS CALCULATED FOR 12 MIDNIGHT GREENWICH MEAN TIME. ALL OTHER DATA AND FACING ASPECTARIAN PAGE IN **EASTERN TIME (BOLD)** AND PACIFIC TIME (REGULAR).

JUNE 2009

☽ Last Aspect day	ET / hr:mn / PT	asp	☽ Ingress sign	day	ET / hr:mn / PT
1	**4:32 am** 1:32 am	☍ ♅	♎	1	**11:17 am** 8:17 am
3	**2:00 pm** 11:00 am	☍ ♀	♏	3	**6:43 pm** 3:43 pm
5	**10:18 pm** 7:18 pm	□ ♃	♐	6	**4:23 am** 1:23 am
8	**9:51 am** 6:51 am	⚹ ♃	♑	8	**3:59 pm** 12:59 pm
10	**11:31 pm** 8:31 pm	△ ☿	♒	11	**4:52 am** 1:52 am
13	**5:04 pm** 2:04 pm	□ ☿	♓	13	**5:32 pm** 2:32 pm
15	**9:17 pm** 6:17 pm	☌ ♅	♈	16	**3:51 am** 12:51 am
18	**5:35 am** 2:35 am	⚹ ☉	♉	18	**10:20 am** 7:20 am
20	**8:02 am** 5:02 am	□ ♃	♊	20	**1:00 pm** 10:00 am
22	**8:20 am** 5:20 am	△ ♃	♋	22	**1:12 pm** 10:12 am
24	**7:24 am** 4:24 am	△ ♅	♌	24	**12:50 pm** 9:50 am
26	**8:28 am** 5:28 am	☍ ♃	♍	26	**1:46 pm** 10:46 am
28	**11:26 am** 8:26 am	☍ ♅	♎	28	**5:24 pm** 2:24 pm
30	**5:59 pm** 2:59 pm	△ ♃	♏	30	9:18 pm
30	**5:59 pm** 2:59 pm	△ ♃	♏	7/1	**12:18 am**

☽ Phases & Eclipses phase	day	ET / hr:mn / PT
Full Moon	7	**2:12 pm** 11:12 am
4th Quarter	15	**6:14 pm** 3:14 pm
New Moon	22	**3:35 pm** 12:35 pm
2nd Quarter	29	**7:28 am** 4:28 am

Planet Ingress		day	ET / hr:mn / PT
♀	♌	3	**10:24 pm** 7:24 pm
♀	♉	6	**5:07 am** 2:07 am
☿	♊	13	**10:47 pm** 7:47 pm
⚳	♋	19	**2:11 pm** 11:11 am
☉	♋	20	10:45 pm
☉	♋	21	**1:45 am**

Planetary Motion	day	ET / hr:mn / PT
♃ ℞	15	**3:50 am** 12:50 am

1 MONDAY
☽ ⚻ ♀ **2:36 am**
☽ ☍ ♅ **4:32 am** 1:32 am
☽ ⚻ ♆ **4:55 am** 1:55 am
☽ ⚻ ♃ **5:20 am** 2:20 am
☽ ⚻ ♂ **12:21 pm** 9:21 am
☽ □ ♇ **3:51 pm** 12:51 pm

2 TUESDAY
♀ ⚺ ♅ **7:10 am** 4:10 am
☽ △ ☉ **9:26 am** 6:26 am
♀ ⚹ ♆ **11:54 am** 8:54 am
☽ ⚺ ♄ **2:59 pm** 11:59 am
♀ ⚹ ♃ **7:39 pm** 4:39 pm

3 WEDNESDAY
☽ ⚻ ☿ **6:07 am** 3:07 am
☽ ⚻ ♅ **11:47 am** 8:47 am
☽ △ ♆ **12:05 pm** 9:05 am
☽ △ ♃ **12:42 pm** 9:42 am
☽ ☍ ♀ **2:00 pm** 11:00 am
☽ ☍ ♂ **11:19 pm** 8:19 pm
☽ ⚹ ♇ **11:23 pm** 8:23 pm
♂ △ ♇ 9:36 pm

4 THURSDAY
♂ △ ♇ **12:36 am**
☽ ⚻ ☉ **10:29 pm** 7:29 pm
☽ ⚹ ♄ **11:44 pm** 8:44 pm

Eastern time in bold type
Pacific time in medium type

5 FRIDAY
☉ □ ♄ **3:10 pm** 12:10 pm
☽ ☍ ☿ **4:56 pm** 1:56 pm
☽ △ ♅ **9:18 pm** 6:18 pm
☽ □ ♆ **9:29 pm** 6:29 pm
☽ □ ♃ **10:18 pm** 7:18 pm

6 SATURDAY
☽ ⚻ ♀ **4:20 am** 1:20 am
☽ ⚺ ♇ **9:07 am** 6:07 am
☽ ⚻ ♂ **12:54 pm** 9:54 am

7 SUNDAY
☽ □ ♄ **10:35 am** 7:35 am
☽ ☍ ☉ **2:12 pm** 11:12 am

8 MONDAY
☽ ⚻ ☿ **6:54 am** 3:54 am
☽ □ ♅ **8:47 am** 5:47 am
☽ ⚹ ♆ **8:51 am** 5:51 am
☽ ⚹ ♃ **9:51 am** 6:51 am
♀ △ ♇ **3:22 pm** 12:22 pm
☽ ☌ ♇ **8:43 pm** 5:43 pm
☽ △ ♀ **9:13 pm** 6:13 pm

9 TUESDAY
☽ △ ♂ **4:43 am** 1:43 am
☿ ⚹ ♅ **5:45 pm** 2:45 pm
☿ □ ♆ **5:53 pm** 2:53 pm
♅ ⚺ ♆ **9:44 pm** 6:44 pm
☽ △ ♄ **11:10 pm** 8:10 pm

10 WEDNESDAY
☽ ⚻ ☉ **7:59 am** 4:59 am
☿ □ ♃ **11:33 am** 8:33 am
☽ ⚺ ♆ **9:36 pm** 6:36 pm
☽ ⚹ ♅ **9:39 pm** 6:39 pm
☽ ⚺ ♃ **10:44 pm** 7:44 pm
☽ △ ☿ **11:31 pm** 8:31 pm

11 THURSDAY
☽ ⚺ ♇ **9:32 am** 6:32 am
☽ □ ♀ **3:43 pm** 12:43 pm
☽ □ ♂ **9:47 pm** 6:47 pm

12 FRIDAY
☽ ⚻ ♄ **12:24 pm** 9:24 am
☽ △ ☉ 11:16 pm

13 SATURDAY
☽ △ ☉ **2:16 am**
☽ ☌ ♆ **10:22 am** 7:22 am
☽ ⚺ ♅ **10:32 am** 7:32 am
☽ ☌ ♃ **11:34 am** 8:34 am
☽ □ ☿ **5:04 pm** 2:04 pm
☽ ⚹ ♇ **9:58 pm** 6:58 pm

14 SUNDAY
☽ ⚹ ♀ **9:34 am** 6:34 am
☽ ⚹ ♂ **1:53 pm** 10:53 am
☽ ☍ ♄ 9:21 pm

15 MONDAY
☽ ☍ ♄ **12:21 am**
☽ □ ☉ **6:14 pm** 3:14 pm

☽ ⚺ ♆ **9:02 pm** 6:02 pm
☽ ☌ ♅ **9:17 pm** 6:17 pm
☽ ⚺ ♃ **10:13 pm** 7:13 pm
☿ ⚻ ♇ 9:48 pm

16 TUESDAY
☿ ⚻ ♇ **12:48 am**
☽ □ ♇ **7:55 am** 4:55 am
☽ ⚹ ☿ **8:37 am** 5:37 am
☽ ⚺ ♀ **11:48 pm** 8:48 pm
☽ ⚺ ♂ 11:23 pm

17 WEDNESDAY
☽ ⚺ ♂ **2:23 am**
☉ △ ♆ **6:45 am** 3:45 am
☽ ⚻ ♄ **8:59 am** 5:59 am
☉ □ ♅ **10:56 am** 7:56 am
☉ △ ♃ **10:28 pm** 7:28 pm

18 THURSDAY
☽ ⚹ ♆ **3:58 am** 12:58 am
☽ ⚺ ♅ **4:17 am** 1:17 am
☽ ⚹ ♃ **5:05 am** 2:05 am
☽ ⚹ ☉ **5:35 am** 2:35 am
☽ △ ♇ **2:00 pm** 11:00 am
☽ ⚺ ☿ **7:51 pm** 4:51 pm

19 FRIDAY
☽ ☌ ♀ **9:00 am** 6:00 am
☽ ☌ ♂ **10:06 am** 7:06 am
☽ △ ♄ **1:33 pm** 10:33 am

20 SATURDAY
☽ □ ♆ **7:00 am** 4:00 am
☽ ⚹ ♅ **7:22 am** 4:22 am
☽ □ ♃ **8:02 am** 5:02 am
☽ ⚺ ☉ **12:07 pm** 9:07 am
☽ ⚻ ♇ **4:21 pm** 1:21 pm
☽ ☌ ☿ 11:52 pm

21 SUNDAY
☽ ☌ ☿ **2:52 am**
♀ ☌ ♂ **9:09 am** 6:09 am
☽ ⚺ ♂ **1:56 pm** 10:56 am
☽ ⚺ ♀ **2:03 pm** 11:03 am
☽ □ ♄ **2:52 pm** 11:52 am
♀ △ ♄ 11:30 pm

22 MONDAY
♀ △ ♄ **2:30 am**
☽ △ ♆ **7:21 am** 4:21 am
☽ □ ♅ **7:47 am** 4:47 am
☽ △ ♃ **8:20 am** 5:20 am
♂ △ ♄ **10:44 am** 7:44 am
☽ ☌ ☉ **3:35 pm** 12:35 pm
☽ ☍ ♇ **4:22 pm** 1:22 pm

23 TUESDAY
☉ ☍ ♇ **3:41 am** 12:41 am
☽ ⚺ ☿ **7:46 am** 4:46 am
☽ ⚹ ♄ **2:43 pm** 11:43 am
☽ ⚹ ♂ **4:00 pm** 1:00 pm
☽ ⚹ ♀ **5:15 pm** 2:15 pm

24 WEDNESDAY
☽ ⚻ ♆ **6:55 am** 3:55 am
☽ △ ♅ **7:24 am** 4:24 am
☽ ⚻ ♃ **7:51 am** 4:51 am
☽ ⚻ ♇ **3:57 pm** 12:57 pm
☽ ⚺ ☉ **6:29 pm** 3:29 pm

25 THURSDAY
☽ ⚹ ☿ **1:25 pm** 10:25 am
☽ ⚺ ♄ **3:03 pm** 12:03 pm
☽ □ ♂ **6:41 pm** 3:41 pm
☽ □ ♀ **9:13 pm** 6:13 pm

26 FRIDAY
☿ □ ♄ **4:32 am** 1:32 am
☽ ☍ ♆ **7:34 am** 4:34 am
☽ ⚻ ♅ **8:08 am** 5:08 am
☽ ☍ ♃ **8:28 am** 5:28 am
☽ △ ♇ **4:57 pm** 1:57 pm
☽ ⚹ ☉ **11:13 pm** 8:13 pm

27 SATURDAY
☽ ☌ ♄ **5:33 pm** 2:33 pm
☽ □ ☿ **10:33 pm** 7:33 pm
☽ △ ♂ **11:56 pm** 8:56 pm

28 SUNDAY
☽ △ ♀ **4:04 am** 1:04 am
☽ ⚻ ♆ **10:45 am** 7:45 am
☽ ☍ ♅ **11:26 am** 8:26 am
☽ ⚻ ♃ **11:37 am** 8:37 am
☿ ⚺ ♂ **3:48 pm** 12:48 pm
☽ □ ♇ **8:40 pm** 5:40 pm

29 MONDAY
☽ □ ☉ **7:28 am** 4:28 am
☽ ⚺ ♄ **11:14 pm** 8:14 pm

30 TUESDAY
☽ ⚻ ♂ **8:54 am** 5:54 am
☽ △ ☿ **1:02 pm** 10:02 am
☽ ⚻ ♀ **3:03 pm** 12:03 pm
☽ △ ♆ **5:11 pm** 2:11 pm
☽ ⚻ ♅ **5:58 pm** 2:58 pm
☽ △ ♃ **5:59 pm** 2:59 pm
♃ ⚺ ♅ **9:03 pm** 6:03 pm

JUNE 2009

DATE	S.TIME	SUN	MOON	N.NODE	MERCURY	VENUS	MARS	JUPITER	SATURN	URANUS	NEPTUNE	PLUTO	CERES	PALLAS	JUNO	VESTA	CHIRON
1 Mon	16:38:27	10♊39 06	21♍30	01≈35	22♊54	24♈56	00♉05	26≈41	15♍06	26♓15	26≈29	02♑33	07♈45	28♋24	21♓05	21♈52	26≈14
2 Tue	16:42:24	11 36 35	04♎48	01 35R	23 11	25 51	00 50	26 44	15 08	26 18	26 28R	02 31R	08 01	28 55	21 24	22 18	26 14R
3 Wed	16:46:20	12 34 04	17 51	01 28	23 27	26 47	01 35	26 47	15 10	26 19	26 28	02 30	08 17	29 26	21 43	22 44	26 13
4 Thu	16:50:17	13 31 31	00♏41	01 22	23 47	27 44	02 19	26 49	15 11	26 21	26 28	02 28	08 34	29 57	22 02	23 10	26 13
5 Fri	16:54:13	14 28 57	13 17	01 15	24 11	28 41	03 04	26 51	15 13	26 22	26 28	02 27	08 51	00♌28	22 21	23 36	26 13
6 Sat	16:58:10	15 26 21	25 42	01 06	24 40	29 38	03 49	26 53	15 15	26 22	26 28	02 25	09 08	00 59	22 40	24 02	26 12
7 Sun	17:02:06	16 23 45	07♐57	00 58	25 12	00♉36	04 33	26 54	15 17	26 23	26 27	02 24	09 25	01 30	22 59	24 28	26 12
8 Mon	17:06:03	17 21 08	20 02	00 51	25 49	01 34	05 18	26 56	15 19	26 24	26 27	02 22	09 42	02 01	23 17	24 54	26 12
9 Tue	17:09:59	18 18 31	01♑59	00 46	26 30	02 33	06 02	26 57	15 22	26 25	26 27	02 21	10 00	02 31	23 35	25 20	26 11
10 Wed	17:13:56	19 15 52	13 51	00 42	27 15	03 32	06 47	26 58	15 24	26 26	26 26	02 20	10 18	03 02	23 54	25 46	26 10
11 Thu	17:17:53	20 13 13	25 39	00 41 D	28 04	04 31	07 31	26 59	15 27	26 27	26 26	02 18	10 36	03 33	24 12	26 12	26 10
12 Fri	17:21:49	21 10 33	07≈26	00 41	28 57	05 30	08 15	27 00	15 29	26 28	26 26	02 17	10 54	04 04	24 29	26 38	26 09
13 Sat	17:25:46	22 07 53	19 16	00 42	29 53	06 30	09 00	27 01	15 32	26 29	26 25	02 15	11 12	04 35	24 47	27 04	26 08
14 Sun	17:29:42	23 05 12	01♓14	00 44	00♋53	07 31	09 44	27 01	15 35	26 30	26 25	02 13	11 30	05 06	25 05	27 30	26 07
15 Mon	17:33:39	24 02 30	13 24	00 45R	01 57	08 31	10 28	27 01R	15 37	26 31	26 24	02 12	11 49	05 37	25 22	27 56	26 06
16 Tue	17:37:35	24 59 49	26 24	00 46	03 04	09 34	11 12	27 01	15 40	26 32	26 24	02 10	12 08	06 08	25 39	28 22	26 05
17 Wed	17:41:32	25 57 07	09♈42	00 45	04 14	10 34	11 56	27 01	15 43	26 32	26 23	02 09	12 27	06 38	25 56	28 48	26 04
18 Thu	17:45:28	26 54 24	23 18	00 43	05 29	11 35	12 40	27 00	15 47	26 33	26 22	02 07	12 46	07 09	26 13	29 14	26 03
19 Fri	17:49:25	27 51 42	07♉12	00 40	06 47	12 37	13 24	27 00	15 50	26 34	26 22	02 06	13 05	07 40	26 29	29 40	26 02
20 Sat	17:53:22	28 48 59	21 24	00 35	08 07	13 39	14 08	26 59	15 53	26 34	26 21	02 04	13 25	08 11	26 46	00♉06	26 01
21 Sun	17:57:18	29 46 16	05♊54	00 30	09 32	14 41	14 52	26 59	15 56	26 35	26 20	02 03	13 44	08 41	27 02	00 32	26 00
22 Mon	18:01:15	00♋43 33	20 42	00 26	10 59	15 44	15 35	26 57	16 00	26 35	26 20	02 01	14 04	09 12	27 18	00 58	25 58
23 Tue	18:05:11	01 40 49	05♋42	00 23	12 30	16 47	16 19	26 55	16 04	26 36	26 19	02 00	14 24	09 43	27 34	01 25	25 57
24 Wed	18:09:08	02 38 05	20 54	00 22 D	14 04	17 50	17 03	26 54	16 07	26 36	26 18	01 58	14 44	10 13	27 49	01 51	25 56
25 Thu	18:13:04	03 35 21	06♌00	00 22	15 41	18 53	17 46	26 52	16 11	26 36	26 17	01 57	15 04	10 44	28 05	02 17	25 54
26 Fri	18:17:01	04 32 36	20 54	00 22	17 21	19 57	18 29	26 50	16 15	26 37	26 17	01 55	15 25	11 15	28 20	02 43	25 53
27 Sat	18:20:58	05 29 50	05♍30	00 24	19 04	21 00	19 13	26 48	16 19	26 37	26 16	01 53	15 45	11 45	28 35	03 09	25 51
28 Sun	18:24:54	06 27 04	19 48	00 25	20 51	22 04	19 56	26 46	16 23	26 37	26 15	01 52	16 06	12 16	28 49	03 35	25 49
29 Mon	18:28:51	07 24 17	03♎48	00 26R	22 40	23 08	20 39	26 43	16 27	26 37	26 14	01 50	16 27	12 47	29 04	04 01	25 48
30 Tue	18:32:47	08 21 30	17 30	00 26	24 31	24 13	21 23	26 40	16 31	26 37	26 13	01 49	16 47	13 17	29 18	04 27	25 46

EPHEMERIS CALCULATED FOR 12 MIDNIGHT GREENWICH MEAN TIME. ALL OTHER DATA AND FACING ASPECTARIAN PAGE IN **EASTERN TIME (BOLD)** AND PACIFIC TIME (REGULAR).

JULY 2009

☽ Last Aspect day	ET / hr:mn	PT	asp	☽ Ingress sign	day	ET / hr:mn	PT
6/30	**5:59 pm**	2:59 pm	△ ♃	♏	1	**12:18 am**	
3	**6:03 am**	3:03 am	☍ ♀	♐	3	**10:10 am**	7:10 am
5	**3:17 pm**	12:17 pm	□ ♅	♑	5	**10:07 pm**	7:07 pm
8	**5:43 am**	2:43 am	△ ♂	♒	8	**11:03 am**	8:03 am
10	**10:17 pm**	7:17 pm	□ ♂	♓	5	**11:44 pm**	8:44 pm
13	**4:03 am**	1:03 am	☌ ♅	♈	13	**10:40 am**	7:40 am
15	**11:07 am**	8:07 am	⚹ ♆	♉	15	**6:30 pm**	3:30 pm
17	**4:48 pm**	1:48 pm	⚹ ♅	♊	17	**10:41 pm**	7:41 pm
19	**6:12 pm**	3:12 pm	□ ♅	♋	19	**11:51 pm**	8:51 pm
21	**10:34 pm**	7:34 pm	☌ ☉	♌	21	**11:27 pm**	8:27 pm
23	**4:28 pm**	1:28 pm	☍ ♆	♍	23	**11:22 pm**	8:22 pm
25	**7:14 pm**	4:14 pm	☍ ♅	♎	25		10:25 pm
25	**7:14 pm**	4:14 pm	☍ ♅	♎	26	**1:25 am**	
27	**10:53 pm**	7:53 pm	△ ♆	♏	28	**6:56 am**	3:56 am
30	**8:54 am**	5:54 am	△ ♅	♐	30	**4:10 pm**	1:10 pm

☽ Phases & Eclipses phase	day	ET / hr:mn	PT
Full Moon	7	**5:21 am**	2:21 am
● (eclipse)	7	15° ♑ 32'	
4th Quarter	15	**5:53 am**	2:53 am
New Moon	21	**10:34 pm**	7:34 pm
● (eclipse)	21	29° ♋ 26'	
2nd Quarter	28	**6:00 pm**	3:00 pm

Planet Ingress	day	ET / hr:mn	PT
✱ ♈	2	**9:43 pm**	6:43 pm
☿ ♋	3	**3:19 pm**	12:19 pm
♀ ♊	5	**4:22 am**	1:22 am
♂ ♊	11	**10:56 pm**	7:56 pm
☿ ♌	17	**7:07 pm**	4:07 pm
☉ ♌	22	**12:36 pm**	9:36 am
♀ ♋	31	**9:28 pm**	6:28 pm

Planetary Motion	day	ET / hr:mn	PT
♅ ℞	1	**3:37 am**	12:37 am

1 WEDNESDAY
☽ ⚹ ♇ **3:40 am** 12:40 am
♀ □ ♆ **4:01 pm** 1:01 pm
☿ △ ♆ **4:48 pm** 1:48 pm
☿ ⚺ ♀ **5:49 pm** 2:49 pm
☽ △ ☉ **7:48 pm** 4:48 pm
☿ △ ♃ **9:34 pm** 6:34 pm
☿ □ ♅ **10:13 pm** 7:13 pm
♀ □ ♃ 9:24 pm
♀ ⚹ ♅ 10:42 pm

2 THURSDAY
♀ □ ♃ **12:24 am**
♀ ⚹ ♅ **1:42 am**
☽ ⚹ ♄ **8:12 am** 5:12 am
☽ ☍ ♂ **9:34 pm** 6:34 pm
☽ □ ♆ 11:38 pm

3 FRIDAY
☽ □ ♆ **2:38 am**
☽ □ ♃ **3:18 am** 12:18 am
☽ △ ♅ **3:32 am** 12:32 am
☽ ☍ ♀ **6:03 am** 3:03 am
☽ ⚻ ☿ **9:10 am** 6:10 am
☽ ⚺ ♇ **1:34 pm** 10:34 am

4 SATURDAY
☿ ☍ ♇ **11:29 am** 8:29 am
☽ ⚻ ☉ **11:32 am** 8:32 am
☽ □ ♄ **7:43 pm** 4:43 pm

Eastern time in bold type
Pacific time in medium type

5 SUNDAY
☽ ⚻ ♂ **12:57 pm** 9:57 am
☽ ⚹ ♆ **2:17 pm** 11:17 am
☽ ⚹ ♃ **2:45 pm** 11:45 am
☽ □ ♅ **3:17 pm** 12:17 pm
☽ ⚻ ♀ **11:55 pm** 8:55 pm
☽ ☌ ♇ 10:28 pm

6 MONDAY
☽ ☌ ♇ **1:28 am**
☽ ☍ ☿ **9:35 am** 6:35 am
♂ □ ♆ **10:43 am** 7:43 am
♀ ⚻ ♇ **4:26 pm** 1:26 pm
♂ □ ♃ **4:47 pm** 1:47 pm

7 TUESDAY
♂ ⚹ ♅ **3:48 am** 12:48 am
☽ ☍ ☉ **5:21 am** 2:21 am
☽ △ ♄ **8:46 am** 5:46 am

8 WEDNESDAY
☽ ⚺ ♆ **3:03 am** 12:03 am
☽ ⚺ ♃ **3:17 am** 12:17 am
☽ ⚹ ♅ **4:08 am** 1:08 am
☽ △ ♂ **5:43 am** 2:43 am
☽ ⚺ ♇ **2:18 pm** 11:18 am
☽ △ ♀ **7:06 pm** 4:06 pm

9 THURSDAY
☉ ⚹ ♄ **3:09 am** 12:09 am
☽ ⚻ ☿ **11:56 am** 8:56 am
☽ ⚻ ♄ **10:08 pm** 7:08 pm
☽ ⚻ ☉ **11:39 pm** 8:39 pm

10 FRIDAY
♃ ☌ ♆ **5:13 am** 2:13 am
☽ ☌ ♃ **3:42 pm** 12:42 pm
☽ ☌ ♆ **3:45 pm** 12:45 pm
☽ ⚺ ♅ **4:53 pm** 1:53 pm
☽ □ ♂ **10:17 pm** 7:17 pm
☽ ⚹ ♇ 11:47 pm

11 SATURDAY
☽ ⚹ ♇ **2:47 am**
☽ □ ♀ **1:44 pm** 10:44 am
☿ ⚹ ♄ **9:55 pm** 6:55 pm

12 SUNDAY
☽ ☍ ♄ **10:24 am** 7:24 am
☽ △ ☿ **12:58 pm** 9:58 am
☽ △ ☉ **4:30 pm** 1:30 pm
☽ ⚺ ♃ 11:34 pm
☽ ⚺ ♆ 11:54 pm

13 MONDAY
☽ ⚺ ♃ **2:34 am**
☽ ⚺ ♆ **2:54 am**
☽ ☌ ♅ **4:03 am** 1:03 am
☽ ⚹ ♂ **12:47 pm** 9:47 am
☽ □ ♇ **1:29 pm** 10:29 am
☉ ☌ ☿ **10:15 pm** 7:15 pm
♂ ⚻ ♇ 9:52 pm

14 TUESDAY
♂ ⚻ ♇ **12:52 am**
☽ ⚹ ♀ **5:38 am** 2:38 am
☽ ⚻ ♄ **8:03 pm** 5:03 pm

15 WEDNESDAY
☽ □ ☉ **5:53 am** 2:53 am
☽ □ ☿ **9:17 am** 6:17 am
☽ ⚹ ♃ **10:31 am** 7:31 am
☽ ⚹ ♆ **11:07 am** 8:07 am
☽ ⚺ ♅ **12:14 pm** 9:14 am
☿ ⚻ ♃ **4:39 pm** 1:39 pm
☿ ⚻ ♆ **8:31 pm** 5:31 pm
☽ △ ♇ **9:03 pm** 6:03 pm
☽ ⚺ ♂ **11:34 pm** 8:34 pm

16 THURSDAY
☿ △ ♅ **3:33 am** 12:33 am
☽ ⚺ ♀ **5:07 pm** 2:07 pm
☽ △ ♄ 11:04 pm

17 FRIDAY
☽ △ ♄ **2:04 am**
☽ ⚹ ☉ **2:46 pm** 11:46 am
☽ □ ♃ **2:53 pm** 11:53 am
☽ □ ♆ **3:43 pm** 12:43 pm
☉ ⚻ ♃ **4:33 pm** 1:33 pm
☽ ⚹ ♅ **4:48 pm** 1:48 pm
☽ ⚹ ☿ **11:18 pm** 8:18 pm
☽ ⚻ ♇ 9:59 pm

18 SATURDAY
☽ ⚻ ♇ **12:59 am**
☉ ⚻ ♆ **4:31 am** 1:31 am
☽ ☌ ♂ **6:05 am** 3:05 am
☿ ⚻ ♇ **10:49 am** 7:49 am
☉ △ ♅ **8:36 pm** 5:36 pm
☽ ☌ ♀ 9:06 pm

19 SUNDAY
☽ ☌ ♀ **12:06 am**
☽ □ ♄ **4:38 am** 1:38 am
☽ △ ♃ **4:07 pm** 1:07 pm
☽ △ ♆ **5:08 pm** 2:08 pm
☽ □ ♅ **6:12 pm** 3:12 pm
☽ ⚺ ☉ **7:42 pm** 4:42 pm
☽ ☍ ♇ 10:58 pm

20 MONDAY
☽ ☍ ♇ **1:58 am**
☽ ⚺ ☿ **8:13 am** 5:13 am
☽ ⚺ ♂ **9:16 am** 6:16 am
☿ ⚹ ♂ **7:32 pm** 4:32 pm

21 TUESDAY
☽ ⚺ ♀ **4:07 am** 1:07 am
☽ ⚹ ♄ **4:57 am** 1:57 am
☽ ⚻ ♃ **3:32 pm** 12:32 pm
♀ □ ♄ **4:05 pm** 1:05 pm
☽ ⚻ ♆ **4:47 pm** 1:47 pm
☽ △ ♅ **5:51 pm** 2:51 pm
☽ ☌ ☉ **10:34 pm** 7:34 pm
☽ ⚻ ♇ 10:29 pm

22 WEDNESDAY
☽ ⚻ ♇ **1:29 am**
☽ ⚹ ♂ **11:04 am** 8:04 am
☽ ☌ ☿ **2:58 pm** 11:58 am

23 THURSDAY
☽ ⚺ ♄ **4:49 am** 1:49 am
☽ ⚹ ♀ **7:34 am** 4:34 am
☽ ☍ ♃ **2:55 pm** 11:55 am
☽ ☍ ♆ **4:28 pm** 1:28 pm
☽ ⚻ ♅ **5:35 pm** 2:35 pm
☉ ⚻ ♇ **7:47 pm** 4:47 pm
☽ △ ♇ 10:23 pm
☽ ⚺ ☉ 10:47 pm

24 FRIDAY
☽ △ ♇ **1:23 am**
☽ ⚺ ☉ **1:47 am**
☽ □ ♂ **1:44 pm** 10:44 am
☽ ⚺ ☿ **10:51 pm** 7:51 pm

25 SATURDAY
☽ ☌ ♄ **6:12 am** 3:12 am
☽ □ ♀ **1:01 pm** 10:01 am
☽ ⚻ ♃ **4:06 pm** 1:06 pm
☽ ⚻ ♆ **6:02 pm** 3:02 pm
☽ ☍ ♅ **7:14 pm** 4:14 pm

26 SUNDAY
☽ □ ♇ **3:29 am** 12:29 am
☽ ⚹ ☉ **7:41 am** 4:41 am
☽ △ ♂ **7:24 pm** 4:24 pm
♀ △ ♃ 9:07 pm

27 MONDAY
♀ △ ♃ **12:07 am**
☿ ⚺ ♄ **10:05 am** 7:05 am
☽ ⚺ ♄ **10:41 am** 7:41 am
☽ ⚹ ☿ **10:47 am** 7:47 am
☽ △ ♃ **8:28 pm** 5:28 pm
☽ △ ♀ **10:36 pm** 7:36 pm
☽ △ ♆ **10:53 pm** 7:53 pm
☽ ⚻ ♅ 9:12 pm
♀ △ ♆ 10:51 pm

28 TUESDAY
☽ ⚻ ♅ **12:12 am**
♀ △ ♆ **1:51 am**
☽ ⚹ ♇ **9:03 am** 6:03 am
♀ □ ♅ **4:38 pm** 1:38 pm
☽ □ ☉ **6:00 pm** 3:00 pm

29 WEDNESDAY
☽ ⚻ ♂ **5:20 am** 2:20 am
☽ ⚹ ♄ **7:03 pm** 4:03 pm

30 THURSDAY
☽ □ ☿ **4:07 am** 1:07 am
☽ □ ♃ **4:30 am** 1:30 am
☿ ☍ ♃ **6:38 am** 3:38 am
☽ □ ♆ **7:30 am** 4:30 am
☽ △ ♅ **8:54 am** 5:54 am
☽ ⚻ ♀ **1:08 pm** 10:08 am
☽ ⚺ ♇ **6:19 pm** 3:19 pm

31 FRIDAY
☿ ☍ ♆ **3:46 am** 12:46 am
☽ △ ☉ **8:51 am** 5:51 am
☿ ⚻ ♅ **1:49 pm** 10:49 am
☽ ☍ ♂ **7:21 pm** 4:21 pm

JULY 2009

DATE	S.TIME	SUN	MOON	N.NODE	MERCURY	VENUS	MARS	JUPITER	SATURN	URANUS	NEPTUNE	PLUTO	CERES	PALLAS	JUNO	VESTA	CHIRON
1 Wed	18:36:44	09♋18 42	27♎43	00♒25	24♊32	25♊17	22♉06	26♒37 R	16♍35	26♓37 R	26♒12 R	01♑47 R	17♍08	13♌48	29♓32	04♋53	25♒44
2 Thu	18:40:40	10 15 49	10♏22	00 23 R	26 22	26 27	22 49	26 34 R	16 37	26 37	26 11 R	01 46 R	17 30	14 18	29 46	05 19	25 42 R
3 Fri	18:44:37	11 13 06	22 46	00 20	28 24	27 27	23 32	26 31	16 44	26 37	26 10	01 44	17 51	14 49	29 59	05 46	25 40
4 Sat	18:48:33	12 10 17	04♐58	00 18	00♋23	28 32	24 14	26 28	16 48	26 37	26 09	01 43	18 12	15 19	00♈12	06 12	25 38
5 Sun	18:52:30	13 07 29	17 01	00 15	02 25	29 37	24 57	26 24	16 53	26 37	26 08	01 41	18 34	15 50	00 25	06 38	25 36
6 Mon	18:56:27	14 04 40	28 57	00 13	04 29	00♋43	25 40	26 20	16 57	26 37	26 07	01 40	18 55	16 20	00 38	07 04	25 34
7 Tue	19:00:23	15 01 51	10♑43	00 11	06 34	01 48	26 23	26 16	17 02	26 37	26 06	01 38	19 17	16 51	00 50	07 30	25 32
8 Wed	19:04:20	15 59 02	22 36	00 10 D	08 41	02 54	27 05	26 12	17 07	26 36	26 05	01 37	19 39	17 21	01 03	07 56	25 30
9 Thu	19:08:16	16 56 14	04♒24	00 10	10 49	04 00	27 48	26 08	17 12	26 36	26 03	01 35	20 01	17 51	01 14	08 22	25 28
10 Fri	19:12:13	17 53 25	16 14	00 11	12 58	05 06	28 30	26 04	17 17	26 36	26 02	01 34	20 23	18 22	01 26	08 48	25 26
11 Sat	19:16:09	18 50 37	28 08	00 12	15 07	06 12	29 13	25 59	17 22	26 35	26 01	01 32	20 45	18 52	01 37	09 14	25 24
12 Sun	19:20:06	19 47 49	10♓11	00 13	17 17	07 19	29 55	25 54	17 27	26 35	26 00	01 31	21 07	19 22	01 48	09 40	25 21
13 Mon	19:24:02	20 45 02	22 25	00 14	19 26	08 25	00♊37	25 49	17 32	26 34	25 59	01 29	21 30	19 53	01 59	10 06	25 19
14 Tue	19:27:59	21 42 15	04♈53	00 14	21 36	09 32	01 19	25 44	17 37	26 34	25 57	01 28	21 52	20 23	02 10	10 32	25 17
15 Wed	19:31:56	22 39 28	17 41	00 15 R	23 44	10 39	02 01	25 39	17 42	26 33	25 56	01 27	22 15	20 53	02 20	10 58	25 14
16 Thu	19:35:52	23 36 42	00♉50	00 15	25 52	11 46	02 43	25 33	17 48	26 32	25 55	01 25	22 37	21 23	02 30	11 24	25 12
17 Fri	19:39:49	24 33 57	14 24	00 15	27 59	12 53	03 25	25 28	17 53	26 31	25 53	01 24	23 00	21 53	02 39	11 50	25 09
18 Sat	19:43:45	25 31 13	28 24	00 14	00♌05	14 01	04 07	25 22	17 59	26 31	25 52	01 22	23 23	22 24	02 48	12 16	25 07
19 Sun	19:47:42	26 28 29	12♊49	00 13	02 09	15 08	04 49	25 16	18 04	26 30	25 51	01 21	23 46	22 54	02 57	12 42	25 04
20 Mon	19:51:38	27 25 47	27 36	00 13	04 11	16 16	05 31	25 10	18 10	26 29	25 49	01 20	24 09	23 24	03 05	13 08	25 01
21 Tue	19:55:35	28 23 04	12♋39	00 13	06 14	17 23	06 12	25 04	18 15	26 28	25 48	01 18	24 32	23 54	03 14	13 34	24 59
22 Wed	19:59:31	29 20 23	27 49	00 13 D	08 14	18 31	06 54	24 58	18 21	26 27	25 47	01 17	24 55	24 24	03 21	14 00	24 56
23 Thu	20:03:28	00♌17 41	12♌57	00 13 R	10 12	19 39	07 35	24 52	18 27	26 26	25 45	01 16	25 19	24 54	03 29	14 26	24 53
24 Fri	20:07:25	01 15 01	27 55	00 13	12 09	20 47	08 17	24 45	18 33	26 25	25 44	01 14	25 42	25 24	03 36	14 52	24 51
25 Sat	20:11:21	02 12 20	12♍35	00 13	14 04	21 55	08 58	24 39	18 39	26 23	25 42	01 13	26 06	25 54	03 43	15 18	24 48
26 Sun	20:15:18	03 09 40	26 50	00 12	15 58	23 04	09 39	24 32	18 44	26 23	25 41	01 12	26 29	26 24	03 49	15 44	24 45
27 Mon	20:19:14	04 07 01	10♎40	00 12	17 49	24 12	10 20	24 25	18 50	26 22	25 39	01 11	26 53	26 54	03 55	16 10	24 42
28 Tue	20:23:11	05 04 22	24 03	00 12 D	19 39	25 21	11 01	24 18	18 57	26 21	25 38	01 09	27 16	27 24	04 00	16 36	24 40
29 Wed	20:27:07	06 01 43	07♏38	00 12	21 28	26 29	11 42	24 11	19 03	26 19	25 36	01 08	27 40	27 54	04 06	17 02	24 37
30 Thu	20:31:04	06 59 05	19 38	00 12	23 14	27 38	12 23	24 04	19 09	26 18	25 35	01 07	28 04	28 24	04 10	17 27	24 34
31 Fri	20:35:00	07 56 28	01♐57	00 12	24 59	28 47	13 04	23 57	19 15	26 17	25 33	01 06	28 28	28 54	04 15	17 53	24 31

EPHEMERIS CALCULATED FOR 12 MIDNIGHT GREENWICH MEAN TIME. ALL OTHER DATA AND FACING ASPECTARIAN PAGE IN **EASTERN TIME (BOLD)** AND PACIFIC TIME (REGULAR).

AUGUST 2009

☽ Last Aspect day	ET / hr:mn / PT	asp	☽ Ingress sign day	ET / hr:mn / PT
1	10:42 pm	△☿	♑ 2	**4:08 am** 1:08 am
2	**1:42 am**	△☿	♑ 2	**4:08 am** 1:08 am
4	**9:21 am** 6:21 am	✶♅	♒ 4	**5:08 pm** 2:08 pm
6	**8:19 pm** 5:19 pm	☌♆	♓ 7	**5:34 am** 2:34 am
9	**8:44 am** 5:44 am	☌♅	♈ 9	**4:23 pm** 1:23 pm
11	**4:03 pm** 1:03 pm	✶♆	♉ 11	9:49 pm
11	**4:03 pm** 1:03 pm	✶♆	♉ 12	**12:49 am**
13	**11:17 pm** 8:17 pm	✶♅	♊ 14	**6:25 am** 3:25 am
15	11:19 pm	□♅	♋ 16	**9:13 am** 6:13 am
16	**2:19 am**	□♅	♋ 16	**9:13 am** 6:13 am

☽ Last Aspect day	ET / hr:mn / PT	asp	☽ Ingress sign day	ET / hr:mn / PT
18	**3:09 am** 12:09 am	△♅	♌ 18	**9:56 am** 6:56 am
20	**6:01 am** 3:01 am	☌☉	♍ 20	**10:00 am** 7:00 am
22	**7:44 am** 4:44 am	□♂	♎ 22	**11:12 am** 8:12 am
24	**2:10 pm** 11:10 am	△♂	♏ 24	**3:16 pm** 12:16 pm
26	**2:34 pm** 11:34 am	△♅	♐ 26	**11:16 pm** 8:16 pm
28	10:26 pm	□♅	♑ 29	**10:44 am** 7:44 am
29	**1:26 am**	□♅	♑ 29	**10:44 am** 7:44 am
31	**2:09 pm** 11:09 am	✶♅	♒ 31	**11:43 pm** 8:43 pm

☽ Phases & Eclipses phase	day	ET / hr:mn / PT
Full Moon	5	**8:55 pm** 5:55 pm
☊ (eclipse)	5	13° ♒ 35'
4th Quarter	13	**2:55 pm** 11:55 am
New Moon	20	**6:01 am** 3:01 am
2nd Quarter	27	**7:42 am** 4:42 am

Planet Ingress	day	ET / hr:mn / PT
♀ ♍	1	10:29 pm
♀ ♍	2	**1:29 am**
☿ ♍	2	**7:07 pm** 4:07 pm
⚳ ♎	3	**3:31 pm** 12:31 pm
☉ ♍	22	**7:38 pm** 4:38 pm
♂ ♋	25	**1:15 pm** 10:15 am
☿ ♎	25	**4:18 pm** 1:18 pm
♀ ♌	26	**12:11 pm** 9:11 am
⚶ ♌	28	**8:45 am** 5:45 am

Planetary Motion	day	ET / hr:mn / PT
⚵ ℞	9	**8:01 pm** 5:01 pm

1 SATURDAY
☽□♄ **6:44 am** 3:44 am
☽✶♃ **3:27 pm** 12:27 pm
☽✶♆ **7:02 pm** 4:02 pm
♀☍♇ **7:35 pm** 4:35 pm
☽□♅ **8:31 pm** 5:31 pm
☽△☿ 10:42 pm

2 SUNDAY
☽△☿ **1:42 am**
☽☌♇ **6:16 am** 3:16 am
☽☍♀ **7:26 am** 4:26 am
☽⚻☉ 11:38 pm

3 MONDAY
☽⚻☉ **2:38 am**
☿△♇ **10:11 am** 7:11 am
☽⚻♂ **11:42 am** 8:42 am
☽△♄ **8:08 pm** 5:08 pm

4 TUESDAY
☽⚺♃ **3:44 am** 12:44 am
☽⚺♆ **7:51 am** 4:51 am
☽✶♅ **9:21 am** 6:21 am
☽⚺♇ **7:10 pm** 4:10 pm
☽⚻☿ 9:26 pm

5 WEDNESDAY
☽⚻☿ **12:26 am**
☽⚻♀ **3:02 am** 12:02 am
☽☍☉ **8:55 pm** 5:55 pm

6 THURSDAY
☽△♂ **4:12 am** 1:12 am
☽⚻♄ **9:27 am** 6:27 am
☽☌♃ **3:47 pm** 12:47 pm
☽☌♆ **8:19 pm** 5:19 pm
☽⚺♅ **9:48 pm** 6:48 pm

7 FRIDAY
☽✶♇ **7:30 am** 4:30 am
☽☍☿ **9:35 pm** 6:35 pm
☽△♀ **9:39 pm** 6:39 pm
☿✶♀ **11:52 pm** 8:52 pm

8 SATURDAY
☽⚻☉ **1:48 pm** 10:48 am
☽□♂ **7:14 pm** 4:14 pm
☽☍♄ **9:27 pm** 6:27 pm
☽⚺♃ 11:26 pm

9 SUNDAY
☽⚺♃ **2:26 am**
☽⚺♆ **7:19 am** 4:19 am
☽☌♅ **8:44 am** 5:44 am
☽□♇ **6:10 pm** 3:10 pm

10 MONDAY
☽□♀ **1:48 pm** 10:48 am
☽⚻☿ **3:29 pm** 12:29 pm
♂□♄ **8:16 pm** 5:16 pm

11 TUESDAY
☽△☉ **4:04 am** 1:04 am
☽⚻♄ **7:14 am** 4:14 am
☽✶♂ **7:43 am** 4:43 am
☽✶♃ **10:56 am** 7:56 am
☽✶♆ **4:03 pm** 1:03 pm
☽⚺♅ **5:24 pm** 2:24 pm
☽△♇ 11:27 pm

12 WEDNESDAY
☽△♇ **2:27 am**
☽✶♀ 11:31 pm

13 THURSDAY
☽✶♀ **2:31 am**
☉⚺♄ **3:44 am** 12:44 am
☽△☿ **5:15 am** 2:15 am
♂△♃ **12:29 pm** 9:29 am
☽△♄ **2:13 pm** 11:13 am
☽□☉ **2:55 pm** 11:55 am
☽□♃ **4:45 pm** 1:45 pm
☽⚺♂ **5:00 pm** 2:00 pm
☽□♆ **10:00 pm** 7:00 pm
☽✶♅ **11:17 pm** 8:17 pm

14 FRIDAY
☽⚻♇ **7:55 am** 4:55 am
☉☍♃ **1:53 pm** 10:53 am

15 SATURDAY
☽⚺♀ **11:27 am** 8:27 am
☽□☿ **2:40 pm** 11:40 am
☽□♄ **6:14 pm** 3:14 pm
☽△♃ **7:45 pm** 4:45 pm
☽✶☉ **10:11 pm** 7:11 pm
☽☌♂ **10:56 pm** 7:56 pm
☽△♆ 10:07 pm
☽□♅ 11:19 pm

16 SUNDAY
☽△♆ **1:07 am**
☽□♅ **2:19 am**
☽☍♇ **10:35 am** 7:35 am

17 MONDAY
☉✶♂ **6:58 am** 3:58 am
☿☌♄ **11:14 am** 8:14 am
☉☍♆ **4:55 pm** 1:55 pm
☽☌♀ **5:11 pm** 2:11 pm
☽✶♄ **7:51 pm** 4:51 pm
☿⚻♃ **8:00 pm** 5:00 pm
☽⚻♃ **8:30 pm** 5:30 pm
☽✶☿ **8:33 pm** 5:33 pm
♂△♆ **9:28 pm** 6:28 pm
☽⚻♆ 11:01 pm
☽⚺♂ 11:14 pm
☽⚺☉ 11:40 pm

18 TUESDAY
☽⚻♆ **2:01 am**
☽⚺♂ **2:14 am**
☽⚺☉ **2:40 am**
☽△♅ **3:09 am** 12:09 am
☉⚻♅ **10:02 am** 7:02 am
☽⚻♇ **11:14 am** 8:14 am
♂□♅ **10:24 pm** 7:24 pm

19 WEDNESDAY
♀✶♄ **6:11 am** 3:11 am
♀⚻♃ **7:06 am** 4:06 am
♃⚻♄ **11:07 am** 8:07 am
☽☍♃ **8:10 pm** 5:10 pm
☽⚺♄ **8:19 pm** 5:19 pm
☽⚺♀ **9:24 pm** 6:24 pm
☽⚺☿ 9:43 pm
☽☍♆ 10:59 pm

20 THURSDAY
☽⚺☿ **12:43 am**
☽☍♆ **1:59 am**
☽⚻♅ **3:06 am** 12:06 am
☽✶♂ **4:28 am** 1:28 am
☽☌☉ **6:01 am** 3:01 am
☽△♇ **11:16 am** 8:16 am
☿⚻♆ **5:07 pm** 2:07 pm

21 FRIDAY
☿☍♅ **7:47 am** 4:47 am
☽⚻♃ **8:25 pm** 5:25 pm
☽☌♄ **9:24 pm** 6:24 pm
☽✶♀ 11:27 pm
☽⚻♆ 11:46 pm

22 SATURDAY
☽✶♀ **2:27 am**
☽⚻♆ **2:46 am**
☽☍♅ **3:54 am** 12:54 am
☽☌☿ **5:34 am** 2:34 am
♀⚻♆ **6:07 am** 3:07 am
☽□♂ **7:44 am** 4:44 am
☽⚺☉ **10:35 am** 7:35 am
☽□♇ **12:28 pm** 9:28 am
♀△♅ **7:31 pm** 4:31 pm

23 SUNDAY
☉△♇ **2:20 pm** 11:20 am
☽△♃ **11:00 pm** 8:00 pm
☽⚺♄ 9:58 pm

24 MONDAY
☽⚺♄ **12:58 am**
☽△♆ **6:09 am** 3:09 am
☽⚻♅ **7:20 am** 4:20 am
☽□♀ **10:53 am** 7:53 am
☽⚺☿ **1:24 pm** 10:24 am
☽△♂ **2:10 pm** 11:10 am
☽✶♇ **4:36 pm** 1:36 pm
☽✶☉ **6:41 pm** 3:41 pm

25 TUESDAY
☿□♂ **11:57 pm** 8:57 pm

26 WEDNESDAY
☽□♃ **5:14 am** 2:14 am
☽✶♄ **8:25 am** 5:25 am
☿□♇ **12:09 pm** 9:09 am
☽□♆ **1:21 pm** 10:21 am
☽△♅ **2:34 pm** 11:34 am
♂☍♇ **4:34 pm** 1:34 pm
☽△♀ 9:27 pm
☽⚺♇ 9:40 pm
☽⚻♂ 10:06 pm
☽✶☿ 10:35 pm
♀⚻♇ 11:43 pm

27 THURSDAY
☽△♀ **12:27 am**
☽⚺♇ **12:40 am**
☽⚻♂ **1:06 am**
☽✶☿ **1:35 am**
♀⚻♇ **2:43 am**
☽□☉ **7:42 am** 4:42 am
♀⚺♂ **2:24 pm** 11:24 am

28 FRIDAY
☿✶♀ **9:25 am** 6:25 am
☽✶♃ **3:10 pm** 12:10 pm
☽□♄ **7:44 pm** 4:44 pm
☽✶♆ 9:11 pm
☽□♅ 10:26 pm

29 SATURDAY
☽✶♆ **12:11 am**
☽□♅ **1:26 am**
☽☌♇ **12:09 pm** 9:09 am
☽☍♂ **4:00 pm** 1:00 pm
☽□☿ **5:12 pm** 2:12 pm
☽⚻♀ **6:37 pm** 3:37 pm
☽△☉ 9:51 pm

30 SUNDAY
☽△☉ **12:51 am**

31 MONDAY
☽⚺♃ **3:19 am** 12:19 am
☽△♄ **9:11 am** 6:11 am
☽⚺♆ **12:56 pm** 9:56 am
☽✶♅ **2:09 pm** 11:09 am
☽⚺♇ 10:06 pm

Eastern time in bold type
Pacific time in medium type

AUGUST 2009

DATE	S.TIME	SUN	MOON	N.NODE	MERCURY	VENUS	MARS	JUPITER	SATURN	URANUS	NEPTUNE	PLUTO	CERES	PALLAS	JUNO	VESTA	CHIRON
1 Sat	20:38:57	08 ♌ 53 51	14 ♐ 03	00 ≈ 13	26 ♌ 42	29 ♊ 57	13 ♊ 44	23 ≈ 50	19 ♍ 21	26 ♓ 15	25 ≈ 32	01 ♑ 05	28 ♏ 52	29 ♋ 23	04 ♏ 19	18 ♋ 19	24 ≈ 28
2 Sun	20:42:54	09 51 14	25 59	00 14	28 24	01 ♋ 05	14 25	23 42 R	19 28	26 14 R	25 30 R	01 04 R	29 16	29 53	04 22	18 45	24 25 R
3 Mon	20:46:50	10 48 39	07 ♑ 49	00 15	00 ♍ 03	02 14	15 05	23 35	19 34	26 13	25 27	01 03	29 40	00 ♌ 23	04 25	19 11	24 22
4 Tue	20:50:47	11 46 04	19 37	00 16 R	01 42	03 23	15 46	23 27	19 40	26 11	25 25	01 02	00 ♐ 05	00 53	04 28	19 36	24 19
5 Wed	20:54:43	12 43 30	01 ≈ 35	00 16	03 18	04 33	16 26	23 20	19 47	26 10	25 24	01 01	00 29	01 23	04 31	20 02	24 16
6 Thu	20:58:40	13 40 57	13 16	00 14	04 53	05 42	17 06	23 12	19 53	26 08	25 22	01 00	00 53	01 52	04 33	20 28	24 13
7 Fri	21:02:36	14 38 24	25 12	00 13	06 27	06 52	17 46	23 05	20 00	26 07	25 21	00 59	01 18	02 22	04 35	20 53	24 10
8 Sat	21:06:33	15 35 53	07 ♓ 16	00 13	07 58	08 01	18 26	22 57	20 06	26 05	25 19	00 57	01 42	02 51	04 36	21 19	24 07
9 Sun	21:10:29	16 33 23	19 29	00 10	09 28	09 11	19 06	22 49	20 13	26 03	25 17	00 56	02 07	03 21	04 36 R	21 45	24 04
10 Mon	21:14:26	17 30 54	01 ♈ 53	00 08	10 56	10 21	19 46	22 41	20 20	26 02	25 16	00 56	02 31	03 51	04 36	22 10	24 01
11 Tue	21:18:23	18 28 27	14 30	00 05	12 23	11 31	20 26	22 34	20 26	26 00	25 14	00 55	02 56	04 20	04 35	22 36	23 58
12 Wed	21:22:19	19 26 01	27 23	00 04	13 48	12 41	21 06	22 26	20 33	25 58	25 12	00 54	03 20	04 50	04 34	23 02	23 55
13 Thu	21:26:16	20 23 36	10 ♉ 33	00 02 D	15 11	13 51	21 45	22 18	20 40	25 56	25 11	00 53	03 45	05 19	04 33	23 27	23 52
14 Fri	21:30:12	21 21 13	24 02	00 02	16 32	15 02	22 25	22 10	20 47	25 54	25 09	00 52	04 10	05 49	04 31	23 53	23 49
15 Sat	21:34:09	22 18 51	07 ♊ 51	00 02	17 51	16 12	23 04	22 02	20 54	25 53	25 08	00 51	04 35	06 18	04 28	24 18	23 46
16 Sun	21:38:05	23 16 31	22 03	00 03	19 09	17 22	23 44	21 54	21 01	25 51	25 06	00 50	05 00	06 48	04 25	24 44	23 43
17 Mon	21:42:02	24 14 13	06 ♋ 33	00 05	20 25	18 33	24 23	21 46	21 07	25 49	25 04	00 50	05 25	07 17	04 22	25 09	23 39
18 Tue	21:45:58	25 11 56	21 20	00 06 R	21 39	19 44	25 02	21 39	21 14	25 47	25 03	00 49	05 50	07 46	04 18	25 34	23 36
19 Wed	21:49:55	26 09 41	06 ♌ 17	00 05	22 50	20 54	25 41	21 31	21 21	25 45	25 01	00 48	06 15	08 16	04 14	26 00	23 33
20 Thu	21:53:52	27 07 26	21 17	00 05	24 00	22 05	26 20	21 23	21 28	25 43	24 59	00 47	06 40	08 45	04 09	26 25	23 30
21 Fri	21:57:48	28 05 14	06 ♍ 06	00 04	25 08	23 16	26 58	21 15	21 36	25 41	24 58	00 47	07 05	09 14	04 04	26 51	23 27
22 Sat	22:01:45	29 03 02	20 52	00 03	26 15	24 27	27 37	21 07	21 43	25 39	24 56	00 46	07 31	09 44	03 58	27 16	23 24
23 Sun	22:05:41	00 ♍ 00 52	05 ♎ 13	29 ♑ 59	27 16	25 38	28 16	21 00	21 50	25 37	24 54	00 45	07 56	10 13	03 52	27 41	23 21
24 Mon	22:09:38	00 58 43	19 09	29 55	28 16	26 49	28 54	20 52	21 57	25 35	24 53	00 45	08 21	10 42	03 45	28 06	23 18
25 Tue	22:13:34	01 56 36	02 ♏ 37	29 52	29 13	28 00	29 33	20 45	22 04	25 32	24 51	00 44	08 47	11 11	03 38	28 31	23 15
26 Wed	22:17:31	02 54 29	15 40	29 49	00 ≏ 08	29 12	00 ♋ 11	20 38	22 11	25 30	24 50	00 44	09 12	11 40	03 31	28 57	23 12
27 Thu	22:21:27	03 52 24	28 18	29 46	01 00	00 ♌ 23	00 49	20 30	22 18	25 28	24 48	00 43	09 37	12 10	03 23	29 22	23 09
28 Fri	22:25:24	04 50 20	10 ♐ 37	29 44	01 49	01 35	01 27	20 22	22 25	25 26	24 46	00 43	10 03	12 39	03 15	29 47	23 06
29 Sat	22:29:21	05 48 18	23 06	29 42 D	02 34	02 46	02 05	20 15	22 33	25 24	24 45	00 42	10 28	13 08	03 06	00 ♌ 12	23 03
30 Sun	22:33:17	06 46 17	05 ♑ 35	29 45	03 16	03 58	02 43	20 08	22 40	25 22	24 45	00 42	10 54	13 37	02 57	00 37	23 00
31 Mon	22:37:14	07 44 17	17 23	29 47	03 54	05 10	03 20	20 00	22 48	25 19	24 45	00 42	11 20	14 06	02 48	01 02	22 57

EPHEMERIS CALCULATED FOR 12 MIDNIGHT GREENWICH MEAN TIME. ALL OTHER DATA AND FACING ASPECTARIAN PAGE IN **EASTERN TIME (BOLD)** AND PACIFIC TIME (REGULAR).

SEPTEMBER 2009

☽ Last Aspect day	ET / hr:mn / PT	asp	☽ Ingress sign day	ET / hr:mn / PT
2	10:19 am	☌ ♆	♓ 3	**11:58 am** 8:58 am
3	**1:19 am**	☌ ♆	♓ 3	**11:58 am** 8:58 am
5	**12:53 pm** 9:53 am	☌ ♅	♈ 5	**10:14 pm** 7:14 pm
7	**8:12 pm** 5:12 pm	⚹ ♆	♉ 8	**6:17 am** 3:17 am
10	**3:17 am** 12:17 am	⚹ ♅	♊ 10	**12:17 pm** 9:17 am
12	**7:30 am** 4:30 am	□ ♅	♋ 12	**4:19 pm** 1:19 pm
14	**9:57 am** 6:57 am	△ ♅	♌ 14	**6:39 pm** 3:39 pm
16	**12:10 pm** 9:10 am	☌ ♀	♍ 16	**7:56 pm** 4:56 pm
18	**7:56 pm** 4:56 pm	☌ ☿	♎ 18	**9:26 pm** 6:26 pm
20	**2:43 pm** 11:43 am	△ ♆	♏ 20	9:52 pm
20	**2:43 pm** 11:43 am	△ ♆	♏ 21	**12:52 am**
22	**11:32 pm** 8:32 pm	⚹ ♄	♐ 23	**7:43 am** 4:43 am
25	**10:15 am** 7:15 am	□ ♄	♑ 25	**6:19 pm** 3:19 pm
27	**11:33 pm** 8:33 pm	△ ♄	♒ 28	**7:06 am** 4:06 am
30	**7:34 am** 4:34 am	☌ ♆	♓ 30	**7:26 pm** 4:26 pm

☽ Phases & Eclipses phase	day	ET / hr:mn / PT
Full Moon	4	**12:02 pm** 9:02 am
4th Quarter	11	**10:16 pm** 7:16 pm
New Moon	18	**2:44 pm** 11:44 am
2nd Quarter	25	9:50 pm
2nd Quarter	26	**12:50 am**

Planet Ingress	day	ET / hr:mn / PT
⚳ ♓	14	**7:00 pm** 4:00 pm
☿ ♍	17	**11:26 pm** 8:26 pm
♀ ♍	20	**9:32 am** 6:32 am
☉ ♎	22	**5:18 pm** 2:18 pm

Planetary Motion	day	ET / hr:mn / PT
☿ ℞	6	9:45 pm
☿ ℞	7	**12:45 am**
♇ D	11	**12:57 pm** 9:57 am
☿ D	29	**9:13 am** 6:13 am

1 TUESDAY
☽ ⚺ ♇ **1:06 am**
☽ ⚻ ♂ **8:24 am** 5:24 am
☽ △ ☿ **9:22 am** 6:22 am
☽ ☍ ♀ **2:27 pm** 11:27 am
☽ ⚻ ☉ **7:14 pm** 4:14 pm

2 WEDNESDAY
☽ ☌ ♃ **3:26 pm** 12:26 pm
☽ ⚻ ♄ **10:24 pm** 7:24 pm
☽ ☌ ♆ 10:19 pm
☽ ⚺ ♅ 11:26 pm

3 THURSDAY
☽ ☌ ♆ **1:19 am**
☽ ⚺ ♅ **2:26 am**
☿ □ ♂ **12:19 pm** 9:19 am
☽ ⚹ ♇ **1:18 pm** 10:18 am
☽ ⚻ ☿ **11:21 pm** 8:21 pm
☽ △ ♂ **11:39 pm** 8:39 pm

4 FRIDAY
☽ ⚻ ♀ **8:47 am** 5:47 am
☽ ☍ ☉ **12:02 pm** 9:02 am
☽ ⚺ ♃ 10:55 pm

5 SATURDAY
☽ ⚺ ♃ **1:55 am**
☽ ☍ ♄ **9:45 am** 6:45 am
☽ ⚺ ♆ **11:52 am** 8:52 am
☽ ☌ ♅ **12:53 pm** 9:53 am
☽ □ ♇ **11:30 pm** 8:30 pm

6 SUNDAY
☽ ☍ ☿ **10:00 am** 7:00 am
☽ □ ♂ **12:25 pm** 9:25 am
☽ △ ♀ 9:14 pm
☽ ⚻ ☉ 11:05 pm

7 MONDAY
☽ △ ♀ **12:14 am**
☽ ⚻ ☉ **2:05 am**
☽ ⚹ ♃ **10:17 am** 7:17 am
☽ ⚻ ♄ **6:50 pm** 3:50 pm
☽ ⚹ ♆ **8:12 pm** 5:12 pm
☽ ⚺ ♅ **9:07 pm** 6:07 pm

8 TUESDAY
☽ △ ♇ **7:30 am** 4:30 am
☽ ⚻ ☿ **5:23 pm** 2:23 pm
☽ ⚹ ♂ **10:38 pm** 7:38 pm

9 WEDNESDAY
☽ □ ♀ **12:47 pm** 9:47 am
☽ △ ☉ **1:25 pm** 10:25 am
☽ □ ♃ **4:35 pm** 1:35 pm
☽ △ ♄ 10:44 pm
☽ □ ♆ 11:27 pm

10 THURSDAY
☽ △ ♄ **1:44 am**
☽ □ ♆ **2:27 am**
☽ ⚹ ♅ **3:17 am** 12:17 am
☽ ⚻ ♇ **1:26 pm** 10:26 am
☉ ⚺ ♀ **9:41 pm** 6:41 pm
☽ △ ☿ **9:50 pm** 6:50 pm

11 FRIDAY
♀ ☍ ♃ **3:54 am** 12:54 am
☉ ⚻ ♃ **5:17 am** 2:17 am
☽ ⚺ ♂ **6:29 am** 3:29 am
☽ △ ♃ **8:58 pm** 5:58 pm
☽ □ ☉ **10:16 pm** 7:16 pm
☽ ⚹ ♀ **10:43 pm** 7:43 pm

12 SATURDAY
☽ □ ♄ **6:38 am** 3:38 am
☽ △ ♆ **6:45 am** 3:45 am
☽ □ ♅ **7:30 am** 4:30 am
☽ ☍ ♇ **5:27 pm** 2:27 pm
♄ ⚻ ♆ **6:58 pm** 3:58 pm
☽ □ ☿ **11:41 pm** 8:41 pm

13 SUNDAY
☽ ☌ ♂ **12:10 pm** 9:10 am
☽ ⚻ ♃ **11:34 pm** 8:34 pm

14 MONDAY
☽ ⚹ ☉ **4:50 am** 1:50 am
☽ ⚺ ♀ **6:16 am** 3:16 am
☽ ⚻ ♆ **9:17 am** 6:17 am
☽ ⚹ ♄ **9:41 am** 6:41 am
☽ △ ♅ **9:57 am** 6:57 am
☽ ⚻ ♇ **7:45 pm** 4:45 pm
☽ ⚹ ☿ **11:22 pm** 8:22 pm

15 TUESDAY
♄ ☍ ♅ **8:51 am** 5:51 am
☽ ⚺ ♂ **4:05 pm** 1:05 pm
♀ ☍ ♆ **5:37 pm** 2:37 pm
♀ ⚻ ♅ 9:48 pm
☽ ☍ ♃ 9:50 pm

16 WEDNESDAY
♀ ⚻ ♅ **12:48 am**
☽ ☍ ♃ **12:50 am**
♀ ⚺ ♄ **3:12 am** 12:12 am
☽ ⚺ ☉ **9:50 am** 6:50 am
☽ ☍ ♆ **10:37 am** 7:37 am
☽ ⚻ ♅ **11:12 am** 8:12 am
☽ ⚺ ♄ **11:30 am** 8:30 am
☽ ☌ ♀ **12:10 pm** 9:10 am
☽ △ ♇ **9:01 pm** 6:01 pm
☉ ⚻ ♆ **9:17 pm** 6:17 pm
☽ ⚺ ☿ **9:42 pm** 6:42 pm

17 THURSDAY
☉ ☍ ♅ **5:41 am** 2:41 am
☿ □ ♇ **7:46 am** 4:46 am
☉ ☌ ♄ **2:22 pm** 11:22 am
☽ ⚹ ♂ **7:21 pm** 4:21 pm
☽ ⚻ ♃ 10:47 pm

18 FRIDAY
☽ ⚻ ♃ **1:47 am**
☽ ⚻ ♆ **11:52 am** 8:52 am
☽ ☍ ♅ **12:25 pm** 9:25 am
☽ ☌ ♄ **1:17 pm** 10:17 am
☽ ☌ ☉ **2:44 pm** 11:44 am
☽ ⚺ ♀ **6:05 pm** 3:05 pm
☽ ☌ ☿ **7:56 pm** 4:56 pm
☽ □ ♇ **10:34 pm** 7:34 pm

19 SATURDAY
☿ ⚺ ♀ **6:34 am** 3:34 am
☽ □ ♂ **11:45 pm** 8:45 pm

20 SUNDAY
☽ △ ♃ **3:59 am** 12:59 am
☉ ☌ ☿ **6:04 am** 3:04 am
☽ △ ♆ **2:43 pm** 11:43 am
☽ ⚻ ♅ **3:13 pm** 12:13 pm
☽ ⚺ ♄ **4:45 pm** 1:45 pm
☽ ⚺ ☿ **7:34 pm** 4:34 pm
☽ ⚺ ☉ **9:44 pm** 6:44 pm
♀ △ ♇ **10:57 pm** 7:57 pm
☽ ⚹ ♇ 11:04 pm
☽ ⚹ ♀ 11:23 pm

21 MONDAY
☽ ⚹ ♇ **2:04 am**
☽ ⚹ ♀ **2:23 am**

22 TUESDAY
☿ ☌ ♄ **5:07 am** 2:07 am
☽ △ ♂ **7:16 am** 4:16 am
☽ □ ♃ **9:03 am** 6:03 am
☽ □ ♆ **8:44 pm** 5:44 pm
☽ △ ♅ **9:12 pm** 6:12 pm
☽ ⚹ ☿ **10:06 pm** 7:06 pm
☽ ⚹ ♄ **11:32 pm** 8:32 pm

23 WEDNESDAY
☽ ⚹ ☉ **8:55 am** 5:55 am
☽ ⚺ ♇ **9:02 am** 6:02 am
☉ □ ♇ **10:22 am** 7:22 am
☿ ☍ ♅ **11:36 am** 8:36 am
☽ □ ♀ **3:14 pm** 12:14 pm
☿ ⚻ ♆ **6:20 pm** 3:20 pm
♂ ⚻ ♃ **7:50 pm** 4:50 pm

24 THURSDAY
☽ ⚹ ♃ **5:55 pm** 2:55 pm
☽ ⚻ ♂ **7:07 pm** 4:07 pm

25 FRIDAY
☽ □ ☿ **4:29 am** 1:29 am
☽ ⚹ ♆ **6:34 am** 3:34 am
☽ □ ♅ **6:58 am** 3:58 am
☽ □ ♄ **10:15 am** 7:15 am
☽ ☌ ♇ **7:44 pm** 4:44 pm
☽ □ ☉ 9:50 pm

26 SATURDAY
☽ □ ☉ **12:50 am**
☽ △ ♀ **9:01 am** 6:01 am

27 SUNDAY
☽ ⚺ ♃ **5:50 am** 2:50 am
☽ ☍ ♂ **10:24 am** 7:24 am
☽ △ ☿ **2:35 pm** 11:35 am
☽ ⚺ ♆ **7:02 pm** 4:02 pm
☽ ⚹ ♅ **7:21 pm** 4:21 pm
☽ △ ♄ **11:33 pm** 8:33 pm

28 MONDAY
☽ ⚺ ♇ **8:36 am** 5:36 am
☽ △ ☉ **7:13 pm** 4:13 pm

29 TUESDAY
☽ ⚻ ♀ **4:58 am** 1:58 am
☽ ☌ ♃ **6:25 pm** 3:25 pm
☽ ⚻ ♂ 11:08 pm
☽ ⚻ ☿ 11:50 pm

30 WEDNESDAY
☽ ⚻ ♂ **2:08 am**
☽ ⚻ ☿ **2:50 am**
☽ ☌ ♆ **7:34 am** 4:34 am
☽ ⚺ ♅ **7:45 am** 4:45 am
☽ ⚻ ♄ **12:41 pm** 9:41 am
☽ ⚹ ♇ **8:55 pm** 5:55 pm
☿ ⚹ ♂ 11:00 pm

Eastern time in bold type
Pacific time in medium type

SEPTEMBER 2009

DATE	S.TIME	SUN	MOON	N.NODE	MERCURY	VENUS	MARS	JUPITER	SATURN	URANUS	NEPTUNE	PLUTO	CERES	PALLAS	JUNO	VESTA	CHIRON
1 Tue	22:41:07	08♍42 18	28♑10	29♒47 Rx	04♎28	06♋21	03♋58	19♒53	22♍55	25♓17	24♒42	00♑41	11♎45	14♍35	02♈48	01♌30	22♒54
2 Wed	22:45:07	09 40 21	10♒01	29 47	04 55	07 33	04 35	19 46 Rx	23 02	25 15 Rx	24 39 Rx	00 41 Rx	12 11	15 04	02 38 Rx	01 54	22 51 Rx
3 Thu	22:49:03	10 38 26	21 58	29 45	05 23	08 45	05 13	19 40	23 10	25 12	24 37	00 41	12 37	15 33	02 27	02 17	22 48
4 Fri	22:53:00	11 36 32	04♓04	29 40	05 44	09 57	05 50	19 33	23 17	25 10	24 35	00 41	13 02	16 02	02 17	02 41	22 46
5 Sat	22:56:56	12 34 40	16 21	29 34	05 59	11 09	06 27	19 26	23 24	25 08	24 34	00 40	13 28	16 30	02 06	03 06	22 43
6 Sun	23:00:53	13 32 49	28 50	29 27	06 09	12 21	07 04	19 20	23 32	25 06	24 32	00 40	13 54	16 59	01 55	03 30	22 40
7 Mon	23:04:50	14 31 00	11♈31	29 19	06 13 Rx	13 33	07 41	19 13	23 39	25 03	24 31	00 40	14 20	17 28	01 43	03 55	22 37
8 Tue	23:08:46	15 29 13	24 24	29 11	06 11	14 46	08 17	19 07	23 47	25 01	24 29	00 40	14 46	17 57	01 31	04 19	22 34
9 Wed	23:12:43	16 27 28	07♉31	29 04	06 03	15 58	08 54	19 01	23 54	24 58	24 28	00 40	15 12	18 26	01 19	04 44	22 32
10 Thu	23:16:39	17 25 45	20 50	28 59	05 49	17 11	09 30	18 55	24 02	24 56	24 26	00 40	15 38	18 54	01 06	05 08	22 29
11 Fri	23:20:36	18 24 04	04♊23	28 57	05 28	18 23	10 07	18 49	24 09	24 54	24 25	00 40 D	16 04	19 23	00 53	05 33	22 26
12 Sat	23:24:32	19 22 26	18 09	28 56 D	05 00	19 36	10 43	18 43	24 16	24 51	24 24	00 40	16 30	19 52	00 40	05 57	22 24
13 Sun	23:28:29	20 20 49	02♋10	28 56	04 25	20 48	11 19	18 37	24 24	24 49	24 24	00 40	16 56	20 20	00 27	06 22	22 21
14 Mon	23:32:25	21 19 15	16 23	28 57 Rx	03 45	22 01	11 55	18 32	24 31	24 47	24 22	00 40	17 22	20 49	00 13	06 46	22 18
15 Tue	23:36:22	22 17 43	00♌49	28 57	02 58	23 14	12 31	18 27	24 39	24 44	24 21	00 40	17 48	21 18	29♓59	07 10	22 16
16 Wed	23:40:19	23 16 12	15 24	28 56	02 06	24 27	13 06	18 22	24 46	24 42	24 19	00 40	18 14	21 46	29 45	07 34	22 13
17 Thu	23:44:15	24 14 44	00♍03	28 53	01 09	25 40	13 42	18 17	24 54	24 39	24 18	00 40	18 40	22 15	29 31	07 58	22 11
18 Fri	23:48:12	25 13 18	14 40	28 47	00 09	26 53	14 17	18 12	25 01	24 37	24 16	00 40	19 06	22 43	29 16	08 22	22 09
19 Sat	23:52:08	26 11 54	29 08	28 39	29♍06	28 06	14 53	18 07	25 09	24 35	24 15	00 40	19 33	23 12	29 02	08 46	22 06
20 Sun	23:56:05	27 10 31	13♎22	28 30	28 02	29 19	15 28	18 03	25 16	24 32	24 14	00 41	19 59	23 40	28 48	09 10	22 04
21 Mon	00:00:01	28 09 11	27 14	28 20	26 58	00♌32	16 03	17 58	25 24	24 30	24 13	00 41	20 25	24 08	28 33	09 34	22 02
22 Tue	00:03:58	29 07 52	10♏43	28 11	25 57	01 45	16 37	17 54	25 31	24 27	24 11	00 41	20 51	24 37	28 19	09 58	21 59
23 Wed	00:07:54	00♎06 35	23 46	28 02	24 59	02 58	17 12	17 50	25 39	24 25	24 10	00 41	21 18	25 05	28 04	10 21	21 57
24 Thu	00:11:51	01 05 20	06♐27	27 58	24 05	04 12	17 46	17 46	25 46	24 23	24 09	00 42	21 44	25 33	27 49	10 45	21 55
25 Fri	00:15:48	02 04 07	18 46	27 55 D	23 19	05 25	18 21	17 43	25 54	24 20	24 08	00 42	22 10	26 02	27 34	11 09	21 53
26 Sat	00:19:44	03 02 55	00♑51	27 55	22 40	06 39	18 55	17 39	26 01	24 18	24 06	00 42	22 37	26 30	27 20	11 32	21 51
27 Sun	00:23:41	04 01 46	12 44	27 55	22 10	07 52	19 29	17 36	26 09	24 15	24 05	00 43	23 03	26 58	27 05	11 55	21 49
28 Mon	00:27:37	05 00 37	24 32	27 55 Rx	21 49	09 06	20 03	17 33	26 16	24 13	24 04	00 44	23 29	27 26	26 51	12 19	21 47
29 Tue	00:31:34	05 59 31	06♒21	27 53	21 38 D	10 19	20 36	17 30	26 23	24 11	24 03	00 44	23 56	27 54	26 36	12 42	21 45
30 Wed	00:35:30	06 58 26	18 15	27 53	21 38	11 33	21 10	17 27	26 31	24 08	24 02	00 45	24 22	28 22	26 22	13 05	21 43

EPHEMERIS CALCULATED FOR 12 MIDNIGHT GREENWICH MEAN TIME. ALL OTHER DATA AND FACING ASPECTARIAN PAGE IN **EASTERN TIME (BOLD)** AND PACIFIC TIME (REGULAR).

OCTOBER 2009

☽ Last Aspect day	ET / hr:mn / PT	asp	☽ Ingress sign day	ET / hr:mn / PT
2	**11:29 pm** 8:29 pm	☍ ♄	♈ 3	**5:20 am** 2:20 am
4	10:46 pm	□ ♂	♉ 5	**12:33 pm** 9:33 am
5	**1:46 am**	□ ♂	♉ 5	**12:33 pm** 9:33 am
7	**1:19 pm** 10:19 am	△ ♄	♊ 7	**5:46 pm** 2:46 pm
9	**9:35 pm** 6:35 pm	□ ☿	♋ 9	**9:48 pm** 6:48 pm
11	**9:37 pm** 6:37 pm	⚹ ♄	♌ 11	10:02 pm
11	**9:37 pm** 6:37 pm	⚹ ♄	♌ 12	**1:02 am**
13	**5:20 pm** 2:20 pm	☍ ♆	♍ 14	**3:45 am** 12:45 am
16	**6:18 am** 3:18 am	⚹ ♂	♎ 16	**6:29 am** 3:29 am
17	10:33 pm	☌ ☉	♏ 18	**10:22 am** 7:22 am
18	**1:33 am**	☌ ☉	♏ 18	**10:22 am** 7:22 am
20	**2:57 pm** 11:57 am	⚹ ♄	♐ 20	**4:49 pm** 1:49 pm
22	10:13 pm	□ ♄	♑ 22	11:39 pm
23	**1:13 am**	□ ♄	♑ 23	**2:39 am**
25	**2:14 pm** 11:14 am	△ ♄	♒ 25	**3:08 pm** 12:08 pm
28	**3:22 am** 12:22 am	△ ☿	♓ 28	**3:45 am** 12:45 am
29	9:56 pm	☌ ♅	♈ 30	**1:56 pm** 10:56 am
30	**12:56 am**	☌ ♅	♈ 30	**1:56 pm** 10:56 am

☽ Phases & Eclipses phase	day	ET / hr:mn / PT
Full Moon	3	11:10 pm
Full Moon	4	**2:10 am**
4th Quarter	11	**4:56 am** 1:56 am
New Moon	17	10:33 pm
New Moon	18	**1:33 am**
2nd Quarter	25	**8:42 pm** 5:42 pm

Planet Ingress	day	ET / hr:mn / PT
♀ ♎	3	**7:45 am** 4:45 am
☿ ♎	9	**11:45 pm** 7:45 pm
⚳ ♏	12	**2:29 pm** 11:29 am
♀ ♎	14	**6:46 pm** 3:46 pm
♂ ♌	16	**11:32 am** 8:32 am
☉ ♏	22	11:43 pm
☉ ♏	23	**2:43 am**
☿ ♏	28	**6:08 am** 3:08 am
♄ ♎	29	**1:09 pm** 10:09 am

Planetary Motion	day	ET / hr:mn / PT
♃ D	12	9:34 pm
♃ D	13	**12:34 am**
⚷ D	30	10:45 pm
⚷ D	31	**1:45 am**

1 THURSDAY
☿ ⚹ ♂ **2:00 am**
☽ ⚻ ☉ **12:22 pm** 9:22 am
☽ ☍ ♀ **11:08 pm** 8:08 pm

2 FRIDAY
☽ ⚺ ♃ **5:17 am** 2:17 am
☽ ☍ ☿ **3:08 pm** 12:08 pm
☽ △ ♂ **3:33 pm** 12:33 pm
☽ ⚺ ♆ **5:57 pm** 2:57 pm
☽ ☌ ♅ **6:02 pm** 3:02 pm
☽ ☍ ♄ **11:29 pm** 8:29 pm

3 SATURDAY
☽ □ ♇ **6:49 am** 3:49 am
☽ ☍ ☉ 11:10 pm

4 SUNDAY
☽ ☍ ☉ **2:10 am**
☿ ⚹ ♂ **7:37 am** 4:37 am
♀ ⚻ ♃ **11:57 am** 8:57 am
☽ ⚹ ♃ **1:27 pm** 10:27 am
☽ ⚻ ♀ **1:36 pm** 10:36 am
☿ ⚻ ♆ **4:57 pm** 1:57 pm
☿ ☍ ♅ **5:06 pm** 2:06 pm
♂ ⚻ ♆ **9:33 pm** 6:33 pm
♂ △ ♅ **9:37 pm** 6:37 pm
♅ ⚺ ♆ **11:08 pm** 8:08 pm
☽ ⚺ ♅ 10:35 pm
☽ ⚹ ♆ 10:36 pm
☽ □ ♂ 10:46 pm
☽ ⚻ ☿ 11:13 pm

5 MONDAY
☽ ⚺ ♅ **1:35 am**
☽ ⚹ ♆ **1:36 am**
☽ □ ♂ **1:46 am**
☽ ⚻ ☿ **2:13 am**
☽ ⚻ ♄ **7:28 am** 4:28 am
☽ △ ♇ **2:01 pm** 11:01 am

6 TUESDAY
☽ ⚻ ☉ **12:49 pm** 9:49 am
☽ □ ♃ **7:18 pm** 4:18 pm
☽ △ ♀ 9:56 pm

7 WEDNESDAY
☽ △ ♀ **12:56 am**
☽ ⚹ ♅ **7:00 am** 4:00 am
☽ □ ♆ **7:05 am** 4:05 am
☽ ⚹ ♂ **9:31 am** 6:31 am
☽ △ ☿ **12:10 pm** 9:10 am
☽ △ ♄ **1:19 pm** 10:19 am
☽ ⚻ ♇ **7:14 pm** 4:14 pm
☿ ☌ ♄ 11:34 pm

8 THURSDAY
☿ ☌ ♄ **2:34 am**
☽ △ ☉ **9:27 pm** 6:27 pm
☽ △ ♃ **11:42 pm** 8:42 pm

9 FRIDAY
☽ □ ♀ **10:23 am** 7:23 am
☽ □ ♅ **11:05 am** 8:05 am
☽ △ ♆ **11:15 am** 8:15 am
☽ ⚺ ♂ **3:45 pm** 12:45 pm
☽ □ ♄ **5:52 pm** 2:52 pm
♀ ☍ ♅ **6:00 pm** 3:00 pm
♀ ⚻ ♆ **8:01 pm** 5:01 pm
☽ □ ☿ **9:35 pm** 6:35 pm
☽ ☍ ♇ **11:17 pm** 8:17 pm

10 SATURDAY
☉ △ ♃ **4:38 am** 1:38 am
☿ □ ♇ **2:44 pm** 11:44 am

11 SUNDAY
☽ ⚻ ♃ **3:12 am** 12:12 am
☽ □ ☉ **4:56 am** 1:56 am
☽ △ ♅ **2:20 pm** 11:20 am
☽ ⚻ ♆ **2:35 pm** 11:35 am
☽ ⚹ ♀ **6:43 pm** 3:43 pm
☽ ☌ ♂ **9:03 pm** 6:03 pm
☽ ⚹ ♄ **9:37 pm** 6:37 pm
☽ ⚻ ♇ 11:34 pm

12 MONDAY
☽ ⚻ ♇ **2:34 am**
☽ ⚹ ☿ **6:43 am** 3:43 am
♂ ⚹ ♄ **4:51 pm** 1:51 pm

13 TUESDAY
☽ ☍ ♃ **6:06 am** 3:06 am
♀ ☌ ♄ **6:52 am** 3:52 am
☽ ⚹ ☉ **11:37 am** 8:37 am
♀ ⚹ ♂ **2:31 pm** 11:31 am
☽ ⚻ ♅ **5:01 pm** 2:01 pm
☽ ☍ ♆ **5:20 pm** 2:20 pm
☽ ⚺ ♄ 9:46 pm
☽ ⚺ ♂ 10:42 pm
☽ ⚺ ♀ 11:19 pm

14 WEDNESDAY
☽ ⚺ ♄ **12:46 am**
☽ ⚺ ♂ **1:42 am**
☽ ⚺ ♀ **2:19 am**
☽ △ ♇ **5:20 am** 2:20 am
☽ ⚺ ☿ **3:42 pm** 12:42 pm

15 THURSDAY
☽ ⚻ ♃ **8:44 am** 5:44 am
♀ □ ♇ **1:21 pm** 10:21 am
☽ ⚺ ☉ **6:04 pm** 3:04 pm
☽ ☍ ♅ **7:33 pm** 4:33 pm
☽ ⚻ ♆ **7:57 pm** 4:57 pm

16 FRIDAY
☽ ☌ ♄ **3:55 am** 12:55 am
☽ ⚹ ♂ **6:18 am** 3:18 am
☽ □ ♇ **8:09 am** 5:09 am
☽ ☌ ♀ **9:56 am** 6:56 am
☉ ⚻ ♅ **2:36 pm** 11:36 am
☉ △ ♆ **8:46 pm** 5:46 pm
☽ ☌ ☿ 10:22 pm

17 SATURDAY
☽ ☌ ☿ **1:22 am**
☽ △ ♃ **12:00 pm** 9:00 am
☽ ⚻ ♅ **10:57 pm** 7:57 pm
☽ △ ♆ **11:27 pm** 8:27 pm
☽ ☌ ☉ 10:33 pm

18 SUNDAY
☽ ☌ ☉ **1:33 am**
☽ ⚺ ♄ **8:09 am** 5:09 am
☽ □ ♂ **12:09 pm** 9:09 am
☽ ⚹ ♇ **12:10 pm** 9:10 am
♂ ⚻ ♇ **12:24 pm** 9:24 am
☽ ⚺ ♀ **7:13 pm** 4:13 pm

19 MONDAY
☽ ⚺ ☿ **1:42 pm** 10:42 am
☽ □ ♃ **5:16 pm** 2:16 pm

20 TUESDAY
☽ △ ♅ **4:35 am** 1:35 am
☽ □ ♆ **5:13 am** 2:13 am
☽ ⚺ ☉ **11:58 am** 8:58 am
☽ ⚹ ♄ **2:57 pm** 11:57 am
☿ △ ♃ **5:49 pm** 2:49 pm
☽ ⚺ ♇ **6:48 pm** 3:48 pm
☽ △ ♂ **8:52 pm** 5:52 pm

21 WEDNESDAY
☽ ⚹ ♀ **8:11 am** 5:11 am
☽ ⚹ ♃ 10:46 pm

22 THURSDAY
☽ ⚹ ♃ **1:46 am**
☽ ⚹ ☿ **6:47 am** 3:47 am
☉ ⚺ ♄ **7:19 am** 4:19 am
☽ □ ♅ **1:32 pm** 10:32 am
☽ ⚹ ♆ **2:18 pm** 11:18 am
☽ □ ♄ 10:13 pm
☉ ⚹ ☽ 11:39 pm

23 FRIDAY
☽ □ ♄ **1:13 am**
☽ ⚹ ☉ **2:39 am**
☽ ☌ ♇ **4:51 am** 1:51 am
☽ ⚻ ♂ **9:21 am** 6:21 am
☽ □ ♀ 10:43 pm

24 SATURDAY
☽ □ ♀ **1:43 am**
☉ ⚹ ♇ **5:57 am** 2:57 am
☿ ⚻ ♅ **6:50 am** 3:50 am
☿ △ ♆ **12:55 pm** 9:55 am
☽ ⚺ ♃ **1:31 pm** 10:31 am
☽ ⚹ ♅ 10:27 pm
☽ ⚺ ♆ 11:21 pm

25 SUNDAY
☽ ⚹ ♅ **1:27 am**
☽ ⚺ ♆ **2:21 am**
☽ □ ☿ **4:37 am** 1:37 am
☽ △ ♄ **2:14 pm** 11:14 am
☽ ⚺ ♇ **5:30 pm** 2:30 pm
☽ □ ☉ **8:42 pm** 5:42 pm
☽ ☍ ♂ 9:30 pm

26 MONDAY
☽ ☍ ♂ **12:30 am**
☽ △ ♀ **9:46 pm** 6:46 pm
☽ ☌ ♃ 11:40 pm

27 TUESDAY
☽ ☌ ♃ **2:40 am**
☽ ⚺ ♅ **2:09 pm** 11:09 am
☽ ☌ ♆ **3:10 pm** 12:10 pm

28 WEDNESDAY
☽ △ ☿ **3:22 am** 12:22 am
☽ ⚻ ♄ **3:27 am** 12:27 am
☿ ⚺ ♄ **3:59 am** 12:59 am
☽ ⚹ ♇ **6:11 am** 3:11 am
☽ △ ☉ **2:37 pm** 11:37 am
☽ ⚻ ♂ **3:15 pm** 12:15 pm
♀ △ ♃ **10:02 pm** 7:02 pm
☿ ⚹ ♇ **11:53 pm** 8:53 pm

29 THURSDAY
☉ □ ♂ **3:56 am** 12:56 am
☽ ⚺ ♃ **2:20 pm** 11:20 am
☽ ⚻ ♀ **4:05 pm** 1:05 pm
☽ ☌ ♅ 9:56 pm
☽ ⚺ ♆ 11:00 pm

30 FRIDAY
☽ ☌ ♅ **12:56 am**
☽ ⚺ ♆ **2:00 am**
☽ ☍ ♄ **2:09 pm** 11:09 am
☽ □ ♇ **4:20 pm** 1:20 pm
☽ ⚻ ☿ **10:17 pm** 7:17 pm
☽ △ ♂ 11:50 pm

31 SATURDAY
☽ △ ♂ **2:50 am**
☽ ⚻ ☉ **5:01 am** 2:01 am
☽ ⚹ ♃ **10:46 pm** 7:46 pm

Eastern time in bold type
Pacific time in medium type

OCTOBER 2009

DATE	S.TIME	SUN	MOON	N.NODE	MERCURY	VENUS	MARS	JUPITER	SATURN	URANUS	NEPTUNE	PLUTO	CERES	PALLAS	JUNO	VESTA	CHIRON
1 Thu	00:39:27	07♎57 23	00 ♓ 17	27 ♑ 49	21 ♍ 47	12 ♍ 47	21 ♋ 43	17 ♒ 25	26 ♍ 38	24 ♓ 06	24 ♒ 01	00 ♑ 45	24 ♎ 48	28 ♍ 50	26 ♓ 08	13 ♌ 28	21 ♒ 41
2 Fri	00:43:23	08 56 22	12 33	27 42℞	22 07	14 00	22 16	17 22℞	26 46	24 04℞	24 00℞	00 46	25 15	29 18	25 53℞	13 51	21 39℞
3 Sat	00:47:20	09 55 23	25 04	27 32	22 37	15 14	22 49	17 20	26 53	24 02	23 59	00 47	25 41	29 46	25 40	14 14	21 38
4 Sun	00:51:16	10 54 26	07 ♈ 50	27 20	23 16	16 28	23 22	17 18	27 00	23 59	23 58	00 47	26 08	00 ♎ 14	25 26	14 37	21 36
5 Mon	00:55:13	11 53 30	20 52	27 08	24 03	17 42	23 55	17 17	27 08	23 57	23 57	00 48	26 34	00 42	25 13	15 00	21 34
6 Tue	00:59:10	12 52 37	04 ♉ 09	26 56	24 59	18 56	24 27	17 15	27 15	23 55	23 56	00 49	27 01	01 10	24 59	15 22	21 33
7 Wed	01:03:06	13 51 46	17 37	26 45	26 02	20 10	24 59	17 14	27 22	23 53	23 55	00 50	27 27	01 38	24 47	15 45	21 31
8 Thu	01:07:03	14 50 58	01 ♊ 16	26 37	27 11	21 24	25 31	17 13	27 29	23 50	23 54	00 50	27 54	02 06	24 34	16 07	21 30
9 Fri	01:10:59	15 50 11	15 04	26 31	28 27	22 38	26 03	17 12	27 37	23 48	23 53	00 51	28 20	02 33	24 22	16 30	21 28
10 Sat	01:14:56	16 49 27	28 57	26 28	29 47	23 52	26 35	17 11	27 44	23 46	23 52	00 52	28 47	03 01	24 10	16 52	21 27
11 Sun	01:18:52	17 48 45	12 ♋ 57	26 27	01 ♎ 12	25 07	27 06	17 10	27 51	23 44	23 52	00 53	29 13	03 29	23 58	17 14	21 26
12 Mon	01:22:49	18 48 06	27 02	26 27	02 40	26 21	27 38	17 10	27 58	23 42	23 51	00 54	29 40	03 56	23 47	17 36	21 25
13 Tue	01:26:45	19 47 29	11 ♌ 11	26 27	04 12	27 35	28 09	17 10 D	28 06	23 40	23 50	00 55	00 ♏ 06	04 24	23 36	17 58	21 24
14 Wed	01:30:42	20 46 54	25 24	26 24	05 46	28 49	28 39	17 10	28 13	23 38	23 49	00 56	00 33	04 51	23 25	18 20	21 22
15 Thu	01:34:39	21 46 21	09 ♍ 38	26 20	07 22	00 ♎ 04	29 10	17 10	28 20	23 36	23 49	00 57	00 59	05 19	23 15	18 41	21 21
16 Fri	01:38:35	22 45 51	23 50	26 12	09 00	01 18	29 40	17 11	28 27	23 34	23 48	00 58	01 26	05 46	23 05	19 03	21 20
17 Sat	01:42:32	23 45 23	07 ♎ 55	26 01	10 40	02 33	00 ♌ 11	17 11	28 34	23 32	23 47	00 59	01 52	06 14	22 56	19 25	21 19
18 Sun	01:46:28	24 44 57	21 48	25 49	12 20	03 47	00 41	17 12	28 41	23 30	23 47	01 00	02 19	06 41	22 47	19 46	21 19
19 Mon	01:50:25	25 44 33	05 ♏ 26	25 36	14 02	05 02	01 10	17 13	28 48	23 28	23 46	01 01	02 45	07 09	22 39	20 07	21 18
20 Tue	01:54:21	26 44 11	18 44	25 24	15 43	06 16	01 40	17 15	28 55	23 26	23 46	01 02	03 12	07 36	22 31	20 28	21 17
21 Wed	01:58:18	27 43 51	01 ♐ 42	25 13	17 25	07 31	02 09	17 16	29 02	23 24	23 45	01 04	03 38	08 03	22 23	20 49	21 16
22 Thu	02:02:14	28 43 32	14 19	25 05	19 07	08 46	02 38	17 18	29 08	23 22	23 45	01 05	04 05	08 30	22 16	21 10	21 16
23 Fri	02:06:11	29 43 16	26 38	25 00	20 50	10 00	03 07	17 20	29 15	23 20	23 44	01 06	04 31	08 58	22 10	21 31	21 15
24 Sat	02:10:08	00♏43 01	08 ♑ 42	24 58	22 32	11 15	03 35	17 22	29 22	23 18	23 44	01 07	04 58	09 25	22 04	21 52	21 15
25 Sun	02:14:04	01 42 48	20 35	24 57 D	24 14	12 30	04 03	17 24	29 29	23 17	23 43	01 09	05 25	09 52	21 58	22 12	21 14
26 Mon	02:18:01	02 42 37	02 ♒ 24	24 57℞	25 55	13 44	04 31	17 26	29 36	23 15	23 43	01 10	05 51	10 19	21 53	22 32	21 14
27 Tue	02:21:57	03 42 28	14 12	24 57	27 37	14 59	04 59	17 29	29 42	23 13	23 43	01 11	06 18	10 46	21 49	22 53	21 14
28 Wed	02:25:54	04 42 20	26 07	24 55	29 17	16 14	05 26	17 32	29 49	23 12	23 42	01 13	06 44	11 13	21 45	23 13	21 13
29 Thu	02:29:50	05 42 13	08 ♓ 13	24 51	00 ♏ 58	17 29	05 53	17 35	29 55	23 10	23 42	01 14	07 11	11 39	21 41	23 33	21 13
30 Fri	02:33:47	06 42 09	20 34	24 44	02 38	18 44	06 20	17 38	00 ♎02	23 09	23 42	01 15	07 37	12 06	21 39	23 52	21 13
31 Sat	02:37:43	07 42 06	03 ♈ 14	24 35	04 18	19 59	06 46	17 42	00 08	23 07	23 42	01 17	08 04	12 33	21 36	24 12	21 13 D

EPHEMERIS CALCULATED FOR 12 MIDNIGHT GREENWICH MEAN TIME. ALL OTHER DATA AND FACING ASPECTARIAN PAGE IN **EASTERN TIME (BOLD)** AND PACIFIC TIME (REGULAR).

NOVEMBER 2009

☽ Last Aspect				☽ Ingress			
day	ET / hr:mn / PT		asp	sign	day	ET / hr:mn / PT	
1	**8:29 am**	5:29 am	✶♆	♉	1	**7:44 pm**	4:44 pm
3	**1:04 pm**	10:04 am	□♆	♊	3	**11:53 pm**	8:53 pm
5	**10:47 pm**	7:47 pm	△♀	♋	5		11:42 pm
5	**10:47 pm**	7:47 pm	△♀	♋	6	**2:42 am**	
7	**5:26 pm**	2:26 pm	△♅	♌	8	**5:23 am**	2:23 am
9	**9:43 pm**	6:43 pm	☍♆	♍	10	**8:30 am**	5:30 am
11		11:13 pm	✶☿	♎	12	**12:22 pm**	9:22 am
12	**2:13 am**		✶☿	♎	12	**12:22 pm**	9:22 am
14	**6:10 am**	3:10 am	△♆	♏	14	**5:24 pm**	2:24 pm
16	**2:14 pm**	11:14 am	☌☉	♐	16		9:22 pm

☽ Last Aspect				☽ Ingress			
day	ET / hr:mn / PT		asp	sign	day	ET / hr:mn / PT	
16	**2:14 pm**	11:14 am	☌☉	♐	17	**12:22 am**	
18	**9:46 pm**	6:46 pm	✶♆	♑	19	**10:00 am**	7:00 am
21	**10:04 pm**	7:04 pm	✶☉	♒	21	**10:11 pm**	7:11 pm
23	**10:35 pm**	7:35 pm	☌♆	♓	24	**11:07 am**	8:07 am
26	**9:17 am**	6:17 am	△♀	♈	26	**10:10 pm**	7:10 pm
28	**6:32 pm**	3:32 pm	✶♆	♉	29	**5:34 am**	2:34 am

☽ Phases & Eclipses			
phase	day	ET / hr:mn / PT	
Full Moon	2	**2:14 pm**	11:14 am
4th Quarter	9	**10:56 am**	7:56 am
New Moon	16	**2:14 pm**	11:14 am
2nd Quarter	24	**4:39 pm**	1:39 pm

Planet Ingress				
		day	ET / hr:mn / PT	
♀	♏	7	**7:23 pm**	4:23 pm
☿	♐	15	**7:28 pm**	4:28 pm
⚶	♍	19	**8:38 am**	5:38 am
☉	♐	21	**11:22 pm**	8:22 pm

Planetary Motion				
		day	ET / hr:mn / PT	
⚵	D	3	**4:17 pm**	1:17 pm
♆	D	4	**1:10 pm**	10:10 am

1 SUNDAY
☽☍♀ **4:59 am** 1:59 am
☽⚺♅ **7:23 am** 4:23 am
☽✶♆ **8:29 am** 5:29 am
☿□♂ **7:50 pm** 4:50 pm
☽⚻♄ **8:22 pm** 5:22 pm
☽△♇ **10:06 pm** 7:06 pm

2 MONDAY
♀⚻♅ **6:12 am** 3:12 am
☽□♂ **9:41 am** 6:41 am
☽☍☿ **11:04 am** 8:04 am
☽☍☉ **2:14 pm** 11:14 am
♀△♆ **6:21 pm** 3:21 pm

3 TUESDAY
☽□♃ **3:06 am** 12:06 am
☽✶♅ **11:56 am** 8:56 am
☽□♆ **1:04 pm** 10:04 am
☽⚻♀ **2:54 pm** 11:54 am
☽△♄ 9:53 pm
☽⚻♇ 11:15 pm

4 WEDNESDAY
☽△♄ **12:53 am**
☽⚻♇ **2:15 am**
☽✶♂ **2:55 pm** 11:55 am
☽⚻☿ **9:24 pm** 6:24 pm
☽⚻☉ **9:40 pm** 6:40 pm

5 THURSDAY
☉☌☿ **3:02 am** 12:02 am
☽△♃ **6:33 am** 3:33 am
☽□♅ **2:52 pm** 11:52 am
☽△♆ **4:04 pm** 1:04 pm
☽△♀ **10:47 pm** 7:47 pm

6 FRIDAY
☽□♄ **4:04 am** 1:04 am
☽☍♇ **5:09 am** 2:09 am
☽⚺♂ **7:06 pm** 4:06 pm

7 SATURDAY
☽△☉ **4:10 am** 1:10 am
☽△☿ **6:33 am** 3:33 am
☽⚻♃ **9:28 am** 6:28 am
☽△♅ **5:26 pm** 2:26 pm
☽⚻♆ **6:42 pm** 3:42 pm

8 SUNDAY
☽□♀ **6:21 am** 3:21 am
☽✶♄ **7:06 am** 4:06 am
☽⚻♇ **7:56 am** 4:56 am
☿□♃ **9:42 am** 6:42 am
♀⚺♄ **3:39 pm** 12:39 pm
☽☌♂ **11:21 pm** 8:21 pm
♀✶♇ 9:34 pm

9 MONDAY
♀✶♇ **12:34 am**
☽□☉ **10:56 am** 7:56 am
☽☍♃ **12:41 pm** 9:41 am

☽□☿ **3:56 pm** 12:56 pm
☽⚻♅ **8:21 pm** 5:21 pm
☽☍♆ **9:43 pm** 6:43 pm

10 TUESDAY
☽⚺♄ **10:37 am** 7:37 am
☽△♇ **11:11 am** 8:11 am
☉□♃ **1:41 pm** 10:41 am
☽✶♀ **2:31 pm** 11:31 am

11 WEDNESDAY
☽⚺♂ **4:09 am** 1:09 am
☿△♅ **6:37 am** 3:37 am
☽⚻♃ **4:34 pm** 1:34 pm
☽✶☉ **6:29 pm** 3:29 pm
☿□♆ **7:11 pm** 4:11 pm
☽☍♅ **11:57 pm** 8:57 pm
☽⚻♆ 10:25 pm
☽✶☿ 11:13 pm

12 THURSDAY
☽⚻♆ **1:25 am**
☽✶☿ **2:13 am**
☽☌♄ **2:53 pm** 11:53 am
☽□♇ **3:12 pm** 12:12 pm
☽⚺♀ **11:43 pm** 8:43 pm

13 FRIDAY
☽✶♂ **9:51 am** 6:51 am
☽△♃ **9:28 pm** 6:28 pm

14 SATURDAY
☽⚺☉ **3:16 am** 12:16 am
☽⚻♅ **4:35 am** 1:35 am
☽△♆ **6:10 am** 3:10 am

☽⚺☿ **1:57 pm** 10:57 am
☽⚺♄ **8:22 pm** 5:22 pm
☽✶♇ **8:26 pm** 5:26 pm
☉△♅ **8:41 pm** 5:41 pm

15 SUNDAY
♄□♇ **10:20 am** 7:20 am
☽☌♀ **10:41 am** 7:41 am
☽□♂ **5:03 pm** 2:03 pm
☉□♆ **6:11 pm** 3:11 pm

16 MONDAY
☽□♃ **4:02 am** 1:02 am
☽△♅ **10:57 am** 7:57 am
☽□♆ **12:40 pm** 9:40 am
☽☌☉ **2:14 pm** 11:14 am
☿⚺♇ **10:29 pm** 7:29 pm
☿✶♄ 9:00 pm

17 TUESDAY
☿✶♄ **12:00 am**
☽⚺♇ **3:40 am** 12:40 am
☽✶♄ **3:52 am** 12:52 am
☽☌☿ **4:22 am** 1:22 am
☽⚺♀ 9:37 pm
☽△♂ 11:40 pm

18 WEDNESDAY
☽⚺♀ **12:37 am**
☽△♂ **2:40 am**
☽✶♃ **1:10 pm** 10:10 am
☽□♅ **7:52 pm** 4:52 pm
☽✶♆ **9:46 pm** 6:46 pm

19 THURSDAY
♀□♂ **3:22 am** 12:22 am
☽⚺☉ **4:29 am** 1:29 am
☽☌♇ **1:37 pm** 10:37 am
☽□♄ **2:07 pm** 11:07 am
☽⚺☿ **10:42 pm** 7:42 pm

20 FRIDAY
☽⚻♂ **3:12 pm** 12:12 pm
☽✶♀ **6:21 pm** 3:21 pm
☽⚺♃ 10:08 pm

21 SATURDAY
☽⚺♃ **1:08 am**
☽✶♅ **7:28 am** 4:28 am
☽⚺♆ **9:32 am** 6:32 am
☽✶☉ **10:04 pm** 7:04 pm
☽⚺♇ 11:04 pm
☽△♄ 11:51 pm

22 SUNDAY
☽⚺♇ **2:04 am**
☽△♄ **2:51 am**
☽✶☿ **8:20 pm** 5:20 pm

23 MONDAY
☽☍♂ **5:39 am** 2:39 am
☽□♀ **2:30 pm** 11:30 am
☽☌♃ **2:45 pm** 11:45 am
♀□♃ **5:02 pm** 2:02 pm
☽⚺♅ **8:26 pm** 5:26 pm
☉⚺♇ **10:14 pm** 7:14 pm
☽☌♆ **10:35 pm** 7:35 pm

24 TUESDAY
☉✶♄ **10:35 am** 7:35 am
☽✶♇ **3:08 pm** 12:08 pm
☽⚻♄ **4:11 pm** 1:11 pm
☽□☉ **4:39 pm** 1:39 pm

25 WEDNESDAY
☽□☿ **5:38 pm** 2:38 pm
☽⚻♂ **7:21 pm** 4:21 pm
♀△♅ **10:00 pm** 7:00 pm

26 THURSDAY
☽⚺♃ **3:22 am** 12:22 am
☽☌♅ **8:08 am** 5:08 am
☽△♀ **9:17 am** 6:17 am
☿△♂ **9:53 am** 6:53 am
☽⚺♆ **10:17 am** 7:17 am
♀□♆ **7:15 pm** 4:15 pm
☽□♇ 11:08 pm

27 FRIDAY
☽□♇ **2:08 am**
☽☍♄ **3:20 am** 12:20 am
☽△☉ **8:31 am** 5:31 am

28 SATURDAY
☽△♂ **5:40 am** 2:40 am
☽△☿ **10:27 am** 7:27 am
☽✶♃ **12:37 pm** 9:37 am
☽⚺♅ **4:28 pm** 1:28 pm
☽✶♆ **6:32 pm** 3:32 pm
☽⚻♀ **11:25 pm** 8:25 pm

29 SUNDAY
☿✶♃ **6:53 am** 3:53 am
☽△♇ **9:24 am** 6:24 am
☽⚻♄ **10:41 am** 7:41 am
☽⚻☉ **7:34 pm** 4:34 pm

30 MONDAY
☽□♂ **11:52 am** 8:52 am
☿□♅ **2:52 pm** 11:52 am
☽□♃ **5:59 pm** 2:59 pm
☽✶♅ **9:03 pm** 6:03 pm
☽⚻☿ **9:47 pm** 6:47 pm
☽□♆ **11:04 pm** 8:04 pm

Eastern time in bold type
Pacific time in medium type

NOVEMBER 2009

DATE	S.TIME	SUN	MOON	N.NODE	MERCURY	VENUS	MARS	JUPITER	SATURN	URANUS	NEPTUNE	PLUTO	CERES	PALLAS	JUNO	VESTA	CHIRON
1 Sun	02:41:40	08 ♏ 42 04	16 ♈ 14	24 ♑ 24	05 ♏ 57	21 ♎ 14	07 ♌ 13	17 ♒ 45	00 ♎ 15	23 ♓ 06	23 ♒ 42	01 ♑ 18	08 ♏ 30	13 ♎ 00	21 ♓ 34	24 ♌ 31	21 ♒ 13
2 Mon	02:45:37	09 42 05	29 35	23 59 R	07 36	22 29	07 39	17 49	00 21	23 04 R	23 41 R	01 20	08 56	13 26	21 33 R	24 51	21 13
3 Tue	02:49:33	10 42 07	13 ♉ 14	23 48	09 14	23 44	08 04	17 53	00 27	23 03	23 41	01 21	09 23	13 53	21 32 D	25 10	21 13
4 Wed	02:53:30	11 42 12	27 09	23 45	10 52	24 59	08 29	17 57	00 34	23 01	23 41 D	01 23	09 49	14 19	21 32	25 29	21 14
5 Thu	02:57:26	12 42 18	11 ♊ 14	23 44	12 30	26 14	08 54	18 02	00 40	23 00	23 41	01 24	10 16	14 46	21 33	25 48	21 14
6 Fri	03:01:23	13 42 26	25 26	23 34	14 07	27 29	09 19	18 06	00 46	22 59	23 41	01 26	10 42	15 12	21 33	26 06	21 14
7 Sat	03:05:19	14 42 36	09 ♋ 40	23 32 D	15 44	28 44	09 43	18 11	00 52	22 58	23 42	01 28	11 09	15 39	21 35	26 25	21 15
8 Sun	03:09:16	15 42 49	23 52	23 31	17 20	29 59	10 07	18 16	00 58	22 56	23 42	01 29	11 35	16 05	21 37	26 43	21 15
9 Mon	03:13:12	16 43 03	08 ♌ 02	23 31 R	18 56	01 ♏ 14	10 31	18 21	01 04	22 55	23 42	01 31	12 01	16 31	21 39	27 01	21 16
10 Tue	03:17:09	17 43 19	22 07	23 31	20 31	02 29	10 54	18 26	01 10	22 54	23 42	01 33	12 28	16 58	21 42	27 19	21 16
11 Wed	03:21:06	18 43 38	06 ♍ 07	23 30	22 07	03 44	11 17	18 31	01 16	22 53	23 42	01 34	12 54	17 24	21 46	27 37	21 17
12 Thu	03:25:02	19 43 58	20 01	23 26	23 42	04 59	11 40	18 37	01 22	22 52	23 42	01 36	13 20	17 50	21 50	27 54	21 17
13 Fri	03:28:59	20 44 20	03 ♎ 48	23 20	25 16	06 15	12 02	18 43	01 28	22 51	23 43	01 38	13 47	18 16	21 54	28 12	21 18
14 Sat	03:32:55	21 44 45	17 26	23 11	26 50	07 30	12 23	18 49	01 33	22 50	23 43	01 40	14 13	18 42	21 59	28 29	21 19
15 Sun	03:36:52	22 45 11	00 ♏ 54	23 01	28 24	08 45	12 45	18 55	01 39	22 49	23 43	01 41	14 39	19 08	22 05	28 46	21 20
16 Mon	03:40:48	23 45 38	14 08	22 50	29 58	10 00	13 06	19 01	01 44	22 49	23 44	01 43	15 06	19 33	22 11	29 03	21 21
17 Tue	03:44:45	24 46 08	27 08	22 40	01 ♐ 32	11 16	13 26	19 08	01 50	22 48	23 44	01 45	15 32	19 59	22 17	29 19	21 22
18 Wed	03:48:41	25 46 39	09 ♐ 52	22 31	03 05	12 31	13 46	19 14	01 55	22 47	23 44	01 47	15 58	20 25	22 24	29 35	21 23
19 Thu	03:52:38	26 47 11	22 20	22 25	04 38	13 46	14 06	19 21	02 01	22 46	23 45	01 49	16 24	20 51	22 32	29 51	21 24
20 Fri	03:56:35	27 47 45	04 ♑ 33	22 20	06 11	15 02	14 25	19 28	02 06	22 46	23 45	01 51	16 50	21 16	22 40	00 ♍ 07	21 26
21 Sat	04:00:31	28 48 21	16 34	22 20	07 43	16 17	14 44	19 35	02 11	22 45	23 46	01 52	17 16	21 42	22 49	00 22	21 27
22 Sun	04:04:28	29 48 57	28 26	22 19	09 16	17 32	15 02	19 42	02 16	22 45	23 47	01 54	17 43	22 07	22 58	00 38	21 28
23 Mon	04:08:24	00 ♐ 49 35	10 ♒ 14	22 20 R	10 48	18 48	15 20	19 50	02 21	22 44	23 47	01 56	18 09	22 32	23 07	00 53	21 30
24 Tue	04:12:21	01 50 14	22 02	22 20	12 20	20 03	15 37	19 57	02 26	22 44	23 48	01 58	18 35	22 58	23 17	01 08	21 31
25 Wed	04:16:17	02 50 54	03 ♓ 55	22 20	13 52	21 18	15 54	20 05	02 31	22 43	23 48	02 00	19 01	23 23	23 28	01 22	21 33
26 Thu	04:20:14	03 51 35	16 00	22 17	15 23	22 34	16 10	20 13	02 36	22 43	23 49	02 02	19 27	23 48	23 39	01 37	21 34
27 Fri	04:24:10	04 52 17	28 21	22 11	16 55	23 49	16 26	20 21	02 41	22 43	23 50	02 04	19 53	24 13	23 50	01 51	21 36
28 Sat	04:28:07	05 53 00	11 ♈ 02	22 05	18 26	25 04	16 41	20 29	02 46	22 43	23 51	02 06	20 19	24 38	24 02	02 04	21 38
29 Sun	04:32:04	06 53 44	24 07	22 05	19 57	26 20	16 56	20 38	02 50	22 42	23 51	02 08	20 44	25 03	24 14	02 18	21 39
30 Mon	04:36:00	07 54 30	07 ♉ 36	21 58	21 27	27 35	17 10	20 46	02 55	22 42	23 52	02 10	21 10	25 27	24 27	02 31	21 41

EPHEMERIS CALCULATED FOR 12 MIDNIGHT GREENWICH MEAN TIME. ALL OTHER DATA AND FACING ASPECTARIAN PAGE IN **EASTERN TIME (BOLD)** AND PACIFIC TIME (REGULAR).

DECEMBER 2009

D Last Aspect / D Ingress

day	ET / hr:mn / PT	asp	sign day	ET / hr:mn / PT
1	9:23 am 6:23 am	☐ ♀	♑ 1	6:42 pm 3:42 pm
3	5:27 am 2:27 am	□ ♂	♒ 3	6:39 am 3:39 am
5	9:08 pm	△ ♄	♓ 5	6:26 pm 3:26 pm
5			♓ 6	12:26 am
8	12:08 am	□ ⊙	♈ 8	8:13 am 5:13 am
9	3:57 am 12:57 am			
9	5:04 am 2:04 am			
11	12:44 pm 9:44 am			
13	8:17 pm 5:17 pm	⚹ ♆	♐ 14	7:25 am 4:25 am
16	7:02 am 4:02 am			
18	3:07 pm 12:07 pm	≈ ♄	♒ 30	9:45 pm 6:45 pm

D Phases & Eclipses

phase	day	ET / hr:mn / PT
Full Moon	1	3:07 pm
Full Moon		5:17 pm
4th Quarter	8	
New Moon	16	
2nd Quarter	24	
Full Moon	31	

Planet Ingress

	day	ET / hr:mn / PT
♀ ♐	1	5:03 pm 2:03 pm
♀ ♐	5	12:24 pm 9:24 am
♀ ♏	10	9:57 pm
♀	10	12:57 pm
☿ ♑	19	5:09 pm 2:09 pm
⊙ ♑	21	12:47 am 9:47 am
☿	25	1:17 pm 10:17 am

Planetary Motion

	day	ET / hr:mn / PT
♅ D	1	3:27 pm 12:27 pm
♆ D	20	8:26 am 5:26 am
♇ R	26	9:38 am 6:38 am

Eastern time in **bold type**
Pacific time in medium type

DECEMBER 2009

DATE	S.TIME	SUN	MOON	N.NODE	MERCURY	VENUS	MARS	JUPITER	SATURN	URANUS	NEPTUNE	PLUTO	CERES	PALLAS	JUNO	VESTA	CHIRON
1 Tue	04:39:57	08♐55 16	21 ♉ 30	21 ♒ 50	22 ♐ 58	28 ♏ 51	17 ♋ 24	20 ♒ 55	02 ♎ 59	22 ♓ 42	23 ♒ 53	02 ♑ 12	21 ♍ 36	25 ♎ 52	24 ♓ 43	02 ♍ 40	21 ♒ 43
2 Wed	04:43:53	09 56 04	04 ♊ 11	21 44 R	24 28	00 ♐ 06	17 37	21 03	03 04	22 42	23 54	02 14	22 02	26 17	24 53	02 57	21 45
3 Thu	04:47:50	10 56 53	18 39	21 39	25 58	01 20	17 49	21 12	03 08	22 42	23 55	02 16	22 28	26 41	25 07	03 09	21 47
4 Fri	04:51:46	11 57 43	02 ♋ 54	21 35	27 27	02 37	18 01	21 21	03 12	22 42	23 56	02 18	22 53	27 06	25 21	03 21	21 49
5 Sat	04:55:43	12 58 34	17 34	21 34 D	28 56	03 52	18 12	21 30	03 16	22 43	23 57	02 20	23 19	27 30	25 36	03 33	21 51
6 Sun	04:59:40	13 59 26	02 ♌ 11	21 35	00 ♑ 24	05 08	18 23	21 40	03 20	22 43	23 58	02 23	23 45	27 54	25 51	03 45	21 53
7 Mon	05:03:36	15 00 20	16 39	21 36	01 52	06 23	18 33	21 49	03 24	22 43	23 59	02 25	24 10	28 18	26 07	03 56	21 55
8 Tue	05:07:33	16 01 15	00 ♍ 54	21 38 R	03 19	07 39	18 43	21 59	03 28	22 44	24 00	02 27	24 36	28 42	26 23	04 07	21 58
9 Wed	05:11:29	17 02 11	14 42	21 38	04 45	08 54	18 51	22 08	03 31	22 44	24 01	02 29	25 01	29 06	26 39	04 18	22 00
10 Thu	05:15:26	18 03 09	28 14	21 35	06 10	10 10	19 00	22 18	03 35	22 44	24 02	02 31	25 27	29 30	26 56	04 28	22 02
11 Fri	05:19:22	19 04 07	11 ♎ 14	21 33	07 34	11 25	19 07	22 28	03 39	22 45	24 04	02 33	25 52	29 54	27 13	04 37	22 05
12 Sat	05:23:19	20 05 07	24 31	21 31	08 56	12 41	19 14	22 38	03 42	22 45	24 05	02 35	26 18	00 ♏ 18	27 30	04 47	22 07
13 Sun	05:27:15	21 06 08	07 ♏ 27	21 27	10 17	13 56	19 20	22 48	03 45	22 45	24 06	02 37	26 43	00 41	27 48	04 56	22 10
14 Mon	05:31:12	22 07 10	20 04	21 21	11 35	15 12	19 25	22 58	03 49	22 46	24 07	02 39	27 08	01 05	28 06	05 05	22 12
15 Tue	05:35:09	23 08 13	02 ♐ 24	21 16	12 52	16 27	19 30	23 09	03 52	22 47	24 09	02 42	27 33	01 28	28 24	05 14	22 15
16 Wed	05:39:05	24 09 17	14 30	21 12	14 06	17 43	19 34	23 19	03 55	22 47	24 10	02 44	27 58	01 51	28 43	05 22	22 18
17 Thu	05:43:02	25 10 21	26 29	21 09	15 16	18 58	19 37	23 30	03 58	22 48	24 11	02 46	28 24	02 15	29 02	05 29	22 21
18 Fri	05:46:58	26 11 26	08 ♑ 24	21 08 D	16 23	20 14	19 39	23 41	04 01	22 49	24 13	02 48	28 49	02 38	29 22	05 37	22 23
19 Sat	05:50:55	27 12 32	20 21	21 07	17 26	21 29	19 41	23 51	04 04	22 50	24 14	02 50	29 14	03 01	29 41	05 44	22 26
20 Sun	05:54:51	28 13 38	02 ♒ 05	21 08	18 24	22 45	19 42 R	24 02	04 06	22 51	24 16	02 52	29 39	03 23	00 ♈ 02	05 50	22 29
21 Mon	05:58:48	29 14 44	15 08	21 10	19 16	24 00	19 42	24 13	04 09	22 52	24 17	02 55	00 ♎ 04	03 46	00 22	05 57	22 32
22 Tue	06:02:44	00 ♑15 51	27 22	21 13	20 02	25 16	19 41	24 25	04 11	22 53	24 19	02 57	00 29	04 09	00 43	06 02	22 35
23 Wed	06:06:41	01 16 58	09 ♓ 52	21 14 R	20 41	26 31	19 39	24 36	04 14	22 54	24 20	02 59	00 53	04 31	01 04	06 08	22 38
24 Thu	06:10:38	02 18 05	22 41	21 14	21 12	27 47	19 37	24 47	04 16	22 55	24 22	03 01	01 18	04 53	01 25	06 13	22 41
25 Fri	06:14:34	03 19 12	05 ♈ 52	21 14	21 26	29 02	19 34	24 59	04 18	22 56	24 23	03 03	01 43	05 15	01 47	06 17	22 44
26 Sat	06:18:31	04 20 19	19 25	21 14	21 46 R	00 ♑ 18	19 30	25 10	04 20	22 57	24 25	03 05	02 07	05 38	02 09	06 22	22 47
27 Sun	06:22:27	05 21 27	03 ♉ 20	21 12	21 47	01 33	19 25	25 22	04 22	22 58	24 26	03 08	02 32	05 59	02 31	06 25	22 50
28 Mon	06:26:24	06 22 34	17 35	21 10	21 37	02 49	19 20	25 34	04 24	23 00	24 28	03 10	02 56	06 21	02 53	06 29	22 54
29 Tue	06:30:20	07 23 42	02 ♊ 07	21 08	21 15	04 05	19 13	25 46	04 25	23 01	24 30	03 12	03 21	06 43	03 16	06 32	22 57
30 Wed	06:34:17	08 24 49	16 50	21 07	20 41	05 20	19 06	25 57	04 27	23 01	24 31	03 14	03 45	07 04	03 39	06 34	23 00
31 Thu	06:38:13	09 25 57	01 ♋ 37	21 05	19 56	06 36	18 58	26 09	04 29	23 04	24 33	03 16	04 09	07 26	04 02	06 36	23 04

EPHEMERIS CALCULATED FOR 12 MIDNIGHT GREENWICH MEAN TIME. ALL OTHER DATA AND FACING ASPECTARIAN PAGE IN **EASTERN TIME (BOLD)** AND PACIFIC TIME (REGULAR).

JANUARY 2010

☽ Last Aspect day	ET / hr:mn / PT	asp	☽ Ingress sign day	ET / hr:mn / PT
1	**10:43 am** 7:43 am	△♅	♌ 1	**9:41 pm** 7:41 pm
3	**4:55 pm** 1:55 pm	☍♃	♍ 3	**9:52 pm** 6:52 pm
5	**12:25 pm** 9:25 am	☍♅	♎ 5	**11:58 pm** 8:58 pm
7	10:07 pm	△♃	♏ 8	**5:00 am** 2:00 am
8	**1:07 am**	△♃	♏ 8	**5:00 am** 2:00 am
10	**10:02 am** 7:02 sm	□♃	♐ 10	**1:10 pm** 10:10 am
12	**9:43 pm** 6:43 pm	⚹♃	♑ 12	**11:54 pm** 8:54 pm
15	**4:02 am** 1:02 am	☌♀	♒ 15	**12:17 pm** 9:17 am
17	**3:22 pm** 12:22 pm	☌♆	♓ 17	10:17 pm
17	**3:22 pm** 12:22 pm	☌♆	♓ 18	**1:17 am**
19	10:06 pm	☌♅	♈ 20	**1:36 pm** 10:36 am
20	**1:06 am**	☌♅	♈ 20	**1:36 pm** 10:36 am
22	**2:46 pm** 11:46 am	⚹♆	♉ 22	**11:39 pm** 8:39 pm
24	**10:03 pm** 7:03 pm	□♆	♊ 25	**6:11 am** 3:11 am
26	10:32 pm	△♆	♋ 27	**9:01 am** 6:01 am
27	**1:32 am**	△♆	♋ 27	**9:01 am** 6:01 am
28	**11:49 pm** 8:49 pm	△♅	♌ 29	**9:10 am** 6:10 am
30	10:27 pm	☍♆	♍ 31	**8:23 am** 5:23 am
31	**1:27 am**	☍♆	♍ 31	**8:23 am** 5:23 am

☽ Phases & Eclipses phase	day	ET / hr:mn / PT
4th Quarter	7	**5:39 am** 2:39 am
New Moon	14	11:11 pm
●	15	25° ♑ 01'
New Moon	15	**2:11 am**
2nd Quarter	23	**5:53 am** 2:53 am
Full Moon	29	10:18 pm
Full Moon	30	**1:18 am**

Planet Ingress	day	ET / hr:mn / PT
♃ ♓	17	**9:10 pm** 6:10 pm
♀ ♒	18	**9:35 am** 6:35 am
☉ ♒	19	**11:28 pm** 8:28 pm

Planetary Motion	day	ET / hr:mn / PT
⚵ ℞	3	**7:13 pm** 4:13 pm
♄ ℞	13	**10:56 am** 7:56 am
☿ D	15	**11:52 am** 8:52 am

1 FRIDAY
☽ ☍ ☿ **3:35 am** 12:35 am
☽ ⚺ ♂ **3:48 am** 12:48 am
☽ △ ♅ **10:43 am** 7:43 am
☽ ⚻ ♆ **1:06 pm** 10:06 am
☽ ⚻ ♃ **4:10 pm** 1:10 pm

2 SATURDAY
☽ ⚻ ♇ **3:02 am** 12:02 am
☽ ⚹ ♄ **4:55 am** 1:55 am
☽ ⚻ ♀ **1:47 pm** 10:47 am
☽ ⚻ ☉ **5:30 pm** 2:30 pm
☽ ⚻ ☿ **11:56 pm** 8:56 pm

3 SUNDAY
☽ ☌ ♂ **3:08 am** 12:08 am
☽ ⚻ ♅ **10:46 am** 7:46 am
☽ ☍ ♆ **1:12 pm** 10:12 am
☽ ☍ ♃ **4:55 pm** 1:55 pm

4 MONDAY
☽ △ ♇ **3:29 am** 12:29 am
☽ ⚺ ♄ **5:21 am** 2:21 am
☉ ☌ ☿ **2:06 pm** 11:06 am
☽ △ ♀ **7:05 pm** 4:05 pm
☽ △ ☿ **8:50 pm** 5:50 pm
☽ △ ☉ **10:02 pm** 7:02 pm

5 TUESDAY
☽ ⚺ ♂ **3:39 am** 12:39 am
☿ ☌ ♀ **5:39 am** 2:39 am
☽ ☍ ♅ **12:25 pm** 9:25 am
☽ ⚻ ♆ **2:58 pm** 11:58 am
☽ ⚻ ♃ **7:30 pm** 4:30 pm

6 WEDNESDAY
☽ □ ♇ **6:00 am** 3:00 am
☽ ☌ ♄ **7:54 am** 4:54 am
☽ □ ☿ **7:40 pm** 4:40 pm

7 THURSDAY
☽ □ ♀ **3:35 am** 12:35 am
☽ □ ☉ **5:39 am** 2:39 am
☽ ⚹ ♂ **6:35 am** 3:35 am
☉ ⚻ ♂ **3:39 pm** 12:39 pm
☽ ⚻ ♅ **4:51 pm** 1:51 pm
☽ △ ♆ **7:34 pm** 4:34 pm
☽ △ ♃ 10:07 pm

8 FRIDAY
☽ △ ♃ **1:07 am**
♀ ⚻ ♂ **6:56 am** 3:56 am
☽ ⚹ ♇ **11:33 am** 8:33 am
☽ ⚺ ♄ **1:28 pm** 10:28 am
☽ ⚹ ☿ **9:26 pm** 6:26 pm

9 SATURDAY
☽ □ ♂ **12:24 pm** 9:24 am
☽ ⚹ ♀ **4:18 pm** 1:18 pm
☽ ⚹ ☉ **5:16 pm** 2:16 pm
☽ △ ♅ 9:29 pm

10 SUNDAY
☽ △ ♅ **12:29 am**
☽ □ ♆ **3:22 am** 12:22 am
☽ □ ♃ **10:02 am** 7:02 am
☽ ⚺ ♇ **8:13 pm** 5:13 pm
☽ ⚹ ♄ **10:07 pm** 7:07 pm
☽ ⚺ ☿ 11:43 pm

11 MONDAY
☽ ⚺ ☿ **2:43 am**
☉ ☌ ♀ **4:06 pm** 1:06 pm
☽ △ ♂ **8:48 pm** 5:48 pm

12 TUESDAY
☽ ⚺ ☉ **8:30 am** 5:30 am
☽ ⚺ ♀ **8:51 am** 5:51 am
☽ □ ♅ **10:52 am** 7:52 am
☽ ⚹ ♆ **1:52 pm** 10:52 am
☽ ⚹ ♃ **9:43 pm** 6:43 pm

13 WEDNESDAY
♀ ⚹ ♅ **4:48 am** 1:48 am
☽ ☌ ♇ **7:23 am** 4:23 am
☽ □ ♄ **9:11 am** 6:11 am
☽ ☌ ☿ **11:35 am** 8:35 am
☉ ⚹ ♅ **1:42 pm** 10:42 am

14 THURSDAY
☽ ⚻ ♂ **7:03 am** 4:03 am
♀ ⚺ ♆ **10:25 am** 7:25 am
☽ ⚹ ♅ **11:09 pm** 8:09 pm
☽ ☌ ☉ 11:11 pm
☽ ⚺ ♆ 11:13 pm
☉ ⚺ ♆ 11:29 pm

15 FRIDAY
☽ ☌ ☉ **2:11 am**
☽ ⚺ ♆ **2:13 am**
☉ ⚺ ♆ **2:29 am**
☽ ☌ ♀ **4:02 am** 1:02 am
☽ ⚺ ♃ **11:12 am** 8:12 am
☽ ⚺ ♇ **8:05 pm** 5:05 pm
☽ △ ♄ **9:43 pm** 6:43 pm
☽ ⚺ ☿ **11:36 pm** 8:36 pm

16 SATURDAY
☽ ☍ ♂ **6:13 pm** 3:13 pm

17 SUNDAY
☽ ⚺ ♅ **12:19 pm** 9:19 am
☽ ☌ ♆ **3:22 pm** 12:22 pm
☽ ⚺ ☉ **8:56 pm** 5:56 pm
☽ ⚺ ♀ 9:18 pm
☽ ☌ ♃ 10:22 pm

18 MONDAY
☽ ⚺ ♀ **12:18 am**
☽ ☌ ♃ **1:22 am**
☽ ⚹ ♇ **9:15 am** 6:15 am
☽ ⚻ ♄ **10:41 am** 7:41 am
♀ ⚺ ♃ **12:15 pm** 9:15 am
☽ ⚹ ☿ **1:48 pm** 10:48 am

19 TUESDAY
☽ ⚻ ♂ **5:18 am** 2:18 am
☽ ☌ ♅ 10:06 pm

20 WEDNESDAY
☽ ☌ ♅ **1:06 am**
☽ ⚺ ♆ **4:05 am** 1:05 am
☉ ⚺ ♃ **1:38 pm** 10:38 am
☽ ⚺ ♃ **2:49 pm** 11:49 am
☽ ⚹ ☉ **2:54 pm** 11:54 am
☽ ⚹ ♀ **7:37 pm** 4:37 pm
☽ □ ♇ **9:32 pm** 6:32 pm
☽ ☍ ♄ **10:42 pm** 7:42 pm

21 THURSDAY
☽ □ ☿ **4:26 am** 1:26 am
♀ ⚺ ♇ **2:36 pm** 11:36 am
☽ △ ♂ **3:02 pm** 12:02 pm
♀ △ ♄ 10:07 pm

22 FRIDAY
♀ △ ♄ **1:07 am**
☽ ⚺ ♅ **11:56 am** 8:56 am
☽ ⚹ ♆ **2:46 pm** 11:46 am
☽ ⚹ ♃ 10:51 pm

23 SATURDAY
☽ ⚹ ♃ **1:51 am**
☽ □ ☉ **5:53 am** 2:53 am
☽ △ ♇ **7:19 am** 4:19 am
☽ ⚻ ♄ **8:12 am** 5:12 am
☽ □ ♀ **11:36 am** 8:36 am
☽ △ ☿ **5:07 pm** 2:07 pm
☽ □ ♂ **10:03 pm** 7:03 pm
☉ ⚺ ♇ 9:30 pm

24 SUNDAY
☉ ⚺ ♇ **12:30 am**
☉ △ ♄ **10:37 am** 7:37 am
☽ ⚹ ♅ **7:25 pm** 4:25 pm
☽ □ ♆ **10:03 pm** 7:03 pm

25 MONDAY
☽ □ ♃ **9:09 am** 6:09 am
☽ ⚻ ♇ **1:27 pm** 10:27 am
☽ △ ♄ **2:04 pm** 11:04 am
☽ △ ☉ **4:17 pm** 1:17 pm
☿ ⚻ ♂ **8:40 pm** 5:40 pm
☽ △ ♀ **10:38 pm** 7:38 pm
☽ ⚹ ♂ 10:36 pm
☽ ⚻ ☿ 11:06 pm

26 TUESDAY
☽ ⚹ ♂ **1:36 am**
☽ ⚻ ☿ **2:06 am**
☽ □ ♅ **11:07 pm** 8:07 pm
♀ ☍ ♂ 9:29 pm
☽ △ ♆ 10:32 pm

27 WEDNESDAY
♀ ☍ ♂ **12:29 am**
☽ △ ♆ **1:32 am**
☽ △ ♃ **12:36 pm** 9:36 am
☽ ☍ ♇ **3:56 pm** 12:56 pm
☽ □ ♄ **4:20 pm** 1:20 pm
☽ ⚻ ☉ **10:12 pm** 7:12 pm
☽ ⚺ ♂ 10:57 pm

28 THURSDAY
☽ ⚺ ♂ **1:57 am**
☽ ⚻ ♀ **5:03 am** 2:03 am
☽ ☍ ☿ **7:21 am** 4:21 am
☽ △ ♅ **11:49 pm** 8:49 pm
☽ ⚻ ♆ 11:06 pm

29 FRIDAY
☽ ⚻ ♆ **2:06 am**
☽ ⚻ ♃ **1:21 pm** 10:21 am
☉ ☍ ♂ **2:43 pm** 11:43 am
☽ ⚻ ♇ **3:56 pm** 12:56 pm
☽ ⚹ ♄ **4:08 pm** 1:08 pm
☽ ☌ ♂ 9:20 pm
☽ ☍ ☉ 10:18 pm

30 SATURDAY
☽ ☌ ♂ **12:20 am**
☽ ☍ ☉ **1:18 am**
☽ ☍ ♀ **8:49 am** 5:49 am
☽ ⚻ ☿ **10:33 am** 7:33 am
☽ ⚻ ♅ **11:11 pm** 8:11 pm
☽ ☍ ♆ 10:27 pm

31 SUNDAY
☽ ☍ ♆ **1:27 am**
☽ ☍ ♃ **1:19 pm** 10:19 am
☽ ⚺ ♄ **3:17 pm** 12:17 pm
☽ △ ♇ **3:17 pm** 12:17 pm
♄ □ ♇ **4:27 pm** 1:27 pm
☽ ⚺ ♂ **10:28 pm** 7:28 pm

Eastern time in bold type
Pacific time in medium type

JANUARY 2010

DATE	S.TIME	SUN	MOON	N.NODE	MERCURY	VENUS	MARS	JUPITER	SATURN	URANUS	NEPTUNE	PLUTO	CERES	PALLAS	JUNO	VESTA	CHRON
1 Fri	06:42:10	10♑27'04	13♋15	21♒05'D	19♑00	07♑51	18♌49	26♒22	04♎33	23♓05	24♒35	03♑19	04♐34	07♏47	04♈26	06♍38	23♒07
2 Sat	06:46:07	11♑28'12	28♋19	21♒05	17♑54'R	09♑06	18♌39'R	26♒34	04♎34	23♓07	24♒37	03♑21	04♐58	08♏08	04♈50	06♍39	23♒10
3 Sun	06:50:03	12♑29'20	13♌02	21♒05	16♑41	10♑22	18♌29	26♒46	04♎35	23♓09	24♒38	03♑23	05♐22	08♏29	05♈14	06♍40	23♒14
4 Mon	06:54:00	13♑30'28	28♌14	21♒06	15♑23	11♑37	18♌18	26♒58	04♎36	23♓10	24♒40	03♑25	05♐46	08♏50	05♈38	06♍40'R	23♒17
5 Tue	06:57:56	14♑31'36	12♍37	21♒07	14♑03	12♑53	18♌05	27♒11	04♎37	23♓12	24♒42	03♑27	06♐10	09♏10	06♈02	06♍40	23♒21
6 Wed	07:01:53	15♑32'45	27♍06	21♒07	12♑42	14♑08	17♌53	27♒23	04♎37	23♓14	24♒44	03♑29	06♐34	09♏31	06♈27	06♍39	23♒24
7 Thu	07:05:49	16♑33'54	11♎59	21♒07'R	11♑23	15♑24	17♌39	27♒36	04♎38	23♓15	24♒46	03♑31	06♐57	09♏51	06♈52	06♍38	23♒28
8 Fri	07:09:46	17♑35'02	24♎29	21♒07	10♑10	16♑39	17♌24	27♒48	04♎38	23♓17	24♒48	03♑34	07♐21	10♏11	07♈17	06♍36	23♒32
9 Sat	07:13:42	18♑36'11	07♏38	21♒07	09♑03	17♑55	17♌09	28♒01	04♎39	23♓19	24♒50	03♑36	07♐45	10♏31	07♈43	06♍34	23♒35
10 Sun	07:17:39	19♑37'21	20♏28	21♒07	08♑05	19♑10	16♌53	28♒14	04♎39	23♓21	24♒52	03♑38	08♐08	10♏51	08♈08	06♍31	23♒39
11 Mon	07:21:36	20♑38'30	03♐02	21♒07'D	07♑15	20♑26	16♌37	28♒27	04♎39	23♓23	24♒54	03♑40	08♐32	11♏11	08♈34	06♍28	23♒43
12 Tue	07:25:32	21♑39'39	15♐23	21♒07	06♑36	21♑41	16♌19	28♒40	04♎39	23♓25	24♒56	03♑42	08♐55	11♏30	09♈00	06♍25	23♒46
13 Wed	07:29:29	22♑40'48	27♐32	21♒07	06♑06	22♑57	16♌01	28♒53	04♎39'R	23♓27	24♒58	03♑44	09♐18	11♏49	09♈26	06♍21	23♒50
14 Thu	07:33:25	23♑41'57	09♑33	21♒07'R	05♑46	24♑12	15♌42	29♒06	04♎39	23♓29	25♒00	03♑46	09♐42	12♏09	09♈53	06♍16	23♒54
15 Fri	07:37:22	24♑43'05	21♑28	21♒07	05♑35'D	25♑28	15♌23	29♒19	04♎38	23♓31	25♒02	03♑48	10♐05	12♏27	10♈20	06♍11	23♒58
16 Sat	07:41:18	25♑44'13	03♒19	21♒06	05♑34	26♑43	15♌03	29♒32	04♎38	23♓33	25♒04	03♑50	10♐28	12♏46	10♈47	06♍06	24♒02
17 Sun	07:45:15	26♑45'21	15♒07	21♒07	05♑40	27♑59	14♌43	29♒45	04♎38	23♓35	25♒06	03♑52	10♐51	13♏05	11♈14	06♍00	24♒06
18 Mon	07:49:12	27♑46'27	26♒54	21♒06	05♑54	29♑14	14♌22	29♒59	04♎38	23♓38	25♒08	03♑54	11♐13	13♏23	11♈41	05♍54	24♒10
19 Tue	07:53:08	28♑47'34	08♓45	21♒05	06♑16	00♒30	14♌02	00♓12	04♎37	23♓40	25♒10	03♑56	11♐36	13♏41	12♈09	05♍47	24♒13
20 Wed	07:57:05	29♑48'39	20♓40	21♒04	06♑43	01♒45	13♌38	00♓26	04♎37	23♓42	25♒12	03♑58	11♐59	13♏59	12♈36	05♍40	24♒17
21 Thu	08:01:01	00♒49'43	02♈44	21♒04	07♑17	03♒00	13♌16	00♓39	04♎36	23♓44	25♒14	04♑00	12♐21	14♏17	13♈04	05♍32	24♒21
22 Fri	08:04:58	01♒50'47	15♈00	21♒01	07♑55	04♒16	12♌53	00♓53	04♎35	23♓46	25♒16	04♑02	12♐44	14♏34	13♈32	05♍24	24♒25
23 Sat	08:08:54	02♒51'50	27♈32	21♒00	08♑39	05♒31	12♌30	01♓06	04♎34	23♓49	25♒18	04♑04	13♐06	14♏52	14♈00	05♍15	24♒29
24 Sun	08:12:51	03♒52'52	10♉24	21♒01	09♑27	06♒47	12♌07	01♓20	04♎32	23♓52	25♒20	04♑06	13♐28	15♏09	14♈28	05♍06	24♒33
25 Mon	08:16:47	04♒53'52	23♉40	21♒01	10♑19	08♒02	11♌43	01♓34	04♎31	23♓54	25♒23	04♑08	13♐50	15♏26	14♈57	04♍57	24♒37
26 Tue	08:20:44	05♒54'52	07♊11	21♒01	11♑14	09♒17	11♌19	01♓47	04♎30	23♓57	25♒25	04♑10	14♐12	15♏42	15♈26	04♍47	24♒42
27 Wed	08:24:41	06♒55'51	20♊57	21♒04	12♑12	10♒33	10♌56	02♓01	04♎29	23♓59	25♒27	04♑12	14♐34	15♏59	15♈55	04♍36	24♒46
28 Thu	08:28:37	07♒56'48	04♋50	21♒05	13♑13	11♒48	10♌32	02♓15	04♎28	24♓02	25♒29	04♑14	14♐56	16♏15	16♈24	04♍26	24♒50
29 Fri	08:32:34	08♒57'45	19♋03	21♒05'R	14♑17	13♒03	10♌08	02♓29	04♎26	24♓05	25♒31	04♑16	15♐18	16♏31	16♈53	04♍15	24♒54
30 Sat	08:36:30	09♒58'40	03♌24	21♒05	15♑24	14♒19	09♌44	02♓43	04♎25	24♓07	25♒33	04♑18	15♐39	16♏46	17♈22	04♍03	24♒58
31 Sun	08:40:27	10♒59'35	17♌31	21♒03	16♑32	15♒34	09♌20	02♓57	04♎23	24♓10	25♒36	04♑20	16♐01	17♏02	17♈52	03♍51	25♒02

EPHEMERIS CALCULATED FOR 12 MIDNIGHT GREENWICH MEAN TIME. ALL OTHER DATA AND FACING ASPECTARIAN PAGE IN **EASTERN TIME (BOLD)** AND PACIFIC TIME (REGULAR).

FEBRUARY 2010

☽ Last Aspect day	ET / hr:mn / PT	asp	☽ Ingress sign day	ET / hr:mn / PT
1	**11:17 pm** 8:17 pm	☍ ♅	♎ 2	**8:42 am** 5:42 am
4	**4:27 am** 1:27 am	△ ♆	♏ 4	**11:55 am** 8:55 am
6	**11:11 am** 8:11 am	□ ♆	♐ 6	**7:04 pm** 4:04 pm
8	**11:58 pm** 8:58 pm	⚹ ♀	♑ 9	**5:44 am** 2:44 am
11	**7:39 am** 4:39 am	⚹ ♅	♒ 11	**6:24 pm** 3:24 pm
13	**11:33 pm** 8:33 pm	☌ ♆	♓ 14	**7:23 am** 4:23 am
16	**9:32 am** 6:32 am	☌ ♅	♈ 16	**7:30 pm** 4:30 pm
18	**10:52 pm** 7:52 pm	⚹ ♆	♉ 19	**5:55 am** 2:55 am
21	**7:15 am** 4:15 am	□ ♆	♊ 21	**1:47 pm** 10:47 am
23	**12:29 pm** 9:29 am	△ ♆	♋ 23	**6:29 pm** 3:29 pm
25	**12:48 pm** 9:48 am	△ ♅	♌ 25	**8:08 pm** 5:08 pm
27	**3:15 pm** 12:15 pm	☍ ☿	♍ 27	**7:52 pm** 4:52 pm

☽ Phases & Eclipses phase	day	ET / hr:mn / PT
4th Quarter	5	**6:48 pm** 3:48 pm
New Moon	13	**9:51 pm** 6:51 pm
2nd Quarter	21	**7:42 pm** 4:42 pm
Full Moon	28	**11:38 am** 8:38 am

Planet Ingress	day	ET / hr:mn / PT
☿ ♒	10	**4:06 am** 1:06 am
♀ ♓	11	**6:24 pm** 3:24 pm
⚴ ♌	15	**10:53 pm** 7:53 pm
☉ ♓	18	**1:36 pm** 10:36 am
⚵ ♉	23	**6:47 am** 3:47 am

Planetary Motion	day	ET / hr:mn / PT

1 MONDAY
☽ ⚻ ☉ **4:05 am** 1:05 am
☽ ⚻ ♀ **12:42 pm** 9:42 am
☽ △ ☿ **2:12 pm** 11:12 am
☽ ☍ ♅ **11:17 pm** 8:17 pm
☽ ⚻ ♆ 10:36 pm

2 TUESDAY
☽ ⚻ ♆ **1:36 am**
☽ ⚻ ♃ **2:40 pm** 11:40 am
☽ ☌ ♄ **3:48 pm** 12:48 pm
☽ □ ♇ **4:01 pm** 1:01 pm
☽ ⚹ ♂ **10:09 pm** 7:09 pm

3 WEDNESDAY
☽ △ ☉ **9:14 am** 6:14 am
☽ △ ♀ **7:30 pm** 4:30 pm
☽ □ ☿ **9:05 pm** 6:05 pm
☽ ⚻ ♅ 11:01 pm

4 THURSDAY
☽ ⚻ ♅ **2:01 am**
☽ △ ♆ **4:27 am** 1:27 am
☽ △ ♃ **7:15 pm** 4:15 pm
☽ ⚺ ♄ **7:25 pm** 4:25 pm
☽ ⚹ ♇ **7:54 pm** 4:54 pm
☽ □ ♂ 9:55 pm

5 FRIDAY
☽ □ ♂ **12:55 am**
♃ ⚻ ♄ **3:14 am** 12:14 am
☽ □ ☉ **6:48 pm** 3:48 pm

6 SATURDAY
☿ ⚹ ♅ **3:02 am** 12:02 am
☽ □ ♀ **7:13 am** 4:13 am
☽ △ ♅ **8:36 am** 5:36 am
☽ ⚹ ☿ **9:14 am** 6:14 am
☽ □ ♆ **11:11 am** 8:11 am
♃ ⚹ ♇ **12:51 pm** 9:51 am
♀ ⚺ ♅ **9:50 pm** 6:50 pm
☽ ⚹ ♄ 11:55 pm

7 SUNDAY
☽ ⚹ ♄ **2:55 am**
☽ ⚺ ♇ **3:45 am** 12:45 am
☽ □ ♃ **4:00 am** 1:00 am
☿ ⚺ ♆ **4:18 am** 1:18 am
☽ △ ♂ **7:21 am** 4:21 am
♀ ☌ ♆ 9:44 pm

8 MONDAY
♀ ☌ ♆ **12:44 am**
☽ ⚹ ☉ **9:17 am** 6:17 am
☽ □ ♅ **6:57 pm** 3:57 pm
☽ ⚹ ♆ **9:37 pm** 6:37 pm
☽ ⚹ ♀ **11:58 pm** 8:58 pm
☽ ⚺ ☿ 11:47 pm

9 TUESDAY
☽ ⚺ ☿ **2:47 am**
☽ □ ♄ **1:45 pm** 10:45 am
☽ ☌ ♇ **2:58 pm** 11:58 am
☽ ⚹ ♃ **4:18 pm** 1:18 pm
☽ ⚻ ♂ **4:52 pm** 1:52 pm

10 WEDNESDAY
♂ ⚻ ♃ **4:24 am** 1:24 am

11 THURSDAY
☽ ⚺ ☉ **3:06 am** 12:06 am
☽ ⚹ ♅ **7:39 am** 4:39 am
☽ ⚺ ♆ **10:19 am** 7:19 am
☽ ⚺ ♀ **7:44 pm** 4:44 pm
☽ ☌ ☿ **11:39 pm** 8:39 pm
☽ △ ♄ 11:18 pm

12 FRIDAY
☽ △ ♄ **2:18 am**
☽ ⚺ ♇ **3:55 am** 12:55 am
☽ ☍ ♂ **4:01 am** 1:01 am
☽ ⚺ ♃ **6:23 am** 3:23 am
♂ ⚻ ♇ **7:00 am** 4:00 am
☿ △ ♄ **8:34 pm** 5:34 pm

13 SATURDAY
☿ ☍ ♂ **5:25 am** 2:25 am
☉ ⚺ ♅ **10:38 am** 7:38 am
☿ ⚺ ♇ **10:51 am** 7:51 am
☽ ⚺ ♅ **8:56 pm** 5:56 pm
☽ ☌ ☉ **9:51 pm** 6:51 pm
☽ ☌ ♆ **11:33 pm** 8:33 pm

14 SUNDAY
♀ ⚻ ♄ **7:24 am** 4:24 am
♀ ⚻ ♂ **11:39 am** 8:39 am
☽ ⚻ ♄ **2:58 pm** 11:58 am
☿ ⚺ ♃ **3:13 pm** 12:13 pm
☽ ⚻ ♂ **3:21 pm** 12:21 pm
☽ ☌ ♀ **3:54 pm** 12:54 pm
☽ ⚹ ♇ **4:58 pm** 1:58 pm
☉ ☌ ♆ **6:19 pm** 3:19 pm
☽ ☌ ♃ **8:32 pm** 5:32 pm
☽ ⚺ ☿ **9:10 pm** 6:10 pm
♀ ⚹ ♇ 11:17 pm

15 MONDAY
♀ ⚹ ♇ **2:17 am**
♂ ⚹ ♄ **10:20 am** 7:20 am

16 TUESDAY
☽ ☌ ♅ **9:32 am** 6:32 am
☽ ⚺ ♆ **12:01 pm** 9:01 am
☽ ⚺ ☉ **3:41 pm** 12:41 pm
♀ ☌ ♃ **9:14 pm** 6:14 pm
☽ △ ♂ 10:55 pm
☽ ☍ ♄ 11:39 pm

17 WEDNESDAY
☽ △ ♂ **1:55 am**
☽ ☍ ♄ **2:39 am**
☽ □ ♇ **5:00 am** 2:00 am
☽ ⚺ ♃ **9:33 am** 6:33 am
☽ ⚺ ♀ **10:41 am** 7:41 am
☽ ⚹ ☿ **5:23 pm** 2:23 pm

18 THURSDAY
☽ ⚺ ♅ **8:33 pm** 5:33 pm
☽ ⚹ ♆ **10:52 pm** 7:52 pm

19 FRIDAY
☽ ⚹ ☉ **7:20 am** 4:20 am
☽ □ ♂ **10:55 am** 7:55 am
☽ ⚻ ♄ **12:32 pm** 9:32 am
☽ △ ♇ **3:10 pm** 12:10 pm
☽ ⚹ ♃ **8:33 pm** 5:33 pm
☽ ⚹ ♀ 11:49 pm

20 SATURDAY
☽ ⚹ ♀ **2:49 am**
☽ □ ☿ **10:53 am** 7:53 am
☉ ⚻ ♂ **8:13 pm** 5:13 pm

21 SUNDAY
☽ ⚹ ♅ **5:07 am** 2:07 am
☽ □ ♆ **7:15 am** 4:15 am
☽ ⚹ ♂ **5:34 pm** 2:34 pm
☽ □ ☉ **7:42 pm** 4:42 pm
☽ △ ♄ **7:48 pm** 4:48 pm
☉ ⚻ ♄ **8:56 pm** 5:56 pm
☽ ⚻ ♇ **10:39 pm** 7:39 pm

22 MONDAY
☽ □ ♃ **4:39 am** 1:39 am
☽ □ ♀ **3:06 pm** 12:06 pm
☽ △ ☿ 9:18 pm

23 TUESDAY
☽ △ ☿ **12:18 am**
☽ □ ♅ **10:32 am** 7:32 am
☉ ⚹ ♇ **11:31 am** 8:31 am
☽ △ ♆ **12:29 pm** 9:29 am
☽ ⚺ ♂ **9:18 pm** 6:18 pm
☽ □ ♄ **11:54 pm** 8:54 pm
☽ ☍ ♇ 11:53 pm

24 WEDNESDAY
☽ ☍ ♇ **2:53 am**
☽ △ ☉ **4:02 am** 1:02 am
☽ △ ♃ **9:20 am** 6:20 am
☽ △ ♀ **11:06 pm** 8:06 pm

25 THURSDAY
☽ ⚻ ☿ **9:17 am** 6:17 am
☽ △ ♅ **12:48 pm** 9:48 am
☽ ⚻ ♆ **2:35 pm** 11:35 am
☽ ☌ ♂ **10:14 pm** 7:14 pm
☽ ⚹ ♄ 10:04 pm

26 FRIDAY
☽ ⚹ ♄ **1:04 am**
☽ ⚻ ♇ **4:12 am** 1:12 am
☽ ⚻ ☉ **8:45 am** 5:45 am
☽ ⚻ ♃ **11:04 am** 8:04 am
☿ ⚺ ♅ **5:19 pm** 2:19 pm

27 SATURDAY
☽ ⚻ ♀ **3:49 am** 12:49 am
☿ ☌ ♆ **9:03 am** 6:03 am
☽ ⚻ ♅ **12:54 pm** 9:54 am
☽ ☍ ♆ **2:35 pm** 11:35 am
☽ ☍ ☿ **3:15 pm** 12:15 pm
☽ ⚺ ♂ **9:28 pm** 6:28 pm
☽ ⚺ ♄ 9:30 pm

28 SUNDAY
☽ ⚺ ♄ **12:30 am**
☽ △ ♇ **3:50 am** 12:50 am
☉ ☌ ♃ **5:44 am** 2:44 am
☽ ☍ ♃ **11:20 am** 8:20 am
☽ ☍ ☉ **11:38 am** 8:38 am

Eastern time in bold type
Pacific time in medium type

FEBRUARY 2010

DATE	S.TIME	SUN	MOON	N.NODE	MERCURY	VENUS	MARS	JUPITER	SATURN	URANUS	NEPTUNE	PLUTO	CERES	PALLAS	JUNO	VESTA	CHIRON
1 Mon	08:44:23	12♒00 28	06♍42	21♑01	17♑43	16♒49	08♌32℞	03♓11	04♎21	24♓13	25♒38	04♑21	16♐22	17♏17	18♈21	03♍39	25♒06
2 Tue	08:48:20	13 01 21	21 38	20 55	18 55	18 05	08 08	03 25	04 19℞	24 15	25 40	04 23	16 43	17 32	18 51	03 26℞	25 10
3 Wed	08:52:16	14 02 12	06♎12	20 55	20 09	19 20	07 45	03 39	04 17	24 18	25 42	04 25	17 04	17 47	19 21	03 13	25 15
4 Thu	08:56:13	15 03 03	20 20	20 50 D	21 25	20 35	07 22	03 53	04 15	24 21	25 45	04 27	17 25	18 01	19 51	03 00	25 19
5 Fri	09:00:10	16 03 53	03♏59	20 50	22 42	21 51	06 59	04 07	04 13	24 24	25 47	04 29	17 46	18 15	20 21	02 47	25 23
6 Sat	09:04:06	17 04 42	17 11	20 50	24 01	23 06	06 37	04 21	04 10	24 27	25 49	04 30	18 07	18 29	20 51	02 33	25 27
7 Sun	09:08:03	18 05 31	29 58	20 50	25 21	24 21	06 14	04 35	04 08	24 30	25 51	04 32	18 27	18 43	21 22	02 19	25 31
8 Mon	09:11:59	19 06 18	12♐26	20 52	26 42	25 36	05 53	04 49	04 05	24 32	25 54	04 34	18 48	18 56	21 52	02 04	25 36
9 Tue	09:15:56	20 07 05	24 37	20 54	28 05	26 51	05 32	05 04	04 02	24 35	25 56	04 35	19 08	19 09	22 23	01 50	25 40
10 Wed	09:19:52	21 07 50	06♑37	20 55	29 28	28 07	05 19	05 18	04 00	24 38	25 58	04 37	19 28	19 22	22 54	01 35	25 44
11 Thu	09:23:49	22 08 34	18 30	20 56℞	00♒53	29 22	05 03	05 32	03 57	24 41	26 01	04 39	19 48	19 34	23 25	01 20	25 48
12 Fri	09:27:45	23 09 17	00♒18	20 56	02 18	00♓37	04 51	05 47	03 54	24 44	26 03	04 40	20 08	19 46	23 56	01 05	25 53
13 Sat	09:31:42	24 09 59	12 05	20 53	03 45	01 52	04 31	06 01	03 51	24 48	26 05	04 42	20 28	19 58	24 27	00 49	25 57
14 Sun	09:35:39	25 10 39	23 53	20 50	05 13	03 07	04 12	06 15	03 48	24 51	26 07	04 43	20 47	20 10	24 58	00 34	26 01
15 Mon	09:39:35	26 11 18	05♓48	20 44	06 41	04 23	03 54	06 30	03 45	24 54	26 10	04 45	21 07	20 21	25 29	00 18	26 05
16 Tue	09:43:32	27 11 56	17 42	20 37	08 11	05 38	03 36	06 44	03 41	24 57	26 12	04 46	21 26	20 32	26 01	00 03	26 10
17 Wed	09:47:28	28 12 32	29 45	20 30	09 42	06 53	03 19	06 58	03 38	25 00	26 14	04 48	21 45	20 42	26 32	29♌47	26 14
18 Thu	09:51:25	29 13 06	12♈06	20 23	11 13	08 08	03 03	07 13	03 35	25 03	26 16	04 49	22 04	20 52	27 04	29 31	26 18
19 Fri	09:55:21	00♓13 38	24 18	20 17	12 46	09 23	02 47	07 27	03 31	25 06	26 19	04 51	22 23	21 02	27 36	29 15	26 22
20 Sat	09:59:18	01 14 09	06♉53	20 12	14 19	10 38	02 32	07 42	03 28	25 09	26 21	04 52	22 41	21 12	28 08	28 59	26 26
21 Sun	10:03:14	02 14 38	19 44	20 09	15 53	11 53	02 18	07 56	03 24	25 13	26 23	04 53	23 00	21 21	28 40	28 43	26 31
22 Mon	10:07:11	03 15 05	02♊53	20 09 D	17 28	13 08	02 05	08 11	03 20	25 16	26 26	04 55	23 18	21 30	29 12	28 27	26 35
23 Tue	10:11:08	04 15 31	16 24	20 09	19 05	14 23	01 52	08 25	03 16	25 19	26 28	04 56	23 36	21 38	29 44	28 12	26 39
24 Wed	10:15:04	05 15 54	00♋16	20 12℞	20 42	15 38	01 41	08 40	03 13	25 22	26 30	04 57	23 54	21 46	00♉16	27 56	26 43
25 Thu	10:19:01	06 16 16	14 37	20 12	22 20	16 53	01 30	08 54	03 09	25 26	26 32	04 59	24 12	21 54	00 49	27 40	26 48
26 Fri	10:22:57	07 16 35	29 18	20 11	23 59	18 08	01 20	09 09	03 05	25 29	26 35	05 00	24 29	22 01	01 21	27 25	26 52
27 Sat	10:26:54	08 16 53	14♌17	20 09	25 39	19 23	01 10	09 23	03 01	25 32	26 37	05 01	24 47	22 08	01 54	27 09	26 56
28 Sun	10:30:50	09 17 08	29 27	20 05	27 20	20 38	01 00	09 38	02 57	25 36	26 39	05 02	25 04	22 15	02 26	26 54	27 00

EPHEMERIS CALCULATED FOR 12 MIDNIGHT GREENWICH MEAN TIME. ALL OTHER DATA AND FACING ASPECTARIAN PAGE IN **EASTERN TIME (BOLD)** AND PACIFIC TIME (REGULAR).

MARCH 2010

☽ Last Aspect day	ET / hr:mn / PT		asp	☽ Ingress sign day	ET / hr:mn / PT	
1	**12:36 pm**	9:36 am	☍ ♅	♎ 1	**7:31 pm**	4:31 pm
3	**3:43 pm**	12:43 pm	△ ♆	♏ 3	**9:11 pm**	6:11 pm
5	**11:31 pm**	8:31 pm	△ ♀	♐ 5		11:36 pm
5	**11:31 pm**	8:31 pm	△ ♀	♐ 6	**2:26 am**	
8	**6:13 am**	3:13 am	⚹ ♆	♑ 8	**12:13 pm**	9:13 am
10	**4:59 pm**	1:59 pm	⚹ ♅	♒ 10		9:42 pm
10	**4:59 pm**	1:59 pm	⚹ ♅	♒ 11	**12:42 am**	
13	**7:57 am**	4:57 am	☌ ♆	♓ 13	**1:44 pm**	10:44 am
15	**8:01 pm**	5:01 pm	☌ ☿	♈ 15		11:32 pm
15	**8:01 pm**	5:01 pm	☌ ☿	♈ 16	**2:32 am**	
18	**7:23 am**	4:23 am	⚹ ♆	♉ 18	**12:29 pm**	9:29 am
20	**3:41 pm**	12:41 pm	□ ♆	♊ 20	**8:28 pm**	5:28 pm
22	**9:49 pm**	6:49 pm	△ ♆	♋ 22		11:16 pm
22	**9:49 pm**	6:49 pm	△ ♆	♋ 23	**2:16 am**	
24		9:39 pm	△ ♅	♌ 25	**5:39 am**	2:39 am
25	**12:39 am**		△ ♅	♌ 25	**5:39 am**	2:39 am
27	**3:04 am**	12:04 am	☍ ♆	♍ 27	**6:57 am**	3:57 am
28		11:55 pm	☍ ♅	♎ 29	**7:21 am**	4:21 am
29	**2:55 am**		☍ ♅	♎ 29	**7:21 am**	4:21 am
31	**8:13 am**	5:13 am	☍ ♀	♏ 31	**8:41 am**	5:41 am

☽ Phases & Eclipses phase	day	ET / hr:mn / PT	
4th Quarter	7	**10:42 am**	7:42 am
New Moon	15	**5:01 pm**	2:01 pm
2nd Quarter	23	**7:00 am**	4:00 am
Full Moon	29	**10:25 pm**	7:25 pm

Planet Ingress	day	ET / hr:mn / PT	
☿ ♓	1	**8:28 am**	5:28 am
♀ ♈	7	**7:33 am**	4:33 am
☿ ♈	17	**12:12 pm**	9:12 am
⚳ ♑	19	**9:44 am**	6:44 am
☉ ♈	20	**1:32 pm**	10:32 am
♀ ♉	31	**1:35 pm**	10:35 am

Planetary Motion	day	ET / hr:mn / PT	
♂ D	10	**12:09 pm**	9:09 am
♀ ℞	14	**8:39 am**	5:39 am

1 MONDAY
☽ ☍ ♀ **7:32 am** 4:32 am
☽ ☍ ♅ **12:36 pm** 9:36 am
☽ ⚻ ♆ **2:15 pm** 11:15 am
☿ ⚻ ♂ **7:14 pm** 4:14 pm
☽ ⚹ ♂ **8:45 pm** 5:45 pm
☽ ⚻ ☿ **8:58 pm** 5:58 pm
☽ ☌ ♄ 9:01 pm

2 TUESDAY
☽ ☌ ♄ **12:01 am**
☽ □ ♇ **3:44 am** 12:44 am
☽ ⚻ ♃ **12:13 pm** 9:13 am
☽ ⚻ ☉ **3:15 pm** 12:15 pm
☿ ⚻ ♄ **10:13 pm** 7:13 pm

3 WEDNESDAY
☽ ⚻ ♀ **1:13 pm** 10:13 am
☽ ⚻ ♅ **2:03 pm** 11:03 am
☽ △ ♆ **3:43 pm** 12:43 pm
☽ □ ♂ **10:09 pm** 7:09 pm
♀ ☌ ♅ **11:07 pm** 8:07 pm
☽ ⚺ ♄ 10:43 pm

4 THURSDAY
☽ ⚺ ♄ **1:43 am**
☽ △ ☿ **5:52 am** 2:52 am
☽ ⚹ ♇ **6:00 am** 3:00 am
☿ ⚹ ♇ **6:55 am** 3:55 am
☽ △ ♃ **3:56 pm** 12:56 pm
♀ ⚺ ♆ **6:34 pm** 3:34 pm
☽ △ ☉ **10:21 pm** 7:21 pm

5 FRIDAY
☽ △ ♅ **7:06 pm** 4:06 pm
☽ □ ♆ **8:50 pm** 5:50 pm
☽ △ ♀ **11:31 pm** 8:31 pm

6 SATURDAY
☽ △ ♂ **3:22 am** 12:22 am
☽ ⚹ ♄ **7:13 am** 4:13 am
☽ ⚺ ♇ **12:13 pm** 9:13 am
☽ □ ☿ **8:55 pm** 5:55 pm
☽ □ ♃ **11:58 pm** 8:58 pm

7 SUNDAY
☽ □ ☉ **10:42 am** 7:42 am
♀ △ ♂ **2:15 pm** 11:15 am
☿ ☌ ♃ **8:45 pm** 5:45 pm

8 MONDAY
☽ □ ♅ **4:27 am** 1:27 am
☽ ⚹ ♆ **6:13 am** 3:13 am
☽ ⚻ ♂ **12:51 pm** 9:51 am
☽ □ ♀ **3:30 pm** 12:30 pm
☽ □ ♄ **4:47 pm** 1:47 pm
☽ ☌ ♇ **10:33 pm** 7:33 pm

9 TUESDAY
♀ ☍ ♄ **3:21 am** 12:21 am
☽ ⚹ ♃ **12:08 pm** 9:08 am
☽ ⚹ ☿ **6:28 pm** 3:28 pm

10 WEDNESDAY
☽ ⚹ ☉ **3:41 am** 12:41 am
☽ ⚹ ♅ **4:59 pm** 1:59 pm

☽ ⚺ ♆ **6:42 pm** 3:42 pm
☽ ☍ ♂ 10:19 pm

11 THURSDAY
☽ ☍ ♂ **1:19 am**
☽ △ ♄ **5:01 am** 2:01 am
☽ ⚹ ♀ **11:14 am** 8:14 am
☽ ⚺ ♇ **11:23 am** 8:23 am
♀ □ ♇ **12:36 pm** 9:36 am
☽ ⚺ ♃ 11:23 pm

12 FRIDAY
☽ ⚺ ♃ **2:23 am**
☽ ⚺ ☿ **7:12 pm** 4:12 pm
☽ ⚺ ☉ **10:25 pm** 7:25 pm

13 SATURDAY
☽ ⚺ ♅ **6:21 am** 3:21 am
☽ ☌ ♆ **7:57 am** 4:57 am
☽ ⚻ ♂ **2:26 pm** 11:26 am
☽ ⚻ ♄ **5:36 pm** 2:36 pm
☽ ⚹ ♇ 9:21 pm

14 SUNDAY
☽ ⚹ ♇ **12:21 am**
☽ ⚺ ♀ **8:13 am** 5:13 am
☉ ☌ ☿ **9:16 am** 6:16 am
☽ ☌ ♃ **5:17 pm** 2:17 pm

15 MONDAY
☽ ☌ ☉ **5:01 pm** 2:01 pm
☿ ☌ ♅ **5:40 pm** 2:40 pm
☽ ☌ ♅ **7:38 pm** 4:38 pm
☽ ☌ ☿ **8:01 pm** 5:01 pm

☽ ⚺ ♆ **9:05 pm** 6:05 pm
☿ ⚺ ♆ 11:44 pm

16 TUESDAY
☿ ⚺ ♆ **2:44 am**
☽ △ ♂ **3:29 am** 12:29 am
☽ ☍ ♄ **5:55 am** 2:55 am
☽ □ ♇ **12:55 pm** 9:55 am
☽ ☌ ♀ 11:08 pm
☉ ☌ ♅ 11:50 pm

17 WEDNESDAY
☽ ☌ ♀ **2:08 am**
☉ ☌ ♅ **2:50 am**
☽ ⚺ ♃ **5:27 am** 2:27 am
☿ △ ♂ **7:33 pm** 4:33 pm
☉ ⚺ ♆ **8:19 pm** 5:19 pm

18 THURSDAY
☽ ⚺ ♅ **6:05 am** 3:05 am
☿ ☍ ♄ **7:04 am** 4:04 am
☽ ⚹ ♆ **7:23 am** 4:23 am
☽ ⚺ ☉ **8:18 am** 5:18 am
☽ □ ♂ **1:47 pm** 10:47 am
☽ ⚻ ♄ **3:25 pm** 12:25 pm
☽ ⚺ ☿ **5:02 pm** 2:02 pm
♀ ⚺ ♃ **6:29 pm** 3:29 pm
☽ △ ♇ **10:34 pm** 7:34 pm

19 FRIDAY
☽ ⚹ ♃ **3:36 pm** 12:36 pm
☽ ⚺ ♀ **5:25 pm** 2:25 pm

20 SATURDAY
☿ □ ♇ **4:16 am** 1:16 am
☽ ⚹ ♅ **2:33 pm** 11:33 am
☽ □ ♆ **3:41 pm** 12:41 pm
☽ ⚹ ☉ **9:02 pm** 6:02 pm
☽ ⚹ ♂ **10:10 pm** 7:10 pm
☽ △ ♄ **10:57 pm** 7:57 pm

21 SUNDAY
☽ ⚻ ♇ **6:14 am** 3:14 am
☽ ⚹ ☿ **10:51 am** 7:51 am
☉ △ ♂ **1:54 pm** 10:54 am
☉ ☍ ♄ **8:37 pm** 5:37 pm
☽ □ ♃ **11:33 pm** 8:33 pm

22 MONDAY
☽ ⚹ ♀ **5:54 am** 2:54 am
☽ □ ♅ **8:49 pm** 5:49 pm
☽ △ ♆ **9:49 pm** 6:49 pm
♂ ⚹ ♄ **11:53 pm** 8:53 pm

23 TUESDAY
☽ □ ♄ **4:20 am** 1:20 am
☽ ⚺ ♂ **4:24 am** 1:24 am
☽ □ ☉ **7:00 am** 4:00 am
☽ ☍ ♇ **11:38 am** 8:38 am
☽ □ ☿ 9:55 pm

24 WEDNESDAY
☽ □ ☿ **12:55 am**
☽ △ ♃ **5:03 am** 2:03 am
☽ □ ♀ **3:14 pm** 12:14 pm

☽ △ ♅ 9:39 pm
☽ ⚻ ♆ 10:31 pm

25 THURSDAY
☽ △ ♅ **12:39 am**
☽ ⚻ ♆ **1:31 am**
☽ ⚹ ♄ **7:21 am** 4:21 am
☽ ☌ ♂ **8:15 am** 5:15 am
☿ ⚺ ♃ **9:46 am** 6:46 am
☽ △ ☉ **1:57 pm** 10:57 am
☽ ⚻ ♇ **2:37 pm** 11:37 am
☉ □ ♇ **11:45 pm** 8:45 pm

26 FRIDAY
☽ ⚻ ♃ **8:06 am** 5:06 am
☽ △ ☿ **11:06 am** 8:06 am
☽ △ ♀ **9:36 pm** 6:36 pm
☽ ⚻ ♅ 11:19 pm

27 SATURDAY
☽ ⚻ ♅ **2:19 am**
☽ ☍ ♆ **3:04 am** 12:04 am
☽ ⚺ ♄ **8:20 am** 5:20 am
☽ ⚺ ♂ **10:03 am** 7:03 am
☽ △ ♇ **3:40 pm** 12:40 pm
☽ ⚻ ☉ **6:30 pm** 3:30 pm

28 SUNDAY
☽ ☍ ♃ **9:30 am** 6:30 am
☽ ⚻ ☿ **6:42 pm** 3:42 pm
☽ ⚻ ♀ 11:26 pm
☽ ☍ ♅ 11:55 pm

29 MONDAY
☽ ⚻ ♀ **2:26 am**
☽ ☍ ♅ **2:55 am**
☽ ⚻ ♆ **3:34 am** 12:34 am
♀ ⚺ ♅ **8:24 am** 5:24 am
☽ ☌ ♄ **8:29 am** 5:29 am
☽ ⚹ ♂ **11:05 am** 8:05 am
☽ □ ♇ **4:06 pm** 1:06 pm
♀ ⚹ ♆ **4:25 pm** 1:25 pm
☽ ☍ ☉ **10:25 pm** 7:25 pm

30 TUESDAY
☽ ⚻ ♃ **10:57 am** 7:57 am
☽ ☍ ☿ 11:27 pm

31 WEDNESDAY
☽ ☍ ☿ **2:27 am**
☽ ⚻ ♅ **4:16 am** 1:16 am
☽ △ ♆ **4:52 am** 1:52 am
☽ ☍ ♀ **8:13 am** 5:13 am
☽ ⚺ ♄ **9:36 am** 6:36 am
☽ □ ♂ **1:19 pm** 10:19 am
☽ ⚹ ♇ **5:50 pm** 2:50 pm
☿ ⚺ ♅ **6:22 pm** 3:22 pm
♀ ⚻ ♄ **11:16 pm** 8:16 pm
☿ ⚹ ♆ **11:21 pm** 8:21 pm

Eastern time in bold type
Pacific time in medium type

MARCH 2010

DATE	S.TIME	SUN	MOON	N.NODE	MERCURY	VENUS	MARS	JUPITER	SATURN	URANUS	NEPTUNE	PLUTO	CERES	PALLAS	JUNO	VESTA	CHIRON
1 Mon	10:34:47	10♓17 22	14 ♍ 38	19 ♑ 58	29 ≈ 02	21 ♓ 52	00 ♌ 54	09 ♒ 52	02 ≏ 53	25 ♓ 39	26 ≈ 41	05 ♑ 04	25 ♐ 21	22 ♏ 12	02 ♉ 59	26 ♌ 39	27 ≈ 04
2 Tue	10:38:43	11 17 34	29 41	19 50 ℞	23 07	23 07	00 46 ℞	10 07	02 48 ℞	25 42	26 44	05 06	25 55	22 26	03 32	26 24 ℞	27 08
3 Wed	10:42:40	12 17 44	14 ♎ 25	19 42	02 30	24 22	00 40	10 21	02 44	25 46	26 46	05 06	26 11	22 37	04 05	26 10	27 12
4 Thu	10:46:36	13 17 53	28 43	19 34	04 15	25 37	00 35	10 36	02 40	25 49	26 48	05 07	26 27	22 41	04 38	25 56	27 17
5 Fri	10:50:33	14 18 00	12 ♏ 33	19 28	06 01	26 51	00 30	10 50	02 36	25 52	26 50	05 08	26 43	22 45	05 11	25 41	27 21
6 Sat	10:54:30	15 18 06	25 53	19 24	07 48	28 06	00 26	11 05	02 31	25 56	26 52	05 09	—	—	05 44	25 28	27 25
7 Sun	10:58:26	16 18 10	08 ♐ 45	19 22 D	09 37	29 21	00 23	11 19	02 27	25 59	26 55	05 10	26 59	22 49	06 17	25 14	27 29
8 Mon	11:02:23	17 18 13	21 14	19 21	11 26	00 ♈ 36	00 21	11 33	02 22	26 03	26 57	05 11	27 15	22 52	06 50	25 01	27 33
9 Tue	11:06:19	18 18 14	03 ♑ 25	19 22	13 17	01 52	00 19	11 48	02 18	26 06	26 59	05 12	27 30	22 55	07 23	24 48	27 37
10 Wed	11:10:16	19 18 13	15 22	19 23 ℞	15 09	03 05	00 18 D	12 02	02 13	26 09	27 01	05 13	27 46	22 57	07 57	24 35	27 41
11 Thu	11:14:12	20 18 11	27 12	19 23	17 02	04 20	00 18	12 17	02 09	26 13	27 03	05 14	28 01	22 59	08 30	24 23	27 45
12 Fri	11:18:09	21 18 07	08 ≈ 58	19 20	18 56	05 34	00 18	12 31	02 04	26 16	27 05	05 14	28 16	23 01	09 03	24 11	27 49
13 Sat	11:22:06	22 18 01	20 46	19 16	20 51	06 49	00 20	12 46	02 00	26 20	27 07	05 15	28 30	23 01	09 37	24 00	27 53
14 Sun	11:26:02	23 17 53	02 ♓ 45	19 08	22 46	08 03	00 22	13 00	01 55	26 23	27 10	05 16	28 44	23 02 ℞	10 10	23 48	27 57
15 Mon	11:29:59	24 17 43	14 55	18 59	24 43	09 18	00 24	13 14	01 50	26 26	27 12	05 17	28 59	23 02	10 44	23 38	28 01
16 Tue	11:33:55	25 17 32	26 41	18 47	26 41	10 32	00 28	13 29	01 46	26 30	27 14	05 17	29 12	23 01	11 18	23 27	28 04
17 Wed	11:37:52	26 17 18	09 ♈ 56	18 34	28 40	11 47	00 32	13 43	01 41	26 33	27 16	05 18	29 26	23 01	11 51	23 17	28 08
18 Thu	11:41:48	27 17 03	21 22	18 21	00 ♈ 39	13 01	00 37	13 57	01 36	26 37	27 18	05 19	29 39	22 59	12 25	23 08	28 12
19 Fri	11:45:45	28 16 45	03 ♉ 58	18 10	02 39	14 16	00 42	14 12	01 31	26 40	27 20	05 19	29 53	22 57	12 59	22 59	28 16
20 Sat	11:49:41	29 16 25	16 45	18 01	04 39	15 30	00 48	14 26	01 27	26 44	27 22	05 20	00 ♑ 05	22 55	13 33	22 50	28 20
21 Sun	11:53:38	00 ♈ 16 04	29 45	17 55	06 39	16 44	00 55	14 40	01 22	26 47	27 24	05 21	00 18	22 52	14 07	22 42	28 23
22 Mon	11:57:34	01 15 39	12 ♊ 58	17 51	08 39	17 59	01 02	14 54	01 17	26 50	27 26	05 21	00 31	22 49	14 41	22 35	28 27
23 Tue	12:01:31	02 15 13	26 26	17 50 D	10 39	19 13	01 10	15 09	01 13	26 54	27 28	05 22	00 43	22 45	15 15	22 27	28 31
24 Wed	12:05:28	03 14 44	10 ♋ 12	17 50 ℞	12 39	20 27	01 19	15 23	01 08	26 57	27 30	05 22	00 55	22 40	15 49	22 21	28 35
25 Thu	12:09:24	04 14 13	24 16	17 50	14 38	21 41	01 28	15 37	01 03	27 01	27 32	05 23	01 06	22 36	16 23	22 14	28 38
26 Fri	12:13:21	05 13 40	08 ♌ 38	17 47	16 35	22 55	01 38	15 51	00 58	27 04	27 34	05 23	01 18	22 30	16 57	22 09	28 42
27 Sat	12:17:17	06 13 04	23 15	17 45	18 31	24 10	01 48	16 05	00 54	27 08	27 35	05 24	01 29	22 24	17 31	22 03	28 45
28 Sun	12:21:14	07 12 26	08 ♍ 05	17 39	20 24	25 24	01 59	16 19	00 49	27 11	27 37	05 24	01 39	22 18	18 06	21 59	28 49
29 Mon	12:25:10	08 11 46	22 58	17 30	22 16	26 38	02 11	16 33	00 44	27 14	27 39	05 24	01 50	22 11	18 40	21 54	28 52
30 Tue	12:29:07	09 11 03	07 ♎ 48	17 20	24 04	27 52	02 23	16 47	00 40	27 17	27 41	05 24	02 00	22 04	19 14	21 50	28 56
31 Wed	12:33:03	10 10 19	22 25	17 07	25 49	29 06	02 35	17 01	00 35	27 21	27 43	05 24	02 10	21 56	19 48	21 47	28 59

EPHEMERIS CALCULATED FOR 12 MIDNIGHT GREENWICH MEAN TIME. ALL OTHER DATA AND FACING ASPECTARIAN PAGE IN **EASTERN TIME (BOLD)** AND PACIFIC TIME (REGULAR).

APRIL 2010

☽ Last Aspect day	ET / hr:mn / PT		asp	☽ Ingress sign	day	ET / hr:mn / PT	
2	**8:54 am**	5:54 am	□ ♆	♐	2	**12:52 pm**	9:52 am
4	**4:57 pm**	1:57 pm	⚹ ♆	♑	4	**9:07 pm**	6:07 pm
7	**4:18 am**	1:18 am	⚹ ♅	♒	7	**8:51 am**	5:51 am
9	**5:44 pm**	2:44 pm	☌ ♆	♓	9	**9:48 pm**	6:48 pm
12	**8:51 am**	5:51 am	☍ ♄	♈	12	**9:31 am**	6:31 am
14	**3:23 pm**	12:23 pm	⚹ ♆	♉	14	**6:55 pm**	3:55 pm
16		9:57 pm	△ ♄	♊	16		11:08 pm
17	**12:57 am**		△ ♄	♊	17	**2:08 am**	
19	**6:21 am**	3:21 am	⚹ ☉	♋	19	**7:39 am**	4:39 am
21	**10:07 am**	7:07 am	⚹ ♄	♌	21	**11:42 am**	8:42 am
23	**11:35 am**	8:35 am	☍ ♆	♍	23	**2:24 pm**	11:24 am
25	**2:21 pm**	11:21 am	☌ ♄	♎	25	**4:16 pm**	1:16 pm
27	**3:45 pm**	12:45 pm	△ ♆	♏	27	**6:28 pm**	3:28 pm
29	**8:39 pm**	5:39 pm	△ ♅	♐	29	**10:36 pm**	7:36 pm

☽ Phases & Eclipses phase	day	ET / hr:mn / PT	
4th Quarter	6	**5:37 am**	2:37 am
New Moon	14	**8:29 am**	5:29 am
2nd Quarter	21	**2:20 pm**	11:20 am
Full Moon	28	**8:18 am**	5:18 am

Planet Ingress		day	ET / hr:mn / PT	
☿	♉	2	**9:06 am**	6:06 am
♄	♍	7	**2:51 pm**	11:51 am
⚵	♊	17	**1:05 pm**	10:05 am
☉	♉	19		9:30 pm
⚷	♓	19		11:28 pm
☉	♉	20	**12:30 am**	
⚷	♓	20	**2:28 am**	
♀	♊	24		10:05 pm
♀	♊	25	**1:05 am**	

Planetary Motion		day	ET / hr:mn / PT	
⚴	D	6	**8:37 am**	5:37 am
♇	℞	6	**10:34 pm**	7:34 pm
☿	℞	17		9:06 pm
☿	℞	18	**12:06 am**	
⚳	℞	28	**7:02 pm**	4:02 pm

1 THURSDAY
☽ ⊼ ☉ **4:15 am** 1:15 am
☽ △ ♃ **2:33 pm** 11:33 am

2 FRIDAY
☽ △ ♅ **8:22 am** 5:22 am
☽ □ ♆ **8:54 am** 5:54 am
☽ ⊼ ☿ **1:22 pm** 10:22 am
☽ ⚹ ♄ **1:33 pm** 10:33 am
☿ ⊼ ♄ **2:53 pm** 11:53 am
☽ ⊼ ♀ **5:43 pm** 2:43 pm
☽ △ ♂ **6:46 pm** 3:46 pm
☽ ⊻ ♇ **10:43 pm** 7:43 pm

3 SATURDAY
♀ □ ♂ **7:25 am** 4:25 am
☽ △ ☉ **2:23 pm** 11:23 am
☽ □ ♃ **10:02 pm** 7:02 pm

4 SUNDAY
☽ □ ♅ **4:30 pm** 1:30 pm
☽ ⚹ ♆ **4:57 pm** 1:57 pm
☽ □ ♄ **9:30 pm** 6:30 pm
♀ △ ♇ **11:12 pm** 8:12 pm
☿ □ ♂ 9:17 pm

5 MONDAY
☿ □ ♂ **12:17 am**
☽ ⊼ ♂ **4:37 am** 1:37 am
☽ △ ☿ **5:02 am** 2:02 am
☽ ☌ ♇ **7:42 am** 4:42 am
☽ △ ♀ **8:39 am** 5:39 am

6 TUESDAY
☽ □ ☉ **5:37 am** 2:37 am
☿ △ ♇ **6:46 am** 3:46 am
☽ ⚹ ♃ **9:42 am** 6:42 am

7 WEDNESDAY
☽ ⚹ ♅ **4:18 am** 1:18 am
☽ ⊻ ♆ **4:39 am** 1:39 am
☽ △ ♄ **8:53 am** 5:53 am
☽ ☍ ♂ **6:02 pm** 3:02 pm
☽ ⊻ ♇ **7:51 pm** 4:51 pm
☽ □ ☿ **11:47 pm** 8:47 pm

8 THURSDAY
☽ □ ♀ **3:50 am** 12:50 am
☉ ⊻ ♃ **9:09 pm** 6:09 pm
☽ ⊻ ♃ **11:42 pm** 8:42 pm
☽ ⚹ ☉ **11:53 pm** 8:53 pm

9 FRIDAY
☽ ⊻ ♅ **5:32 pm** 2:32 pm
☽ ☌ ♆ **5:44 pm** 2:44 pm
☽ ⊼ ♄ **9:28 pm** 6:28 pm

10 SATURDAY
☽ ⊼ ♂ **8:25 am** 5:25 am
☽ ⚹ ♇ **8:43 am** 5:43 am
☽ ⚹ ☿ **5:38 pm** 2:38 pm
♂ ⊼ ♇ **8:51 pm** 5:51 pm
☽ ⚹ ♀ **11:33 pm** 8:33 pm

11 SUNDAY
☽ ☌ ♃ **1:13 pm** 10:13 am
☽ ⊻ ☉ **5:34 pm** 2:34 pm

12 MONDAY
☽ ☌ ♅ **5:40 am** 2:40 am
☽ ⊻ ♆ **5:43 am** 2:43 am
☽ ☍ ♄ **8:51 am** 5:51 am
☽ □ ♇ **8:03 pm** 5:03 pm
☽ △ ♂ **9:15 pm** 6:15 pm

13 TUESDAY
♅ ⊻ ♆ **3:43 am** 12:43 am
☽ ⊻ ☿ **7:47 am** 4:47 am
☽ ⊻ ♀ **4:41 pm** 1:41 pm
☽ ⊻ ♃ 9:29 pm

14 WEDNESDAY
☽ ⊻ ♃ **12:29 am**
☽ ☌ ☉ **8:29 am** 5:29 am
☽ ⚹ ♆ **3:23 pm** 12:23 pm
☽ ⊻ ♅ **3:27 pm** 12:27 pm
☽ ⊼ ♄ **5:58 pm** 2:58 pm

15 THURSDAY
☽ △ ♇ **5:00 am** 2:00 am
☽ □ ♂ **7:36 am** 4:36 am
☽ ☌ ☿ **5:55 pm** 2:55 pm

16 FRIDAY
☽ ☌ ♀ **6:39 am** 3:39 am
☽ ⚹ ♃ **9:18 am** 6:18 am
☽ ⊻ ☉ **8:31 pm** 5:31 pm
☽ □ ♆ **10:49 pm** 7:49 pm
☽ ⚹ ♅ **11:01 pm** 8:01 pm
☽ △ ♄ 9:57 pm

17 SATURDAY
☽ △ ♄ **12:57 am**
☽ ⊼ ♇ **11:52 am** 8:52 am
☽ ⚹ ♂ **3:48 pm** 12:48 pm
♀ ⚹ ♃ **4:43 pm** 1:43 pm
☽ ⊻ ☿ 9:51 pm

18 SUNDAY
☽ ⊻ ☿ **12:51 am**
☉ ⚹ ♆ **4:16 am** 1:16 am
☉ ⊻ ♅ **7:58 am** 4:58 am
☽ □ ♃ **4:11 pm** 1:11 pm
☽ ⊻ ♀ **6:06 pm** 3:06 pm

19 MONDAY
☽ △ ♆ **4:31 am** 1:31 am
☽ □ ♅ **4:49 am** 1:49 am
☉ ⊼ ♄ **5:06 am** 2:06 am
☽ □ ♄ **6:15 am** 3:15 am
☽ ⚹ ☉ **6:21 am** 3:21 am
☽ ☍ ♇ **5:05 pm** 2:05 pm
☽ ⊻ ♂ **10:18 pm** 7:18 pm

20 TUESDAY
☽ ⚹ ☿ **5:19 am** 2:19 am
☽ △ ♃ **9:29 pm** 6:29 pm

21 WEDNESDAY
☽ ⚹ ♀ **3:33 am** 12:33 am
☽ ⊼ ♆ **8:44 am** 5:44 am
☽ △ ♅ **9:08 am** 6:08 am
☽ ⚹ ♄ **10:07 am** 7:07 am
☽ □ ☉ **2:20 pm** 11:20 am
☽ ⊼ ♇ **8:51 pm** 5:51 pm

22 THURSDAY
☽ ☌ ♂ **3:18 am** 12:18 am
☽ □ ☿ **7:43 am** 4:43 am
☽ ⊼ ♃ 10:18 pm

23 FRIDAY
☽ ⊼ ♃ **1:18 am**
☽ □ ♀ **11:11 am** 8:11 am
☽ ☍ ♆ **11:35 am** 8:35 am
☽ ⊼ ♅ **12:05 pm** 9:05 am
☽ ⊻ ♄ **12:39 pm** 9:39 am
♀ □ ♆ **3:54 pm** 12:54 pm
☽ △ ☉ **8:40 pm** 5:40 pm
♀ ⚹ ♅ **10:06 pm** 7:06 pm
☽ △ ♇ **11:20 pm** 8:20 pm

24 SATURDAY
♀ △ ♄ **3:44 am** 12:44 am
☽ ⊻ ♂ **6:59 am** 3:59 am
☽ △ ☿ **8:27 am** 5:27 am

25 SUNDAY
☽ ☍ ♃ **4:02 am** 1:02 am
☿ □ ♂ **6:41 am** 3:41 am
☉ △ ♇ **11:44 am** 8:44 am
☽ ⊼ ♆ **1:32 pm** 10:32 am
☽ ☍ ♅ **2:08 pm** 11:08 am
☽ ☌ ♄ **2:21 pm** 11:21 am
☽ △ ♀ **5:40 pm** 2:40 pm
☽ □ ♇ 10:07 pm
☽ ⊼ ☉ 11:06 pm

26 MONDAY
☽ □ ♇ **1:07 am**
☽ ⊼ ☉ **2:06 am**
☽ ⊼ ☿ **8:23 am** 5:23 am
☽ ⚹ ♂ **10:10 am** 7:10 am
♄ ☍ ♅ **7:23 pm** 4:23 pm

27 TUESDAY
☽ ⊼ ♃ **6:45 am** 3:45 am
☽ △ ♆ **3:45 pm** 12:45 pm
☽ ⊻ ♄ **4:19 pm** 1:19 pm
☽ ⊼ ♅ **4:28 pm** 1:28 pm
☽ ⊼ ♀ 9:38 pm

28 WEDNESDAY
☽ ⊼ ♀ **12:38 am**
☽ ⚹ ♇ **3:30 am** 12:30 am
☽ ☍ ☉ **8:18 am** 5:18 am
☽ ☍ ☿ **8:48 am** 5:48 am
☉ ☌ ☿ **12:44 pm** 9:44 am
☽ □ ♂ **2:20 pm** 11:20 am

29 THURSDAY
♀ ⊼ ♇ **9:32 am** 6:32 am
☽ △ ♃ **11:04 am** 8:04 am
☽ □ ♆ **7:48 pm** 4:48 pm
☽ ⚹ ♄ **8:07 pm** 5:07 pm
☽ △ ♅ **8:39 pm** 5:39 pm

30 FRIDAY
☽ ⊻ ♇ **8:05 am** 5:05 am
☽ ☍ ♀ **10:22 am** 7:22 am
☽ ⊼ ☿ **11:13 am** 8:13 am
☿ ⊻ ♀ **4:39 pm** 1:39 pm
☽ ⊼ ☉ **5:26 pm** 2:26 pm
☽ △ ♂ **9:17 pm** 6:17 pm

Eastern time in bold type
Pacific time in medium type

APRIL 2010

DATE	S.TIME	SUN	MOON	N.NODE	MERCURY	VENUS	MARS	JUPITER	SATURN	URANUS	NEPTUNE	PLUTO	CERES	PALLAS	JUNO	VESTA	CHIRON
1 Thu	12:37:00	11♈09 32	06♏41	16♑41	27♈31	00♉20	02♌48	17♓15	00♎30	27♓24	27♒45	05♑25	02♑20	21♏48	20♓23	21♌44	29♒03
2 Fri	12:40:57	12 08 44	20 32	16 40R	29 09	01 34	03 02	17 29	00 26R	27 28	27 46	05 25	02 30	21 39R	20 57	21 42R	29 06
3 Sat	12:44:53	13 07 54	03♐56	16 39	00♉42	02 48	03 16	17 43	00 21	27 31	27 48	05 25	02 38	21 30	21 31	21 40	29 09
4 Sun	12:48:50	14 07 02	16 53	16 35	02 10	04 01	03 30	17 56	00 17	27 34	27 50	05 25	02 47	21 20	22 06	21 38	29 13
5 Mon	12:52:46	15 06 08	29 26	16 33	03 34	05 15	03 45	18 10	00 12	27 38	27 52	05 25	02 56	21 10	22 40	21 37	29 16
6 Tue	12:56:43	16 05 13	11♑39	16 32	04 52	06 29	04 01	18 24	00 08	27 41	27 53	05 25R	03 04	21 00	23 15	21 37	29 19
7 Wed	13:00:39	17 04 16	23 39	16 31	06 05	07 43	04 17	18 37	00 03	27 44	27 55	05 25	03 12	20 49	23 49	21 37D	29 22
8 Thu	13:04:36	18 03 17	05♒30	16 29	07 11	08 57	04 33	18 51	29♍59	27 48	27 57	05 25	03 19	20 37	24 24	21 37	29 25
9 Fri	13:08:32	19 02 16	17 17	16 27	08 12	10 10	04 50	19 04	29 55	27 51	27 58	05 25	03 26	20 25	24 58	21 38	29 28
10 Sat	13:12:29	20 01 13	29 07	16 24	09 07	11 24	05 07	19 18	29 50	27 54	28 00	05 25	03 33	20 13	25 33	21 40	29 31
11 Sun	13:16:26	21 00 09	11♓02	16 16	09 56	12 38	05 24	19 31	29 46	27 57	28 01	05 25	03 40	20 00	26 08	21 42	29 34
12 Mon	13:20:22	21 59 02	23 07	16 06	10 38	13 51	05 42	19 45	29 42	28 01	28 03	05 25	03 46	19 46	26 42	21 44	29 37
13 Tue	13:24:19	22 57 54	05♈23	15 54	11 14	15 05	06 01	19 58	29 38	28 04	28 04	05 24	03 52	19 33	27 17	21 47	29 40
14 Wed	13:28:15	23 56 44	17 52	15 40	11 44	16 18	06 19	20 11	29 34	28 07	28 06	05 24	03 57	19 19	27 51	21 50	29 43
15 Thu	13:32:12	24 55 32	00♉35	15 27	12 07	17 32	06 39	20 25	29 30	28 10	28 07	05 24	04 03	19 04	28 26	21 54	29 46
16 Fri	13:36:08	25 54 18	13 30	15 15	12 23	18 45	06 58	20 38	29 26	28 13	28 09	05 23	04 08	18 49	29 01	21 58	29 49
17 Sat	13:40:05	26 53 02	26 37	15 15	12 34	19 59	07 18	20 51	29 22	28 16	28 10	05 23	04 12	18 34	29 35	22 02	29 51
18 Sun	13:44:01	27 51 44	09♊55	14 58	12 38R	21 12	07 38	21 04	29 18	28 19	28 11	05 23	04 16	18 19	00♈10	22 07	29 54
19 Mon	13:47:58	28 50 24	23 24	14 54	12 36	22 25	07 59	21 17	29 14	28 23	28 13	05 23	04 20	18 03	00 45	22 13	29 57
20 Tue	13:51:55	29 49 01	07♋09	14 53D	12 28	23 38	08 20	21 30	29 10	28 26	28 14	05 22	04 24	17 47	01 19	22 19	29 59
21 Wed	13:55:51	00♉47 52	20 52	14 53R	12 15	24 52	08 41	21 43	29 07	28 29	28 15	05 22	04 27	17 30	01 54	22 25	00♓02
22 Thu	13:59:48	01 46 10	04♌21	14 52	11 56	26 05	09 03	21 55	29 03	28 32	28 17	05 21	04 29	17 14	02 29	22 32	00 04
23 Fri	14:03:44	02 45 17	18 02	14 51	11 33	27 18	09 24	22 08	29 00	28 35	28 18	05 20	04 32	16 57	03 04	22 39	00 07
24 Sat	14:07:41	03 43 09	17♍47	14 49	11 05	28 31	09 47	22 21	28 56	28 38	28 19	05 20	04 34	16 40	03 38	22 46	00 09
25 Sun	14:11:37	04 41 36	02♎15	14 43	10 34	29 45	10 09	22 33	28 53	28 41	28 20	05 19	04 35	16 22	04 13	22 54	00 12
26 Mon	14:15:34	05 40 00	16 39	14 35	10 00	00♊58	10 32	22 46	28 49	28 43	28 21	05 18	04 37	16 05	04 48	23 03	00 14
27 Tue	14:19:30	06 38 23	00♏58	14 26	09 23	02 11	10 55	22 58	28 46	28 46	28 23	05 18	04 38	15 47	05 22	23 11	00 16
28 Wed	14:23:27	07 36 43	14 53	14 15	08 45	03 23	11 18	23 10	28 43	28 49	28 24	05 17	04 38R	15 29	05 57	23 20	00 18
29 Thu	14:27:23	08 35 02	28 33	14 03	08 05	04 36	11 42	23 23	28 40	28 52	28 25	05 17	04 38	15 11	06 32	23 30	00 20
30 Fri	14:31:20	09 33 18	13♐56	13 56	07 26	05 49	12 06	23 35	28 37	28 55	28 26	05 17	04 38	14 53	07 06	23 40	00 22

EPHEMERIS CALCULATED FOR 12 MIDNIGHT GREENWICH MEAN TIME. ALL OTHER DATA AND FACING ASPECTARIAN PAGE IN **EASTERN TIME (BOLD)** AND PACIFIC TIME (REGULAR).

☽ Last Aspect day	ET / hr:mn / PT		asp	☽ Ingress sign	day	ET / hr:mn / PT	
2	**4:08 am**	1:08 am	□ ♅	♑	2	**6:00 am**	3:00 am
4	**3:07 pm**	12:07 pm	✶ ♅	♒	4	**4:52 pm**	1:52 pm
6		11:36 pm	☌ ♆	♓	7	**5:34 am**	2:34 am
7	**2:36 am**		☌ ♆	♓	7	**5:34 am**	2:34 am
9	**4:12 pm**	1:12 pm	☌ ♅	♈	9	**5:29 pm**	2:29 pm
11		9:11 pm	✶ ♆	♉	11		11:48 pm
12	**12:11 am**		✶ ♆	♉	12	**2:48 am**	
14	**8:28 am**	5:28 am	✶ ♅	♊	14	**9:18 am**	6:18 am
16	**1:06 pm**	10:06 am	□ ♅	♋	16	**1:46 pm**	10:46 am
18	**4:35 pm**	1:35 pm	△ ♅	♌	18	**5:06 pm**	2:06 pm
20	**7:43 pm**	4:43 pm	□ ☉	♍	20	**7:58 pm**	4:58 pm
22	**10:34 pm**	7:34 pm	☍ ♅	♎	22	**10:50 pm**	7:50 pm
24		9:01 pm	△ ♆	♏	24		11:17 pm
25	**12:01 am**		△ ♆	♏	25	**2:17 am**	
27	**7:13 am**	4:13 am	△ ♅	♐	27	**7:15 am**	4:15 am
29	**12:40 pm**	9:40 am	□ ♃	♑	29	**2:44 pm**	11:44 am
31	**11:41 pm**	8:41 pm	✶ ♃	♒	31		10:08 pm
31	**11:41 pm**	8:41 pm	✶ ♃	♒	6/1	**1:08 am**	

☽ Phases & Eclipses phase	day	ET / hr:mn / PT	
4th Quarter	5		9:15 pm
4th Quarter	6	**12:15 am**	
New Moon	13	**9:04 pm**	6:04 pm
2nd Quarter	20	**7:43 pm**	4:43 pm
Full Moon	27	**7:07 pm**	4:07 pm

Planet Ingress		day	ET / hr:mn / PT	
♀	♋	19	**9:05 pm**	6:05 pm
☉	♊	20	**11:34 pm**	8:34 pm
⚳	♍	26	**10:46 am**	7:46 am
♅	♈	27	**9:44 pm**	6:44 pm

Planetary Motion		day	ET / hr:mn / PT	
☿	D	11	**6:26 pm**	3:26 pm
♄	D	30	**2:08 pm**	11:08 am
♆	R	31	**2:48 pm**	11:48 am

1 SATURDAY
☽ □ ♃ **6:34 pm** 3:34 pm

2 SUNDAY
☽ ✶ ♆ **3:05 am** 12:05 am
☽ □ ♄ **3:09 am** 12:09 am
☽ □ ♅ **4:08 am** 1:08 am
☽ ☌ ♇ **4:04 pm** 1:04 pm
☽ △ ☿ **4:46 pm** 1:46 pm
♄ ⊼ ♆ **6:22 pm** 3:22 pm
☽ ⊼ ♀ 9:41 pm

3 MONDAY
☽ ⊼ ♀ **12:41 am**
☽ △ ☉ **6:57 am** 3:57 am
☿ △ ♇ **8:01 am** 5:01 am
☽ ⊼ ♂ **8:10 am** 5:10 am

4 TUESDAY
☽ ✶ ♃ **5:47 am** 2:47 am
☉ □ ♂ **9:09 am** 6:09 am
☽ △ ♄ **1:39 pm** 10:39 am
☽ ⊻ ♆ **1:52 pm** 10:52 am
☽ ✶ ♅ **3:07 pm** 12:07 pm
☽ □ ☿ 10:35 pm

5 WEDNESDAY
☽ □ ☿ **1:35 am**
☽ ⊻ ♇ **3:22 am** 12:22 am
☽ △ ♀ **7:11 pm** 4:11 pm
☽ ☍ ♂ **10:23 pm** 7:23 pm
☽ □ ☉ 9:15 pm

6 THURSDAY
☽ □ ☉ **12:15 am**
☽ ⊻ ♃ **7:21 pm** 4:21 pm
☽ ⊼ ♄ 11:07 pm
☽ ☌ ♆ 11:36 pm

7 FRIDAY
☽ ⊼ ♄ **2:07 am**
☽ ☌ ♆ **2:36 am**
☽ ⊻ ♅ **4:02 am** 1:02 am
☽ ✶ ☿ **12:21 pm** 9:21 am
☽ ✶ ♇ **4:03 pm** 1:03 pm
♀ ✶ ♂ **5:55 pm** 2:55 pm

8 SATURDAY
☽ ⊼ ♂ **1:17 pm** 10:17 am
☽ □ ♀ **2:40 pm** 11:40 am
☽ ✶ ☉ **6:10 pm** 3:10 pm

9 SUNDAY
☽ ☌ ♃ **8:32 am** 5:32 am
☽ ☍ ♄ **1:58 pm** 10:58 am
☽ ⊻ ♆ **2:41 pm** 11:41 am
☽ ☌ ♅ **4:12 pm** 1:12 pm
☽ ⊻ ☿ **10:56 pm** 7:56 pm

10 MONDAY
☽ □ ♇ **3:32 am** 12:32 am
☽ △ ♂ 11:05 pm

11 TUESDAY
☽ △ ♂ **2:05 am**
☽ ✶ ♀ **7:28 am** 4:28 am

☽ ⊻ ☉ **9:27 am** 6:27 am
☽ ⊻ ♃ **7:09 pm** 4:09 pm
☽ ⊼ ♄ **11:18 pm** 8:18 pm
☽ ✶ ♆ 9:11 pm
☽ ⊻ ♅ 10:46 pm

12 WEDNESDAY
☽ ✶ ♆ **12:11 am**
☽ ⊻ ♅ **1:46 am**
☽ ☌ ☿ **7:46 am** 4:46 am
☽ △ ♇ **12:16 pm** 9:16 am

13 THURSDAY
☽ □ ♂ **11:42 am** 8:42 am
☽ ⊻ ♀ **8:22 pm** 5:22 pm
☽ ☌ ☉ **9:04 pm** 6:04 pm
☽ ✶ ♃ 11:45 pm

14 FRIDAY
☽ ✶ ♃ **2:45 am**
☽ △ ♄ **5:50 am** 2:50 am
☽ □ ♆ **6:51 am** 3:51 am
☽ ✶ ♅ **8:28 am** 5:28 am
☽ ⊻ ☿ **2:34 pm** 11:34 am
☽ ⊼ ♇ **6:17 pm** 3:17 pm

15 SATURDAY
☉ ⊻ ♀ **9:13 am** 6:13 am
☽ ✶ ♂ **6:42 pm** 3:42 pm

16 SUNDAY
☽ ⊻ ☉ **5:52 am** 2:52 am
☽ ☌ ♀ **6:15 am** 3:15 am
☽ □ ♃ **8:06 am** 5:06 am
☽ □ ♄ **10:19 am** 7:19 am

☽ △ ♆ **11:25 am** 8:25 am
☽ □ ♅ **1:06 pm** 10:06 am
☽ ✶ ☿ **8:02 pm** 5:02 pm
☽ ☍ ♇ **10:25 pm** 7:25 pm

17 MONDAY
♀ □ ♃ **6:57 am** 3:57 am
☉ ✶ ♃ **8:41 pm** 5:41 pm
☽ ⊻ ♂ 9:07 pm

18 TUESDAY
☽ ⊻ ♂ **12:07 am**
♀ □ ♄ **4:18 am** 1:18 am
☽ △ ♃ **12:11 pm** 9:11 am
☽ ✶ ☉ **1:07 pm** 10:07 am
☽ ✶ ♄ **1:37 pm** 10:37 am
☽ ⊻ ♀ **2:30 pm** 11:30 am
☽ ⊼ ♆ **2:49 pm** 11:49 am
☽ △ ♅ **4:35 pm** 1:35 pm
♀ △ ♆ **6:12 pm** 3:12 pm
☉ △ ♄ **8:27 pm** 5:27 pm
☽ □ ☿ 10:01 pm
☽ ⊼ ♇ 10:35 pm

19 WEDNESDAY
☽ □ ☿ **1:01 am**
☽ ⊼ ♇ **1:35 am**
☉ □ ♆ **2:14 pm** 11:14 am
☿ △ ♇ **2:47 pm** 11:47 am
♀ □ ♅ **3:41 pm** 12:41 pm

20 THURSDAY
☽ ☌ ♂ **4:51 am** 1:51 am
☽ ⊼ ♃ **3:42 pm** 12:42 pm
☽ ⊻ ♄ **4:27 pm** 1:27 pm

☽ ☍ ♆ **5:43 pm** 2:43 pm
☉ ✶ ♅ **5:48 pm** 2:48 pm
☽ ⊼ ♅ **7:35 pm** 4:35 pm
☽ □ ☉ **7:43 pm** 4:43 pm
☽ ✶ ♀ **10:05 pm** 7:05 pm

21 FRIDAY
☽ △ ♇ **4:21 am** 1:21 am
☽ △ ☿ **6:09 am** 3:09 am

22 SATURDAY
☽ ⊻ ♂ **9:26 am** 6:26 am
☽ ☍ ♃ **7:09 pm** 4:09 pm
☽ ☌ ♄ **7:14 pm** 4:14 pm
☽ ⊼ ♆ **8:35 pm** 5:35 pm
☽ ☍ ♅ **10:34 pm** 7:34 pm
♃ ☍ ♄ 10:36 pm
☽ △ ☉ 11:17 pm

23 SUNDAY
♃ ☍ ♄ **1:36 am**
☽ △ ☉ **2:17 am**
☽ □ ♀ **5:40 am** 2:40 am
☽ □ ♇ **7:11 am** 4:11 am
☽ ⊼ ☿ **11:56 am** 8:56 am
♀ ☍ ♇ **11:15 pm** 8:15 pm

24 MONDAY
☽ ✶ ♂ **2:30 pm** 11:30 am
☽ ⊻ ♄ **10:34 pm** 7:34 pm
☽ ⊼ ♃ **11:09 pm** 8:09 pm
☽ △ ♆ 9:01 pm
☽ ⊼ ♅ 11:08 pm

25 TUESDAY
☽ △ ♆ **12:01 am**
☽ ⊼ ♅ **2:08 am**
☽ ⊼ ☉ **9:40 am** 6:40 am
☽ ✶ ♇ **10:44 am** 7:44 am
☽ △ ♀ **2:10 pm** 11:10 am
☽ ☍ ☿ **7:15 pm** 4:15 pm
☉ ⊼ ♇ 9:39 pm

26 WEDNESDAY
☉ ⊼ ♇ **12:39 am**
☽ □ ♂ **9:02 pm** 6:02 pm

27 THURSDAY
☽ ✶ ♄ **3:22 am** 12:22 am
☽ △ ♃ **4:38 am** 1:38 am
☽ □ ♆ **4:55 am** 1:55 am
☽ △ ♅ **7:13 am** 4:13 am
☽ ⊻ ♇ **3:58 pm** 12:58 pm
☽ ☍ ☉ **7:07 pm** 4:07 pm
☽ ⊼ ♀ 9:58 pm

28 FRIDAY
☽ ⊼ ♀ **12:58 am**
♃ ⊻ ♆ **4:14 am** 1:14 am
☽ ⊼ ☿ **5:28 am** 2:28 am

29 SATURDAY
☽ △ ♂ **6:12 am** 3:12 am
☽ □ ♄ **10:38 am** 7:38 am
☽ ✶ ♆ **12:16 pm** 9:16 am
☽ □ ♃ **12:40 pm** 9:40 am
☽ □ ♅ **2:50 pm** 11:50 am
☽ ☌ ♇ **11:49 pm** 8:49 pm

30 SUNDAY
☽ ⊼ ☉ **7:55 am** 4:55 am
☽ ☍ ♀ **3:23 pm** 12:23 pm
☽ △ ☿ **7:55 pm** 4:55 pm

31 MONDAY
☽ ⊼ ♂ **6:42 pm** 3:42 pm
☽ △ ♄ **8:50 pm** 5:50 pm
☽ ⊻ ♆ **10:33 pm** 7:33 pm
☽ ✶ ♃ **11:41 pm** 8:41 pm
☽ ✶ ♅ 10:22 pm

Eastern time in bold type
Pacific time in medium type

MAY 2010

DATE	S.TIME	SUN	MOON	N.NODE	MERCURY	VENUS	MARS	JUPITER	SATURN	URANUS	NEPTUNE	PLUTO	CERES	PALLAS	JUNO	VESTA	CHIRON
1 Sat	14:35:17	10♉31	11♐50	13♑50 R	06♉08 R	07♊02	12♌02	23♓47	28♍31 R	28♓58	28♒28	05♑16 R	04♑37 R	14♏46 R	07♊41	23♌50	00♓26
2 Sun	14:39:13	11 29 47	24 44	13 46	05 32	08 15	12 55	23 59	28 28	29 00	28 29	05 15	04 35	14 17	08 16	24 01	00 28
3 Mon	14:43:10	12 27 59	07♑17	13 44	04 58	09 28	13 19	24 11	28 26	29 03	28 30	05 14	04 34	13 58	08 51	24 11	00 30
4 Tue	14:47:06	13 26 10	19 32	13 45	04 27	10 40	13 44	24 23	28 23	29 06	28 30	05 13	04 31	13 40	09 25	24 23	00 32
5 Wed	14:51:03	14 24 19	01♒34	13 45	03 59	11 53	14 09	24 35	28 21	29 08	28 31	05 13	04 29	13 22	10 00	24 34	00 34
6 Thu	14:54:59	15 22 27	13 27	13 45	03 35	13 05	14 35	24 46	28 18	29 11	28 31	05 12	04 26	13 03	10 35	24 46	00 35
7 Fri	14:58:56	16 20 33	25 17	13 45	03 15	14 18	15 01	24 58	28 16	29 14	28 32	05 11	04 23	12 45	11 09	24 59	00 37
8 Sat	15:02:53	17 18 37	07♓09	13 43	03 00	15 30	15 26	25 09	28 14	29 16	28 33	05 10	04 19	12 27	11 44	25 11	00 39
9 Sun	15:06:49	18 16 41	19 07	13 38	02 53	16 43	15 53	25 21	28 12	29 19	28 34	05 09	04 15	12 09	12 19	25 24	00 40
10 Mon	15:10:46	19 14 42	01♈17	13 32	02 46	17 55	16 19	25 32	28 10	29 21	28 34	05 07	04 11	11 51	12 53	25 37	00 42
11 Tue	15:14:42	20 12 43	13 41	13 24	02 42 D	19 08	16 45	25 43	28 08	29 24	28 35	05 06	04 06	11 33	13 28	25 51	00 43
12 Wed	15:18:39	21 10 42	26 21	13 15	02 40	20 20	17 12	25 55	28 06	29 26	28 36	05 05	04 01	11 15	14 03	26 05	00 45
13 Thu	15:22:35	22 08 40	09♉19	13 06	02 42	21 32	17 39	26 06	28 04	29 28	28 36	05 04	03 56	10 57	14 37	26 19	00 46
14 Fri	15:26:32	23 06 36	22 33	12 57	02 49	22 44	18 06	26 17	28 03	29 31	28 37	05 03	03 50	10 40	15 12	26 33	00 47
15 Sat	15:30:28	24 04 31	06♊03	12 51	03 01	23 57	18 34	26 27	28 01	29 33	28 38	05 03	03 44	10 23	15 46	26 48	00 48
16 Sun	15:34:25	25 02 24	19 45	12 46	03 18	25 09	19 01	26 38	28 00	29 35	28 38	05 02	03 37	10 06	16 21	27 03	00 49
17 Mon	15:38:22	26 00 16	03♋37	12 44	03 39	26 21	19 29	26 49	27 58	29 38	28 39	05 01	03 30	09 49	16 56	27 19	00 50
18 Tue	15:42:18	26 58 06	17 37	12 44	04 04	27 33	19 57	26 59	27 57	29 40	28 39	04 59	03 23	09 33	17 30	27 34	00 51
19 Wed	15:46:15	27 55 54	01♌42	12 45	04 33	28 45	20 25	27 10	27 56	29 42	28 40	04 58	03 15	09 17	18 05	27 50	00 52
20 Thu	15:50:11	28 53 41	15 51	12 46	05 06	29 57	20 54	27 20	27 55	29 44	28 40	04 57	03 07	09 01	18 39	28 06	00 53
21 Fri	15:54:08	29 51 26	00♍03	12 47	05 44	01♋09	21 22	27 30	27 53	29 46	28 41	04 56	02 59	08 45	19 14	28 23	00 54
22 Sat	15:58:04	00♊49 11	14 11	12 46	06 25	02 20	21 51	27 41	27 52	29 48	28 41	04 55	02 51	08 30	19 48	28 40	00 55
23 Sun	16:02:01	01 46 50	28 20	12 43	07 10	03 32	22 20	27 51	27 51	29 50	28 41	04 54	02 42	08 15	20 22	28 57	00 56
24 Mon	16:05:57	02 44 27	12♎25	12 39	07 58	04 44	22 49	28 00	27 51	29 52	28 41	04 52	02 33	08 01	20 57	29 14	00 56
25 Tue	16:09:54	03 42 09	26 21	12 34	08 50	05 55	23 18	28 10	27 50	29 54	28 42	04 51	02 23	07 46	21 31	29 31	00 57
26 Wed	16:13:51	04 39 46	10♏10	12 28	09 46	07 07	23 48	28 20	27 50	29 56	28 42	04 50	02 13	07 33	22 06	29 49	00 57
27 Thu	16:17:47	05 37 22	23 44	12 22	10 44	08 18	24 17	28 29	27 50	29 58	28 42	04 50	02 03	07 19	22 40	00♍07	00 58
28 Fri	16:21:44	06 34 56	07♐02	12 17	11 46	09 30	24 47	28 39	27 50	00♈00	28 42	04 49	01 53	07 06	23 14	00 25	00 58
29 Sat	16:25:40	07 32 30	20 03	12 14	12 51	10 41	25 17	28 48	27 50 D	00 02	28 42	04 47	01 53	06 54	23 49	00 44	00 59
30 Sun	16:29:37	08 30 02	02♑50	12 12	13 59	11 53	25 47	28 57	27 50	00 03	28 42	04 46	01 42	06 42	24 23	01 02	00 59
31 Mon	16:33:33	09 27 33	15 13	12 11	15 11	13 04	26 17	29 06	27 50	00 05	28 42 R	04 45	01 32	06 30	24 57	01 21	00 59

EPHEMERIS CALCULATED FOR 12 MIDNIGHT GREENWICH MEAN TIME. ALL OTHER DATA AND FACING ASPECTARIAN PAGE IN **EASTERN TIME (BOLD)** AND PACIFIC TIME (REGULAR).

JUNE 2010

☽ Last Aspect day	ET / hr:mn / PT	asp	☽ Ingress sign day	ET / hr:mn / PT
5/31	**11:41 pm** 8:41 pm	✶ ♃	♒ 1	**1:08 am**
3	**10:56 am** 7:56 am	☌ ♆	♓ 3	**1:34 pm** 10:34 am
5	10:49 pm	☌ ♃	♈ 5	10:50 pm
6	**1:49 am**	☌ ♃	♈ 6	**1:50 am**
8	**9:13 am** 6:13 am	✶ ♆	♉ 8	**11:41 am** 7:41 am
10	**3:50 pm** 12:50 pm	□ ♆	♊ 10	**6:11 pm** 3:11 pm
12	**7:35 pm** 4:35 pm	△ ♆	♋ 12	**9:50 pm** 6:50 pm
14	**8:38 pm** 5:38 pm	✶ ♄	♌ 14	**11:54 pm** 8:54 pm
16	**11:24 pm** 8:24 pm	☍ ♆	♍ 16	10:41 pm
16	**11:24 pm** 8:24 pm	☍ ♆	♍ 16	**1:41 am**
18	10:04 pm	☌ ♄	♎ 19	**4:13 am** 1:13 am
19	**1:04 am**	☌ ♄	♎ 19	**4:13 am** 1:13 am
21	**5:44 am** 2:44 am	△ ♆	♏ 21	**8:14 am** 5:14 am
23	**11:32 am** 8:32 am	□ ♆	♐ 23	**2:10 pm** 11:10 am
25	**7:33 pm** 4:33 pm	✶ ♆	♑ 25	**10:21 pm** 7:21 pm
28	**5:56 am** 2:56 am	△ ♄	♒ 28	**8:52 am** 5:52 am
30	**6:03 pm** 3:03 pm	☌ ♆	♓ 30	**9:10 pm** 6:10 pm

☽ Phases & Eclipses phase	day	ET / hr:mn / PT
4th Quarter	4	**6:13 pm** 3:13 pm
New Moon	12	**7:15 am** 4:15 am
2nd Quarter	18	9:29 pm
2nd Quarter	19	**12:29 am**
Full Moon	26	**7:30 am** 4:30 am
●	26	4° ♑ 50'

Planet Ingress	day	ET / hr:mn / PT
♃ ♈	5	11:28 pm
♃ ♈	6	**2:28 am**
♂ ♍	6	11:11 pm
♂ ♍	7	**2:11 am**
⚳ ♐	7	**2:28 pm** 11:28 am
⚵ ♋	8	**5:08 pm** 2:08 pm
☿ ♊	9	10:41 pm
☿ ♊	10	**1:41 am**
♀ ♌	14	**4:50 am** 1:50 am
☉ ♋	21	**7:28 am** 4:28 am
☿ ♋	25	**6:32 am** 3:32 am

Planetary Motion	day	ET / hr:mn / PT
⚷ ℞	4	**3:05 am** 12:05 am
♀ D	24	**10:30 am** 7:30 am

1 TUESDAY
- ☽ ✶ ♅ **1:22 am**
- ☽ ⚺ ♇ **10:31 am** 7:31 am
- ☽ △ ☉ 9:15 pm

2 WEDNESDAY
- ☽ △ ☉ **12:15 am**
- ☽ ⚻ ♀ **9:25 am** 6:25 am
- ☽ □ ☿ **2:44 pm** 11:44 am
- ♂ ⚺ ♄ **9:50 pm** 6:50 pm

3 THURSDAY
- ☽ ⚻ ♄ **9:12 am** 6:12 am
- ☽ ☍ ♂ **9:42 am** 6:42 am
- ☽ ☌ ♆ **10:56 am** 7:56 am
- ☽ ⚺ ♃ **12:50 pm** 9:50 am
- ☽ ⚺ ♅ **1:56 pm** 10:56 am
- ☽ ✶ ♇ **10:58 pm** 7:58 pm

4 FRIDAY
- ♂ ☍ ♆ **1:52 pm** 10:52 am
- ☽ □ ☉ **6:13 pm** 3:13 pm

5 SATURDAY
- ☽ △ ♀ **4:44 am** 1:44 am
- ☽ ✶ ☿ **11:25 am** 8:25 am
- ☽ ☍ ♄ **9:36 pm** 6:36 pm
- ☽ ⚺ ♆ **11:15 pm** 8:15 pm
- ☽ ⚻ ♂ 9:44 pm
- ☽ ☌ ♃ 10:49 pm
- ☽ ☌ ♅ 11:19 pm

6 SUNDAY
- ☽ ⚻ ♂ **12:44 am**
- ☽ ☌ ♃ **1:49 am**
- ☽ ☌ ♅ **2:19 am**
- ☽ □ ♇ **10:53 am** 7:53 am

7 MONDAY
- ♂ ⚻ ♃ **10:26 am** 7:26 am
- ☽ ✶ ☉ **10:31 am** 7:31 am
- ♂ ⚻ ♅ **3:03 pm** 12:03 pm
- ☽ □ ♀ **9:44 pm** 6:44 pm

8 TUESDAY
- ☽ ⚺ ☿ **6:05 am** 3:05 am
- ♃ ☌ ♅ **7:27 am** 4:27 am
- ☽ ⚻ ♄ **7:44 am** 4:44 am
- ☽ ✶ ♆ **9:13 am** 6:13 am
- ☽ ⚺ ♅ **12:14 pm** 9:14 am
- ☽ ⚺ ♃ **12:17 pm** 9:17 am
- ☽ △ ♂ **1:06 pm** 10:06 am
- ☿ △ ♄ **7:14 pm** 4:14 pm
- ☽ △ ♇ **8:08 pm** 5:08 pm

9 WEDNESDAY
- ☿ □ ♆ **6:39 am** 3:39 am
- ☽ ⚺ ☉ **10:51 pm** 7:51 pm

10 THURSDAY
- ☿ ✶ ♅ **6:28 am** 3:28 am
- ☿ ✶ ♃ **9:42 am** 6:42 am
- ☽ ✶ ♀ **10:21 am** 7:21 am
- ☽ △ ♄ **2:32 pm** 11:32 am
- ☽ □ ♆ **3:50 pm** 12:50 pm
- ☽ ✶ ♅ **6:47 pm** 3:47 pm
- ☽ ✶ ♃ **7:16 pm** 4:16 pm
- ☽ ☌ ☿ **8:31 pm** 5:31 pm
- ☽ □ ♂ **9:42 pm** 6:42 pm
- ☽ ⚻ ♇ 11:03 pm

11 FRIDAY
- ☽ ⚻ ♇ **2:03 am**
- ☿ □ ♂ **9:27 am** 6:27 am

12 SATURDAY
- ☽ ☌ ☉ **7:15 am** 4:15 am
- ♀ ✶ ♄ **11:18 am** 8:18 am
- ☿ ⚻ ♇ **3:05 pm** 12:05 pm
- ☽ □ ♄ **6:25 pm** 3:25 pm
- ☽ ⚺ ♀ **7:03 pm** 4:03 pm
- ☽ △ ♆ **7:35 pm** 4:35 pm
- ☽ □ ♅ **10:29 pm** 7:29 pm
- ☽ □ ♃ **11:19 pm** 8:19 pm
- ♀ ⚻ ♆ 10:23 pm

13 SUNDAY
- ♀ ⚻ ♆ **1:23 am**
- ☽ ✶ ♂ **3:13 am** 12:13 am
- ☽ ☍ ♇ **5:17 am** 2:17 am
- ☽ ⚺ ☿ **7:22 am** 4:22 am

14 MONDAY
- ☽ ⚺ ☉ **1:12 pm** 10:12 am
- ♀ △ ♅ **1:20 pm** 10:20 am
- ☽ ✶ ♄ **8:38 pm** 5:38 pm
- ☽ ⚻ ♆ **9:40 pm** 6:40 pm
- ☽ △ ♅ 9:36 pm
- ☽ ☌ ♀ 10:35 pm
- ☽ △ ♃ 10:46 pm

15 TUESDAY
- ☽ △ ♅ **12:36 am**
- ☽ ☌ ♀ **1:35 am**
- ☽ △ ♃ **1:46 am**
- ♀ △ ♃ **4:07 am** 1:07 am
- ☽ ⚺ ♂ **7:06 am** 4:06 am
- ☽ ⚻ ♇ **7:09 am** 4:09 am
- ♂ △ ♇ **8:12 am** 5:12 am
- ☽ ✶ ☿ **4:41 pm** 1:41 pm

16 WEDNESDAY
- ☽ ✶ ☉ **6:27 pm** 3:27 pm
- ☽ ⚺ ♄ **10:29 pm** 7:29 pm
- ☽ ☍ ♆ **11:24 pm** 8:24 pm
- ☽ ⚻ ♅ 11:26 pm

17 THURSDAY
- ☽ ⚻ ♅ **2:26 am**
- ☽ ⚻ ♃ **3:56 am** 12:56 am
- ☽ ⚺ ♀ **7:46 am** 4:46 am
- ☽ △ ♇ **8:53 am** 5:53 am
- ☽ ☌ ♂ **10:53 am** 7:53 am
- ♀ ⚻ ♇ **9:23 pm** 6:23 pm
- ☽ □ ☿ 11:35 pm

18 FRIDAY
- ☽ □ ☿ **2:35 am**
- ☽ □ ☉ 9:29 pm
- ☽ ☌ ♄ 10:04 pm
- ☽ ⚻ ♆ 10:51 pm

19 SATURDAY
- ☽ □ ☉ **12:29 am**
- ☽ ☌ ♄ **1:04 am**
- ☽ ⚻ ♆ **1:51 am**
- ☽ ☍ ♅ **5:03 am** 2:03 am
- ☽ ☍ ♃ **6:55 am** 3:55 am
- ☉ □ ♄ **9:18 am** 6:18 am
- ☽ □ ♇ **11:31 am** 8:31 am
- ☽ ✶ ♀ **3:03 pm** 12:03 pm
- ☽ ⚺ ♂ **3:43 pm** 12:43 pm
- ☉ △ ♆ **8:21 pm** 5:21 pm

20 SUNDAY
- ♀ ⚺ ♂ **5:29 am** 2:29 am
- ☽ △ ☿ **2:43 pm** 11:43 am

21 MONDAY
- ☽ ⚺ ♄ **5:06 am** 2:06 am
- ☽ △ ♆ **5:44 am** 2:44 am
- ☽ △ ☉ **8:17 am** 5:17 am
- ☽ ⚻ ♅ **9:08 am** 6:08 am
- ☽ ⚻ ♃ **11:24 am** 8:24 am
- ☽ ✶ ♇ **3:40 pm** 12:40 pm
- ☉ □ ♅ **8:27 pm** 5:27 pm
- ☽ ✶ ♂ **10:20 pm** 7:20 pm
- ☽ □ ♀ 9:22 pm

22 TUESDAY
- ☽ □ ♀ **12:22 am**

23 WEDNESDAY
- ☽ ⚻ ☿ **6:11 am** 3:11 am
- ☉ □ ♃ **9:21 am** 6:21 am
- ☽ ✶ ♄ **11:04 am** 8:04 am
- ☽ □ ♆ **11:32 am** 8:32 am
- ☽ △ ♅ **3:09 pm** 12:09 pm
- ☽ △ ♃ **5:52 pm** 2:52 pm
- ☽ ⚻ ☉ **6:28 pm** 3:28 pm
- ☽ ⚺ ♇ **9:48 pm** 6:48 pm

24 THURSDAY
- ☽ □ ♂ **7:17 am** 4:17 am
- ☽ △ ♀ **12:20 pm** 9:20 am
- ☿ □ ♄ **12:23 pm** 9:23 am
- ☿ △ ♆ **2:33 pm** 11:33 am

25 FRIDAY
- ☿ □ ♅ **12:36 pm** 9:36 am
- ☉ ☍ ♇ **2:55 pm** 11:55 am
- ☽ □ ♄ **7:19 pm** 4:19 pm
- ☽ ✶ ♆ **7:33 pm** 4:33 pm
- ☽ □ ♅ **11:25 pm** 8:25 pm
- ☽ ☍ ☿ 10:41 pm
- ☽ □ ♃ 11:37 pm

26 SATURDAY
- ☽ ☍ ☿ **1:41 am**
- ☽ □ ♃ **2:37 am**
- ☽ ☌ ♇ **6:12 am** 3:12 am
- ☿ □ ♃ **7:08 am** 4:08 am
- ☽ ☍ ☉ **7:30 am** 4:30 am
- ☽ △ ♂ **6:53 pm** 3:53 pm

27 SUNDAY
- ☿ ☍ ♇ **3:15 am** 12:15 am
- ☽ ⚻ ♀ **3:22 am** 12:22 am
- ♄ ⚻ ♆ **10:46 pm** 7:46 pm

28 MONDAY
- ☽ ⚺ ♆ **5:54 am** 2:54 am
- ☽ △ ♄ **5:56 am** 2:56 am
- ☉ ☌ ☿ **8:07 am** 5:07 am
- ☽ ✶ ♅ **10:00 am** 7:00 am
- ☽ ✶ ♃ **1:41 pm** 10:41 am
- ☽ ⚺ ♇ **4:53 pm** 1:53 pm
- ☽ ⚻ ☉ **11:26 pm** 8:26 pm
- ☽ ⚻ ☿ 10:21 pm

29 TUESDAY
- ☽ ⚻ ☿ **1:21 am**
- ☽ ⚻ ♂ **9:04 am** 6:04 am
- ☽ ☍ ♀ **9:14 pm** 6:14 pm

30 WEDNESDAY
- ☽ ☌ ♆ **6:03 pm** 3:03 pm
- ☽ ⚻ ♄ **6:25 pm** 3:25 pm
- ☽ ⚺ ♅ **10:20 pm** 7:20 pm
- ☽ ⚺ ♃ 11:27 pm

Eastern time in bold type
Pacific time in medium type

JUNE 2010

DATE	S.TIME	SUN	MOON	N. NODE	MERCURY	VENUS	MARS	JUPITER	SATURN	URANUS	NEPTUNE	PLUTO	CERES	PALLAS	JUNO	VESTA	CHIRON
1 Tue	16:37:30	10♊25 04	27♑25	12♑17	16♉25	14♋15	26♌47	29♓15	27♍50	00♈07	28≈42 ℞	04♑43 ℞	01♑09 ℞	06♏21 ℞	25♊31	01♍38	00♓59
2 Wed	16:41:26	11 22 33	09≈25	12 14	17 41	15 26	27 18	29 33	27 50	00 08	28 42	04 42	01 09	06 08	26 06	01 59	00 59
3 Thu	16:45:23	12 19 02	21 20	12 15	19 01	16 37	27 48	29 41	27 50	00 10	28 42	04 41	00 58	05 58	26 40	02 19	00 59
4 Fri	16:49:20	13 17 30	03♓01	12 17 ℞	20 24	17 48	28 19	29 50	27 51	00 11	28 42	04 39	00 46	05 48	27 14	02 39	00 59 ℞
5 Sat	16:53:16	14 14 57	15 04	12 17	21 49	18 59	28 50	29 58	27 51	00 13	28 42	04 38	00 34	05 38	27 48	02 59	00 59
6 Sun	16:57:13	15 12 24	27 04	12 17	23 17	20 10	29 21	00♈06	27 52	00 14	28 42	04 36	00 22	05 29	28 22	03 19	00 59
7 Mon	17:01:09	16 09 49	09♈15	12 15	24 48	21 21	29 52	00 14	27 53	00 16	28 41	04 35	00 10	05 21	28 56	03 39	00 59
8 Tue	17:05:06	17 07 14	21 42	12 12	26 21	22 31	00♍23	00 22	27 53	00 17	28 41	04 33	29♐57	05 13	29 30	04 00	00 59
9 Wed	17:09:02	18 04 39	04♉28	12 09	27 57	23 42	00 55	00 29	27 54	00 18	28 41	04 32	29 45	05 05	00♋04	04 20	00 59
10 Thu	17:12:59	19 02 03	17 34	12 05	29 36	24 53	01 26	00 37	27 55	00 20	28 40	04 31	29 32	04 58	00 38	04 41	00 58
11 Fri	17:16:55	19 59 26	01♊02	12 02	01♊18	26 03	01 58	00 44	27 56	00 21	28 40	04 29	29 19	04 51	01 12	05 02	00 58
12 Sat	17:20:52	20 56 49	14 50	12 02	03 02	27 14	02 30	00 52	27 58	00 22	28 40	04 28	29 06	04 45	01 46	05 24	00 58
13 Sun	17:24:49	21 54 11	28 55	11 58 D	04 48	28 24	03 02	00 59	27 59	00 23	28 40	04 26	28 53	04 40	02 20	05 45	00 57
14 Mon	17:28:45	22 51 33	13♋13	11 58	06 38	29 34	03 34	01 06	28 00	00 24	28 39	04 25	28 40	04 34	02 54	06 07	00 57
15 Tue	17:32:42	23 48 53	27 39	11 59	08 30	00♌44	04 06	01 13	28 02	00 25	28 39	04 23	28 26	04 30	03 27	06 29	00 56
16 Wed	17:36:38	24 46 13	12♌02	11 59	10 24	01 54	04 38	01 19	28 03	00 26	28 38	04 22	28 13	04 25	04 01	06 51	00 55
17 Thu	17:40:35	25 43 32	26 05	12 00	12 20	03 05	05 11	01 26	28 05	00 27	28 38	04 20	28 00	04 22	04 35	07 13	00 55
18 Fri	17:44:31	26 40 50	10♍02	12 01	14 19	04 14	05 43	01 32	28 07	00 28	28 37	04 19	27 47	04 18	05 08	07 35	00 54
19 Sat	17:48:28	27 38 07	25 10	12 02 ℞	16 20	05 24	06 16	01 38	28 09	00 29	28 37	04 17	27 33	04 16	05 42	07 58	00 53
20 Sun	17:52:24	28 35 23	09♎51	12 01	18 24	06 34	06 49	01 44	28 11	00 30	28 36	04 16	27 20	04 13	06 16	08 20	00 52
21 Mon	17:56:21	29 32 39	23 02	12 01	20 29	07 44	07 22	01 50	28 13	00 30	28 36	04 14	27 07	04 11	06 49	08 43	00 51
22 Tue	18:00:18	00♋29 53	06♏39	11 59	22 35	08 53	07 55	01 56	28 15	00 31	28 35	04 12	26 54	04 10	07 23	09 06	00 50
23 Wed	18:04:14	01 27 07	20 02	11 58	24 43	10 03	08 28	02 01	28 17	00 32	28 34	04 11	26 40	04 09 D	07 56	09 29	00 49
24 Thu	18:08:11	02 24 20	03♐10	11 57	26 53	11 12	09 01	02 07	28 20	00 32	28 34	04 09	26 27	04 09	08 30	09 52	00 48
25 Fri	18:12:07	03 21 33	16 05	11 56	29 03	12 22	09 34	02 12	28 22	00 33	28 33	04 08	26 14	04 09	09 03	10 16	00 47
26 Sat	18:16:04	04 18 46	28 46	11 55	01♋13	13 31	10 08	02 17	28 25	00 33	28 32	04 06	26 01	04 09	09 36	10 39	00 46
27 Sun	18:20:00	05 15 58	11♑14	11 55 D	03 25	14 40	10 41	02 22	28 27	00 34	28 31	04 05	25 49	04 10	10 10	11 03	00 44
28 Mon	18:23:57	06 13 11	23 30	11 56	05 36	15 49	11 15	02 27	28 30	00 34	28 30	04 03	25 36	04 11	10 43	11 27	00 43
29 Tue	18:27:53	07 10 22	05≈36	11 56	07 47	16 58	11 48	02 31	28 33	00 34	28 30	04 02	25 23	04 13	11 16	11 51	00 42
30 Wed	18:31:50	08 07 34	17 33	11 56	09 57	18 06	12 22	02 36	28 36	00 35	28 29	04 00	25 11	04 15	11 49	12 15	00 40

☽ Last Aspect day	ET / hr:mn / PT		asp	☽ Ingress sign	day	ET / hr:mn / PT	
3	**7:17 am**	4:17 am	☍ ♄	♈	3	**9:44 am**	6:44 am
5	**5:24 pm**	2:24 pm	⚹ ♆	♉	5	**8:29 pm**	5:29 pm
7		11:10 pm	△ ♄	♊	8	**3:51 am**	12:51 am
8	**2:10 am**		△ ♄	♊	8	**3:51 am**	12:51 am
10	**6:17 am**	3:17 am	□ ♄	♋	10	**7:38 am**	4:38 am
12	**7:48 am**	4:48 am	⚹ ♄	♌	12	**8:53 am**	5:53 am
14	**6:23 am**	3:23 am	☍ ♆	♍	14	**9:15 am**	6:15 am
16	**9:46 am**	6:46 am	☌ ♄	♎	16	**10:24 am**	7:24 am
18	**10:26 am**	7:26 am	△ ♆	♏	18	**1:42 pm**	10:42 am
20	**7:43 pm**	4:43 pm	⚹ ♄	♐	20	**7:48 pm**	4:48 pm
22		9:50 pm	⚹ ♆	♑	23	**4:39 am**	1:39 am
23	**12:50 am**		⚹ ♆	♑	23	**4:39 am**	1:39 am
25	**10:20 am**	7:20 am	△ ♂	♒	25	**3:38 pm**	12:38 pm
27	**11:46 pm**	8:46 pm	☌ ♆	♓	28	**4:00 am**	1:00 am
29	**11:44 pm**	8:44 pm	☍ ♀	♈	30	**4:42 pm**	1:42 pm

☽ Phases & Eclipses phase	day	ET / hr:mn / PT	
4th Quarter	4	**10:35 am**	7:35 am
New Moon	11	**3:40 pm**	12:40 pm
●	11	19° ♋ 24'	
2nd Quarter	18	**6:11 am**	3:11 am
Full Moon	25	**9:37 pm**	6:37 pm

Planet Ingress		day	ET / hr:mn / PT	
☿	♌	9	**12:29 pm**	9:29 am
♀	♍	10	**7:32 am**	4:32 am
⚷	♒	20	**5:46 am**	2:46 am
♄	♎	21	**11:10 am**	8:10 am
☉	♌	22	**6:21 pm**	3:21 pm
☿	♍	27	**5:43 pm**	2:43 pm
♂	♎	29	**7:46 pm**	4:46 pm

Planetary Motion		day	ET / hr:mn / PT	
♅	℞	5	**12:48 pm**	9:48 am
♃	℞	23	**8:03 am**	5:03 am

1 THURSDAY
- ☽ ⊻ ♃ **2:27 am**
- ☽ ⚹ ♇ **5:12 am** 2:12 am
- ☿ ⚹ ♂ **8:19 am** 5:19 am
- ☽ △ ☉ **5:16 pm** 2:16 pm
- ☽ ☍ ♂ 9:44 pm

2 FRIDAY
- ☽ ☍ ♂ **12:44 am**
- ☽ △ ☿ **3:24 am** 12:24 am
- ☽ ⚻ ♀ **4:23 pm** 1:23 pm

3 SATURDAY
- ☽ ⊻ ♆ **6:35 am** 3:35 am
- ☽ ☍ ♄ **7:17 am** 4:17 am
- ☽ ☌ ♅ **10:55 am** 7:55 am
- ☽ ☌ ♃ **3:17 pm** 12:17 pm
- ☽ □ ♇ **5:32 pm** 2:32 pm

4 SUNDAY
- ☽ □ ☉ **10:35 am** 7:35 am
- ☽ ⚻ ♂ **3:41 pm** 12:41 pm

5 MONDAY
- ☽ □ ☿ **3:40 am** 12:40 am
- ☽ △ ♀ **9:52 am** 6:52 am
- ☽ ⚹ ♆ **5:24 pm** 2:24 pm
- ☽ ⚻ ♄ **6:25 pm** 3:25 pm
- ☽ ⊻ ♅ **9:37 pm** 6:37 pm
- ☽ ⊻ ♃ 11:02 pm

6 TUESDAY
- ☽ ⊻ ♃ **2:02 am**
- ☽ △ ♇ **3:47 am** 12:47 am
- ☽ ⚹ ☉ 9:36 pm

7 WEDNESDAY
- ☽ ⚹ ☉ **12:36 am**
- ☽ △ ♂ **3:29 am** 12:29 am
- ☽ ⚹ ☿ **10:15 pm** 7:15 pm
- ☽ □ ♀ **11:06 pm** 8:06 pm
- ☽ □ ♆ 9:53 pm
- ☽ △ ♄ 11:10 pm

8 THURSDAY
- ☽ □ ♆ **12:53 am**
- ☽ △ ♄ **2:10 am**
- ☽ ⚹ ♅ **4:54 am** 1:54 am
- ☽ ⚹ ♃ **9:15 am** 6:15 am
- ☿ ⊻ ♀ **10:33 am** 7:33 am
- ☽ ⚻ ♇ **10:34 am** 7:34 am
- ☿ ⚻ ♆ **3:58 pm** 12:58 pm
- ♀ ☍ ♆ **7:55 pm** 4:55 pm
- ☿ ⚹ ♄ 10:35 pm

9 FRIDAY
- ☿ ⚹ ♄ **1:35 am**
- ☽ ⊻ ☉ **10:02 am** 7:02 am
- ☽ □ ♂ **11:06 am** 8:06 am
- ♀ ⊻ ♄ **1:21 pm** 10:21 am
- ☿ △ ♅ **7:45 pm** 4:45 pm

10 SATURDAY
- ☽ △ ♆ **4:47 am** 1:47 am
- ☽ □ ♄ **6:17 am** 3:17 am
- ☽ ⚹ ♀ **7:39 am** 4:39 am
- ☽ □ ♅ **8:37 am** 5:37 am
- ☽ ⊻ ☿ **10:36 am** 7:36 am
- ☽ □ ♃ **12:53 pm** 9:53 am
- ☽ ☍ ♇ **1:52 pm** 10:52 am
- ♀ ⚻ ♅ **7:55 pm** 4:55 pm
- ☉ ⚹ ♂ 9:13 pm

11 SUNDAY
- ☉ ⚹ ♂ **12:13 am**
- ☿ △ ♃ **4:13 am** 1:13 am
- ☿ ⚻ ♇ **11:13 am** 8:13 am
- ☽ ⚹ ♂ **3:16 pm** 12:16 pm
- ☽ ☌ ☉ **3:40 pm** 12:40 pm

12 MONDAY
- ☽ ⚻ ♆ **6:05 am** 3:05 am
- ☽ ⚹ ♄ **7:48 am** 4:48 am
- ☽ △ ♅ **9:49 am** 6:49 am
- ☽ ⊻ ♀ **12:55 pm** 9:55 am
- ☽ △ ♃ **2:05 pm** 11:05 am
- ☽ ⚻ ♇ **2:50 pm** 11:50 am
- ☽ ☌ ☿ **6:50 pm** 3:50 pm

13 TUESDAY
- ♀ ⚻ ♃ **4:48 am** 1:48 am
- ♀ △ ♇ **1:55 pm** 10:55 am
- ☽ ⊻ ♂ **5:44 pm** 2:44 pm
- ☽ ⊻ ☉ **7:28 pm** 4:28 pm

14 WEDNESDAY
- ☽ ☍ ♆ **6:23 am** 3:23 am
- ☽ ⊻ ♄ **8:23 am** 5:23 am
- ☽ ⚻ ♅ **10:09 am** 7:09 am
- ☽ ⚻ ♃ **2:33 pm** 11:33 am
- ☽ △ ♇ **3:08 pm** 12:08 pm
- ☽ ☌ ♀ **5:14 pm** 2:14 pm
- ☽ ⊻ ☿ 10:55 pm

15 THURSDAY
- ☽ ⊻ ☿ **1:55 am**
- ☽ ☌ ♂ **8:31 pm** 5:31 pm
- ☽ ⚹ ☉ **11:40 pm** 8:40 pm

16 FRIDAY
- ☽ ⚻ ♆ **7:22 am** 4:22 am
- ☽ ☌ ♄ **9:46 am** 6:46 am
- ☽ ☍ ♅ **11:19 am** 8:19 am
- ☽ ☍ ♃ **3:58 pm** 12:58 pm
- ☽ □ ♇ **4:24 pm** 1:24 pm
- ☽ ⊻ ♀ **10:50 pm** 7:50 pm

17 SATURDAY
- ☽ ⚹ ☿ **10:36 am** 7:36 am
- ☽ ⊻ ♂ 10:22 pm

18 SUNDAY
- ☽ ⊻ ♂ **1:22 am**
- ☽ □ ☉ **6:11 am** 3:11 am
- ☽ △ ♆ **10:26 am** 7:26 am
- ☽ ⊻ ♄ **1:18 pm** 10:18 am
- ☽ ⚻ ♅ **2:37 pm** 11:37 am
- ☽ ⚻ ♃ **7:38 pm** 4:38 pm
- ☽ ⚹ ♇ **7:55 pm** 4:55 pm

19 MONDAY
- ☽ ⚹ ♀ **7:26 am** 4:26 am
- ☽ □ ☿ **10:40 pm** 7:40 pm

20 TUESDAY
- ☽ ⚹ ♂ **9:20 am** 6:20 am
- ☽ △ ☉ **4:07 pm** 1:07 pm
- ☽ □ ♆ **4:16 pm** 1:16 pm
- ☉ ⚻ ♆ **6:09 pm** 3:09 pm
- ☽ ⚹ ♄ **7:43 pm** 4:43 pm
- ☽ △ ♅ **8:44 pm** 5:44 pm
- ☽ △ ♃ 11:06 pm
- ☽ ⊻ ♇ 11:17 pm

21 WEDNESDAY
- ☽ △ ♃ **2:06 am**
- ☽ ⊻ ♇ **2:17 am**
- ☽ □ ♀ **7:42 pm** 4:42 pm

22 THURSDAY
- ☽ △ ☿ **2:26 pm** 11:26 am
- ☽ □ ♂ **8:31 pm** 5:31 pm
- ☉ ⚹ ♄ **9:12 pm** 6:12 pm
- ☽ ⚹ ♆ 9:50 pm

23 FRIDAY
- ☽ ⚹ ♆ **12:50 am**
- ☽ □ ♄ **4:55 am** 1:55 am
- ☽ ⚻ ☉ **5:30 am** 2:30 am
- ☽ □ ♅ **5:33 am** 2:33 am
- ☉ △ ♅ **6:06 am** 3:06 am
- ☽ □ ♃ **11:14 am** 8:14 am
- ☽ ☌ ♇ **11:18 am** 8:18 am

24 SATURDAY
- ☽ △ ♀ **11:12 am** 8:12 am
- ♃ □ ♇ 9:20 pm

25 SUNDAY
- ♃ □ ♇ **12:20 am**
- ☽ ⚻ ☿ **9:06 am** 6:06 am
- ☽ △ ♂ **10:20 am** 7:20 am
- ☽ ⊻ ♆ **11:36 am** 8:36 am
- ☽ △ ♄ **4:19 pm** 1:19 pm
- ☽ ⚹ ♅ **4:30 pm** 1:30 pm
- ☽ ☍ ☉ **9:37 pm** 6:37 pm
- ☽ ⊻ ♇ **10:23 pm** 7:23 pm
- ☽ ⚹ ♃ **10:24 pm** 7:24 pm
- ☿ ⊻ ♂ 11:25 pm

26 MONDAY
- ☿ ⊻ ♂ **2:25 am**
- ☿ ☍ ♆ **6:03 am** 3:03 am
- ☉ ⚻ ♇ **7:04 am** 4:04 am
- ☉ △ ♃ **7:30 am** 4:30 am
- ♂ ⚻ ♆ **10:41 am** 7:41 am
- ♄ ☍ ♅ **1:07 pm** 10:07 am

27 TUESDAY
- ☽ ⚻ ♀ **4:59 am** 1:59 am
- ☽ ☌ ♆ **11:46 pm** 8:46 pm
- ☿ ⚻ ♅ 9:42 pm
- ☽ ⚻ ♂ 10:51 pm

28 WEDNESDAY
- ☿ ⚻ ♅ **12:42 am**
- ☽ ⚻ ♂ **1:51 am**
- ☿ ⊻ ♄ **3:37 am** 12:37 am
- ☽ ⊻ ♅ **4:47 am** 1:47 am
- ☽ ⚻ ♄ **5:08 am** 2:08 am
- ☽ ☍ ☿ **5:19 am** 2:19 am
- ☽ ⚹ ♇ **10:44 am** 7:44 am
- ☽ ⊻ ♃ **10:48 am** 7:48 am
- ☽ ⚻ ☉ **3:22 pm** 12:22 pm

29 THURSDAY
- ☽ ☍ ♀ **11:44 pm** 8:44 pm

30 FRIDAY
- ☿ △ ♇ **6:04 am** 3:04 am
- ☿ ⚻ ♃ **6:44 am** 3:44 am
- ♂ ☍ ♅ **9:31 am** 6:31 am
- ☽ ⊻ ♆ **12:22 pm** 9:22 am
- ☽ ☌ ♅ **5:23 pm** 2:23 pm
- ☽ ☍ ♂ **5:49 pm** 2:49 pm
- ☽ ☍ ♄ **6:16 pm** 3:16 pm
- ☽ □ ♇ **11:17 pm** 8:17 pm
- ☽ ☌ ♃ **11:21 pm** 8:21 pm
- ☽ ⚻ ☿ 10:19 pm

31 SATURDAY
- ☽ ⚻ ☿ **1:19 am**
- ♂ ☌ ♄ **4:07 am** 1:07 am
- ☽ △ ☉ **9:13 am** 6:13 am

Eastern time in bold type
Pacific time in medium type

JULY 2010

DATE	S.TIME	SUN	MOON	N.NODE	MERCURY	VENUS	MARS	JUPITER	SATURN	URANUS	NEPTUNE	PLUTO	CERES	PALLAS	JUNO	VESTA	CHIRON
1 Thu	18:35:47	09♋00'46	29≈26	11♑56℞	12♋56	19♌56	12♍56	02♈35	28♍37℞	00♈39	28≈28	03♑59℞	24♐59℞	04♍17	12♋23	12♍39	00♓39℞
2 Fri	18:39:43	10 01 58	11♓17	11 57	14 16	20 24	13 30	02 40	28 42	00 35	28 27	03 57℞	24 47℞	04 20	12 56	13 04	00 37℞
3 Sat	18:43:40	10 59 09	23 09	11 57	16 24	21 32	14 00	02 44	28 45	00 35	28 26	03 56	24 35	04 24	13 29	13 28	00 35
4 Sun	18:47:36	11 56 22	05♈09	11 57	18 31	22 40	14 39	02 47	28 48	00 35	28 25	03 54	24 23	04 27	14 02	13 53	00 34
5 Mon	18:51:33	12 53 34	17 19	11 57	20 36	23 48	15 13	02 51	28 52	00 35℞	28 24	03 53	24 12	04 32	14 35	14 18	00 32
6 Tue	18:55:29	13 50 46	29 45	11 57	22 39	24 57	15 47	02 54	28 55	00 35	28 23	03 51	24 00	04 36	15 08	14 43	00 30
7 Wed	18:59:26	14 47 59	12♉30	11 57	24 41	26 04	16 22	02 58	28 59	00 35	28 22	03 50	23 49	04 41	15 41	15 08	00 28
8 Thu	19:03:22	15 45 12	25 37	11 57	26 41	27 12	16 56	03 01	29 02	00 35	28 21	03 48	23 39	04 47	16 13	15 33	00 27
9 Fri	19:07:19	16 42 26	09♊06	11 58	28 40	28 20	17 31	03 04	29 06	00 35	28 20	03 47	23 28	04 52	16 46	15 58	00 25
10 Sat	19:11:16	17 39 40	23 06	11 58	00♌36	29 28	18 05	03 06	29 10	00 35	28 19	03 45	23 18	04 58	17 19	16 23	00 23
11 Sun	19:15:12	18 36 54	07♋35℞	11 58℞	02 31	00♍37	18 41	03 09	29 14	00 35	28 17	03 44	23 08	05 05	17 52	16 49	00 21
12 Mon	19:19:09	19 34 09	22 03	11 57	04 24	01 42	19 16	03 11	29 18	00 35	28 16	03 42	22 58	05 12	18 24	17 15	00 19
13 Tue	19:23:05	20 31 23	06♌53	11 58	06 15	02 50	19 51	03 13	29 22	00 34	28 15	03 41	22 49	05 19	18 57	17 40	00 17
14 Wed	19:27:02	21 28 38	21 47	11 57	08 05	03 57	20 26	03 15	29 26	00 34	28 14	03 39	22 39	05 26	19 29	18 06	00 15
15 Thu	19:30:58	22 25 53	06♍38	11 56	09 51	05 03	21 01	03 17	29 30	00 33	28 13	03 38	22 31	05 34	20 02	18 32	00 12
16 Fri	19:34:55	23 23 08	21 19	11 56	11 36	06 10	21 37	03 19	29 34	00 33	28 11	03 36	22 22	05 42	20 34	18 58	00 10
17 Sat	19:38:52	24 20 23	05♎44	11 55	13 19	07 17	22 12	03 20	29 39	00 32	28 10	03 34	22 14	05 51	21 07	19 24	00 08
18 Sun	19:42:48	25 17 38	19 50	11 53 D	15 00	08 23	22 48	03 21	29 43	00 32	28 09	03 34	22 06	06 00	21 39	19 51	00 06
19 Mon	19:46:45	26 14 53	03♏35	11 54	16 40	09 29	23 23	03 22	29 48	00 31	28 08	03 32	21 58	06 09	22 11	20 17	00 03
20 Tue	19:50:41	27 12 08	17 00	11 54	18 17	10 35	23 59	03 23	29 52	00 30	28 06	03 31	21 51	06 19	22 44	20 44	00 01
21 Wed	19:54:38	28 09 24	00♐06	11 55	19 50	11 41	24 35	03 24	29 57	00 29	28 05	03 29	21 44	06 29	23 16	21 10	29≈59
22 Thu	19:58:34	29 06 40	12 56	11 56	21 26	12 47	25 11	03 24℞	00♎02	00 28	28 04	03 28	21 38	06 39	23 48	21 37	29 56
23 Fri	20:02:31	00♌03 56	25 31	11 58	22 58	13 53	25 47	03 24	00 07	00 27	28 02	03 27	21 32	06 49	24 20	22 04	29 54
24 Sat	20:06:27	01 01 13	07♑54	11 58	24 28	14 58	26 23	03 24	00 11	00 26	28 01	03 25	21 26	07 00	24 52	22 31	29 51
25 Sun	20:10:24	01 58 30	20 07	11 58	25 56	16 03	26 59	03 24	00 16	00 24	27 59	03 24	21 20	07 11	25 24	22 58	29 49
26 Mon	20:14:21	02 55 47	02≈11	11 57	27 22	17 08	27 35	03 23	00 21	00 23	27 58	03 23	21 15	07 22	25 56	23 25	29 46
27 Tue	20:18:17	03 53 06	14 09	11 55	28 46	18 13	28 11	03 23	00 26	00 22	27 56	03 21	21 09	07 34	26 28	23 52	29 43
28 Wed	20:22:14	04 50 25	26 03	11 53	00♍08	19 17	28 47	03 22	00 32	00 21	27 55	03 20	21 06	07 46	27 00	24 19	29 41
29 Thu	20:26:10	05 47 44	07♓54	11 51	01 28	20 22	29 24	03 21	00 37	00 20	27 53	03 19	21 02	07 58	27 31	24 46	29 38
30 Fri	20:30:07	06 45 05	19 45	11 44	02 45	21 26	00♎00	03 20	00 42	00 19	27 52	03 18	20 58	08 11	28 03	25 14	29 35
31 Sat	20:34:03	07 42 26	01♈39	11 39	04 01	22 30	00 37	03 19	00 48	00 18	27 50	03 17	20 55	08 23	28 35	25 41	29 33

EPHEMERIS CALCULATED FOR 12 MIDNIGHT GREENWICH MEAN TIME. ALL OTHER DATA AND FACING ASPECTARIAN PAGE IN **EASTERN TIME (BOLD)** AND PACIFIC TIME (REGULAR).

AUGUST 2010

☽ Last Aspect day	ET / hr:mn / PT	asp	☽ Ingress sign day	ET / hr:mn / PT
1	**11:54 pm** 8:54 pm	⚹♆	♉ 2	**4:13 am** 1:13 am
4	**8:44 am** 5:44 am	□♆	♊ 4	**12:54 pm** 9:54 am
6	**5:22 pm** 2:22 pm	□♀	♋ 6	**5:50 pm** 2:50 pm
7	**2:46 pm** 11:46 am	⚹☿	♌ 8	**7:23 pm** 4:23 pm
10	**3:10 pm** 12:10 pm	☍♆	♍ 10	**7:01 pm** 4:01 pm
11	**8:04 pm** 5:04 pm	☌☿	♎ 12	**6:43 pm** 3:43 pm
14	**4:06 pm** 1:06 pm	△♆	♏ 14	**8:26 pm** 5:26 pm
16	10:24 pm	△♅	♐ 16	10:34 pm
17	**1:24 am**	△♅	♐ 17	**1:34 am**
19	**9:58 am** 6:58 am	□♅	♑ 19	**10:17 am** 7:17 am

☽ Last Aspect day	ET / hr:mn / PT	asp	☽ Ingress sign day	ET / hr:mn / PT
21	**9:08 pm** 6:08 pm	⚹♅	♒ 21	**9:37 pm** 6:37 pm
24	**4:29 am** 1:29 am	☌♆	♓ 24	**10:11 am** 7:11 am
26	**10:00 pm** 7:00 pm	☌♅	♈ 26	**10:49 pm** 7:49 pm
29	**4:47 am** 1:47 am	⚹♆	♉ 29	**10:35 am** 7:35 am
31	**7:13 pm** 4:13 pm	⚹♅	♊ 31	**8:19 pm** 5:19 pm

☽ Phases & Eclipses phase	day	ET / hr:mn / PT
4th Quarter	2	9:59 pm
4th Quarter	3	**12:59 am**
New Moon	9	**11:08 pm** 8:08 pm
2nd Quarter	16	**2:14 pm** 11:14 am
Full Moon	24	**1:05 pm** 10:05 am

Planet Ingress	day	ET / hr:mn / PT
⚵ ♌	2	**1:00 pm** 10:00 am
♀ ♎	6	**11:47 pm** 8:47 pm
⚶ ♎	8	11:08 pm
⚶ ♎	9	**2:08 am**
♅ ♓	13	**11:36 pm** 8:36 pm
☉ ♍	22	10:27 pm
☉ ♍	23	**1:27 am**

Planetary Motion	day	ET / hr:mn / PT
⚳ D	8	**2:32 pm** 11:32 am
☿ R	20	**3:59 pm** 12:59 pm

1 SUNDAY
☽⚻♀ **5:28 pm** 2:28 pm
☽⚹♆ **11:54 pm** 8:54 pm

2 MONDAY
☽⚺♅ **4:47 am** 1:47 am
☽⚻♄ **6:11 am** 3:11 am
☽⚻♂ **8:24 am** 5:24 am
☽△♇ **10:28 am** 7:28 am
☽⚺♃ **10:29 am** 7:29 am
☽△☿ **6:44 pm** 3:44 pm
☽□☉ 9:59 pm
♃□♇ 10:32 pm

3 TUESDAY
☽□☉ **12:59 am**
♃□♇ **1:32 am**
♂☍♃ 9:20 pm
♂□♇ 9:58 pm

4 WEDNESDAY
♂☍♃ **12:20 am**
♂□♇ **12:58 am**
☽△♀ **7:49 am** 4:49 am
☽□♆ **8:44 am** 5:44 am
☽⚹♅ **1:21 pm** 10:21 am
☽△♄ **3:09 pm** 12:09 pm
☽⚹♃ **6:38 pm** 3:38 pm
☽⚻♇ **6:42 pm** 3:42 pm
♀⚻♆ **6:57 pm** 3:57 pm
☽△♂ **7:36 pm** 4:36 pm

5 THURSDAY
☽□☿ **7:23 am** 4:23 am
☽⚹☉ **12:35 pm** 9:35 am

6 FRIDAY
☽△♆ **1:51 pm** 10:51 am
☽□♀ **5:22 pm** 2:22 pm
☽□♅ **6:09 pm** 3:09 pm
☽□♄ **8:17 pm** 5:17 pm
☽□♃ **11:01 pm** 8:01 pm
☽☍♇ **11:10 pm** 8:10 pm
☽□♂ 11:27 pm

7 SATURDAY
☽□♂ **2:27 am**
♀☍♅ **3:59 am** 12:59 am
☽⚹☿ **2:46 pm** 11:46 am
☽⚺☉ **7:32 pm** 4:32 pm

8 SUNDAY
♀☌♄ **1:24 pm** 10:24 am
☽⚻♆ **3:32 pm** 12:32 pm
☽△♅ **7:36 pm** 4:36 pm
☽⚹♄ **10:02 pm** 7:02 pm
☽⚹♀ **10:36 pm** 7:36 pm
☽△♃ 9:07 pm
☽⚻♇ 9:22 pm

9 MONDAY
☽△♃ **12:07 am**
☽⚻♇ **12:22 am**
☽⚹♂ **5:40 am** 2:40 am
☽⚺☿ **6:13 pm** 3:13 pm

♀☍♃ **7:40 pm** 4:40 pm
☽☌☉ **11:08 pm** 8:08 pm
♀□♇ 9:05 pm

10 TUESDAY
♀□♇ **12:05 am**
☽☍♆ **3:10 pm** 12:10 pm
☽⚻♅ **7:09 pm** 4:09 pm
☽⚺♄ **9:56 pm** 6:56 pm
☽⚻♃ **11:29 pm** 8:29 pm
☽△♇ **11:52 pm** 8:52 pm
☽⚺♀ 10:36 pm

11 WEDNESDAY
☽⚺♀ **1:36 am**
☽⚺♂ **7:10 am** 4:10 am
☽☌☿ **8:04 pm** 5:04 pm
☽⚺☉ 10:47 pm

12 THURSDAY
☽⚺☉ **1:47 am**
☽⚻♆ **2:42 pm** 11:42 am
☽☍♅ **6:46 pm** 3:46 pm
☽☌♄ **10:01 pm** 7:01 pm
☽☍♃ **11:06 pm** 8:06 pm
☽□♇ **11:38 pm** 8:38 pm

13 FRIDAY
☽☌♀ **4:58 am** 1:58 am
☽☌♂ **9:21 am** 6:21 am
☽⚺☿ **10:46 pm** 7:46 pm

14 SATURDAY
☽⚹☉ **6:06 am** 3:06 am
☽△♆ **4:06 pm** 1:06 pm

☽⚻♅ **8:24 pm** 5:24 pm
☽⚺♄ 9:19 pm
☽⚻♃ 9:50 pm
☽⚹♇ 10:36 pm

15 SUNDAY
☽⚺♄ **12:19 am**
☽⚻♃ **12:50 am**
☽⚹♇ **1:36 am**
☽⚺♀ **11:15 am** 8:15 am
☽⚺♂ **2:27 pm** 11:27 am

16 MONDAY
☽⚹☿ **4:10 am** 1:10 am
☽□☉ **2:14 pm** 11:14 am
♃☍♄ **4:45 pm** 1:45 pm
☽□♆ **8:48 pm** 5:48 pm
☽△♅ 10:24 pm

17 TUESDAY
☽△♅ **1:24 am**
☽△♃ **5:59 am** 2:59 am
☽⚹♄ **6:10 am** 3:10 am
☽⚺♇ **7:03 am** 4:03 am
☽⚹♀ **9:56 pm** 6:56 pm
☽⚹♂ **11:42 pm** 8:42 pm

18 WEDNESDAY
☽□☿ **12:50 pm** 9:50 am
☽△☉ 11:57 pm

19 THURSDAY
☽△☉ **2:57 am**
☽⚹♆ **5:06 am** 2:06 am
☽□♅ **9:58 am** 6:58 am

☽□♃ **2:35 pm** 11:35 am
☽□♄ **3:39 pm** 12:39 pm
☽☌♇ **4:02 pm** 1:02 pm

20 FRIDAY
☉☍♆ **6:07 am** 3:07 am
☽□♀ **12:45 pm** 9:45 am
☽□♂ **12:49 pm** 9:49 am
♀☌♂ **2:49 pm** 11:49 am
☽△☿ **11:46 pm** 8:46 pm

21 SATURDAY
♄□♇ **6:16 am** 3:16 am
☽⚺♆ **4:08 pm** 1:08 pm
☽⚻☉ **7:11 pm** 4:11 pm
☽⚹♅ **9:08 pm** 6:08 pm
☽⚹♃ 10:37 pm

22 SUNDAY
☽⚹♃ **1:37 am**
☽⚺♇ **3:29 am** 12:29 am
☽△♄ **3:42 am** 12:42 am
☉⚻♅ **6:42 pm** 3:42 pm

23 MONDAY
☽△♂ **4:17 am** 1:17 am
☽△♀ **6:00 am** 3:00 am
☽⚻☿ **11:17 am** 8:17 am

24 TUESDAY
☽☌♆ **4:29 am** 1:29 am
☽⚺♅ **9:31 am** 6:31 am
☽☍☉ **1:05 pm** 10:05 am
☽⚺♃ **1:44 pm** 10:44 am
☽⚹♇ **4:03 pm** 1:03 pm

☽⚻♄ **4:53 pm** 1:53 pm
☉⚻♃ **8:28 pm** 5:28 pm

25 WEDNESDAY
☿⚺♀ **8:09 am** 5:09 am
☽⚻♂ **8:28 pm** 5:28 pm
☽☍☿ **10:04 pm** 7:04 pm
☽⚻♀ **11:51 pm** 8:51 pm
☉△♇ 10:12 pm

26 THURSDAY
☉△♇ **1:12 am**
☿⚺♂ **1:18 pm** 10:18 am
☽⚺♆ **5:01 pm** 2:01 pm
☉⚺♄ **5:31 pm** 2:31 pm
☽☌♅ **10:00 pm** 7:00 pm
☽☌♃ 10:51 pm

27 FRIDAY
☽☌♃ **1:51 am**
☽□♇ **4:36 am** 1:36 am
☽☍♄ **6:03 am** 3:03 am
☽⚻☉ **7:01 am** 4:01 am

28 SATURDAY
☽⚻☿ **7:23 am** 4:23 am
☽☍♂ **12:09 pm** 9:09 am
☽☍♀ **4:55 pm** 1:55 pm

29 SUNDAY
☽⚹♆ **4:47 am** 1:47 am
☽⚺♅ **9:36 am** 6:36 am
☽⚺♃ **1:02 pm** 10:02 am
☽△♇ **4:11 pm** 1:11 pm

☽⚻♄ **6:12 pm** 3:12 pm
☽△☉ **11:40 pm** 8:40 pm

30 MONDAY
☽△☿ **2:40 pm** 11:40 am
☽⚻♂ 11:00 pm

31 TUESDAY
☽⚻♂ **2:00 am**
☽⚻♀ **7:45 am** 4:45 am
☽□♆ **2:39 pm** 11:39 am
☽⚹♅ **7:13 pm** 4:13 pm
☽⚹♃ **10:09 pm** 7:09 pm
☽⚻♇ 10:37 pm

Eastern time in bold type
Pacific time in medium type

AUGUST 2010

DATE	S.TIME	SUN	MOON	N.NODE	MERCURY	VENUS	MARS	JUPITER	SATURN	URANUS	NEPTUNE	PLUTO	CERES	PALLAS	JUNO	VESTA	CHIRON
1 Sun	20:38:00	08♌39 49	13 ♈ 37	11 ♑ 37	05 ♍ 14	23 ♍ 33	01 ♎ 14	03 ♈ 17	00 ♎ 53	00 ♈ 19	27 ♒ 49	03 ♑ 15	20 ♐ 52	20 ♍ 36	29 ♋ 06	26 ♍ 09	29 ♒ 30
2 Mon	20:41:56	09 37 13	25 47	11 34 R.	06 25	24 37	01 50	03 15 R.	00 58	00 18 R.	27 47 R.	03 14 R.	20 47	09 03	09 38	26 37	29 27 R.
3 Tue	20:45:53	10 34 38	08 ♉ 10	11 34 D	07 38	25 40	02 27	03 13	01 10	00 17	27 46	03 13	20 47	09 17	00 ♌ 09	27 32	29 22
4 Wed	20:49:50	11 32 04	20 51	11 34	08 41	26 43	03 04	03 11	01 15	00 15	27 44	03 12	20 45	09 31	00 41	28 00	29 19
5 Thu	20:53:46	12 29 31	03 ♊ 54	11 35	09 44	27 46	03 41	03 09	01 21	00 14	27 43	03 11	20 43	09 45	01 12	28 28	29 16
6 Fri	20:57:43	13 27 00	17 22	11 37	10 46	28 48	04 18	03 06	01 27	00 13	27 41	03 10	20 42	09 45	01 43	28 28	29 16
7 Sat	21:01:39	14 24 29	01 ♋ 17	11 38 R.	11 44	29 50	04 55	03 04	01 33	00 11	27 40	03 09	20 41	09 59	02 14	28 56	29 13
8 Sun	21:05:36	15 22 00	15 38	11 38	12 40	00 ♎ 52	05 32	03 01	01 38	00 10	27 38	03 08	20 41 D	10 14	02 46	29 25	29 10
9 Mon	21:09:32	16 19 33	00 ♌ 23	11 37	13 32	01 54	06 09	02 57	01 44	00 08	27 36	03 07	20 41	10 29	03 17	29 53	29 07
10 Tue	21:13:29	17 17 06	15 26	11 34 D	14 22	02 55	06 47	02 54	01 50	00 07	27 35	03 06	20 41	10 44	03 48	00 ♎ 21	29 04
11 Wed	21:17:25	18 14 41	00 ♍ 38	11 30	15 08	03 56	07 25	02 51	01 56	00 05	27 33	03 05	20 42	10 59	04 19	00 50	29 01
12 Thu	21:21:22	19 12 16	15 48	11 25	15 50	04 57	08 03	02 47	02 03	00 04	27 32	03 04	20 43	11 15	04 50	01 18	28 58
13 Fri	21:25:19	20 09 52	00 ♎ 48	11 19	16 29	05 57	08 40	02 43	02 09	00 02	27 30	03 03	20 44	11 30	05 20	01 47	28 56
14 Sat	21:29:15	21 07 30	15 29	11 14	17 05	06 57	09 18	02 39	02 15	00 00	27 28	03 02	20 46	11 46	05 51	02 15	28 53
15 Sun	21:33:12	22 05 08	29 45	11 11	17 36	07 57	09 55	02 35	02 21	29 ♓ 59	27 27	03 01	20 48	12 02	06 22	02 44	28 50
16 Mon	21:37:08	23 02 48	13 ♏ 34	11 09 D	18 02	08 56	10 33	02 31	02 27	29 57	27 25	03 00	20 50	12 19	06 53	03 13	28 47
17 Tue	21:41:05	24 00 28	26 57	11 08	18 22	09 55	11 11	02 26	02 33	29 55	27 24	02 59	20 53	12 35	07 23	03 42	28 44
18 Wed	21:45:01	24 58 09	09 ♐ 57	11 09	18 42	10 54	11 49	02 21	02 39	29 53	27 22	02 59	20 56	12 52	07 54	04 10	28 41
19 Thu	21:48:58	25 55 52	22 36	11 10	18 54	11 52	12 27	02 16	02 45	29 51	27 20	02 58	20 59	13 09	08 24	04 39	28 38
20 Fri	21:52:54	26 53 35	04 ♑ 59	11 11 R.	19 02 R.	12 50	13 05	02 11	02 51	29 49	27 19	02 57	21 03	13 26	08 54	05 08	28 35
21 Sat	21:56:51	27 51 20	17 10	11 11	19 03	13 48	13 43	02 06	02 56	29 48	27 17	02 56	21 07	13 43	09 25	05 38	28 32
22 Sun	22:00:48	28 49 06	29 11	11 09	18 59	14 45	14 22	02 01	03 00	29 46	27 15	02 56	21 12	14 01	09 55	06 07	28 29
23 Mon	22:04:44	29 46 53	11 ♒ 07	11 06	18 50	15 41	15 00	01 55	03 06	29 44	27 14	02 55	21 16	14 18	10 25	06 36	28 26
24 Tue	22:08:41	00 ♍ 44 41	23 00	11 00	18 35	16 37	15 39	01 50	03 13	29 42	27 12	02 54	21 21	14 36	10 55	07 05	28 23
25 Wed	22:12:37	01 42 31	04 ♓ 51	10 52	18 14	17 33	16 17	01 44	03 20	29 40	27 10	02 53	21 27	14 54	11 25	07 35	28 20
26 Thu	22:16:34	02 40 22	16 42	10 42	17 46	18 28	16 56	01 38	03 26	29 38	27 09	02 53	21 32	15 12	11 55	08 04	28 17
27 Fri	22:20:30	03 38 15	28 36	10 32	17 14	19 22	17 34	01 32	03 33	29 36	27 07	02 52	21 38	15 31	12 25	08 34	28 14
28 Sat	22:24:27	04 36 09	10 ♈ 37	10 22	16 36	20 16	18 13	01 25	03 40	29 33	27 06	02 52	21 45	15 49	12 55	09 03	28 11
29 Sun	22:28:23	05 34 06	22 36	10 14	15 52	21 10	18 52	01 19	03 47	29 31	27 04	02 51	21 51	16 08	13 25	09 33	28 08
30 Mon	22:32:20	06 32 03	04 ♉ 48	10 07	15 05	22 03	19 31	01 13	03 53	29 29	27 03	02 51	21 58	16 26	13 54	10 02	28 05
31 Tue	22:36:16	07 30 03	17 11	10 03	14 13	22 55	20 09	01 06	04 00	29 27	27 01	02 51	22 05	16 45	14 24	10 32	28 02

EPHEMERIS CALCULATED FOR 12 MIDNIGHT GREENWICH MEAN TIME. ALL OTHER DATA AND FACING ASPECTARIAN PAGE IN **EASTERN TIME (BOLD)** AND PACIFIC TIME (REGULAR).

SEPTEMBER 2010

☽ Last Aspect day	ET / hr:mn / PT	asp	☽ Ingress sign day	ET / hr:mn / PT
2	10:40 pm	□ ♅	♋ 2	11:50 pm
3	**1:40 am**	□ ♅	♋ 3	**2:50 am**
5	**4:31 am** 1:31 am	△ ♅	♌ 5	**5:45 am** 2:45 am
7	**4:17 am** 1:17 am	⚹ ♀	♍ 7	**5:53 am** 2:53 am
9	**4:59 am** 1:59 am	☍ ♃	♎ 9	**5:01 am** 2:01 am
10	10:16 pm	☌ ♂	♏ 11	**5:21 am** 2:21 am
11	**1:16 am**	☌ ♂	♏ 11	**5:21 am** 2:21 am
13	**7:53 am** 4:53 am	△ ♃	♐ 13	**8:52 am** 5:52 am
15	**2:52 pm** 11:52 am	□ ♃	♑ 15	**4:30 pm** 1:30 pm
17	10:13 pm	⚹ ♃	♒ 18	**3:35 am** 12:35 am
18	**1:13 am**	⚹ ♃	♒ 18	**3:35 am** 12:35 am
20	**9:09 am** 6:09 am	☌ ♆	♓ 20	**4:15 pm** 1:15 pm
22	10:52 pm	☌ ♅	♈ 23	**4:47 am** 1:47 am
23	**1:52 am**	☌ ♅	♈ 23	**4:47 am** 1:47 am
25	**9:12 am** 6:12 am	⚹ ♆	♉ 25	**4:17 pm** 1:17 pm
27	**11:03 pm** 8:03 pm	⚹ ♅	♊ 27	11:10 pm
27	**11:03 pm** 8:03 pm	⚹ ♅	♊ 28	**2:10 am**
30	**6:37 am** 3:37 am	□ ♅	♋ 30	**9:46 am** 6:46 am

☽ Phases & Eclipses phase	day	ET / hr:mn / PT
4th Quarter	1	**1:22 pm** 10:22 am
New Moon	8	**6:30 am** 3:30 am
2nd Quarter	14	10:50 pm
2nd Quarter	15	**1:50 am**
Full Moon	23	**5:17 am** 2:17 am
4th Quarter	30	**11:52 pm** 8:52 pm

Planet Ingress	day	ET / hr:mn / PT
♀ ♏	8	**11:44 am** 8:44 am
♃ ♓	8	9:50 pm
♃ ♓	9	**12:50 am**
♂ ♏	14	**6:38 pm** 3:38 pm
☉ ♎	22	**11:09 pm** 8:09 pm

Planetary Motion	day	ET / hr:mn / PT
☿ D	12	**7:09 pm** 4:09 pm
♇ D	13	9:36 pm
♇ D	14	**12:36 am**

1 WEDNESDAY
☽ ⚻ ♇ **1:37 am**
☽ △ ♄ **4:05 am** 1:05 am
☽ □ ☉ **1:22 pm** 10:22 am
☽ □ ☿ **7:17 pm** 4:17 pm

2 THURSDAY
☽ △ ♂ **12:30 pm** 9:30 am
☽ △ ♀ **6:46 pm** 3:46 pm
☽ △ ♆ **9:26 pm** 6:26 pm
☽ □ ♅ 10:40 pm

3 FRIDAY
☽ □ ♅ **1:40 am**
☽ □ ♃ **4:06 am** 1:06 am
☽ ☍ ♇ **7:47 am** 4:47 am
☉ ☌ ☿ **8:35 am** 5:35 am
☽ □ ♄ **10:34 am** 7:34 am
☽ ⚹ ☿ **8:56 pm** 5:56 pm
☽ ⚹ ☉ **10:44 pm** 7:44 pm

4 SATURDAY
♀ △ ♆ **1:11 pm** 10:11 am
☽ □ ♂ **6:49 pm** 3:49 pm
☽ ⚻ ♆ 9:36 pm
☽ □ ♀ 10:18 pm

5 SUNDAY
☽ ⚻ ♆ **12:36 am**
☽ □ ♀ **1:18 am**
☽ △ ♅ **4:31 am** 1:31 am
☽ △ ♃ **6:31 am** 3:31 am
☽ ⚻ ♇ **10:21 am** 7:21 am
☽ ⚹ ♄ **1:23 pm** 10:23 am
☽ ⚺ ☿ **7:52 pm** 4:52 pm

6 MONDAY
☽ ⚺ ☉ **3:52 am** 12:52 am
☽ ⚹ ♂ **9:38 pm** 6:38 pm
☽ ☍ ♆ 9:52 pm

7 TUESDAY
☽ ☍ ♆ **12:52 am**
☽ ⚹ ♀ **4:17 am** 1:17 am
☽ ⚻ ♅ **4:35 am** 1:35 am
☽ ⚻ ♃ **6:14 am** 3:14 am
♀ ⚻ ♅ **9:49 am** 6:49 am
☽ △ ♇ **10:17 am** 7:17 am
☽ ⚺ ♄ **1:36 pm** 10:36 am
☽ ☌ ☿ **5:13 pm** 2:13 pm

8 WEDNESDAY
☽ ☌ ☉ **6:30 am** 3:30 am
♀ ⚻ ♃ **1:36 pm** 10:36 am
☽ ⚺ ♂ **10:55 pm** 7:55 pm
☽ ⚻ ♆ **11:55 pm** 8:55 pm

9 THURSDAY
☽ ☍ ♅ **3:35 am** 12:35 am
☽ ☍ ♃ **4:59 am** 1:59 am
☽ ⚺ ♀ **5:55 am** 2:55 am
☽ □ ♇ **9:26 am** 6:26 am
☽ ☌ ♄ **1:09 pm** 10:09 am
☽ ⚺ ☿ **2:42 pm** 11:42 am
♂ △ ♆ **9:16 pm** 6:16 pm

10 FRIDAY
☽ ⚺ ☉ **9:18 am** 6:18 am
☽ △ ♆ **11:57 pm** 8:57 pm
☽ ☌ ♂ 10:16 pm

11 SATURDAY
☽ ☌ ♂ **1:16 am**
☽ ⚻ ♅ **3:44 am** 12:44 am
☽ ⚻ ♃ **4:54 am** 1:54 am
☽ ☌ ♀ **8:54 am** 5:54 am
☽ ⚹ ♇ **9:59 am** 6:59 am
☽ ⚺ ♄ **2:19 pm** 11:19 am
☽ ⚹ ☿ **2:28 pm** 11:28 am
☿ ⚺ ♄ **9:54 pm** 6:54 pm

12 SUNDAY
♀ ⚹ ♇ **6:43 am** 3:43 am
☽ ⚹ ☉ **3:06 pm** 12:06 pm
☽ □ ♆ 11:57 pm

13 MONDAY
☽ □ ♆ **2:57 am**
♂ ⚻ ♅ **4:30 am** 1:30 am
☽ △ ♅ **6:58 am** 3:58 am
☽ ⚺ ♂ **7:06 am** 4:06 am
☽ △ ♃ **7:53 am** 4:53 am
☽ ⚺ ♇ **1:52 pm** 10:52 am
☽ ⚺ ♀ **3:34 pm** 12:34 pm
☽ □ ☿ **6:38 pm** 3:38 pm
☽ ⚹ ♄ **7:02 pm** 4:02 pm
♂ ⚻ ♃ **8:19 pm** 5:19 pm

14 TUESDAY
☽ □ ☉ 10:50 pm

15 WEDNESDAY
☽ □ ☉ **1:50 am**
☿ ⚺ ♄ **5:48 am** 2:48 am
☽ ⚹ ♆ **10:01 am** 7:01 am
☽ □ ♅ **2:17 pm** 11:17 am
☽ □ ♃ **2:52 pm** 11:52 am
☽ ⚹ ♂ **5:44 pm** 2:44 pm
☽ ☌ ♇ **9:52 pm** 6:52 pm
☽ ⚹ ♀ 11:53 pm

16 THURSDAY
☽ ⚹ ♀ **2:53 am**
☽ □ ♄ **3:58 am** 12:58 am
☽ △ ☿ **4:35 am** 1:35 am

17 FRIDAY
♀ ⚺ ♄ **5:17 am** 2:17 am
☽ △ ☉ **5:19 pm** 2:19 pm
☽ ⚺ ♆ **8:41 pm** 5:41 pm
☽ ⚹ ♅ 10:04 pm
☽ ⚹ ♃ 10:13 pm

18 SATURDAY
☽ ⚹ ♅ **1:04 am**
☽ ⚹ ♃ **1:13 am**
☽ □ ♂ **8:23 am** 5:23 am
☽ ⚺ ♇ **9:12 am** 6:12 am
☽ △ ♄ **4:09 pm** 1:09 pm
☽ □ ♀ **5:37 pm** 2:37 pm
☽ ⚻ ☿ **7:57 pm** 4:57 pm
♃ ☌ ♅ **9:03 pm** 6:03 pm
♂ ⚹ ♇ **10:48 pm** 7:48 pm

19 SUNDAY
☉ ⚻ ♆ **9:43 am** 6:43 am

20 MONDAY
☽ ☌ ♆ **9:09 am** 6:09 am
☽ ⚻ ☉ **11:18 am** 8:18 am
☽ ⚺ ♃ **1:11 pm** 10:11 am
☽ ⚺ ♅ **1:30 pm** 10:30 am
☽ ⚹ ♇ **9:56 pm** 6:56 pm
☽ △ ♂ 9:45 pm

21 TUESDAY
☽ △ ♂ **12:45 am**
☽ ⚻ ♄ **5:32 am** 2:32 am
☉ ☍ ♃ **7:36 am** 4:36 am
☽ △ ♀ **9:23 am** 6:23 am
☉ ☍ ♅ **12:58 pm** 9:58 am
☽ ☍ ☿ **2:42 pm** 11:42 am

22 WEDNESDAY
☽ ⚺ ♆ **9:39 pm** 6:39 pm
☽ ☌ ♃ 10:06 pm
☽ ☌ ♅ 10:52 pm

23 THURSDAY
☽ ☌ ♃ **1:06 am**
☽ ☌ ♅ **1:52 am**
☽ ☍ ☉ **5:17 am** 2:17 am
☽ □ ♇ **10:25 am** 7:25 am
☽ ⚻ ♂ **4:47 pm** 1:47 pm
☽ ☍ ♄ **6:31 pm** 3:31 pm
☽ ⚻ ♀ 9:16 pm

24 FRIDAY
☽ ⚻ ♀ **12:16 am**
☽ ⚻ ☿ **10:30 am** 7:30 am

25 SATURDAY
♂ ⚺ ♄ **5:55 am** 2:55 am
☽ ⚹ ♆ **9:12 am** 6:12 am
☽ ⚺ ♃ **12:01 pm** 9:01 am
☽ ⚺ ♅ **1:14 pm** 10:14 am
☉ □ ♇ **8:26 pm** 5:26 pm
☽ △ ♇ **9:48 pm** 6:48 pm
☽ ⚻ ☉ **9:56 pm** 6:56 pm

26 SUNDAY
☽ ⚻ ♄ **6:18 am** 3:18 am
☽ ☍ ♂ **7:28 am** 4:28 am
☽ ☍ ♀ **1:25 pm** 10:25 am

27 MONDAY
☽ △ ☿ **5:39 am** 2:39 am
☽ □ ♆ **7:13 pm** 4:13 pm
☽ ⚹ ♃ **9:27 pm** 6:27 pm
☽ ⚹ ♅ **11:03 pm** 8:03 pm

28 TUESDAY
☽ ⚻ ♇ **7:33 am** 4:33 am
☽ △ ☉ **12:27 pm** 9:27 am
☽ △ ♄ **4:16 pm** 1:16 pm
☽ ⚻ ♂ **8:04 pm** 5:04 pm
☽ ⚻ ♀ 9:12 pm

29 WEDNESDAY
☽ ⚻ ♀ **12:12 am**
☽ □ ☿ **10:30 pm** 7:30 pm

30 THURSDAY
☽ △ ♆ **3:03 am** 12:03 am
☽ □ ♃ **4:43 am** 1:43 am
☽ □ ♅ **6:37 am** 3:37 am
☽ ☍ ♇ **2:55 pm** 11:55 am
☉ ☌ ♄ **8:42 pm** 5:42 pm
☽ □ ♄ **11:40 pm** 8:40 pm
☽ □ ☉ **11:52 pm** 8:52 pm

Eastern time in bold type
Pacific time in medium type

SEPTEMBER 2010

DATE	S.TIME	SUN	MOON	N.NODE	MERCURY	VENUS	MARS	JUPITER	SATURN	URANUS	NEPTUNE	PLUTO	CERES	PALLAS	JUNO	VESTA	CHIRON
1 Wed	22:40:13	08♍28 05	29 ♌50	10♍01 D	13 ♍19	23 ♎47	20 ♎49	00♈59	04 ♎07	29 ♓25	26 ♒59	02 ♑50	22 ♐13	17 ♏04	14 ♌53	11 ♎02	27 ♒59
2 Thu	22:44:10	09 26 09	12 ♍47	10 00	12 22 R	24 38	21 28	00 52 R	04 14	29 23 R	26 57 R	02 50 R	22 28	17 23	15 23	11 32	27 56 R
3 Fri	22:48:06	10 24 14	26 07	10 01	11 25	25 28	22 07	00 45	04 21	29 21	26 56	02 49	22 28	17 43	15 52	12 02	27 52
4 Sat	22:52:03	11 22 22	09 ♎53	10 01 R	10 28	26 18	22 46	00 38	04 28	29 18	26 54	02 49	22 37	18 02	16 21	12 32	27 50
5 Sun	22:55:59	12 20 31	24 06	10 01	09 32	27 07	23 25	00 31	04 35	29 16	26 53	02 49	22 45	18 22	16 51	13 02	27 47
6 Mon	22:59:56	13 18 43	08 ♏45	09 58	08 40	27 55	24 05	00 24	04 42	29 14	26 51	02 48	22 54	18 41	17 20	13 32	27 44
7 Tue	23:03:52	14 16 56	23 45	09 53	07 51	28 43	24 44	00 17	04 49	29 11	26 50	02 48	23 03	19 01	17 49	14 02	27 41
8 Wed	23:07:49	15 15 11	08 ♐59	09 45	07 08	29 30	25 24	00 09	04 56	29 09	26 48	02 48	23 13	19 21	18 18	14 32	27 39
9 Thu	23:11:45	16 13 28	24 17	09 35	06 31	00 ♏16	26 03	00 02	05 03	29 07	26 47	02 48	23 23	19 41	18 47	15 02	27 36
10 Fri	23:15:42	17 11 47	09 ♑27	09 25	06 01	01 01	26 43	29 ♓54	05 11	29 04	26 45	02 48	23 33	20 02	19 15	15 32	27 33
11 Sat	23:19:39	18 10 07	24 19	09 16	05 39	01 45	27 23	29 46	05 18	29 02	26 44	02 48	23 43	20 22	19 44	16 03	27 30
12 Sun	23:23:35	19 08 29	08 ♒46	09 09	05 26	02 28	28 02	29 39	05 25	29 00	26 42	02 47	23 53	20 42	20 13	16 33	27 27
13 Mon	23:27:32	20 06 53	22 43	09 04	05 22 D	03 11	28 42	29 31	05 32	28 57	26 41	02 47 D	24 04	21 03	20 41	17 03	27 25
14 Tue	23:31:28	21 05 18	06 ♓11	09 01	05 27	03 52	29 22	29 23	05 39	28 55	26 39	02 47	24 15	21 24	21 10	17 33	27 22
15 Wed	23:35:25	22 03 45	19 12	09 00 D	05 41	04 32	00 ♏02	29 15	05 47	28 53	26 38	02 47	24 26	21 45	21 38	18 04	27 19
16 Thu	23:39:21	23 02 13	01 ♈49	09 00 R	06 05	05 12	00 42	29 07	05 54	28 50	26 36	02 47	24 38	22 06	22 06	18 35	27 17
17 Fri	23:43:18	24 00 43	14 08	09 00	06 39	05 50	01 22	29 00	06 01	28 48	26 35	02 48	24 49	22 27	22 34	19 06	27 14
18 Sat	23:47:14	24 59 14	26 13	08 59	07 18	06 27	02 03	28 51	06 09	28 45	26 33	02 48	25 01	22 48	23 03	19 36	27 12
19 Sun	23:51:11	25 57 48	08 ♉09	08 55	08 08	07 02	02 43	28 43	06 16	28 43	26 32	02 48	25 13	23 09	23 31	20 07	27 09
20 Mon	23:55:08	26 56 23	20 01	08 49	09 05	07 37	03 23	28 35	06 23	28 41	26 31	02 48	25 26	23 30	23 58	20 38	27 07
21 Tue	23:59:04	27 54 59	01 ♊51	08 41	10 10	08 10	04 04	28 27	06 31	28 38	26 29	02 48	25 38	23 52	24 26	21 08	27 04
22 Wed	00:03:01	28 53 38	13 43	08 29	11 21	08 41	04 44	28 19	06 38	28 36	26 28	02 48	25 51	24 13	24 54	21 39	27 02
23 Thu	00:06:57	29 52 18	25 37	08 16	12 39	09 10	05 25	28 11	06 45	28 33	26 27	02 49	26 04	24 35	25 22	22 10	27 00
24 Fri	00:10:54	00♎51 00	07 ♋37	08 02	14 02	09 40	06 06	28 03	06 53	28 31	26 25	02 49	26 18	24 57	25 49	22 41	26 57
25 Sat	00:14:50	01 49 44	19 42	07 48	15 29	10 07	06 46	27 55	07 00	28 29	26 24	02 49	26 31	25 18	26 17	23 12	26 55
26 Sun	00:18:47	02 48 31	01 ♌54	07 36	17 01	10 33	07 27	27 47	07 07	28 26	26 23	02 50	26 45	25 40	26 44	23 43	26 53
27 Mon	00:22:43	03 47 19	14 15	07 26	18 36	10 57	08 08	27 39	07 15	28 24	26 21	02 50	26 59	26 02	27 11	24 14	26 50
28 Tue	00:26:40	04 46 10	26 45	07 19	20 14	11 19	08 49	27 31	07 22	28 21	26 20	02 50	27 13	26 24	27 38	24 45	26 48
29 Wed	00:30:37	05 45 03	09 ♍28	07 15	21 55	11 40	09 30	27 24	07 30	28 19	26 19	02 51	27 27	26 46	28 05	25 16	26 46
30 Thu	00:34:33	06 43 58	22 26	07 13	23 37	11 58	10 11	27 16	07 37	28 17	26 17	02 51	27 41	27 09	28 32	25 47	26 44

EPHEMERIS CALCULATED FOR 12 MIDNIGHT GREENWICH MEAN TIME. ALL OTHER DATA AND FACING ASPECTARIAN PAGE IN **EASTERN TIME (BOLD)** AND PACIFIC TIME (REGULAR).

OCTOBER 2010

☽ Last Aspect day	ET / hr:mn / PT		asp	☽ Ingress sign	day	ET / hr:mn / PT	
2	**11:22 am**	8:22 am	✶ ☿	♌	2	**2:21 pm**	11:21 am
4	**9:52 am**	6:52 am	☍ ♆	♍	4	**4:00 pm**	1:00 pm
6	**12:43 pm**	9:43 am	☍ ♅	♎	6	**3:52 pm**	12:52 pm
8	**9:37 am**	6:37 am	△ ♆	♏	8	**3:52 pm**	12:52 pm
10	**2:27 pm**	11:27 am	△ ♅	♐	10	**6:09 pm**	3:09 pm
12	**8:08 pm**	5:08 pm	□ ♅	♑	12		9:17 pm
12	**8:08 pm**	5:08 pm	□ ♅	♑	13	**12:17 am**	
15	**5:49 am**	2:49 am	✶ ♅	♒	15	**10:24 am**	7:24 am
17	**2:49 pm**	11:49 am	☌ ♆	♓	17	**10:52 pm**	7:52 pm
20	**6:25 am**	3:25 am	☌ ♅	♈	20	**11:23 am**	8:23 am

☽ Last Aspect day	ET / hr:mn / PT		asp	☽ Ingress sign	day	ET / hr:mn / PT	
22	**9:37 pm**	6:37 pm	☍ ☉	♉	22	**10:30 pm**	7:30 pm
25	**3:49 am**	12:49 am	☍ ♂	♊	25	**7:47 am**	4:47 am
27	**10:19 am**	7:19 am	□ ♅	♋	27	**3:14 pm**	12:14 pm
29	**3:48 pm**	12:48 pm	△ ♅	♌	29	**8:39 pm**	5:39 pm
31	**5:01 pm**	2:01 pm	☍ ♆	♍	31	**11:51 pm**	8:51 pm

☽ Phases & Eclipses phase	day	ET / hr:mn / PT	
New Moon	7	**2:44 pm**	11:44 am
2nd Quarter	14	**5:27 pm**	2:27 pm
Full Moon	22	**9:37 pm**	6:37 pm
4th Quarter	30	**8:46 am**	5:46 am

Planet Ingress		day	ET / hr:mn / PT	
⚵	♍	2		11:44 pm
⚵	♍	3	**2:44 am**	
☿	♎	3	**11:04 am**	8:04 am
♀	♐	7	**10:10 am**	7:10 am
⚶	♏	7	**9:55 pm**	6:55 pm
⚳	♑	8	**8:15 pm**	5:15 pm
☿	♏	20	**5:19 pm**	2:19 pm
☉	♏	23	**8:35 am**	5:35 am
♂	♐	27		11:48 pm
♂	♐	28	**2:48 am**	

Planetary Motion		day	ET / hr:mn / PT	
♀	℞	8	**3:05 am**	12:05 am

1 FRIDAY
☽ △ ♂ **5:40 am** 2:40 am
☽ △ ♀ **7:50 am** 4:50 am
☿ ⚻ ♆ **8:32 am** 5:32 am
☿ ☍ ♃ **6:36 pm** 3:36 pm

2 SATURDAY
☽ ⚻ ♆ **7:57 am** 4:57 am
☽ △ ♃ **9:07 am** 6:07 am
☿ ☍ ♅ **10:23 am** 7:23 am
☽ △ ♅ **11:14 am** 8:14 am
☽ ✶ ☿ **11:22 am** 8:22 am
☽ ⚻ ♇ **7:14 pm** 4:14 pm

3 SUNDAY
☽ ✶ ♄ **3:54 am** 12:54 am
☽ ✶ ☉ **7:27 am** 4:27 am
☽ □ ♂ **11:40 am** 8:40 am
☽ □ ♀ **11:54 am** 8:54 am
♀ ☌ ♂ **5:58 pm** 2:58 pm

4 MONDAY
☽ ☍ ♆ **9:52 am** 6:52 am
☽ ⚻ ♃ **10:37 am** 7:37 am
☽ ⚻ ♅ **12:55 pm** 9:55 am
☽ ⚺ ☿ **7:56 pm** 4:56 pm
☽ △ ♇ **8:41 pm** 5:41 pm
☿ □ ♇ 11:08 pm

5 TUESDAY
☿ □ ♇ **2:08 am**
☽ ⚺ ♄ **5:19 am** 2:19 am
☽ ⚺ ☉ **11:44 am** 8:44 am
☽ ✶ ♀ **1:01 pm** 10:01 am
☽ ✶ ♂ **2:42 pm** 11:42 am

6 WEDNESDAY
☉ ⚺ ♀ **9:02 am** 6:02 am
☽ ⚻ ♆ **9:49 am** 6:49 am
☽ ☍ ♃ **10:12 am** 7:12 am
☽ ☍ ♅ **12:43 pm** 9:43 am
☽ □ ♇ **8:30 pm** 5:30 pm
☽ ☌ ☿ 11:08 pm

7 THURSDAY
☽ ☌ ☿ **2:08 am**
☽ ☌ ♄ **5:24 am** 2:24 am
☽ ⚺ ♀ **12:53 pm** 9:53 am
☽ ☌ ☉ **2:44 pm** 11:44 am
☽ ⚺ ♂ **4:40 pm** 1:40 pm

8 FRIDAY
☿ ☌ ♄ **7:35 am** 4:35 am
☽ △ ♆ **9:37 am** 6:37 am
☽ ⚻ ♃ **9:41 am** 6:41 am
☽ ⚻ ♅ **12:31 pm** 9:31 am
♃ ⚺ ♆ **6:14 pm** 3:14 pm
☽ ✶ ♇ **8:40 pm** 5:40 pm

9 SATURDAY
☽ ⚺ ♄ **6:15 am** 3:15 am
☽ ⚺ ☿ **9:12 am** 6:12 am
☽ ☌ ♀ **1:35 pm** 10:35 am
☽ ⚺ ☉ **7:12 pm** 4:12 pm
☽ ☌ ♂ **8:06 pm** 5:06 pm

10 SUNDAY
☽ △ ♃ **11:09 am** 8:09 am
☽ □ ♆ **11:27 am** 8:27 am
☽ △ ♅ **2:27 pm** 11:27 am
☿ ⚺ ♀ **7:39 pm** 4:39 pm
☽ ⚺ ♇ **11:20 pm** 8:20 pm

11 MONDAY
☽ ✶ ♄ **10:01 am** 7:01 am
☉ ⚺ ♂ **1:04 pm** 10:04 am
☽ ⚺ ♀ **5:03 pm** 2:03 pm
☽ ✶ ☿ **8:31 pm** 5:31 pm

12 TUESDAY
☽ ⚺ ♂ **3:23 am** 12:23 am
☽ ✶ ☉ **3:43 am** 12:43 am
☽ □ ♃ **4:15 pm** 1:15 pm
☽ ✶ ♆ **4:59 pm** 1:59 pm
☽ □ ♅ **8:08 pm** 5:08 pm

13 WEDNESDAY
☽ ☌ ♇ **5:57 am** 2:57 am
☽ □ ♄ **5:58 pm** 2:58 pm
☽ ✶ ♀ 9:09 pm

14 THURSDAY
☽ ✶ ♀ **12:09 am**
☽ □ ☿ **1:57 pm** 10:57 am
☽ ✶ ♂ **3:32 pm** 12:32 pm
☽ □ ☉ **5:27 pm** 2:27 pm
☽ ✶ ♃ 10:21 pm
☽ ⚺ ♆ 11:35 pm

15 FRIDAY
☽ ✶ ♃ **1:21 am**
☽ ⚺ ♆ **2:35 am**
☽ ✶ ♅ **5:49 am** 2:49 am
☿ ⚺ ♂ **8:05 am** 5:05 am
☽ ⚺ ♇ **4:28 pm** 1:28 pm

16 SATURDAY
☽ △ ♄ **5:40 am** 2:40 am
☽ □ ♀ **10:09 am** 7:09 am
☉ ☌ ☿ **9:05 pm** 6:05 pm

17 SUNDAY
☽ □ ♂ **7:17 am** 4:17 am
☽ △ ☉ **10:58 am** 7:58 am
☽ △ ☿ **11:56 am** 8:56 am
☽ ⚺ ♃ **1:06 pm** 10:06 am
☽ ☌ ♆ **2:49 pm** 11:49 am
☽ ⚺ ♅ **6:00 pm** 3:00 pm
☿ ⚻ ♃ **7:42 pm** 4:42 pm

18 MONDAY
☽ ✶ ♇ **5:08 am** 2:08 am
☿ △ ♆ **8:03 am** 5:03 am
☉ ⚻ ♃ **10:12 am** 7:12 am
☽ ⚻ ♄ **7:00 pm** 4:00 pm
☽ △ ♀ **9:02 pm** 6:02 pm

19 TUESDAY
☿ ⚻ ♅ **6:00 am** 3:00 am
☉ △ ♆ **8:18 am** 5:18 am
☽ △ ♂ **11:48 pm** 8:48 pm
☽ ☌ ♃ 10:15 pm

20 WEDNESDAY
☽ ☌ ♃ **1:15 am**
☽ ⚺ ♆ **3:23 am** 12:23 am
☽ ⚻ ☉ **5:08 am** 2:08 am
☽ ☌ ♅ **6:25 am** 3:25 am
☽ ⚻ ☿ **10:26 am** 7:26 am
♀ ⚺ ♄ **3:03 pm** 12:03 pm
☽ □ ♇ **5:39 pm** 2:39 pm
☉ ⚻ ♅ **8:17 pm** 5:17 pm
♂ △ ♃ **9:42 pm** 6:42 pm

21 THURSDAY
☽ ⚻ ♀ **6:58 am** 3:58 am
☽ ☍ ♄ **7:46 am** 4:46 am

22 FRIDAY
♂ □ ♆ **11:35 am** 8:35 am
☽ ⚺ ♃ **12:13 pm** 9:13 am
☽ ✶ ♆ **2:41 pm** 11:41 am
☽ ⚻ ♂ **2:52 pm** 11:52 am
☿ ✶ ♇ **3:38 pm** 12:38 pm
☽ ⚺ ♅ **5:31 pm** 2:31 pm
☽ ☍ ☉ **9:37 pm** 6:37 pm

23 SATURDAY
☽ △ ♇ **4:40 am** 1:40 am
☽ ☍ ☿ **6:37 am** 3:37 am
☽ ☍ ♀ **3:07 pm** 12:07 pm
☽ ⚻ ♄ **6:49 pm** 3:49 pm

24 SUNDAY
♂ △ ♅ **10:56 am** 7:56 am
☽ ✶ ♃ **9:27 pm** 6:27 pm
☽ □ ♆ 9:11 pm
☽ ✶ ♅ 11:50 pm

25 MONDAY
☽ □ ♆ **12:11 am**
☽ ✶ ♅ **2:50 am**
☽ ☍ ♂ **3:49 am** 12:49 am
☿ ☌ ♀ **9:17 am** 6:17 am
☽ ⚻ ☉ **11:47 am** 8:47 am
☽ ⚻ ♇ **1:51 pm** 10:51 am
☽ ⚻ ♀ **9:29 pm** 6:29 pm
☽ ⚻ ☿ **11:51 pm** 8:51 pm

26 TUESDAY
☽ △ ♄ **4:00 am** 1:00 am
☉ ✶ ♇ **3:01 pm** 12:01 pm

27 WEDNESDAY
☽ □ ♃ **4:56 am** 1:56 am
☽ △ ♆ **7:52 am** 4:52 am
☽ □ ♅ **10:19 am** 7:19 am
☿ ⚺ ♄ **11:45 am** 8:45 am
☽ ⚻ ♂ **2:35 pm** 11:35 am
☽ ☍ ♇ **9:11 pm** 6:11 pm
☽ △ ☉ **11:35 pm** 8:35 pm
☽ △ ♀ 11:05 pm

28 THURSDAY
☽ △ ♀ **2:05 am**
☽ □ ♄ **11:14 am** 8:14 am
☽ △ ☿ **2:08 pm** 11:08 am
☉ ☌ ♀ **9:10 pm** 6:10 pm

29 FRIDAY
☽ △ ♃ **10:28 am** 7:28 am
☽ ⚻ ♆ **1:32 pm** 10:32 am
☽ △ ♅ **3:48 pm** 12:48 pm
☽ △ ♂ **10:56 pm** 7:56 pm
☽ ⚻ ♇ 11:26 pm

30 SATURDAY
☽ ⚻ ♇ **2:26 am**
☽ □ ♀ **4:49 am** 1:49 am
☽ □ ☉ **8:46 am** 5:46 am
☽ ✶ ♄ **4:15 pm** 1:15 pm
☽ □ ☿ 10:13 pm

31 SUNDAY
☽ □ ☿ **1:13 am**
☽ ⚻ ♃ **1:51 pm** 10:51 am
☽ ☍ ♆ **5:01 pm** 2:01 pm
☽ ⚻ ♅ **7:07 pm** 4:07 pm

Eastern time in bold type
Pacific time in medium type

OCTOBER 2010

DATE	S.TIME	SUN	MOON	N.NODE	MERCURY	VENUS	MARS	JUPITER	SATURN	URANUS	NEPTUNE	PLUTO	CERES	PALLAS	JUNO	VESTA	CHIRON
1 Fri	00:38:30	07♎42 56	05♋42	07♑13	25♍27	12♏15	10♏52	27♓08	07♎44	28♓14	26♒17	02♑52	27♐56	27♏31	28♎59	26♎18	26♒42
2 Sat	00:42:26	08 41 56	19 20	07 13R	27 07	12 30	11 33	27 00R	07 52	28 12R	26 16R	02 52	28 11	27 53	29 26	26 50	26 40R
3 Sun	00:46:23	09 40 58	03♌20	07 11	28 53	12 42	12 14	26 53	07 59	28 10	26 15	02 53	28 26	28 16	29 53	27 21	26 38
4 Mon	00:50:19	10 40 02	17 44	07 08	00♎27	12 53	12 56	26 45	08 07	28 07	26 14	02 53	28 41	28 38	00♏19	27 52	26 36
5 Tue	00:54:16	11 39 09	02♍29	07 02	02 27	13 02	13 37	26 37	08 14	28 05	26 13	02 54	28 57	29 01	00 45	28 23	26 34
6 Wed	00:58:12	12 38 18	17 29	06 55	04 14	13 08	14 19	26 30	08 21	28 03	26 12	02 54	29 12	29 24	01 12	28 55	26 33
7 Thu	01:02:09	13 37 29	02♎37	06 42	06 01	13 12	15 00	26 23	08 29	28 00	26 11	02 55	29 28	29 47	01 38	29 26	26 31
8 Fri	01:06:06	14 36 42	17 41	06 31	07 48	13 14R	15 42	26 15	08 36	27 58	26 10	02 56	29 44	00♐09	02 04	29 57	26 29
9 Sat	01:10:02	15 35 57	02♏32	06 25	09 35	13 13	16 23	26 08	08 44	27 56	26 09	02 57	00♑00	00 32	02 30	00♏29	26 27
10 Sun	01:13:59	16 35 14	17 02	06 11	11 21	13 11	17 05	26 01	08 51	27 53	26 08	02 58	00 16	00 55	02 56	01 00	26 26
11 Mon	01:17:55	17 34 33	01♐04	06 04	13 07	13 05	17 47	25 54	08 58	27 51	26 07	02 59	00 33	01 18	03 22	01 32	26 24
12 Tue	01:21:52	18 33 54	14 37	05 59D	14 52	12 58	18 29	25 48	09 06	27 49	26 06	02 59	00 49	01 41	03 47	02 03	26 23
13 Wed	01:25:48	19 33 17	27 43	05 59R	16 37	12 48	19 11	25 41	09 13	27 47	26 06	03 00	01 06	02 05	04 13	02 35	26 21
14 Thu	01:29:45	20 32 42	10♑23	05 59	18 21	12 35	19 53	25 34	09 20	27 45	26 05	03 01	01 23	02 28	04 38	03 07	26 20
15 Fri	01:33:41	21 32 08	22 44	05 55	20 04	12 20	20 35	25 28	09 28	27 42	26 04	03 02	01 40	02 51	05 03	03 38	26 19
16 Sat	01:37:38	22 31 36	04♒49	05 58	21 47	12 03	21 17	25 22	09 35	27 40	26 03	03 03	01 57	03 14	05 29	04 10	26 17
17 Sun	01:41:35	23 31 06	16 45	05 56	23 29	11 43	21 59	25 15	09 42	27 38	26 02	03 04	02 14	03 38	05 54	04 42	26 16
18 Mon	01:45:31	24 30 37	28 35	05 51	25 11	11 22	22 42	25 09	09 49	27 36	26 02	03 05	02 32	04 01	06 18	05 13	26 15
19 Tue	01:49:28	25 30 10	10♓26	05 43	26 51	10 58	23 24	25 03	09 57	27 34	26 01	03 06	02 49	04 25	06 43	05 45	26 14
20 Wed	01:53:24	26 29 45	22 19	05 33	28 32	10 32	24 06	24 58	10 04	27 32	26 00	03 07	03 07	04 48	07 08	06 17	26 13
21 Thu	01:57:21	27 29 22	04♈19	05 21	00♏16	10 04	24 49	24 52	10 11	27 30	26 00	03 08	03 25	05 12	07 32	06 49	26 12
22 Fri	02:01:17	28 29 01	16 27	05 06	01 54	09 34	25 31	24 47	10 18	27 28	25 59	03 09	03 43	05 36	07 57	07 20	26 11
23 Sat	02:05:14	29 28 42	28 43	04 56	03 28	09 03	26 14	24 41	10 25	27 26	25 59	03 11	04 01	05 59	08 21	07 52	26 10
24 Sun	02:09:10	00♏28 25	11♉09	04 45	05 06	08 30	26 57	24 36	10 33	27 24	25 58	03 12	04 20	06 23	08 45	08 24	26 09
25 Mon	02:13:07	01 28 09	23 45	04 36	06 43	07 56	27 39	24 31	10 40	27 22	25 58	03 13	04 38	06 47	09 09	08 56	26 08
26 Tue	02:17:03	02 27 56	06♊31	04 31	08 20	07 21	28 22	24 27	10 47	27 21	25 57	03 14	04 57	07 11	09 33	09 28	26 08
27 Wed	02:21:00	03 27 45	19 28	04 26D	09 56	06 45	29 05	24 22	10 54	27 19	25 57	03 16	05 15	07 35	09 56	10 00	26 07
28 Thu	02:24:57	04 27 37	02♋38	04 26	11 31	06 09	29 48	24 18	11 01	27 17	25 56	03 17	05 34	07 59	10 20	10 32	26 07
29 Fri	02:28:53	05 27 30	16 00	04 27	13 06	05 32	00♐31	24 14	11 08	27 15	25 56	03 18	05 53	08 23	10 43	11 04	26 06
30 Sat	02:32:50	06 27 26	29 38	04 27R	14 41	04 56	01 14	24 09	11 15	27 14	25 56	03 20	06 12	08 47	11 06	11 36	26 06
31 Sun	02:36:46	07 27 24	13♌32	04 27	16 15	04 19	01 57	24 06	11 22	27 12	25 56	03 21	06 31	09 11	11 29	12 08	26 05

EPHEMERIS CALCULATED FOR 12 MIDNIGHT GREENWICH MEAN TIME. ALL OTHER DATA AND FACING ASPECTARIAN PAGE IN **EASTERN TIME (BOLD)** AND PACIFIC TIME (REGULAR).

NOVEMBER 2010

☽ Last Aspect day	ET / hr:mn / PT	asp	☽ Ingress sign day	ET / hr:mn / PT
2	**8:36 pm** 5:36 pm	☍♅	♎ 2	10:19 pm
2	**8:36 pm** 5:36 pm	☍♅	♎ 3	**1:19 am**
4	**7:34 pm** 4:34 pm	△♆	♏ 4	11:16 pm
4	**7:34 pm** 4:34 pm	△♆	♏ 5	**2:16 am**
6	**10:44 pm** 7:44 pm	☌☿	♐ 7	**3:27 am** 12:27 am
9	**7:35 am** 4:35 am	✶♀	♑ 9	**8:36 am** 5:36 am
11	**2:57 pm** 11:57 am	□♀	♒ 11	**5:32 pm** 2:32 pm
13	10:33 pm	△♀	♓ 14	**5:24 am** 2:24 am
14	**1:33 am**	△♀	♓ 14	**5:24 am** 2:24 am
16	**11:37 am** 8:37 am	☌♅	♈ 16	**5:59 pm** 2:59 pm
18	9:33 pm	☍♀	♉ 19	**5:04 am** 2:04 am
19	**12:33 am**	☍♀	♉ 19	**5:04 am** 2:04 am
21	**12:27 pm** 9:27 am	☍☉	♊ 21	**1:46 pm** 10:46 am
23	**4:56 pm** 1:56 pm	△♀	♋ 23	**8:14 pm** 5:14 pm
25	**10:44 pm** 7:44 pm	□♀	♌ 25	10:01 pm
25	**10:44 pm** 7:44 pm	□♀	♌ 26	**1:01 am**
28	**3:30 am** 12:30 am	✶♀	♍ 28	**4:34 am** 1:34 am
30	**6:17 am** 3:17 am	□☿	♎ 30	**7:15 am** 4:15 am

☽ Phases & Eclipses phase	day	ET / hr:mn / PT
New Moon	5	9:52 pm
New Moon	6	**12:52 am**
2nd Quarter	13	**11:39 am** 8:39 am
Full Moon	21	**12:27 pm** 9:27 am
4th Quarter	28	**3:36 pm** 12:36 pm

Planet Ingress	day	ET / hr:mn / PT
♀ ♎	7	**10:06 pm** 7:06 pm
☿ ♐	8	**6:43 pm** 3:43 pm
☉ ♐	22	**5:15 am** 2:15 am
♀ ♏	29	**7:33 pm** 4:33 pm
☿ ♑	30	**7:10 pm** 4:10 pm

Planetary Motion	day	ET / hr:mn / PT
⚷ D	5	**2:40 pm** 11:40 am
♆ D	6	11:04 pm
♆ D	7	**1:04 am**
♃ D	18	**11:53 am** 8:53 am
♀ D	18	**4:18 pm** 1:18 pm

1 MONDAY
☽□♂ **4:45 am** 1:45 am
☽△♇ **5:30 am** 2:30 am
☽✶♀ **5:40 am** 2:40 am
♀✶♇ **9:37 am** 6:37 am
☽✶☉ **3:16 pm** 12:16 pm
♀⚺♂ **3:16 pm** 12:16 pm
☽⚺♄ **7:07 pm** 4:07 pm
♂⚺♇ **8:11 pm** 5:11 pm

2 TUESDAY
☽✶☿ **9:18 am** 6:18 am
☽☍♃ **3:24 pm** 12:24 pm
☽⚻♆ **6:39 pm** 3:39 pm
☽☍♅ **8:36 pm** 5:36 pm

3 WEDNESDAY
☽⚺♀ **5:08 am** 2:08 am
☽□♇ **6:54 am** 3:54 am
☽✶♂ **8:38 am** 5:38 am
☽⚺☉ **7:59 pm** 4:59 pm
☽☌♄ **8:34 pm** 5:34 pm

4 THURSDAY
☉⚺♄ **5:37 am** 2:37 am
☽⚺☿ **3:57 pm** 12:57 pm
☽⚻♃ **4:09 pm** 1:09 pm
☿△♃ **5:46 pm** 2:46 pm
☽△♆ **7:34 pm** 4:34 pm
☽⚻♅ **9:27 pm** 6:27 pm

5 FRIDAY
☽☌♀ **4:24 am** 1:24 am
☽✶♇ **7:59 am** 4:59 am
☽⚺♂ **12:13 pm** 9:13 am
☽⚺♄ **10:10 pm** 7:10 pm
☽☌☉ 9:52 pm
☿□♆ 11:44 pm

6 SATURDAY
☽☌☉ **12:52 am**
☿□♆ **2:44 am**
☽△♃ **5:47 pm** 2:47 pm
☿△♅ **8:15 pm** 5:15 pm
☽□♆ **9:29 pm** 6:29 pm
☽△♅ **11:21 pm** 8:21 pm
☽☌☿ **11:44 pm** 8:44 pm

7 SUNDAY
☽⚺♀ **4:01 am** 1:01 am
☽⚺♇ **9:33 am** 6:33 am
☽☌♂ **4:42 pm** 1:42 pm
☽✶♄ 9:48 pm

8 MONDAY
☽✶♄ **12:48 am**
☽⚺☉ **7:20 am** 4:20 am
☿⚺♀ **2:16 pm** 11:16 am
☽□♃ **9:03 pm** 6:03 pm
☽✶♆ 10:09 pm

9 TUESDAY
☽✶♆ **1:09 am**
☽□♅ **3:04 am** 12:04 am
☽✶♀ **7:35 am** 4:35 am
☽⚺☿ **10:24 am** 7:24 am
☽☌♇ **3:14 pm** 12:14 pm
☽⚺♂ 11:04 pm

10 WEDNESDAY
☽⚺♂ **2:04 am**
☽□♄ **7:57 am** 4:57 am
☽✶☉ **7:16 pm** 4:16 pm

11 THURSDAY
☽✶♃ **5:03 am** 2:03 am
☿⚺♇ **5:17 am** 2:17 am
☽⚺♆ **9:35 am** 6:35 am
☽✶♅ **11:31 am** 8:31 am
☽□♀ **2:57 pm** 11:57 am
☽⚺♇ 9:43 pm

12 FRIDAY
☽⚺♇ **12:43 am**
☽✶☿ **3:21 am** 12:21 am
☽✶♂ **3:49 pm** 12:49 pm
☽△♄ **6:50 pm** 3:50 pm

13 SATURDAY
☽□☉ **11:39 am** 8:39 am
☽⚺♃ **4:21 pm** 1:21 pm
☽☌♆ **9:10 pm** 6:10 pm
☽⚺♅ **11:05 pm** 8:05 pm
☽△♀ 10:33 pm

14 SUNDAY
☽△♀ **1:33 am**
☽✶♇ **12:57 pm** 9:57 am
☽□☿ 9:00 pm
♂✶♄ 9:58 pm

15 MONDAY
☽□☿ **12:00 am**
♂✶♄ **12:58 am**
☽⚻♄ **7:51 am** 4:51 am
☽□♂ **8:15 am** 5:15 am
☉△♃ **6:44 pm** 3:44 pm

16 TUESDAY
☽☌♃ **4:56 am** 1:56 am
☽△☉ **5:52 am** 2:52 am
☽⚺♆ **9:50 am** 6:50 am
☽☌♅ **11:37 am** 8:37 am
☽⚻♀ **1:28 pm** 10:28 am
☽□♇ 10:35 pm

17 WEDNESDAY
☽□♇ **1:35 am**
☽△☿ **8:26 pm** 5:26 pm
☽☍♄ **8:30 pm** 5:30 pm
☿✶♄ **9:09 pm** 6:09 pm
☽△♂ 9:15 pm

18 THURSDAY
☽△♂ **12:15 am**
☉□♆ **4:54 am** 1:54 am
☽⚺♃ **4:27 pm** 1:27 pm
☽✶♆ **9:14 pm** 6:14 pm
☽⚻☉ **10:41 pm** 7:41 pm
☽⚺♅ **10:52 pm** 7:52 pm
☽☍♀ 9:33 pm
☉△♅ 9:57 pm

19 FRIDAY
☽☍♀ **12:33 am**
☉△♅ **12:57 am**
☽△♇ **12:33 pm** 9:33 am
☉⚺♀ **10:17 pm** 7:17 pm

20 SATURDAY
☽⚻♄ **7:02 am** 4:02 am
☽⚻♂ **1:43 pm** 10:43 am
☽⚻☿ **1:43 pm** 10:43 am
☿☌♂ **1:53 pm** 10:53 am
☽✶♃ 10:42 pm

21 SUNDAY
☽✶♃ **1:42 am**
☽□♆ **6:17 am** 3:17 am
☽✶♅ **7:46 am** 4:46 am
☽⚻♀ **9:42 am** 6:42 am
☽☍☉ **12:27 pm** 9:27 am
☽⚻♇ **9:03 pm** 6:03 pm

22 MONDAY
☽△♄ **3:04 pm** 12:04 pm
☽☍♂ 9:22 pm

23 TUESDAY
☽☍♂ **12:22 am**
☽☍☿ **3:25 am** 12:25 am
☽□♃ **8:39 am** 5:39 am
☽△♆ **1:04 pm** 10:04 am
☽□♅ **2:24 pm** 11:24 am
☽△♀ **4:56 pm** 1:56 pm
☽⚻☉ **11:24 pm** 8:24 pm

24 WEDNESDAY
☽☍♇ **3:24 am** 12:24 am
☽□♄ **9:05 pm** 6:05 pm

25 THURSDAY
☽⚻♂ **8:46 am** 5:46 am
☿□♃ **9:18 am** 6:18 am
☽△♃ **1:51 pm** 10:51 am
☽⚻☿ **2:18 pm** 11:18 am
☽⚻♆ **6:05 pm** 3:05 pm
☽△♅ **7:18 pm** 4:18 pm
☽□♀ **10:44 pm** 7:44 pm

26 FRIDAY
☉⚺♇ **6:23 am** 3:23 am
☽⚻♇ **8:07 am** 5:07 am
☽△☉ **8:15 am** 5:15 am
☽✶♄ 10:36 pm

27 SATURDAY
☽✶♄ **1:36 am**
☿✶♆ **8:13 am** 5:13 am
☽△♂ **3:34 pm** 12:34 pm
☽⚻♃ **5:43 pm** 2:43 pm
☿□♅ **9:27 pm** 6:27 pm
☽☍♆ **9:49 pm** 6:49 pm
☽⚻♅ **10:56 pm** 7:56 pm
☽△☿ **11:05 pm** 8:05 pm

28 SUNDAY
☽✶♀ **3:30 am** 12:30 am
☽△♇ **11:38 am** 8:38 am
☽□☉ **3:36 pm** 12:36 pm

29 MONDAY
☽⚺♄ **5:00 am** 2:00 am
♂□♃ **9:51 am** 6:51 am
☽☍♃ **8:41 pm** 5:41 pm
☽□♂ **9:15 pm** 6:15 pm
☽⚻♆ 9:38 pm
☽☍♅ 10:41 pm

30 TUESDAY
☽⚻♆ **12:38 am**
☽☍♅ **1:41 am**
☽□☿ **6:17 am** 3:17 am
☽⚺♀ **7:36 am** 4:36 am
☽□♇ **2:22 pm** 11:22 am
☽✶☉ **10:03 pm** 7:03 pm

Eastern time in bold type
Pacific time in medium type

NOVEMBER 2010

DATE	S.TIME	SUN	MOON	N.NODE	MERCURY	VENUS	MARS	JUPITER	SATURN	URANUS	NEPTUNE	PLUTO	CERES	PALLAS	JUNO	VESTA	CHIRON
1 Mon	02:40:43	08♏27'23	27♌42	04♑25℞	17♏48	03♏43	02♐40	24♓02	11♎29	27♓10	25≈56	03♑22	06♑51	11♐35	11♏52	12♏40	26≈05
2 Tue	02:44:39	09 27 26	12♍08	04 21℞	19 21	03 08℞	03 23	23 58℞	11 35	27 09℞	25 55℞	03 24	07 10	11 59	12 15	13 12	26 05℞
3 Wed	02:48:36	10 27 30	26 45	04 15	20 54	02 34	04 07	23 55	11 42	27 07	25 55	03 25	07 29	10 23	12 38	13 44	26 04
4 Thu	02:52:32	11 27 36	11♎28	04 07	22 26	02 01	04 50	23 52	11 49	27 06	25 55	03 27	07 49	10 47	13 00	14 16	26 04
5 Fri	02:56:29	12 27 44	26 11	04 01	23 56	01 29	05 34	23 49	11 56	27 04	25 55	03 28	08 09	11 11	13 23	14 48	26 04 D
6 Sat	03:00:26	13 27 55	10♏45	03 51	25 29	00 58	06 17	23 46	12 02	27 03	25 55	03 30	08 29	11 36	13 45	15 20	26 04
7 Sun	03:04:22	14 28 07	25 03	03 44	27 00	00 30	07 01	23 44	12 09	27 01	25 55 D	03 31	08 49	12 00	14 07	15 52	26 04
8 Mon	03:08:19	15 28 21	08♐59	03 39	28 31	00 03	07 44	23 42	12 16	27 00	25 55	03 33	09 09	12 24	14 28	16 24	26 04
9 Tue	03:12:15	16 28 36	22 31	03 36 D	00♐01	29♎16	08 28	23 40	12 22	26 59	25 55	03 34	09 29	12 49	14 50	16 56	26 04
10 Wed	03:16:12	17 28 53	05♑38	03 36	01 31	29 16	09 11	23 38	12 29	26 57	25 55	03 36	09 49	13 13	15 11	17 28	26 05
11 Thu	03:20:08	18 29 12	18 21	03 36	03 00	28 56	09 56	23 36	12 35	26 56	25 55	03 38	10 09	13 37	15 33	18 01	26 05
12 Fri	03:24:05	19 29 32	00≈45	03 38	04 29	28 38	10 39	23 34	12 42	26 55	25 56	03 39	10 30	14 02	15 54	18 33	26 05
13 Sat	03:28:02	20 29 54	12 53	03 39℞	05 58	28 22	11 23	23 33	12 48	26 54	25 56	03 41	10 50	14 26	16 15	19 05	26 06
14 Sun	03:31:58	21 30 17	24 51	03 39	07 26	28 09	12 07	23 32	12 55	26 53	25 56	03 43	11 11	14 51	16 35	19 37	26 06
15 Mon	03:35:55	22 30 41	06♓43	03 38	08 53	27 58	12 51	23 31	13 01	26 52	25 56	03 44	11 32	15 15	16 56	20 09	26 07
16 Tue	03:39:51	23 31 06	18 35	03 36	10 20	27 50	13 36	23 30	13 07	26 50	25 56	03 46	11 53	15 40	17 16	20 42	26 07
17 Wed	03:43:48	24 31 33	00♈31	03 30	11 47	27 44	14 20	23 30 D	13 13	26 50	25 56	03 48	12 13	16 04	17 36	21 14	26 08
18 Thu	03:47:44	25 32 01	12 34	03 17	13 12	27 40 D	15 04	23 30	13 19	26 49	25 57	03 50	12 34	16 29	17 56	21 46	26 09
19 Fri	03:51:41	26 32 31	24 48	03 17	14 37	27 39	15 48	23 30	13 25	26 48	25 57	03 51	12 55	16 53	18 16	22 18	26 10
20 Sat	03:55:37	27 33 02	07♉15	03 10	16 02	27 41	16 33	23 30	13 32	26 47	25 58	03 53	13 17	17 18	18 36	22 51	26 10
21 Sun	03:59:34	28 33 35	19 56	03 04	17 25	27 45	17 17	23 30	13 37	26 46	25 58	03 55	13 38	17 42	18 55	23 23	26 11
22 Mon	04:03:30	29 34 09	02♊50	03 00	18 48	27 51	18 01	23 31	13 43	26 45	25 59	03 57	13 59	18 07	19 14	23 55	26 12
23 Tue	04:07:27	00♐34 44	15 58	02 57	20 09	28 00	18 46	23 32	13 49	26 45	25 59	03 59	14 20	18 32	19 33	24 27	26 13
24 Wed	04:11:24	01 35 21	29 19	02 56 D	21 29	28 10	19 30	23 33	13 55	26 44	26 00	04 01	14 42	18 56	19 52	25 00	26 14
25 Thu	04:15:20	02 36 00	12♋50	02 56	22 48	28 23	20 15	23 34	14 01	26 43	26 00	04 03	15 03	19 21	20 10	25 32	26 16
26 Fri	04:19:17	03 36 40	26 32	02 57	24 06	28 39	21 00	23 35	14 06	26 43	26 01	04 05	15 25	19 45	20 28	26 04	26 17
27 Sat	04:23:13	04 37 22	10♌22	02 59	25 21	28 56	21 45	23 37	14 12	26 42	26 02	04 06	15 47	20 10	20 46	26 36	26 18
28 Sun	04:27:10	05 38 05	24 23	03 00℞	26 35	29 15	22 29	23 39	14 18	26 42	26 02	04 08	16 08	20 35	21 04	27 09	26 19
29 Mon	04:31:06	06 38 50	08♍32	03 01	27 46	29 36	23 14	23 41	14 23	26 41	26 03	04 10	16 30	20 59	21 22	27 41	26 21
30 Tue	04:35:03	07 39 37	22 43	03 00	28 54	29 59	23 59	23 43	14 28	26 41	26 04	04 12	16 52	21 24	21 39	28 13	26 22

EPHEMERIS CALCULATED FOR 12 MIDNIGHT GREENWICH MEAN TIME. ALL OTHER DATA AND FACING ASPECTARIAN PAGE IN **EASTERN TIME (BOLD)** AND PACIFIC TIME (REGULAR).

DECEMBER 2010

☽ Last Aspect day	ET / hr:mn / PT		asp	☽ Ingress sign	day	ET / hr:mn / PT	
2	**3:08 am**	12:08 am	△♆	♏	2	**9:44 am**	6:44 am
4	**7:13 am**	4:13 am	△♅	♐	4	**12:59 pm**	9:59 am
6	**4:46 pm**	1:46 pm	☌♂	♑	6	**6:16 pm**	3:16 pm
8	**8:07 pm**	5:07 pm	⚹♅	♒	8		11:30 pm
8	**8:07 pm**	5:07 pm	⚹♅	♒	9	**2:30 am**	
11	**6:09 am**	3:09 am	☌♆	♓	11	**1:41 pm**	10:41 am
13	**7:35 pm**	4:35 pm	☌♅	♈	13		11:15 pm
13	**7:35 pm**	4:35 pm	☌♅	♈	14	**2:15 am**	
16	**6:41 am**	3:41 am	⚹♆	♉	16	**1:49 pm**	10:49 am
18	**4:37 pm**	1:37 pm	⚹♅	♊	18	**10:37 pm**	7:37 pm
21	**3:13 am**	12:13 am	☍☉	♋	21	**4:22 am**	1:22 am
22		11:25 pm	△♅	♌	23	**7:51 am**	4:51 am
23	**2:25 am**		△♅	♌	23	**7:51 am**	4:51 am
25	**4:28 am**	1:28 am	☍♆	♍	25	**10:14 am**	7:14 am
27	**7:20 am**	4:20 am	☍♅	♎	27	**12:38 pm**	9:38 am
29	**10:05 am**	7:05 am	△♆	♏	29	**3:49 pm**	12:49 pm
31	**2:57 pm**	11:57 am	△♅	♐	31	**8:21 pm**	5:21 pm

☽ Phases & Eclipses phase	day	ET / hr:mn / PT	
New Moon	5	**12:36 pm**	9:36 am
2nd Quarter	13	**8:59 am**	5:59 am
Full Moon	21	**3:13 am**	12:13 am
●	21	29° ♊ 22'	
4th Quarter	27	**11:18 pm**	8:18 pm

Planet Ingress		day	ET / hr:mn / PT	
⚵	♐	2		11:27 pm
⚵	♐	3	**2:27 am**	
♂	♑	7	**6:49 pm**	3:49 pm
☿	♐	18	**9:53 am**	6:53 am
♀	♑	20	**5:27 pm**	2:27 pm
☉	♑	21	**6:38 pm**	3:38 pm

Planetary Motion		day	ET / hr:mn / PT	
♅	D	5	**8:50 pm**	5:50 pm
☿	℞	10	**7:04 am**	4:04 am
☿	D	29		11:21 pm
☿	D	30	**2:21 am**	

1 WEDNESDAY
☽ ☌ ♄ **7:48 am** 4:48 am
☿ ⚹ ♀ **11:34 am** 8:34 am
☽ ⚻ ♃ **11:17 pm** 8:17 pm
☽ ⚹ ♂ 11:30 pm

2 THURSDAY
☽ ⚹ ♂ **2:30 am**
☽ △ ♆ **3:08 am** 12:08 am
☽ ⚻ ♅ **4:07 am** 1:07 am
☽ ☌ ♀ **11:43 am** 8:43 am
☽ ⚹ ☿ **12:40 pm** 9:40 am
♂ ⚹ ♆ **2:39 pm** 11:39 am
☽ ⚹ ♇ **5:00 pm** 2:00 pm

3 FRIDAY
☽ ⚺ ☉ **4:33 am** 1:33 am
♂ □ ♅ **9:01 am** 6:01 am
☽ ⚺ ♄ **10:50 am** 7:50 am
☽ △ ♃ 11:28 pm

4 SATURDAY
☽ △ ♃ **2:28 am**
☽ □ ♆ **6:17 am** 3:17 am
☽ △ ♅ **7:13 am** 4:13 am
☽ ⚺ ♂ **8:30 am** 5:30 am
☽ ⚺ ♀ **5:00 pm** 2:00 pm
☽ ⚺ ☿ **7:24 pm** 4:24 pm
☽ ⚺ ♇ **8:36 pm** 5:36 pm

5 SUNDAY
☽ ☌ ☉ **12:36 pm** 9:36 am
☽ ⚹ ♄ **3:16 pm** 12:16 pm
☿ ☌ ♇ **8:20 pm** 5:20 pm

6 MONDAY
☽ □ ♃ **7:27 am** 4:27 am
☽ ⚹ ♆ **11:17 am** 8:17 am
☽ □ ♅ **12:13 pm** 9:13 am
☽ ☌ ♂ **4:46 pm** 1:46 pm
☽ ⚹ ♀ 9:53 pm
☽ ☌ ♇ 11:24 pm

7 TUESDAY
☽ ⚹ ♀ **12:53 am**
☽ ☌ ♇ **2:24 am**
☉ ⚹ ♄ **3:00 am** 12:00 am
☽ ☌ ☿ **3:41 am** 12:41 am
☽ □ ♄ **10:18 pm** 7:18 pm
☽ ⚺ ☉ **11:50 pm** 8:50 pm

8 WEDNESDAY
♀ ⚹ ♇ **11:19 am** 8:19 am
☽ ⚹ ♃ **3:21 pm** 12:21 pm
☽ ⚺ ♆ **7:12 pm** 4:12 pm
☽ ⚹ ♅ **8:07 pm** 5:07 pm

9 THURSDAY
☽ ⚺ ♂ **4:34 am** 1:34 am
☽ ⚺ ♇ **11:17 am** 8:17 am
☽ □ ♀ **12:31 pm** 9:31 am
☽ ⚺ ☿ **1:55 pm** 10:55 am

10 FRIDAY
☽ △ ♄ **8:29 am** 5:29 am
☽ ⚹ ☉ **3:02 pm** 12:02 pm
☿ ⚹ ♀ **4:01 pm** 1:01 pm
☽ ⚺ ♃ 11:23 pm

11 SATURDAY
☽ ⚺ ♃ **2:23 am**
☽ ☌ ♆ **6:09 am** 3:09 am
☽ ⚺ ♅ **7:02 am** 4:02 am
☽ ⚹ ♂ **7:50 pm** 4:50 pm
☽ ⚹ ♇ **10:58 pm** 7:58 pm
☽ ⚹ ☿ 10:04 pm

12 SUNDAY
☽ ⚹ ☿ **1:04 am**
☽ △ ♀ **3:39 am** 12:39 am
☽ ⚻ ♄ **9:02 pm** 6:02 pm

13 MONDAY
☽ □ ☉ **8:59 am** 5:59 am
☽ ☌ ♃ **3:16 pm** 12:16 pm
☽ ⚺ ♆ **6:46 pm** 3:46 pm
☽ ☌ ♅ **7:35 pm** 4:35 pm
☿ ☌ ♇ **11:05 pm** 8:05 pm
☿ ☌ ♂ **11:10 pm** 8:10 pm
♂ ☌ ♇ **11:15 pm** 8:15 pm

14 TUESDAY
☽ □ ☿ **10:57 am** 7:57 am
☽ □ ♇ **11:43 am** 8:43 am
☽ □ ♂ **12:32 pm** 9:32 am
☽ ⚻ ♀ **8:06 pm** 5:06 pm

15 WEDNESDAY
☽ ☍ ♄ **9:44 am** 6:44 am
☽ △ ☉ 11:32 pm

16 THURSDAY
☽ △ ☉ **2:32 am**
☽ ⚺ ♃ **3:37 am** 12:37 am
☽ ⚹ ♆ **6:41 am** 3:41 am
☽ ⚺ ♅ **7:25 am** 4:25 am
☉ □ ♃ **4:47 pm** 1:47 pm
☽ △ ☿ **5:52 pm** 2:52 pm
☽ △ ♇ **11:07 pm** 8:07 pm

17 FRIDAY
☽ △ ♂ **3:34 am** 12:34 am
☽ ☍ ♀ **10:49 am** 7:49 am
☽ ⚻ ♄ **8:18 pm** 5:18 pm

18 SATURDAY
☉ ⚹ ♆ **5:29 am** 2:29 am
☽ ⚹ ♃ **1:24 pm** 10:24 am
☉ □ ♅ **1:48 pm** 10:48 am
☽ □ ♆ **3:58 pm** 12:58 pm
☽ ⚹ ♅ **4:37 pm** 1:37 pm
☽ ⚻ ☉ **4:51 pm** 1:51 pm
☽ ⚻ ☿ **9:26 pm** 6:26 pm

19 SUNDAY
☽ ⚻ ♇ **7:34 am** 4:34 am
☽ ⚻ ♂ **3:04 pm** 12:04 pm
☉ ☌ ☿ **8:23 pm** 5:23 pm
☽ ⚻ ♀ **10:04 pm** 7:04 pm

20 MONDAY
☽ △ ♄ **3:42 am** 12:42 am
☿ □ ♅ **6:30 pm** 3:30 pm
☽ □ ♃ **8:01 pm** 5:01 pm
☽ △ ♆ **10:09 pm** 7:09 pm
☽ ☍ ☿ **10:19 pm** 7:19 pm
☽ □ ♅ **10:43 pm** 7:43 pm
☿ ⚹ ♆ 9:03 pm

21 TUESDAY
☿ ⚹ ♆ **12:03 am**
☽ ☍ ☉ **3:13 am** 12:13 am
☽ ☍ ♇ **1:00 pm** 10:00 am
☿ □ ♃ **7:59 pm** 4:59 pm
☽ ☍ ♂ **11:06 pm** 8:06 pm

22 WEDNESDAY
☽ △ ♀ **6:05 am** 3:05 am
☽ □ ♄ **8:19 am** 5:19 am
☽ ⚻ ☿ **9:41 pm** 6:41 pm
☽ △ ♃ 9:11 pm
☽ ⚻ ♆ 10:55 pm
☽ △ ♅ 11:25 pm

23 THURSDAY
☽ △ ♃ **12:11 am**
☽ ⚻ ♆ **1:55 am**
☽ △ ♅ **2:25 am**
☽ ⚻ ☉ **10:43 am** 7:43 am
☽ ⚻ ♇ **4:21 pm** 1:21 pm
♀ ⚺ ♄ **8:43 pm** 5:43 pm

24 FRIDAY
☽ ⚻ ♂ **4:56 am** 1:56 am
☽ ⚹ ♄ **11:16 am** 8:16 am
☽ □ ♀ **12:10 pm** 9:10 am
☽ △ ☿ **8:45 pm** 5:45 pm

25 SATURDAY
☽ ⚻ ♃ **3:04 am** 12:04 am
☽ ☍ ♆ **4:28 am** 1:28 am
☽ ⚻ ♅ **4:56 am** 1:56 am
☽ △ ☉ **4:56 pm** 1:56 pm
☽ △ ♇ **6:48 pm** 3:48 pm

26 SUNDAY
☽ △ ♂ **10:04 am** 7:04 am
☽ ⚺ ♄ **1:44 pm** 10:44 am
☽ ⚹ ♀ **5:49 pm** 2:49 pm
☉ ☌ ♇ **8:04 pm** 5:04 pm
☽ □ ☿ **8:36 pm** 5:36 pm

27 MONDAY
☽ ☍ ♃ **5:49 am** 2:49 am
☽ ⚻ ♆ **6:54 am** 3:54 am
☽ ☍ ♅ **7:20 am** 4:20 am
☽ □ ♇ **9:25 pm** 6:25 pm
☽ □ ☉ **11:18 pm** 8:18 pm
☿ ⚺ ♀ **11:53 pm** 8:53 pm

28 TUESDAY
☽ □ ♂ **3:42 pm** 12:42 pm
☽ ☌ ♄ **4:40 pm** 1:40 pm
☽ ⚹ ☿ **10:11 pm** 7:11 pm
☽ ⚺ ♀ 9:13 pm

29 WEDNESDAY
☽ ⚺ ♀ **12:13 am**
☽ ⚻ ♃ **9:20 am** 6:20 am
☽ △ ♆ **10:05 am** 7:05 am
♂ □ ♄ **10:29 am** 7:29 am
☽ ⚻ ♅ **10:30 am** 7:30 am
☽ ⚹ ♇ 9:56 pm

30 THURSDAY
☽ ⚹ ♇ **12:56 am**
☽ ⚹ ☉ **6:51 am** 3:51 am
☽ ⚺ ♄ **8:44 pm** 5:44 pm
☽ ⚹ ♂ **10:39 pm** 7:39 pm
☽ ⚺ ☿ 11:08 pm

31 FRIDAY
☽ ⚺ ☿ **2:08 am**
☽ ☌ ♀ **8:11 am** 5:11 am
☽ △ ♃ **2:11 pm** 11:11 am
☽ □ ♆ **2:33 pm** 11:33 am
☽ △ ♅ **2:57 pm** 11:57 am

Eastern time in bold type
Pacific time in medium type

DECEMBER 2010

DATE	S.TIME	SUN	MOON	N.NODE	MERCURY	VENUS	MARS	JUPITER	SATURN	URANUS	NEPTUNE	PLUTO	CERES	PALLAS	JUNO	VESTA	CHIRON
1 Wed	04:39:00	08♐40 24	06♎59	02♑58	00♑01	00♏24	24♐44	23♓45	14♎34	26♓41	26♒04	04♑14	17♑14	21♎49	21♍56	28♏45	26♒24
2 Thu	04:42:56	09 41 14	21 16	02 55 R	01 01	00 51	25 29	23 48	14 39	26 40	26 05	04 16	17 36	22 13	22 13	29 18	26 25
3 Fri	04:46:53	10 42 05	05♏39	02 52	01 59	01 19	26 14	23 51	14 44	26 40	26 06	04 18	17 58	22 38	22 30	29 50	26 27
4 Sat	04:50:49	11 42 57	19 34	02 48	02 52	01 50	26 59	23 54	14 49	26 40	26 07	04 20	18 20	23 03	22 46	00♐22	26 29
5 Sun	04:54:46	12 43 50	03♐27	02 46	03 40	02 21	27 44	23 57	14 54	26 40	26 08	04 22	18 42	23 28	23 02	00 55	26 30
6 Mon	04:58:42	13 44 45	17 05	02 44	04 22	02 54	28 30	24 00	14 59	26 40 D	26 09	04 24	19 04	23 52	23 18	01 27	26 32
7 Tue	05:02:39	14 45 41	00♑23	02 43 D	04 58	03 29	29 15	24 04	15 04	26 40	26 10	04 26	19 27	24 17	23 34	01 59	26 34
8 Wed	05:06:35	15 46 38	13 24	02 44	05 25	04 05	00♑00	24 08	15 09	26 40	26 11	04 29	19 49	24 42	23 49	02 31	26 36
9 Thu	05:10:32	16 47 35	26 06	02 45	05 45	04 42	00 46	24 12	15 14	26 40	26 12	04 31	20 11	25 06	24 04	03 04	26 38
10 Fri	05:14:29	17 48 33	08♒40	02 46	05 55 R	05 21	01 31	24 16	15 19	26 41	26 13	04 33	20 34	25 31	24 19	03 36	26 40
11 Sat	05:18:25	18 49 32	20 39	02 47	05 55	06 00	02 17	24 20	15 23	26 41	26 14	04 35	20 56	25 56	24 34	04 08	26 42
12 Sun	05:22:22	19 50 32	02♓40	02 49	05 44	06 41	03 02	24 25	15 28	26 41	26 15	04 37	21 19	26 21	24 48	04 40	26 44
13 Mon	05:26:18	20 51 32	14 32	02 49 R	05 22	07 24	03 48	24 30	15 32	26 42	26 16	04 39	21 42	26 45	25 02	05 12	26 46
14 Tue	05:30:15	21 52 32	26 25	02 49	04 48	08 07	04 33	24 35	15 37	26 42	26 18	04 41	22 04	27 10	25 16	05 45	26 49
15 Wed	05:34:11	22 53 33	08♈20	02 49	04 03	08 51	05 19	24 40	15 41	26 42	26 19	04 43	22 27	27 34	25 29	06 17	26 51
16 Thu	05:38:08	23 54 35	20 24	02 48	03 08	09 36	06 05	24 45	15 45	26 42	26 20	04 45	22 50	27 59	25 42	06 49	26 53
17 Fri	05:42:04	24 55 37	02♉40	02 47	02 02	10 23	06 51	24 50	15 49	26 43	26 21	04 48	23 13	28 23	25 55	07 21	26 56
18 Sat	05:46:01	25 56 40	15 12	02 46	00 49	11 10	07 36	24 56	15 53	26 44	26 23	04 50	23 35	28 48	26 07	07 53	26 58
19 Sun	05:49:58	26 57 43	28 02	02 45	29♐29 R	11 58	08 22	25 02	15 57	26 45	26 24	04 52	23 58	29 12	26 20	08 25	27 01
20 Mon	05:53:54	27 58 46	11Ⅱ11	02 44	28 07	12 47	09 08	25 08	16 01	26 45	26 25	04 54	24 21	29 37	26 32	08 58	27 03
21 Tue	05:57:51	28 59 50	24 40	02 44 D	26 44	13 37	09 54	25 14	16 05	26 46	26 27	04 56	24 44	00♏02	26 43	09 30	27 06
22 Wed	06:01:47	00♑00 55	08♋29	02 44	25 24	14 28	10 40	25 21	16 08	26 47	26 28	04 58	25 07	00 27	26 54	10 02	27 08
23 Thu	06:05:44	01 02 00	22 28	02 44	24 09	15 19	11 26	25 27	16 12	26 48	26 30	05 00	25 30	00 51	27 05	10 34	27 11
24 Fri	06:09:40	02 03 06	06♌37	02 44 R	23 00	16 12	12 12	25 34	16 15	26 49	26 31	05 03	25 53	01 15	27 16	11 06	27 14
25 Sat	06:13:37	03 04 12	20 54	02 44	22 01	17 05	12 58	25 41	16 19	26 50	26 33	05 05	26 16	01 40	27 26	11 38	27 17
26 Sun	06:17:33	04 05 19	05♍09	02 44	21 11	17 58	13 44	25 48	16 22	26 51	26 34	05 07	26 39	02 04	27 36	12 10	27 19
27 Mon	06:21:30	05 06 26	19 32	02 44	20 31	18 53	14 31	25 55	16 25	26 52	26 36	05 09	27 03	02 28	27 46	12 42	27 22
28 Tue	06:25:27	06 07 34	03♎46	02 44 D	20 04	19 48	15 17	26 02	16 28	26 53	26 37	05 11	27 26	02 53	27 55	13 14	27 25
29 Wed	06:29:23	07 08 42	17 53	02 44	19 46	20 43	16 03	26 10	16 31	26 54	26 39	05 13	27 49	03 17	28 04	13 46	27 28
30 Thu	06:33:20	08 09 51	01♏50	02 44	19 38 D	21 40	16 50	26 17	16 34	26 55	26 41	05 16	28 12	03 42	28 12	14 18	27 31
31 Fri	06:37:16	09 11 01	15 38	02 45	19 40	22 37	17 36	26 25	16 37	26 56	26 42	05 18	28 36	04 06	28 20	14 50	27 34

EPHEMERIS CALCULATED FOR 12 MIDNIGHT GREENWICH MEAN TIME. ALL OTHER DATA AND FACING ASPECTARIAN PAGE IN **EASTERN TIME (BOLD)** AND PACIFIC TIME (REGULAR).

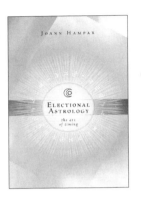

Notes

Notes

Notes